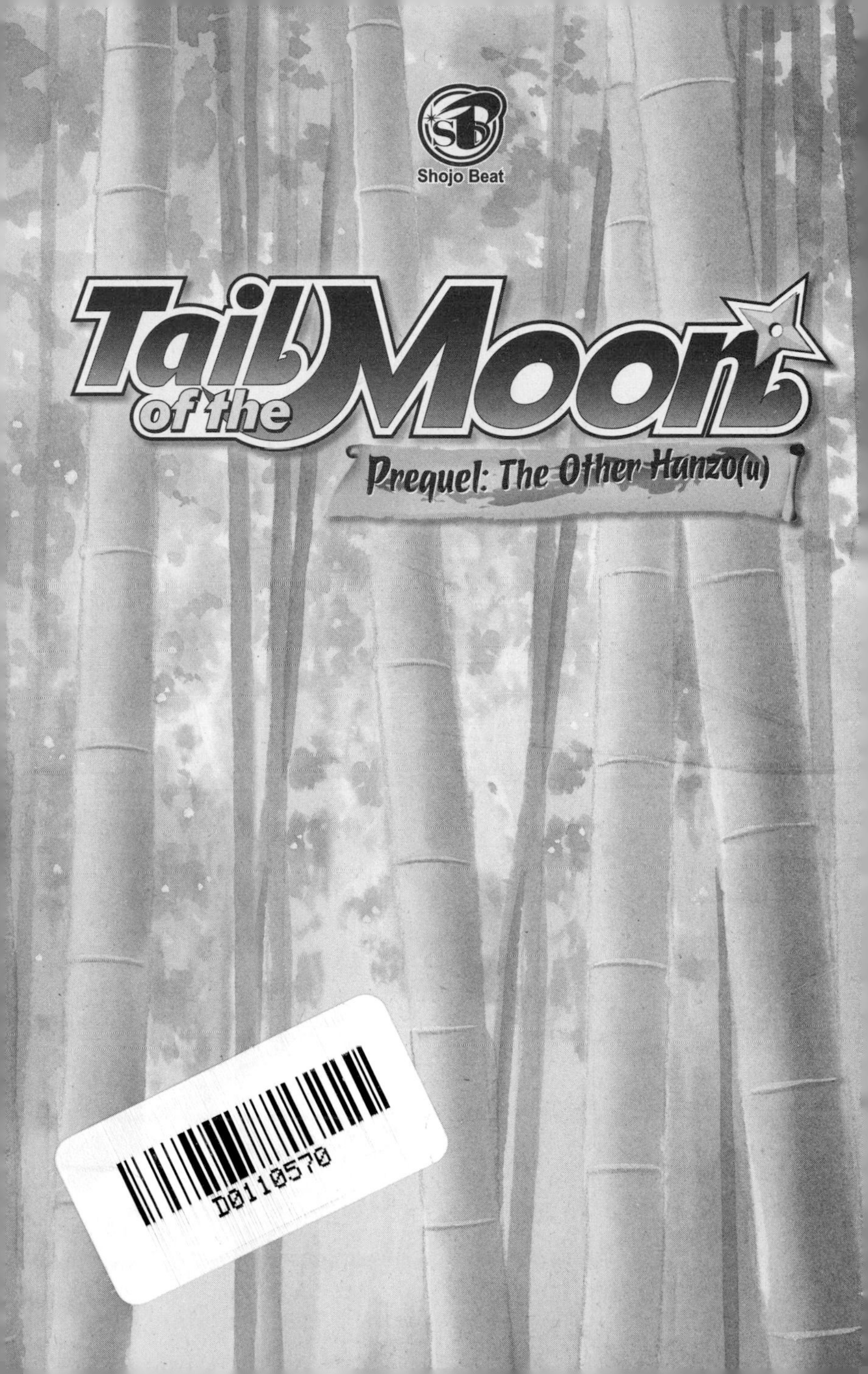
Shojo Beat
Tail of the Moon
Prequel: The Other Hanzo(u)

Tail of the Moon

Prequel: The Other Hanzo(u)

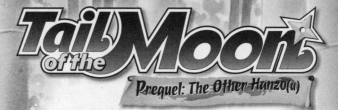

CONTENTS

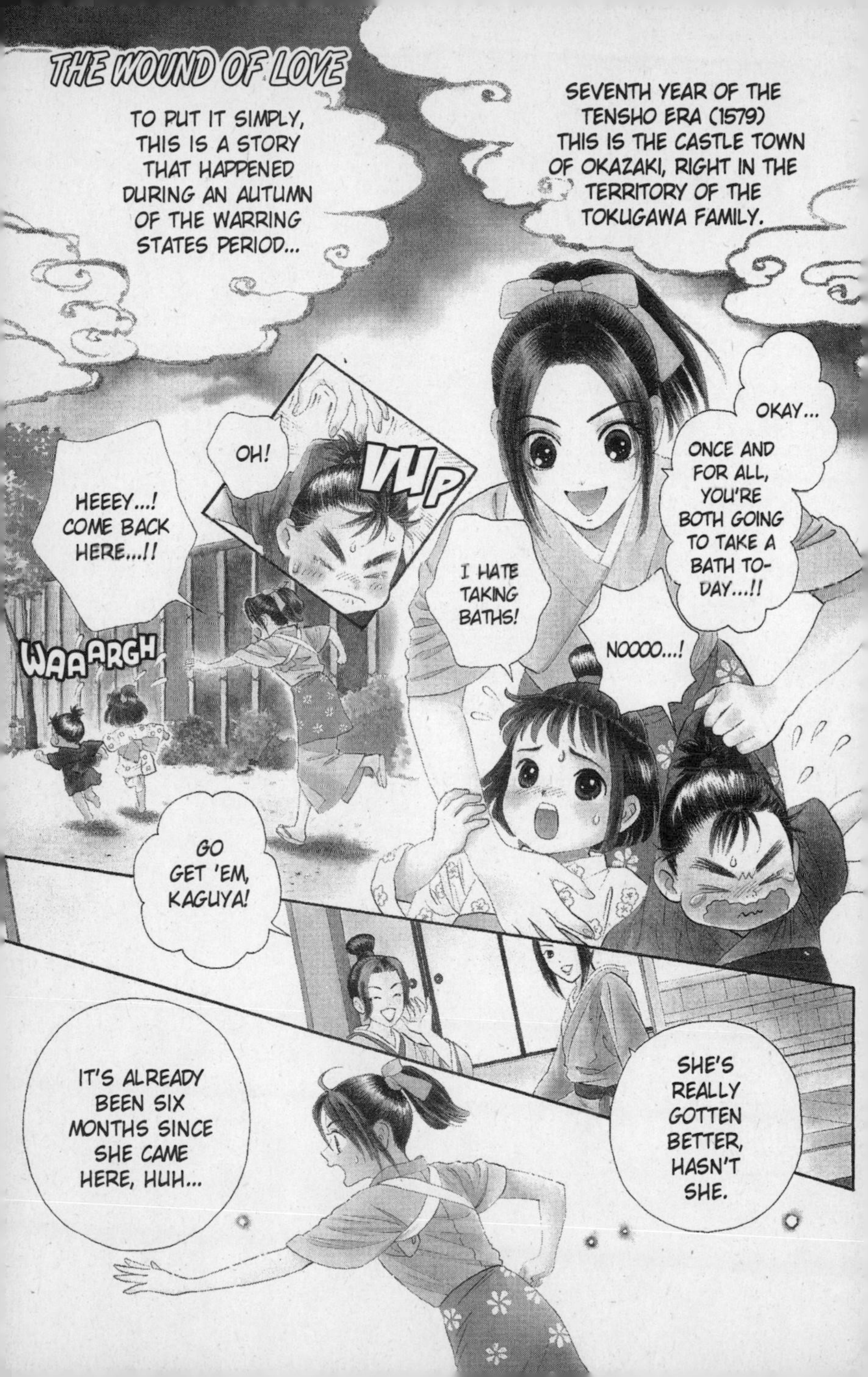
THE WOUND OF LOVE
SEVENTH YEAR OF THE TENSHO ERA (1579) THIS IS THE CASTLE TOWN OF OKAZAKI, RIGHT IN THE TERRITORY OF THE TOKUGAWA FAMILY.
TO PUT IT SIMPLY, THIS IS A STORY THAT HAPPENED DURING AN AUTUMN OF THE WARRING STATES PERIOD...
OKAY...
ONCE AND FOR ALL, YOU'RE BOTH GOING TO TAKE A BATH TO-DAY...!!
NOOOO...!
I HATE TAKING BATHS!
VUP
OH!
HEEEY...! COME BACK HERE...!!
WAAARGH
GO GET 'EM, KAGUYA!
SHE'S REALLY GOTTEN BETTER, HASN'T SHE.
IT'S ALREADY BEEN SIX MONTHS SINCE SHE CAME HERE, HUH...

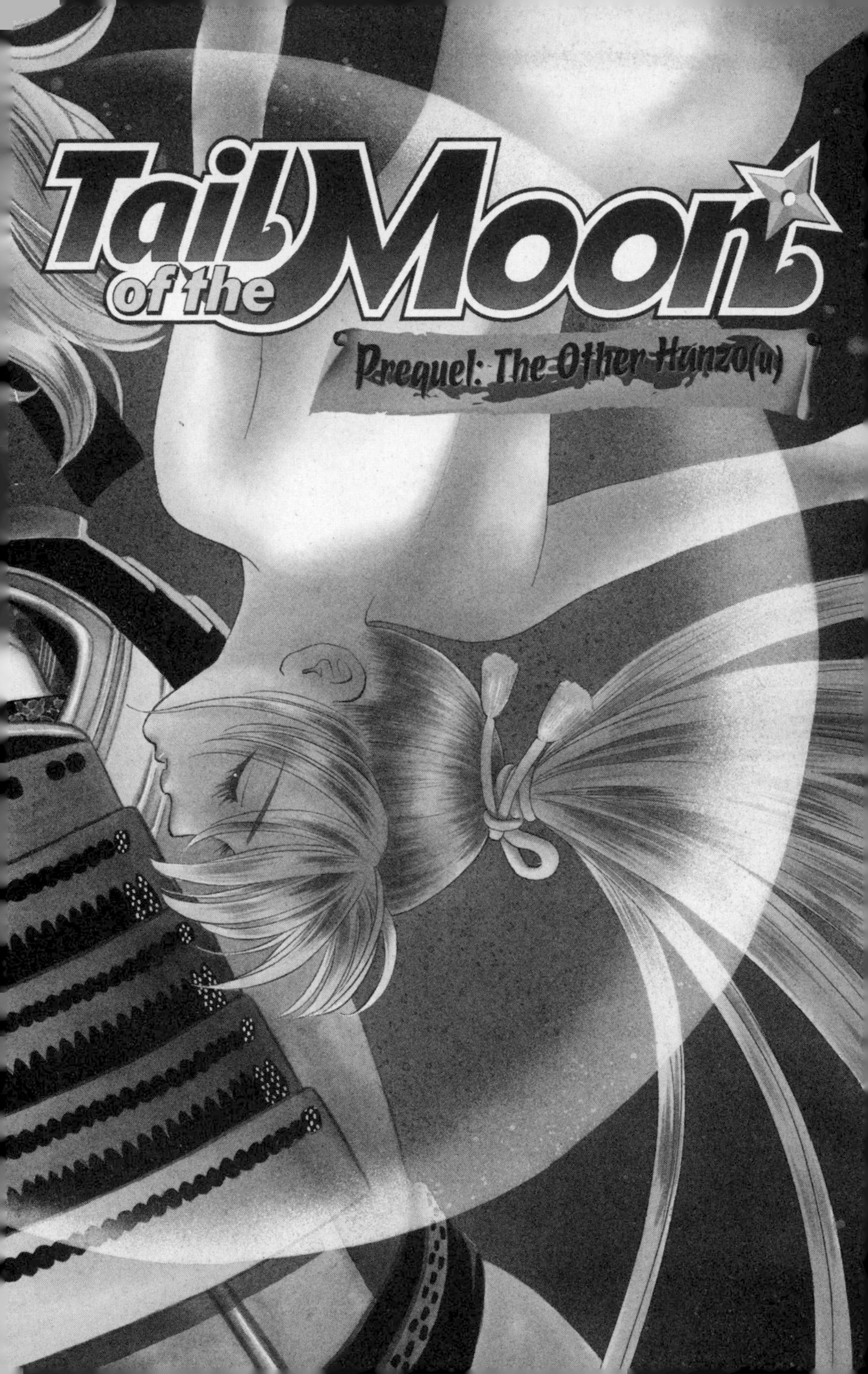
Tail of the Moon
Prequel: The Other Hanzo(u)

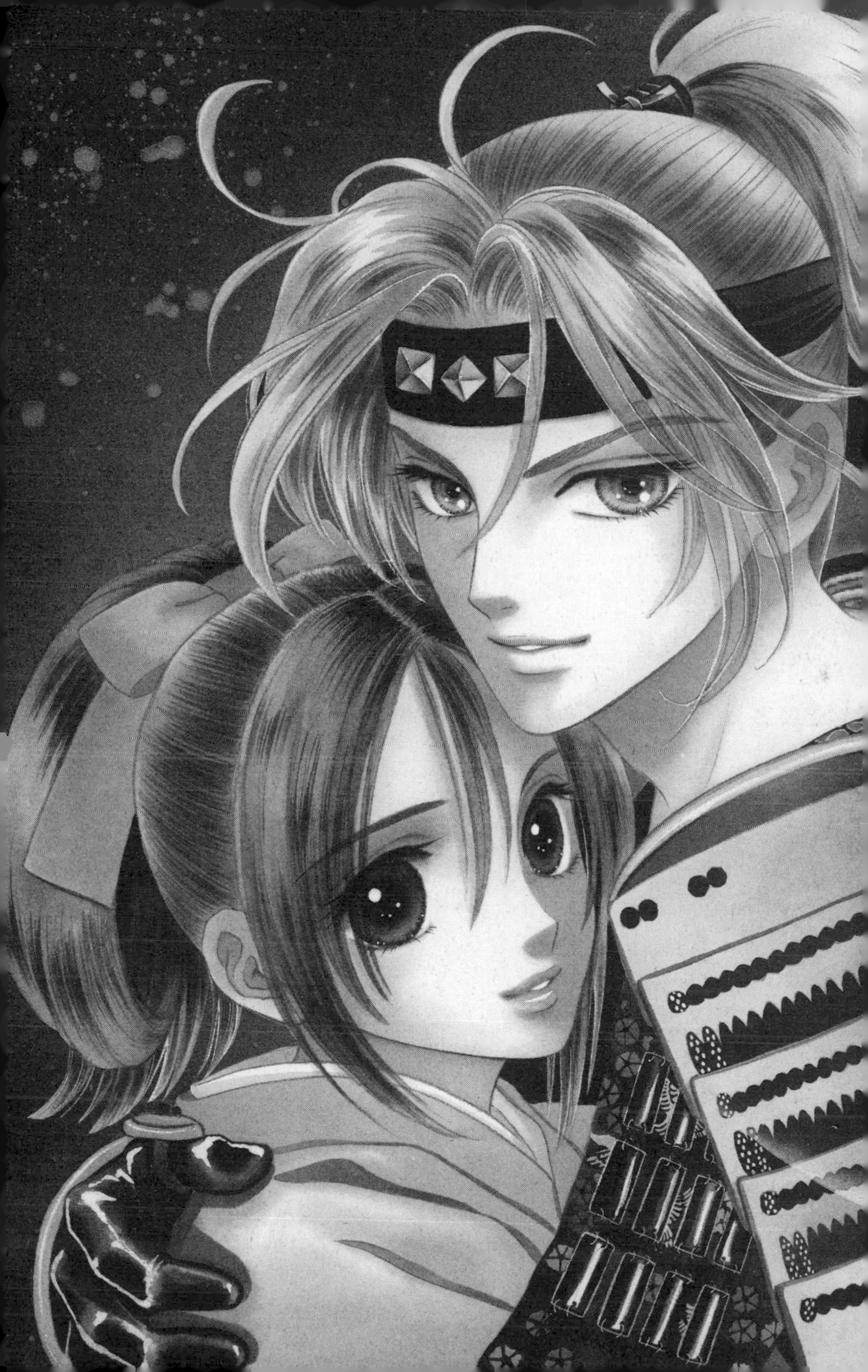

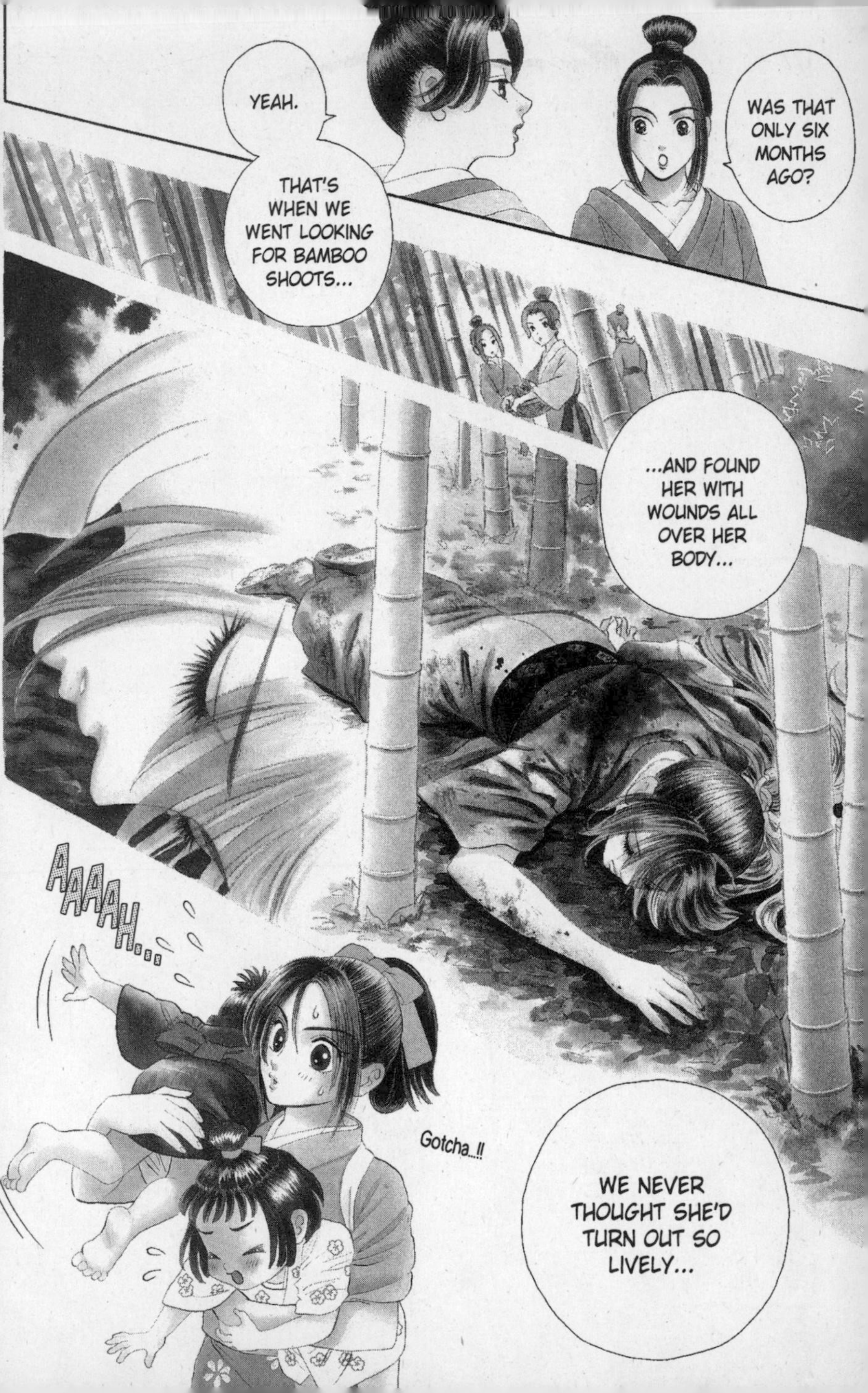
WAS THAT ONLY SIX MONTHS AGO?
YEAH.
THAT'S WHEN WE WENT LOOKING FOR BAMBOO SHOOTS...
...AND FOUND HER WITH WOUNDS ALL OVER HER BODY...
WE NEVER THOUGHT SHE'D TURN OUT SO LIVELY...
Gotcha...!!
AAAAH...

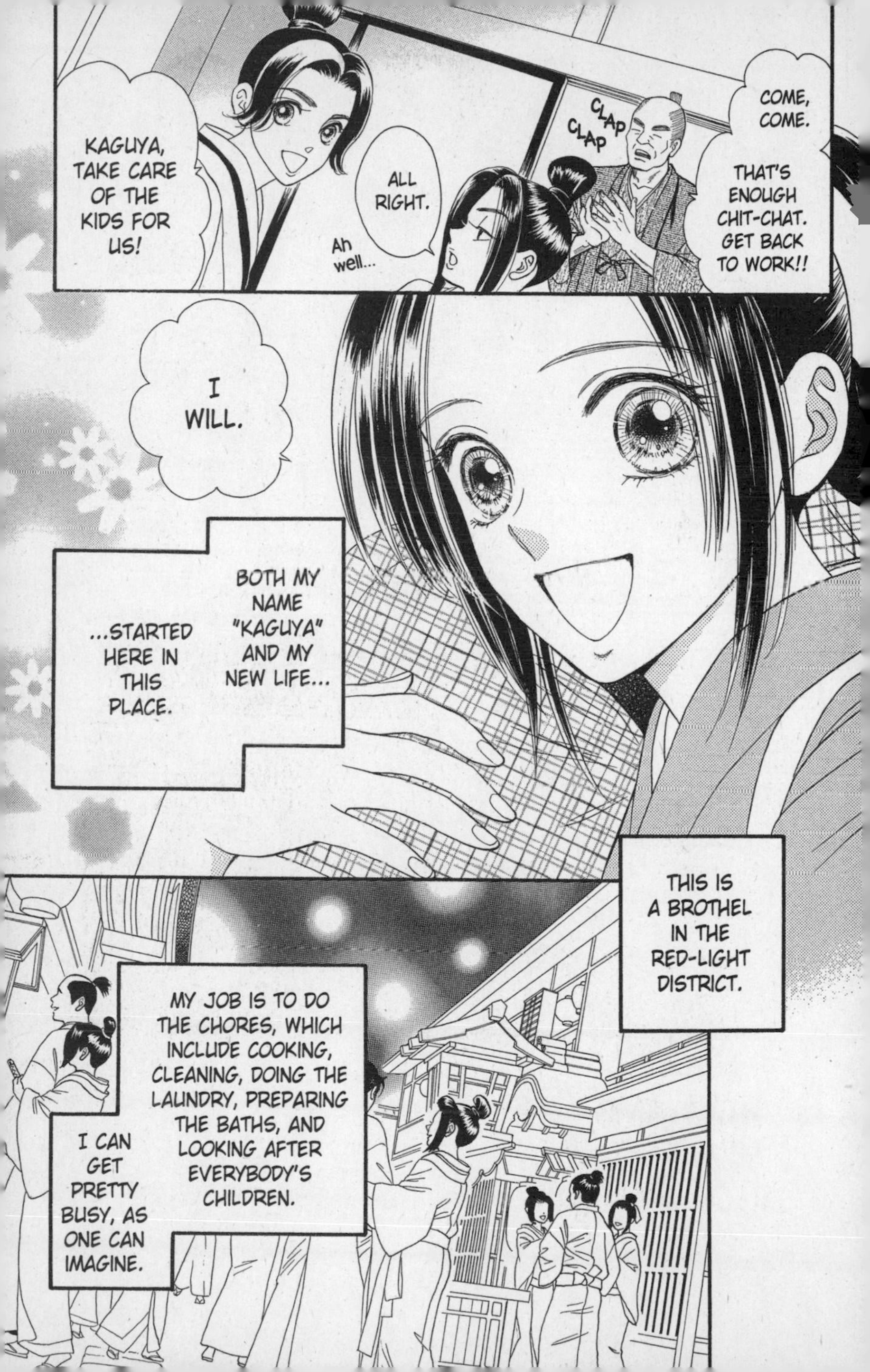
COME, COME. THAT'S ENOUGH CHIT-CHAT. GET BACK TO WORK!!
CLAP CLAP
KAGUYA, TAKE CARE OF THE KIDS FOR US!
ALL RIGHT.
Ah well...
I WILL.
BOTH MY NAME "KAGUYA" AND MY NEW LIFE...
...STARTED HERE IN THIS PLACE.
THIS IS A BROTHEL IN THE RED-LIGHT DISTRICT.
MY JOB IS TO DO THE CHORES, WHICH INCLUDE COOKING, CLEANING, DOING THE LAUNDRY, PREPARING THE BATHS, AND LOOKING AFTER EVERYBODY'S CHILDREN.
I CAN GET PRETTY BUSY, AS ONE CAN IMAGINE.

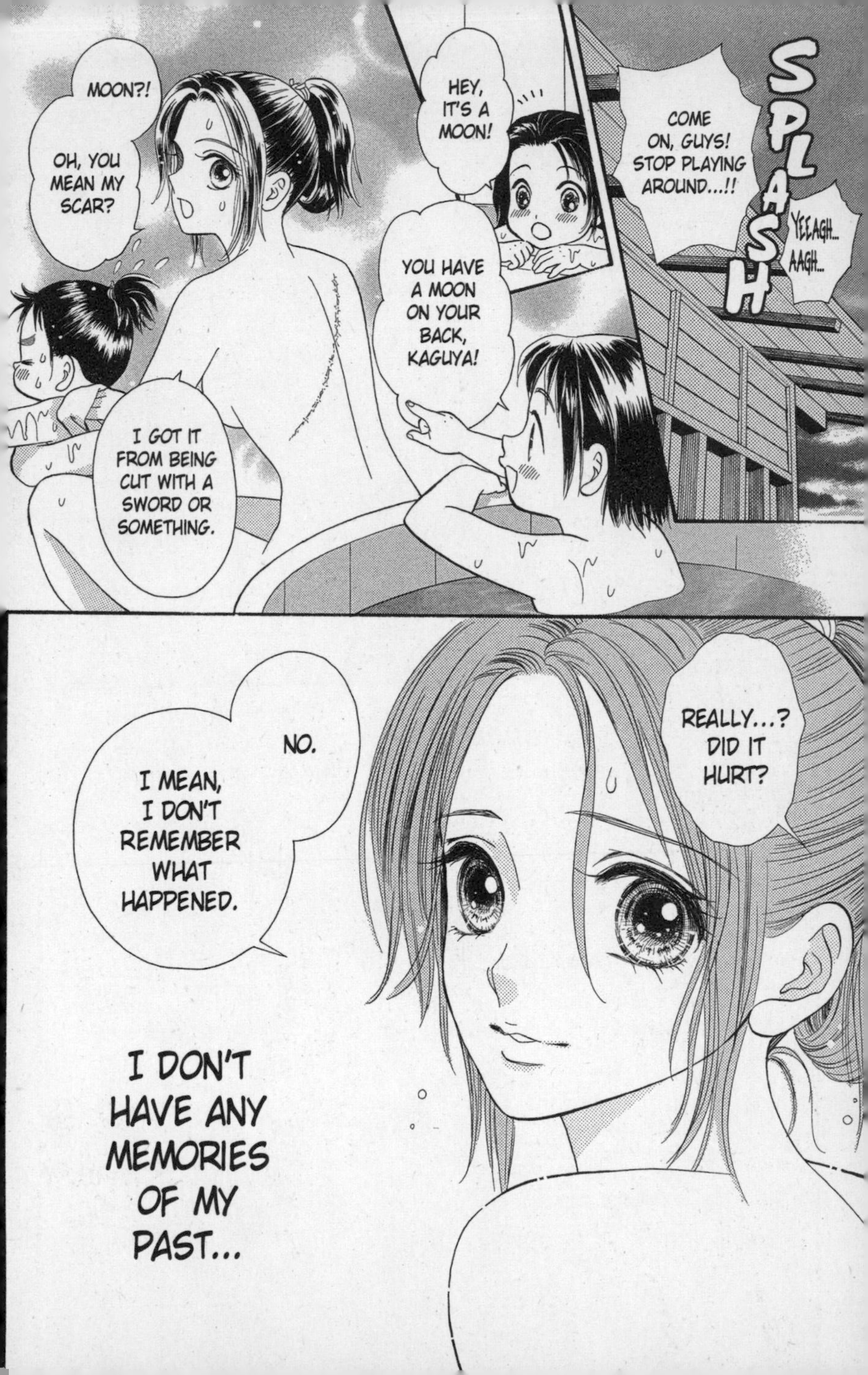
SPLASH
COME ON, GUYS! STOP PLAYING AROUND...!!
YEEAGH... AAGH...
HEY, IT'S A MOON!
YOU HAVE A MOON ON YOUR BACK, KAGUYA!
MOON?!
OH, YOU MEAN MY SCAR?
I GOT IT FROM BEING CUT WITH A SWORD OR SOMETHING.
REALLY...? DID IT HURT?
NO.
I MEAN, I DON'T REMEMBER WHAT HAPPENED.
I DON'T HAVE ANY MEMORIES OF MY PAST...

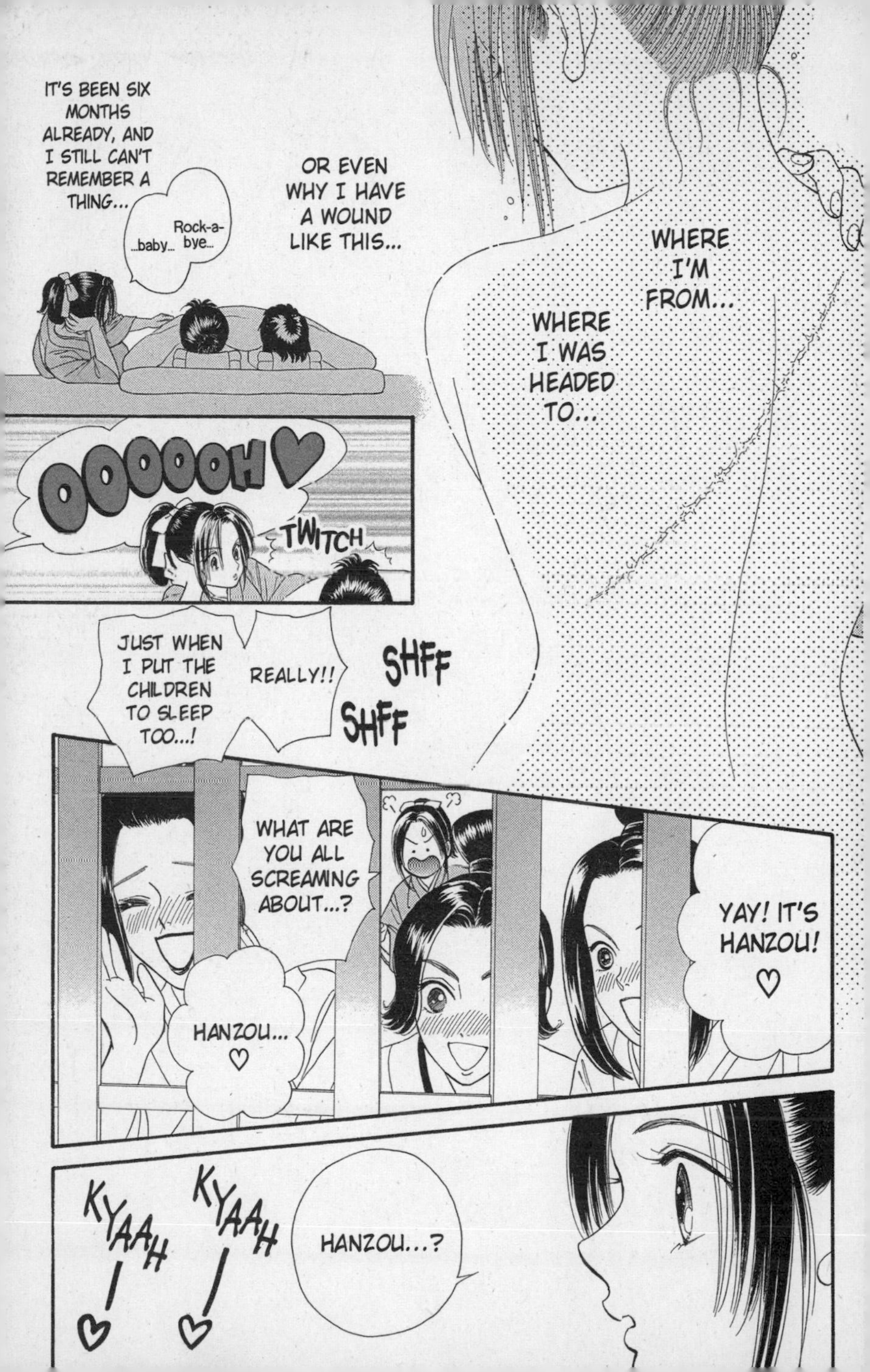
WHERE I'M FROM...
WHERE I WAS HEADED TO...
OR EVEN WHY I HAVE A WOUND LIKE THIS...
IT'S BEEN SIX MONTHS ALREADY, AND I STILL CAN'T REMEMBER A THING...
Rock-a-bye... ...baby...
OOOOOH ♥
TWITCH
REALLY!!
JUST WHEN I PUT THE CHILDREN TO SLEEP TOO...!
SHFF
SHFF
YAY! IT'S HANZOU! ♡
WHAT ARE YOU ALL SCREAMING ABOUT...?
HANZOU... ♡
HANZOU...?
KYAAH! ♡
KYAAH! ♡

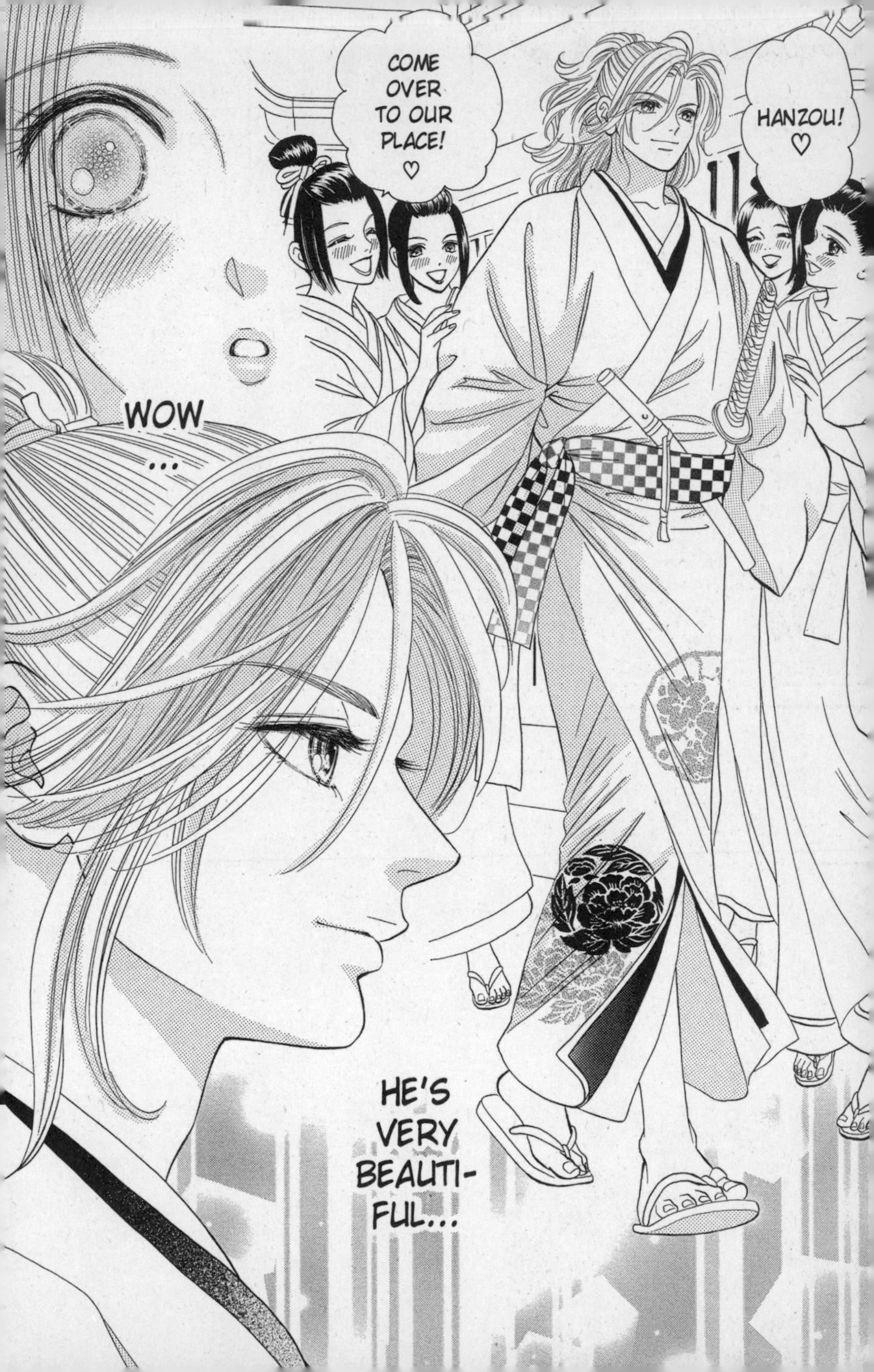
HANZOU! ♡
COME OVER TO OUR PLACE! ♡
WOW ...
HE'S VERY BEAUTI-FUL...

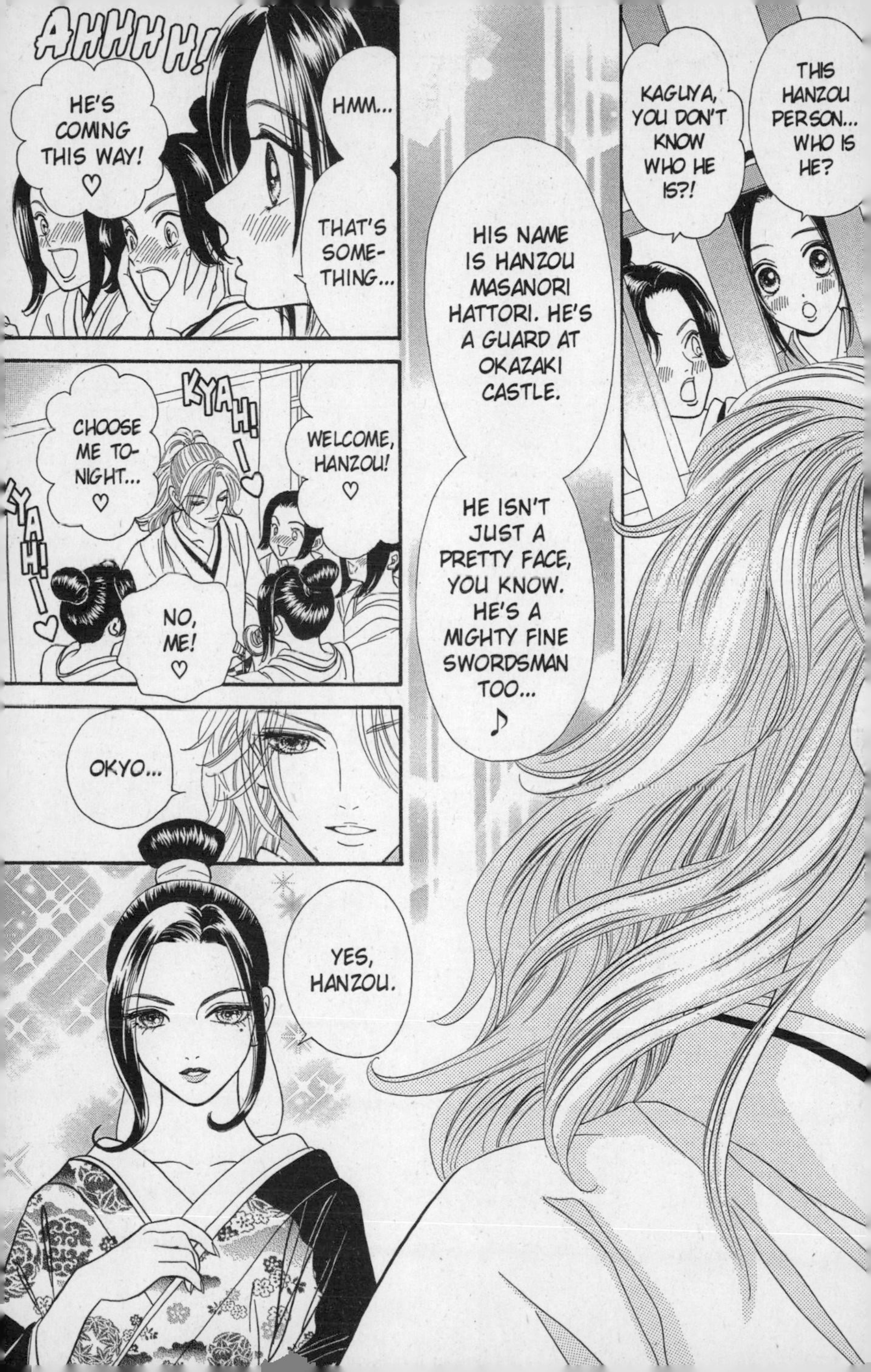
THIS HANZOU PERSON... WHO IS HE?
KAGUYA, YOU DON'T KNOW WHO HE IS?!
HIS NAME IS HANZOU MASANORI HATTORI. HE'S A GUARD AT OKAZAKI CASTLE.
HE ISN'T JUST A PRETTY FACE, YOU KNOW. HE'S A MIGHTY FINE SWORDSMAN TOO... ♪
AHHHH!
HE'S COMING THIS WAY! ♡
HMM...
THAT'S SOME-THING...
WELCOME, HANZOU! ♡
KYAH!
CHOOSE ME TO-NIGHT... ♡
KYAH!
NO, ME! ♡
OKYO...
YES, HANZOU.

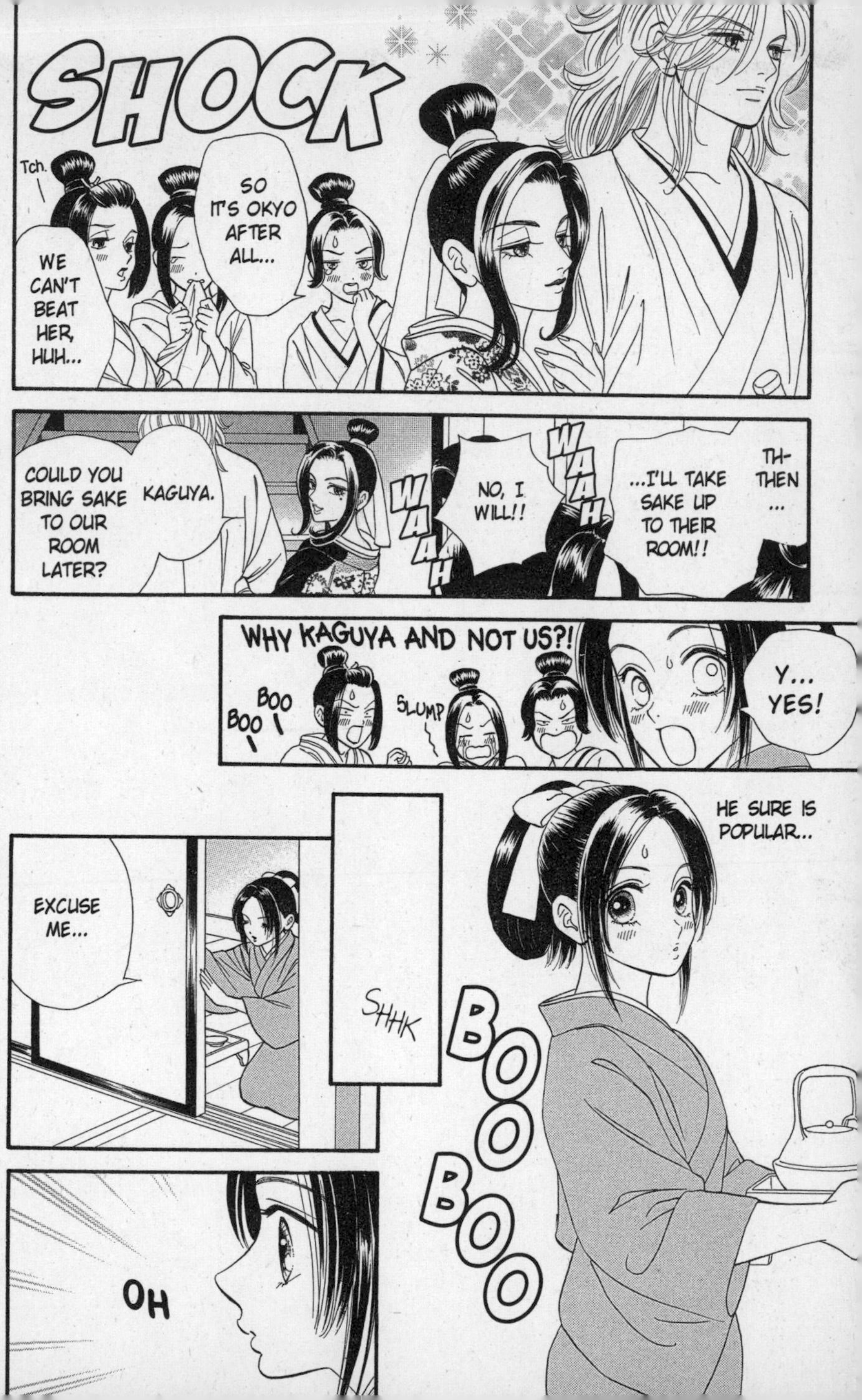
SHOCK
SO IT'S OKYO AFTER ALL...
Tch.
WE CAN'T BEAT HER, HUH...
TH-THEN...
...I'LL TAKE SAKE UP TO THEIR ROOM!!
WAAH
NO, I WILL!!
WAAAH
KAGUYA.
COULD YOU BRING SAKE TO OUR ROOM LATER?
Y... YES!
WHY KAGUYA AND NOT US?!
SLUMP
BOO BOO
HE SURE IS POPULAR...
BOOBOOBOO
SHHK
EXCUSE ME...
OH

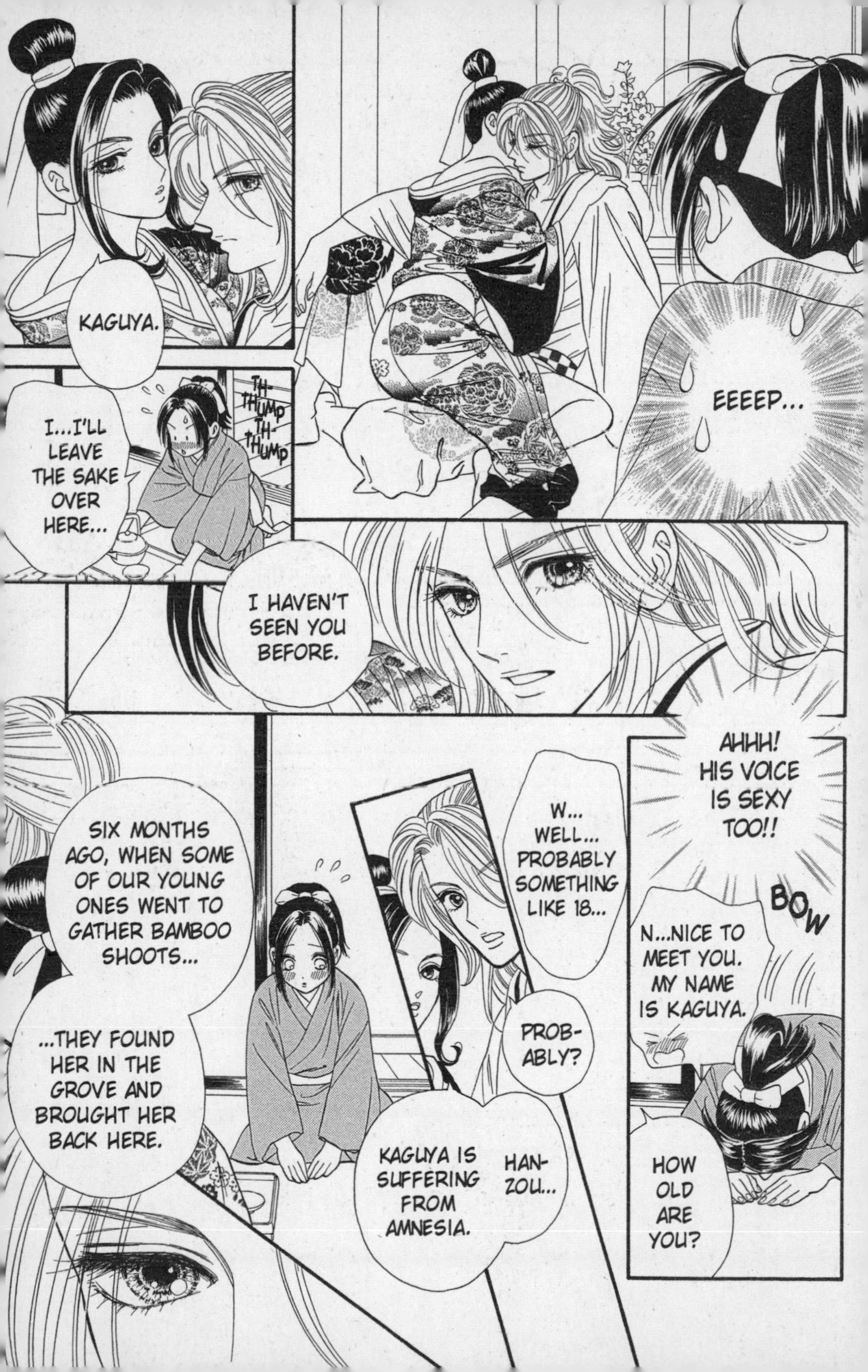
EEEEP...
KAGUYA.
TH-THUMP TH-THUMP
I...I'LL LEAVE THE SAKE OVER HERE...
I HAVEN'T SEEN YOU BEFORE.
AHHH! HIS VOICE IS SEXY TOO!!
BOW
N...NICE TO MEET YOU. MY NAME IS KAGUYA.
HOW OLD ARE YOU?
W... WELL... PROBABLY SOMETHING LIKE 18...
PROB-ABLY?
HAN-ZOU...
KAGUYA IS SUFFERING FROM AMNESIA.
SIX MONTHS AGO, WHEN SOME OF OUR YOUNG ONES WENT TO GATHER BAMBOO SHOOTS...
...THEY FOUND HER IN THE GROVE AND BROUGHT HER BACK HERE.

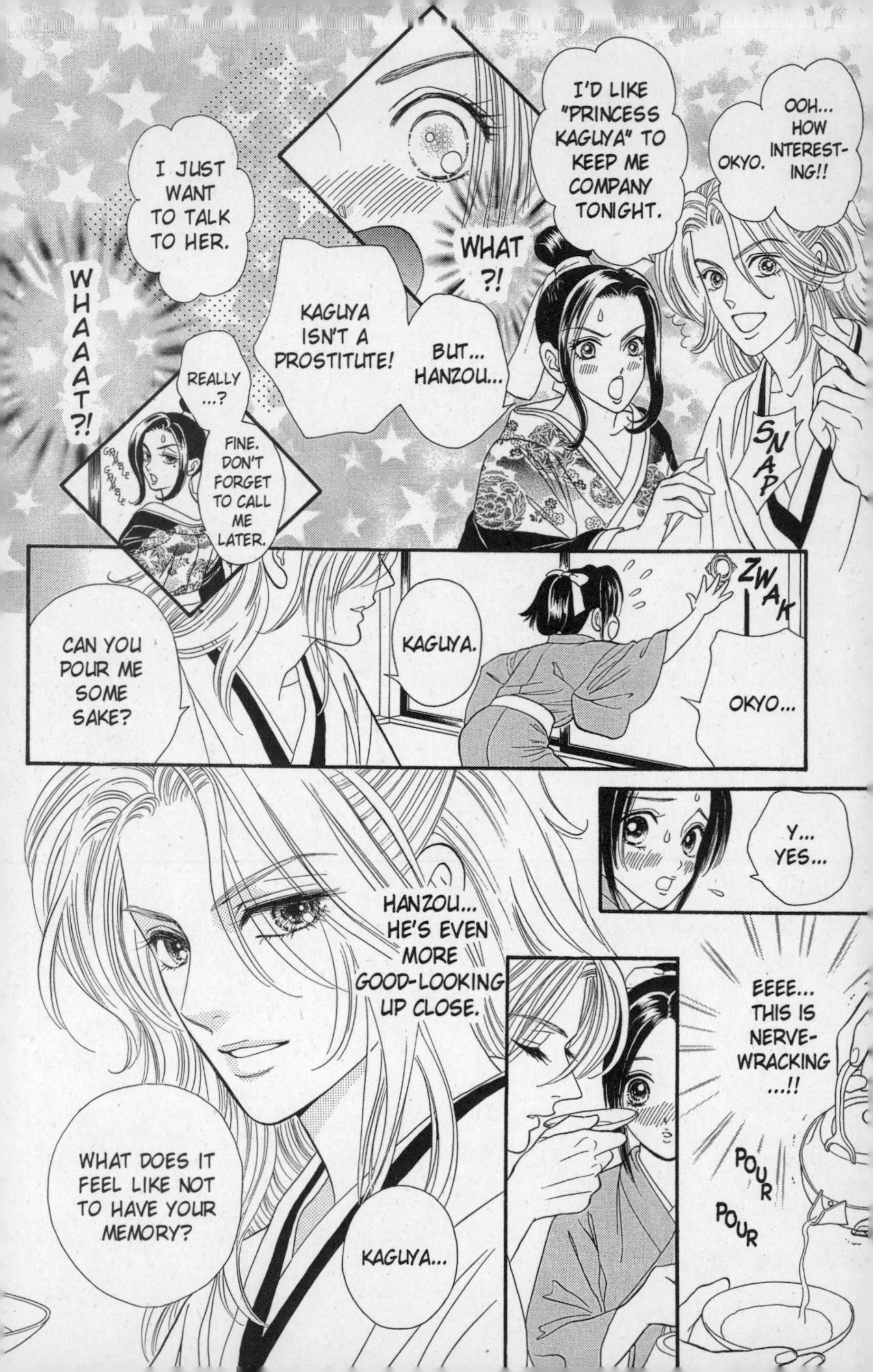
OOH... HOW INTERESTING!!
OKYO.
I'D LIKE "PRINCESS KAGUYA" TO KEEP ME COMPANY TONIGHT.
SNAP
WHAT ?!
BUT... HANZOU...
KAGUYA ISN'T A PROSTITUTE!
I JUST WANT TO TALK TO HER.
WHAAAAT?!
REALLY ...?
FINE. DON'T FORGET TO CALL ME LATER.
GRUMBLE GRUMBLE
ZWAK
OKYO...
KAGUYA.
CAN YOU POUR ME SOME SAKE?
Y... YES...
HANZOU... HE'S EVEN MORE GOOD-LOOKING UP CLOSE.
EEEE... THIS IS NERVE-WRACKING ...!!
POUR
POUR
KAGUYA...
WHAT DOES IT FEEL LIKE NOT TO HAVE YOUR MEMORY?

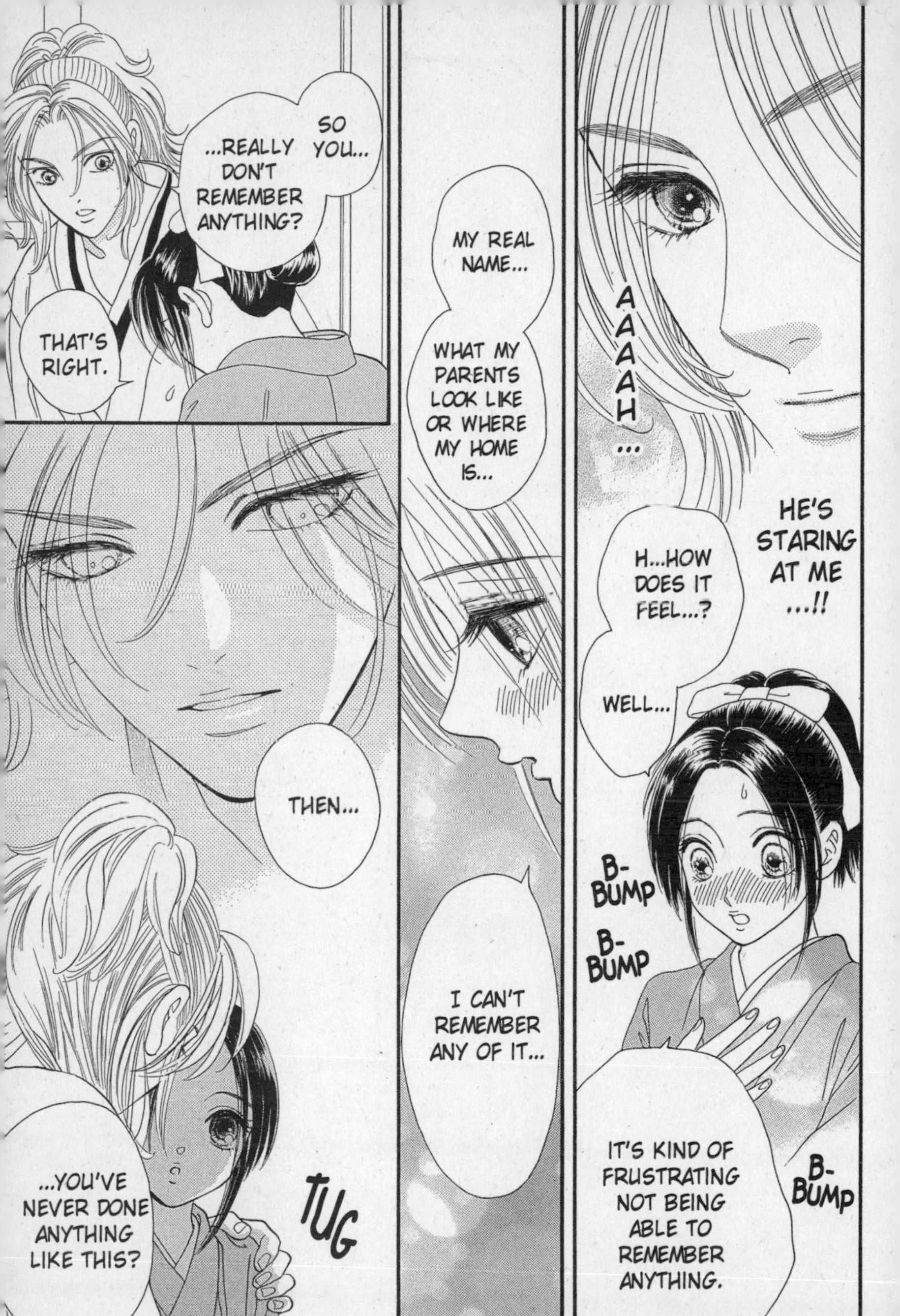
AAAAH...
HE'S STARING AT ME ...!!
H...HOW DOES IT FEEL...?
WELL...
B-BUMP
B-BUMP
IT'S KIND OF FRUSTRATING NOT BEING ABLE TO REMEMBER ANYTHING.
B-BUMP
MY REAL NAME...
WHAT MY PARENTS LOOK LIKE OR WHERE MY HOME IS...
I CAN'T REMEMBER ANY OF IT...
SO YOU...
...REALLY DON'T REMEMBER ANYTHING?
THAT'S RIGHT.
THEN...
TUG
...YOU'VE NEVER DONE ANYTHING LIKE THIS?

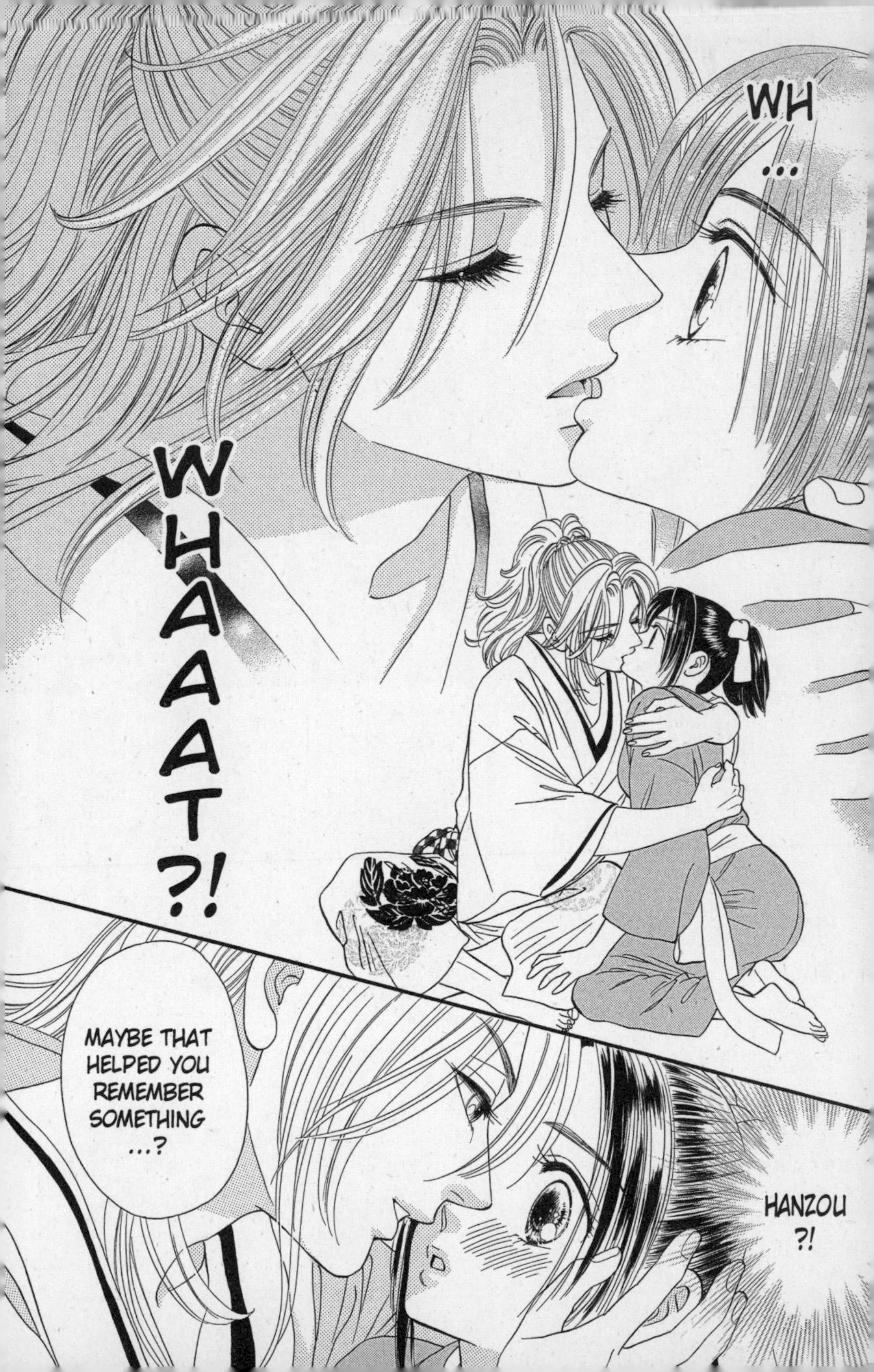
WH ...
WHAAAT?!
MAYBE THAT HELPED YOU REMEMBER SOMETHING ...?
HANZOU ?!

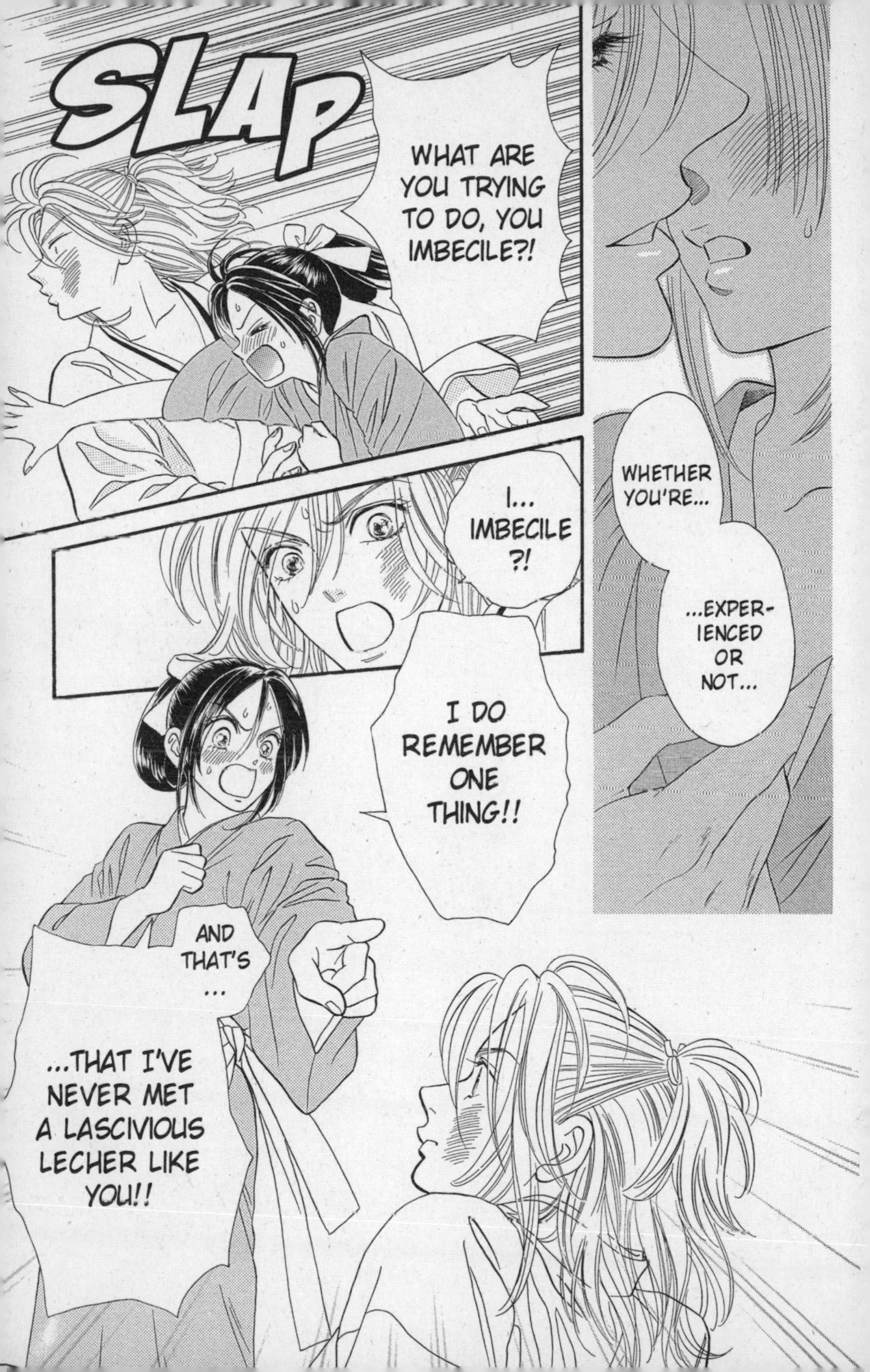
WHETHER YOU'RE...
...EXPER-IENCED OR NOT...
SLAP
WHAT ARE YOU TRYING TO DO, YOU IMBECILE?!
I... IMBECILE?!
I DO REMEMBER ONE THING!!
AND THAT'S...
...THAT I'VE NEVER MET A LASCIVIOUS LECHER LIKE YOU!!

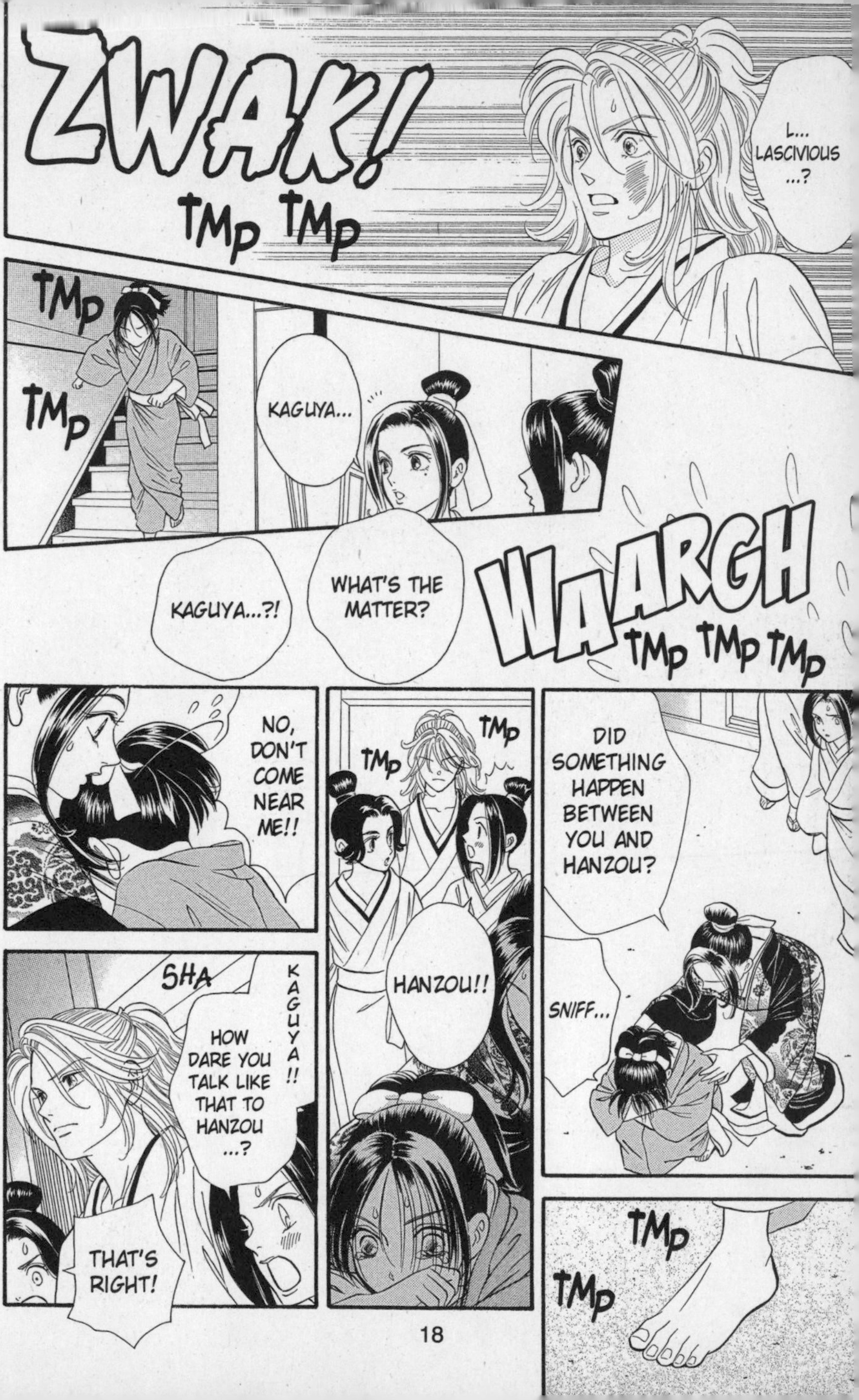
L... LASCIVIOUS ...?
ZWAK!
TMp TMp
KAGUYA...
TMp
TMp
WAARGH
TMp TMp TMp
WHAT'S THE MATTER?
KAGUYA...?!
DID SOMETHING HAPPEN BETWEEN YOU AND HANZOU?
SNIFF...
TMp
TMp
TMp
TMp
HANZOU!!
NO, DON'T COME NEAR ME!!
SHA
KAGUYA!!
HOW DARE YOU TALK LIKE THAT TO HANZOU ...?
THAT'S RIGHT!

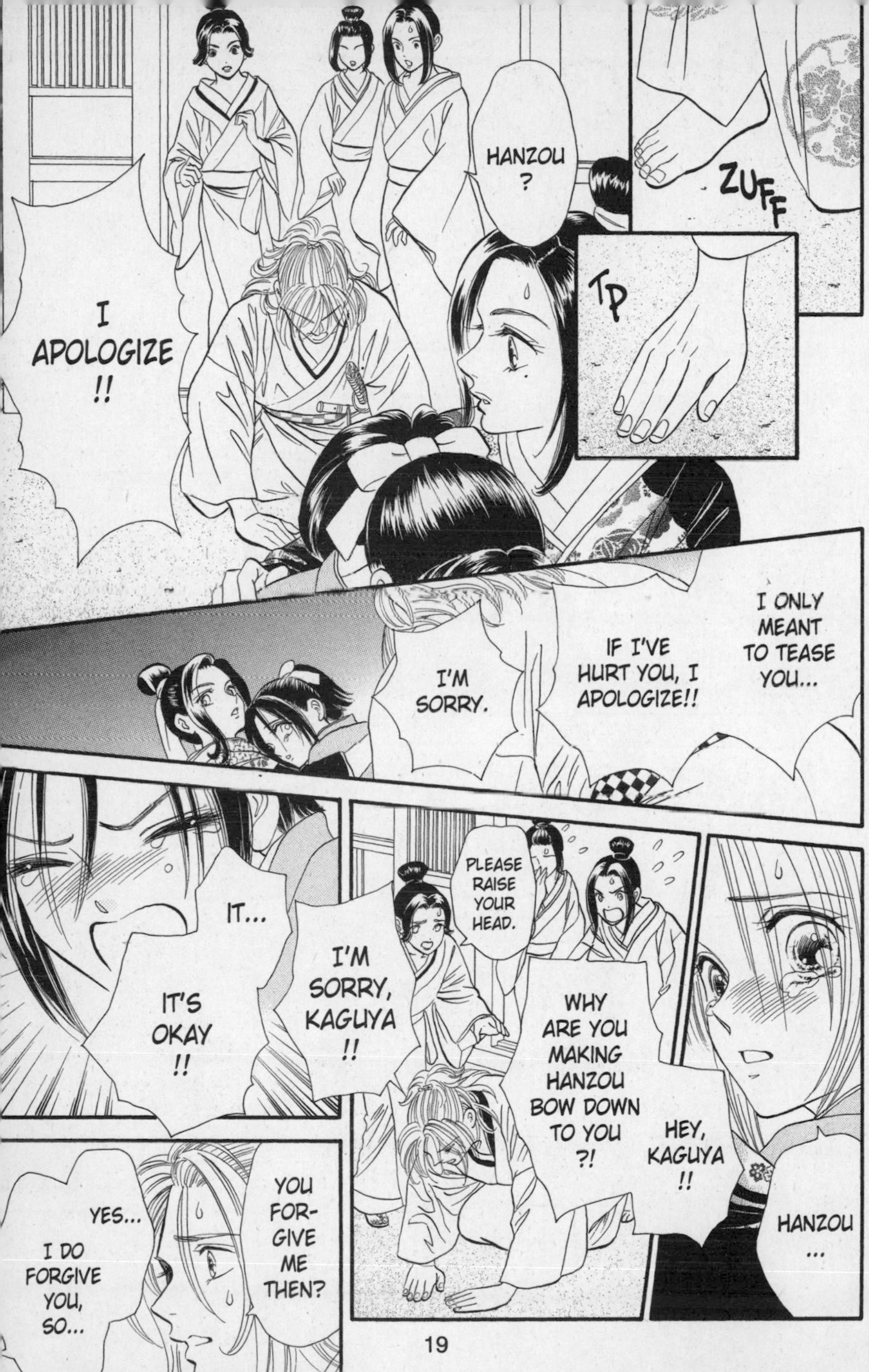

ZUFF
TP
HANZOU ?
I APOLOGIZE !!
I ONLY MEANT TO TEASE YOU...
IF I'VE HURT YOU, I APOLOGIZE!!
I'M SORRY.
HANZOU ...
HEY, KAGUYA !!
PLEASE RAISE YOUR HEAD.
WHY ARE YOU MAKING HANZOU BOW DOWN TO YOU ?!
I'M SORRY, KAGUYA !!
IT...
IT'S OKAY !!
YOU FOR-GIVE ME THEN?
YES...
I DO FORGIVE YOU, SO...

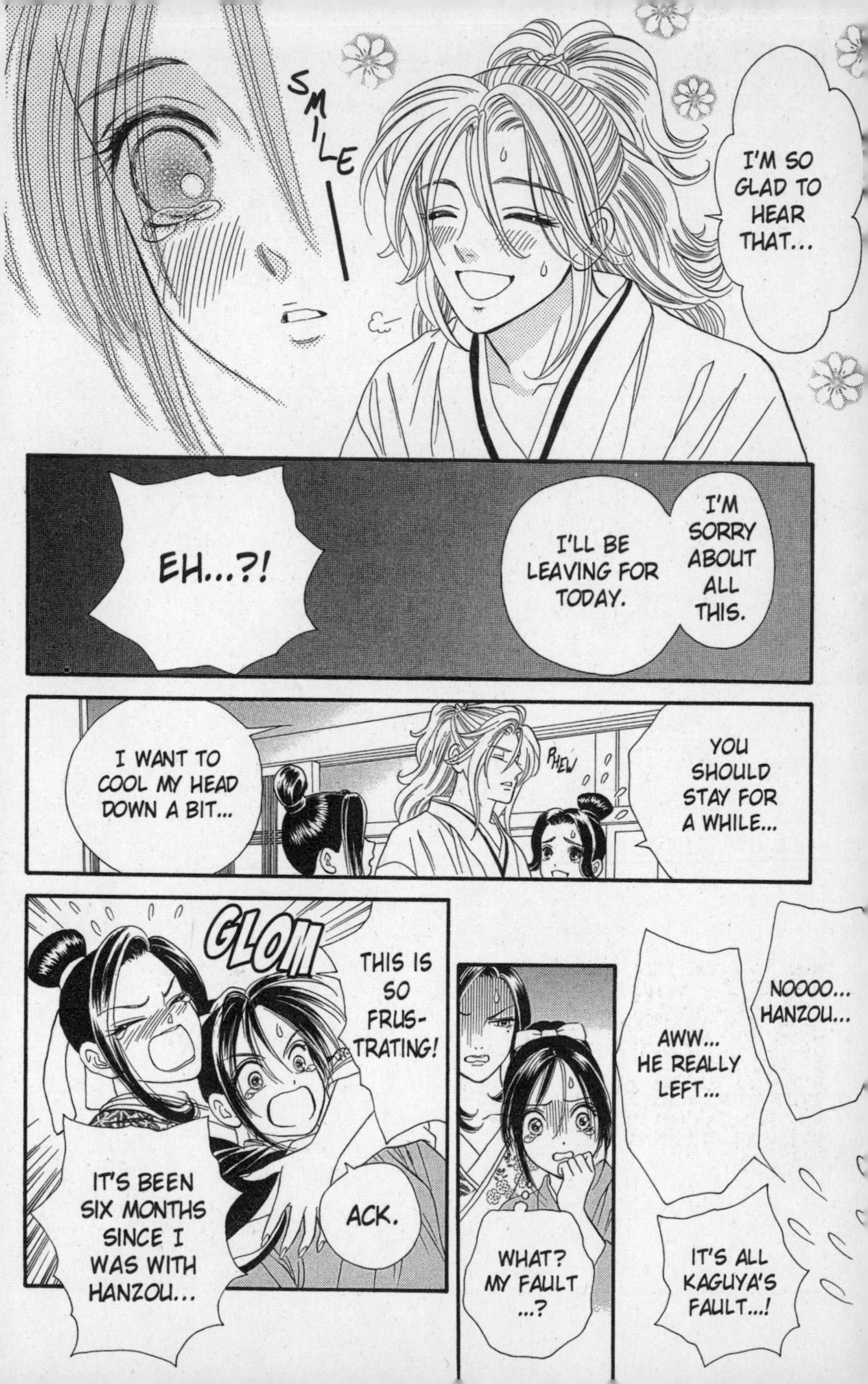
I'M SO GLAD TO HEAR THAT...
SMILE
I'M SORRY ABOUT ALL THIS.
I'LL BE LEAVING FOR TODAY.
EH...?!
YOU SHOULD STAY FOR A WHILE...
RHEW
I WANT TO COOL MY HEAD DOWN A BIT...
NOOOO... HANZOU...
AWW... HE REALLY LEFT...
IT'S ALL KAGUYA'S FAULT...!
WHAT? MY FAULT ...?
THIS IS SO FRUS-TRATING!
GLOM
ACK.
IT'S BEEN SIX MONTHS SINCE I WAS WITH HANZOU...

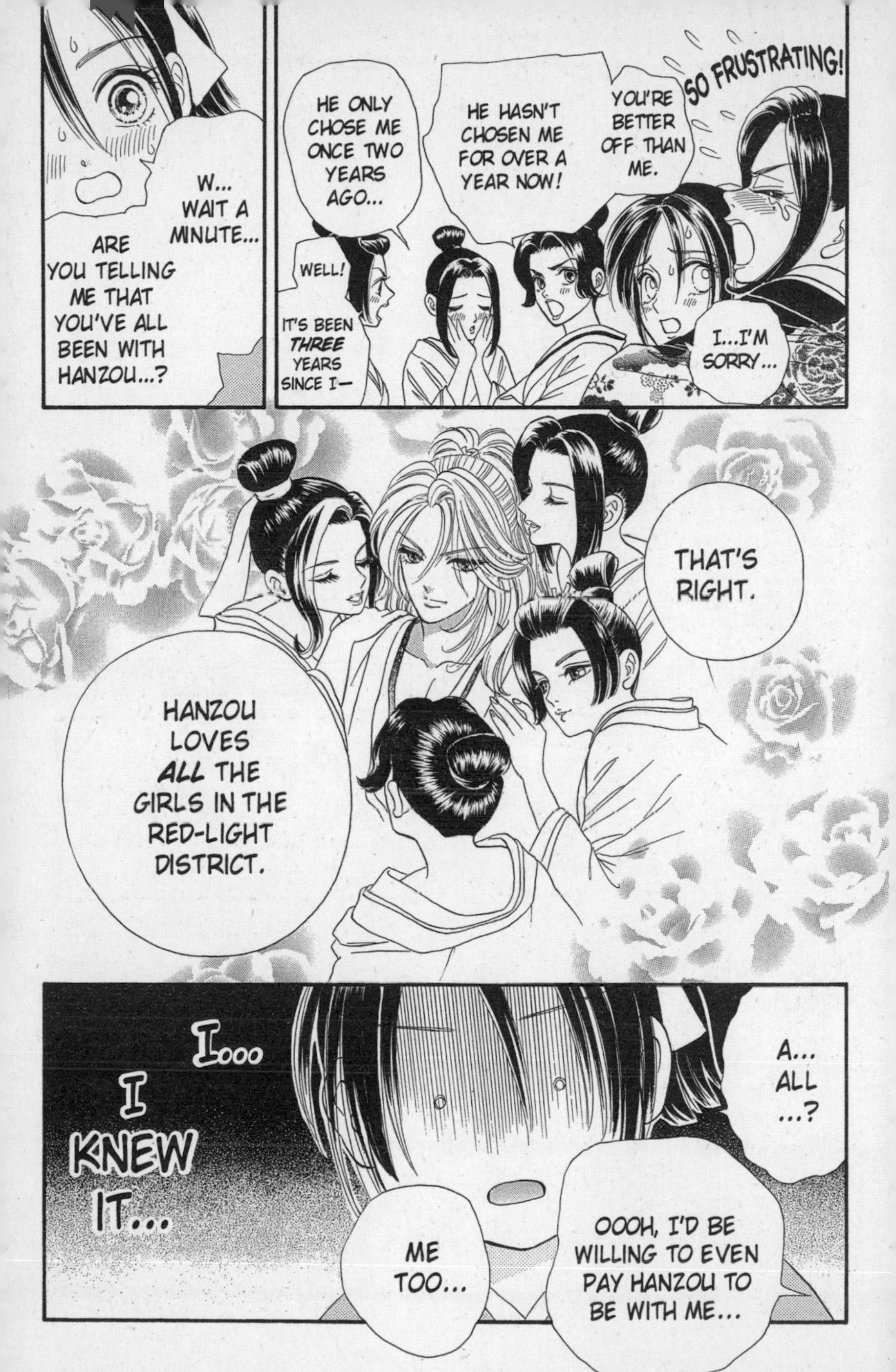
SO FRUSTRATING!
YOU'RE BETTER OFF THAN ME.
HE HASN'T CHOSEN ME FOR OVER A YEAR NOW!
HE ONLY CHOSE ME ONCE TWO YEARS AGO...
I...I'M SORRY...
WELL!
IT'S BEEN THREE YEARS SINCE I—
W... WAIT A MINUTE...
ARE YOU TELLING ME THAT YOU'VE ALL BEEN WITH HANZOU...?
THAT'S RIGHT.
HANZOU LOVES ALL THE GIRLS IN THE RED-LIGHT DISTRICT.
A... ALL ...?
OOOH, I'D BE WILLING TO EVEN PAY HANZOU TO BE WITH ME...
ME TOO...
I...
I KNEW IT...

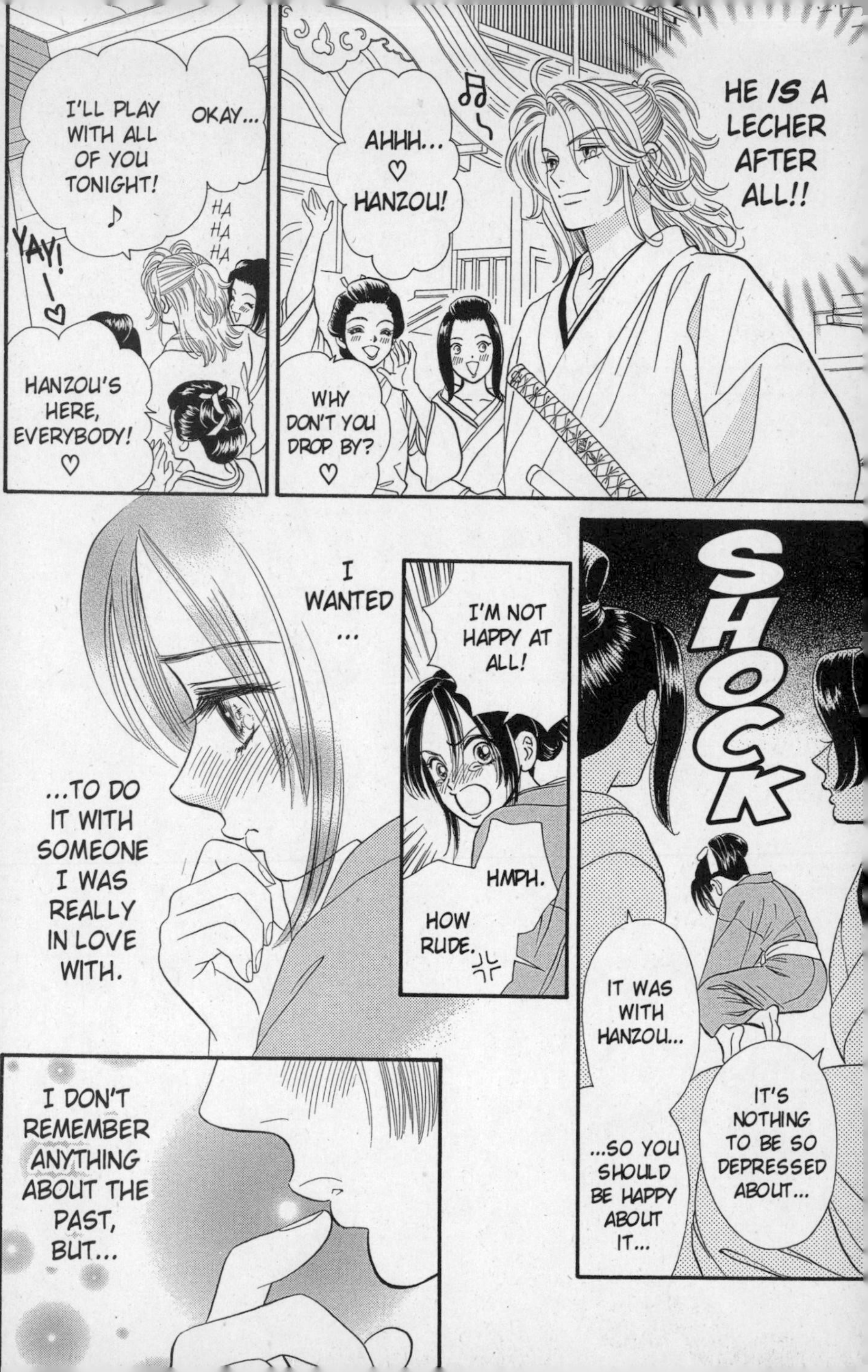
HE IS A LECHER AFTER ALL!!
AHHH... ♡ HANZOU!
WHY DON'T YOU DROP BY? ♡
OKAY...
I'LL PLAY WITH ALL OF YOU TONIGHT! ♪
HA HA HA
YAY! ♡
HANZOU'S HERE, EVERYBODY! ♡
SHOCK
IT WAS WITH HANZOU...
...SO YOU SHOULD BE HAPPY ABOUT IT...
IT'S NOTHING TO BE SO DEPRESSED ABOUT...
I'M NOT HAPPY AT ALL!
HMPH.
HOW RUDE.
I WANTED...
...TO DO IT WITH SOMEONE I WAS REALLY IN LOVE WITH.
I DON'T REMEMBER ANYTHING ABOUT THE PAST, BUT...

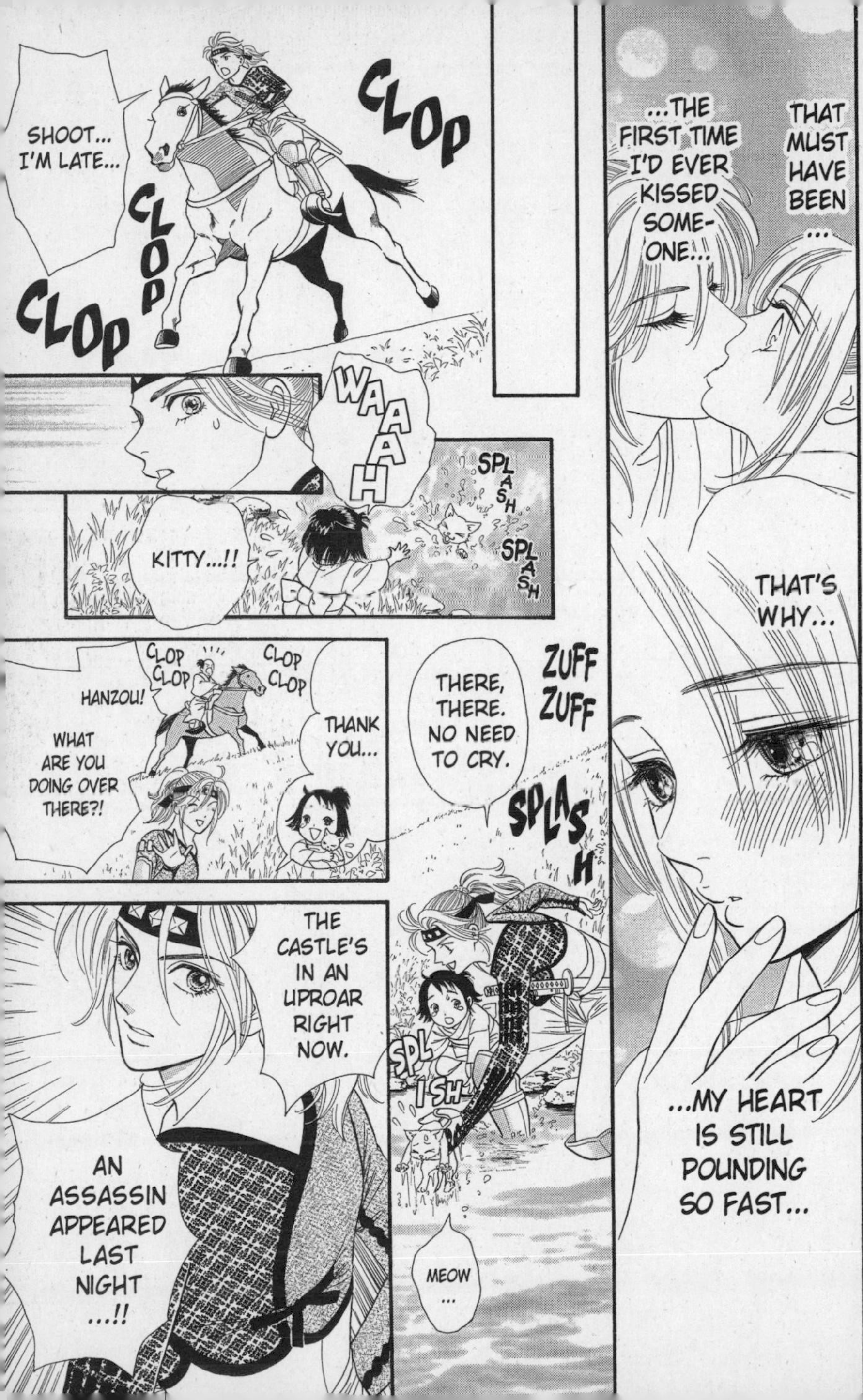
THAT MUST HAVE BEEN ...
...THE FIRST TIME I'D EVER KISSED SOME-ONE...
THAT'S WHY...
...MY HEART IS STILL POUNDING SO FAST...
CLOP
SHOOT... I'M LATE...
CLOP
CLOP
WAAAAH
SPLASH
SPLASH
KITTY...!!
ZUFF ZUFF
THERE, THERE. NO NEED TO CRY.
SPLASH
THANK YOU...
CLOP CLOP
CLOP CLOP
HANZOU!
WHAT ARE YOU DOING OVER THERE?!
SPLISH
MEOW ...
THE CASTLE'S IN AN UPROAR RIGHT NOW.
AN ASSASSIN APPEARED LAST NIGHT ...!!

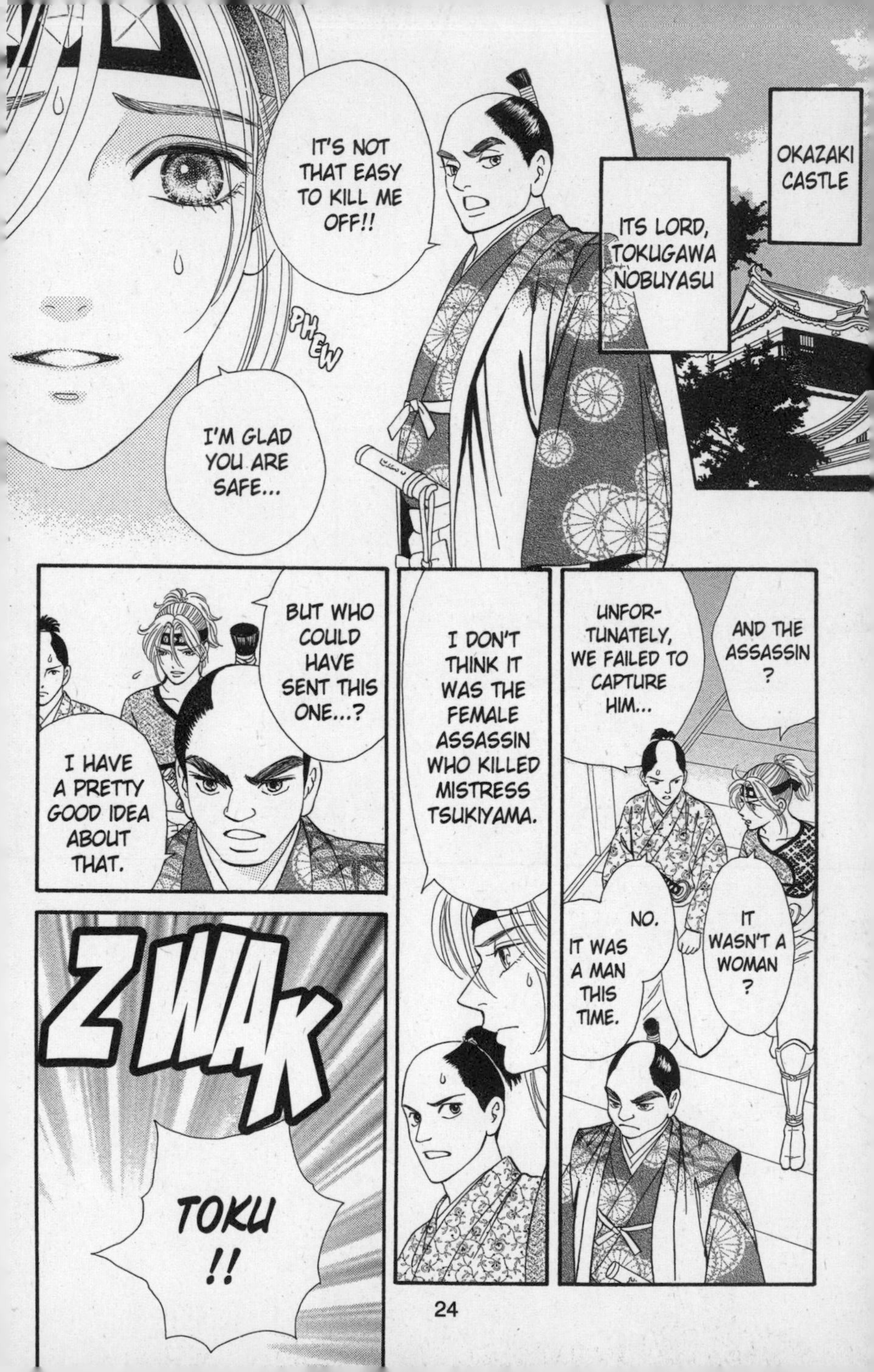
OKAZAKI CASTLE
ITS LORD, TOKUGAWA NOBUYASU
IT'S NOT THAT EASY TO KILL ME OFF!!
PHEW
I'M GLAD YOU ARE SAFE...
AND THE ASSASSIN ?
UNFOR-TUNATELY, WE FAILED TO CAPTURE HIM...
IT WASN'T A WOMAN ?
NO.
IT WAS A MAN THIS TIME.
I DON'T THINK IT WAS THE FEMALE ASSASSIN WHO KILLED MISTRESS TSUKIYAMA.
BUT WHO COULD HAVE SENT THIS ONE...?
I HAVE A PRETTY GOOD IDEA ABOUT THAT.
ZWAK
TOKU !!

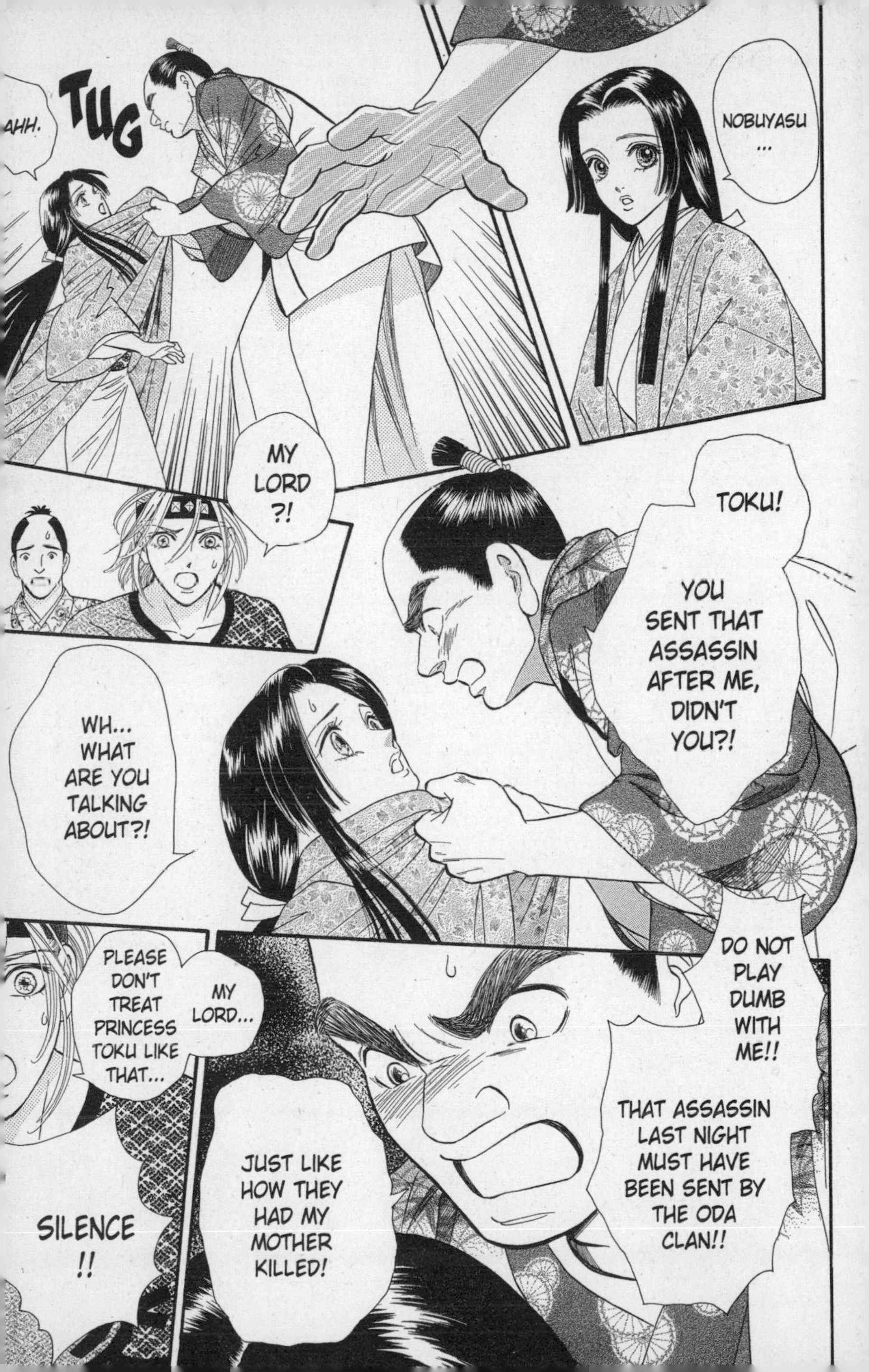
NOBUYASU ...
TUG
AHH.
TOKU!
YOU SENT THAT ASSASSIN AFTER ME, DIDN'T YOU?!
WH... WHAT ARE YOU TALKING ABOUT?!
MY LORD ?!
DO NOT PLAY DUMB WITH ME!!
THAT ASSASSIN LAST NIGHT MUST HAVE BEEN SENT BY THE ODA CLAN!!
JUST LIKE HOW THEY HAD MY MOTHER KILLED!
MY LORD...
PLEASE DON'T TREAT PRINCESS TOKU LIKE THAT...
SILENCE !!

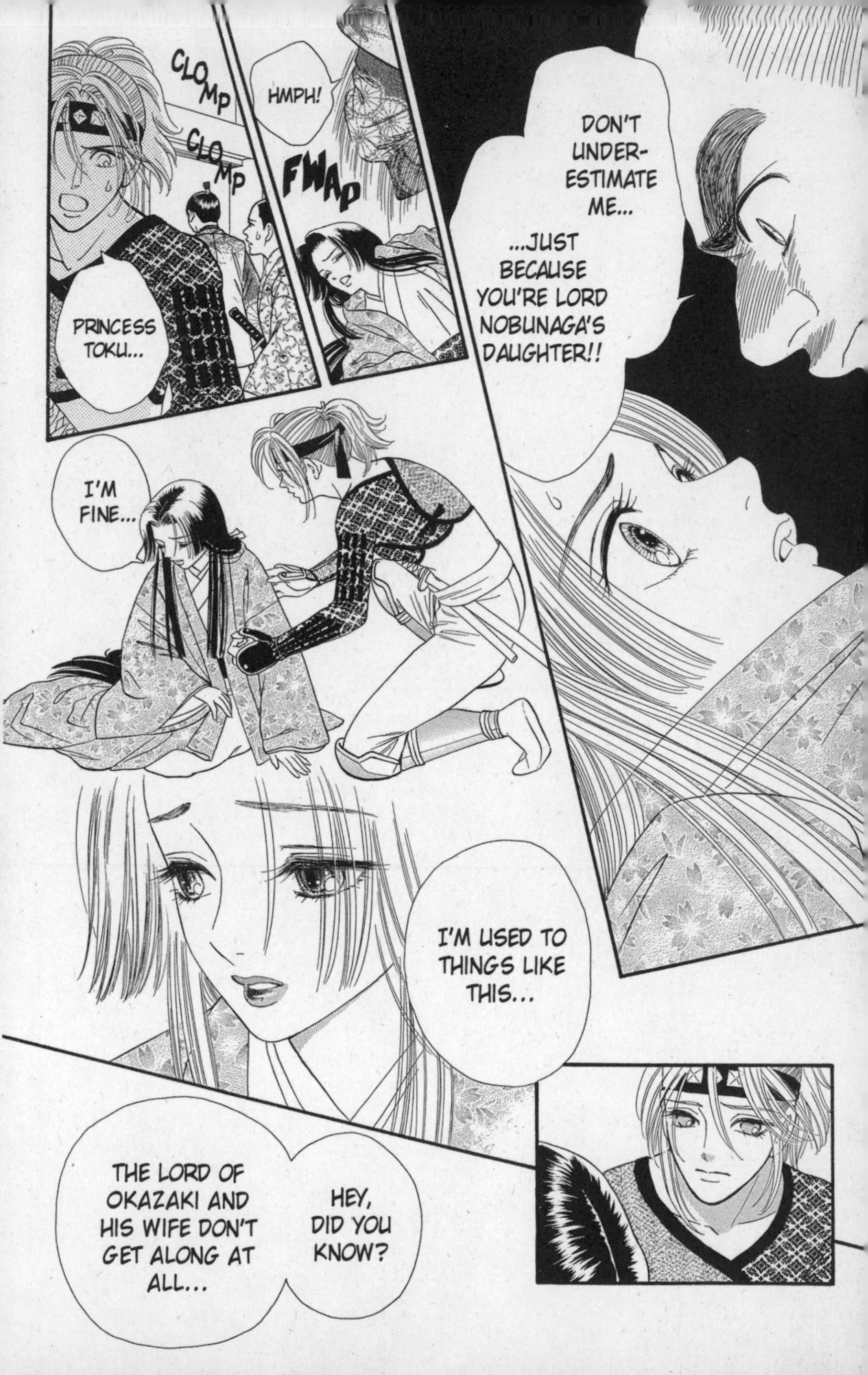
DON'T UNDER-ESTIMATE ME...
...JUST BECAUSE YOU'RE LORD NOBUNAGA'S DAUGHTER!!
HMPH!
FWAP
CLOMP
CLOMP
PRINCESS TOKU...
I'M FINE...
I'M USED TO THINGS LIKE THIS...
HEY, DID YOU KNOW?
THE LORD OF OKAZAKI AND HIS WIFE DON'T GET ALONG AT ALL...

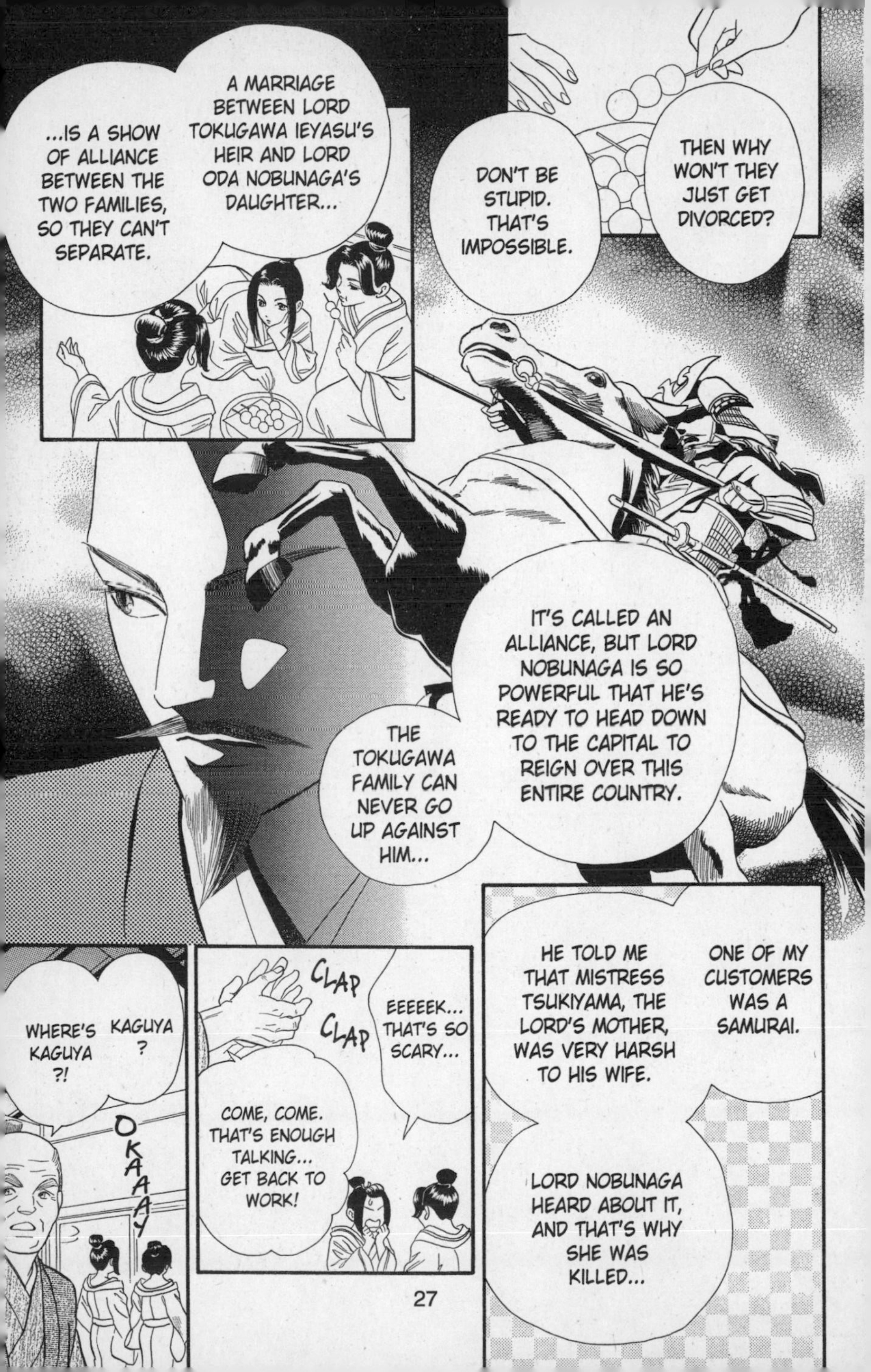
THEN WHY WON'T THEY JUST GET DIVORCED?
DON'T BE STUPID. THAT'S IMPOSSIBLE.
A MARRIAGE BETWEEN LORD TOKUGAWA IEYASU'S HEIR AND LORD ODA NOBUNAGA'S DAUGHTER...
...IS A SHOW OF ALLIANCE BETWEEN THE TWO FAMILIES, SO THEY CAN'T SEPARATE.
IT'S CALLED AN ALLIANCE, BUT LORD NOBUNAGA IS SO POWERFUL THAT HE'S READY TO HEAD DOWN TO THE CAPITAL TO REIGN OVER THIS ENTIRE COUNTRY.
THE TOKUGAWA FAMILY CAN NEVER GO UP AGAINST HIM...
ONE OF MY CUSTOMERS WAS A SAMURAI.
HE TOLD ME THAT MISTRESS TSUKIYAMA, THE LORD'S MOTHER, WAS VERY HARSH TO HIS WIFE.
LORD NOBUNAGA HEARD ABOUT IT, AND THAT'S WHY SHE WAS KILLED...
EEEEEK... THAT'S SO SCARY...
CLAP
CLAP
COME, COME. THAT'S ENOUGH TALKING... GET BACK TO WORK!
KAGUYA?
WHERE'S KAGUYA?!
OKAAAAY

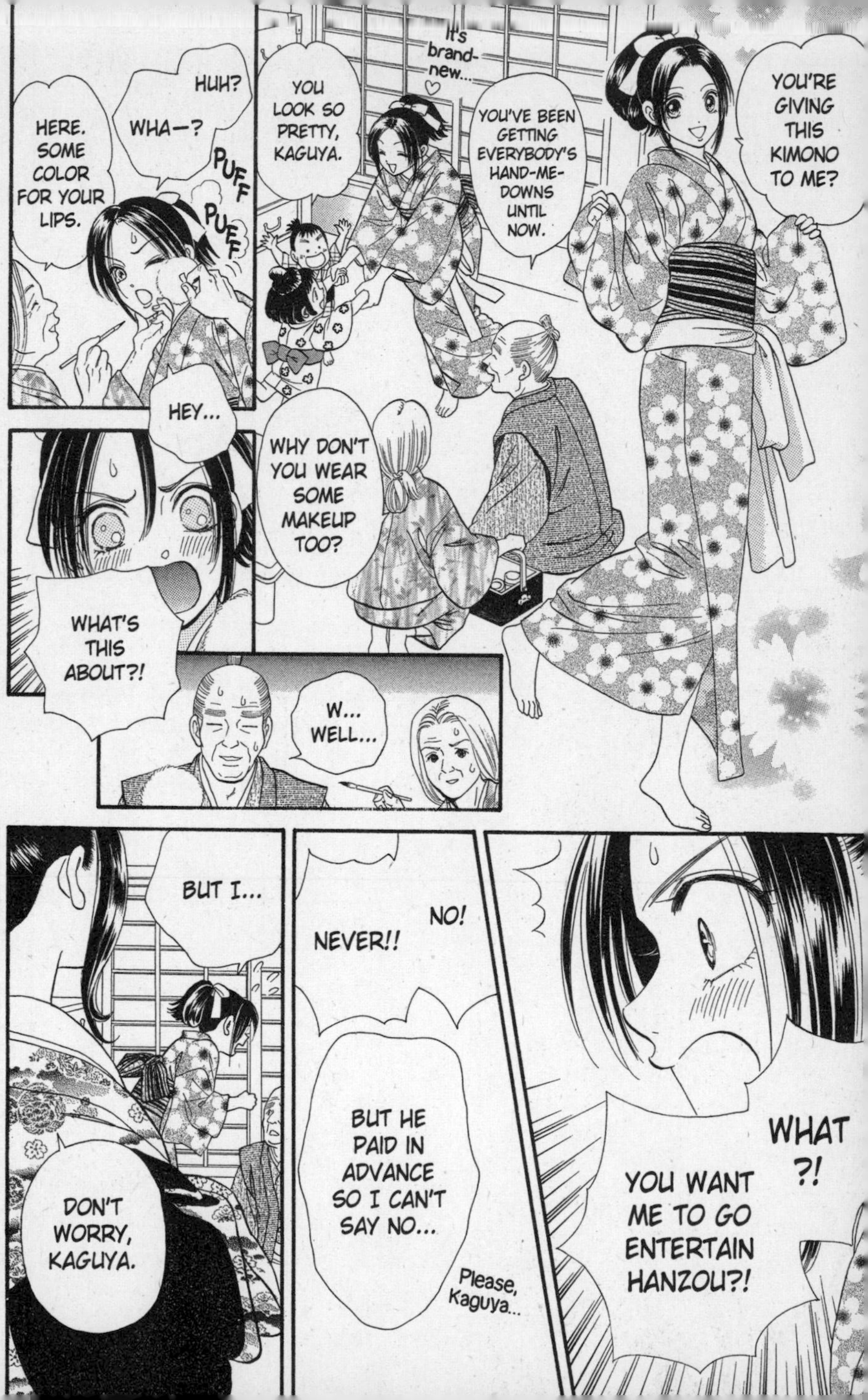

YOU'RE GIVING THIS KIMONO TO ME?
It's brand-new...
YOU'VE BEEN GETTING EVERYBODY'S HAND-ME-DOWNS UNTIL NOW.
YOU LOOK SO PRETTY, KAGUYA.
WHY DON'T YOU WEAR SOME MAKEUP TOO?
HUH?
WHA—?
HERE. SOME COLOR FOR YOUR LIPS.
PUFF PUFF
HEY...
WHAT'S THIS ABOUT?!
W... WELL...
WHAT ?!
YOU WANT ME TO GO ENTERTAIN HANZOU?!
NO!
NEVER!!
BUT HE PAID IN ADVANCE SO I CAN'T SAY NO...
Please, Kaguya...
BUT I...
DON'T WORRY, KAGUYA.

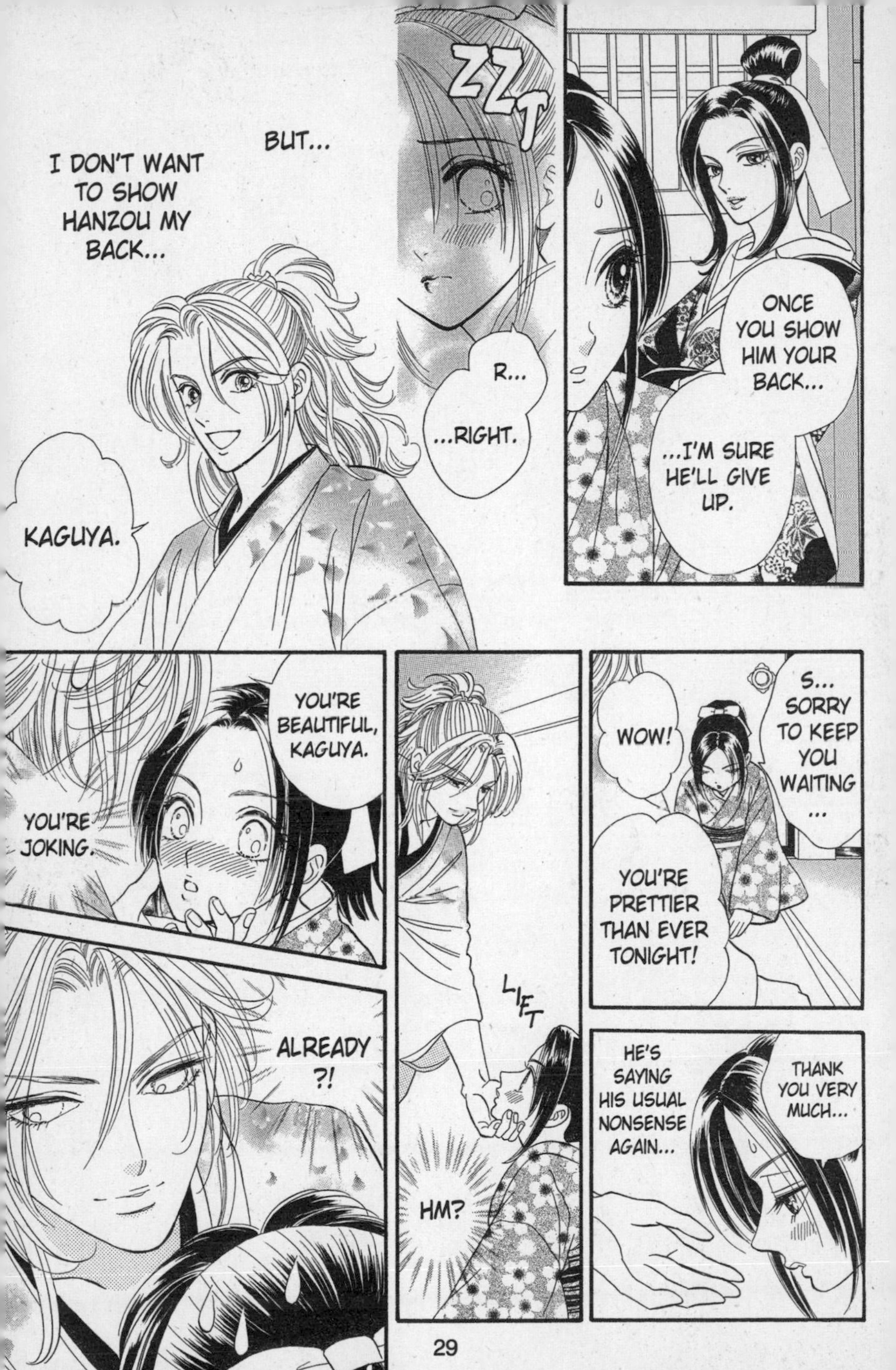
ONCE YOU SHOW HIM YOUR BACK...
...I'M SURE HE'LL GIVE UP.
ZZT
R...
...RIGHT.
BUT...
I DON'T WANT TO SHOW HANZOU MY BACK...
KAGUYA.
S... SORRY TO KEEP YOU WAITING...
WOW!
YOU'RE PRETTIER THAN EVER TONIGHT!
THANK YOU VERY MUCH...
HE'S SAYING HIS USUAL NONSENSE AGAIN...
LIFT
HM?
YOU'RE BEAUTIFUL, KAGUYA.
YOU'RE JOKING.
ALREADY ?!

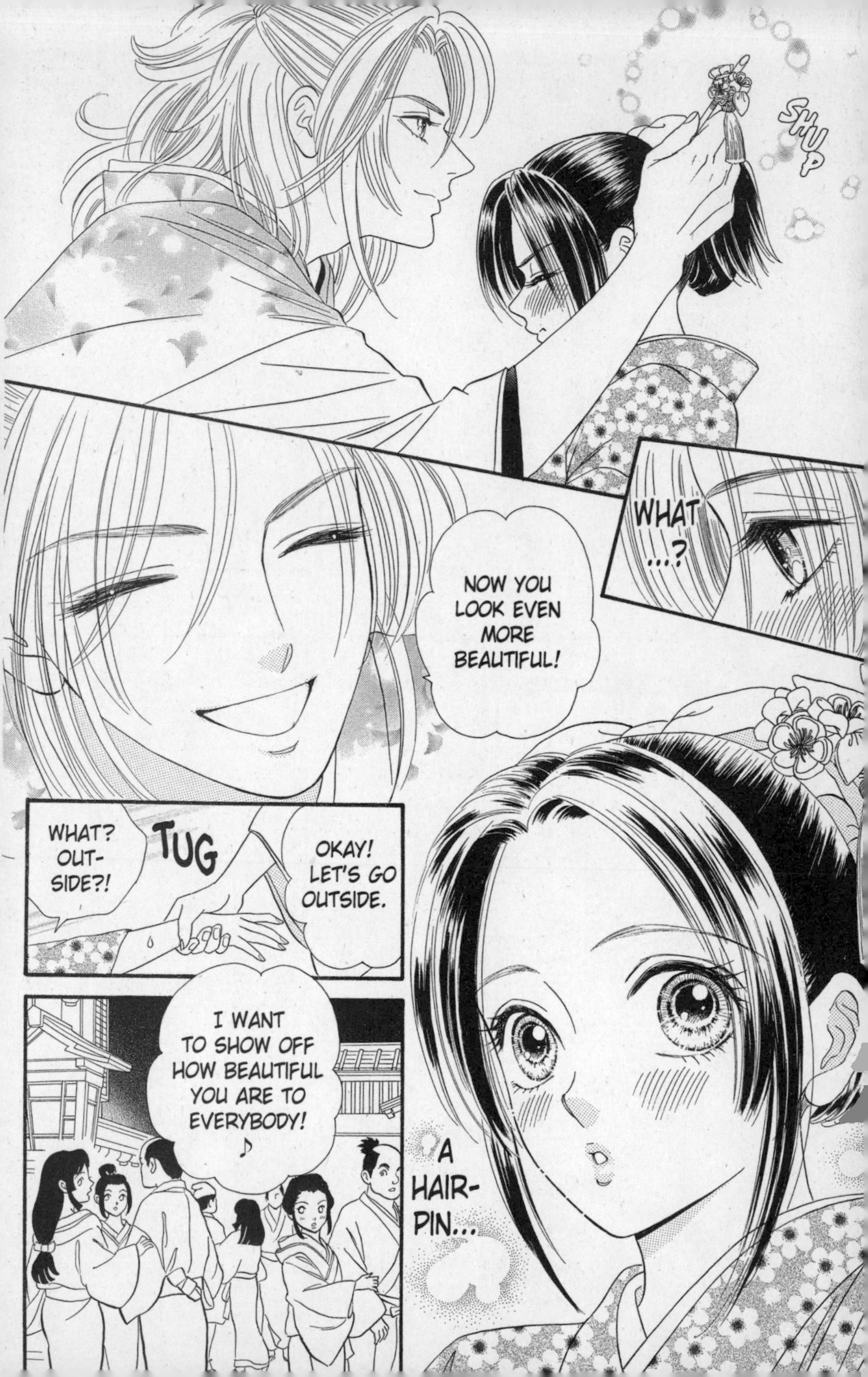
SHUP
WHAT...?
NOW YOU LOOK EVEN MORE BEAUTIFUL!
A HAIR-PIN...
OKAY! LET'S GO OUTSIDE.
TUG
WHAT? OUT-SIDE?!
I WANT TO SHOW OFF HOW BEAUTIFUL YOU ARE TO EVERYBODY! ♪

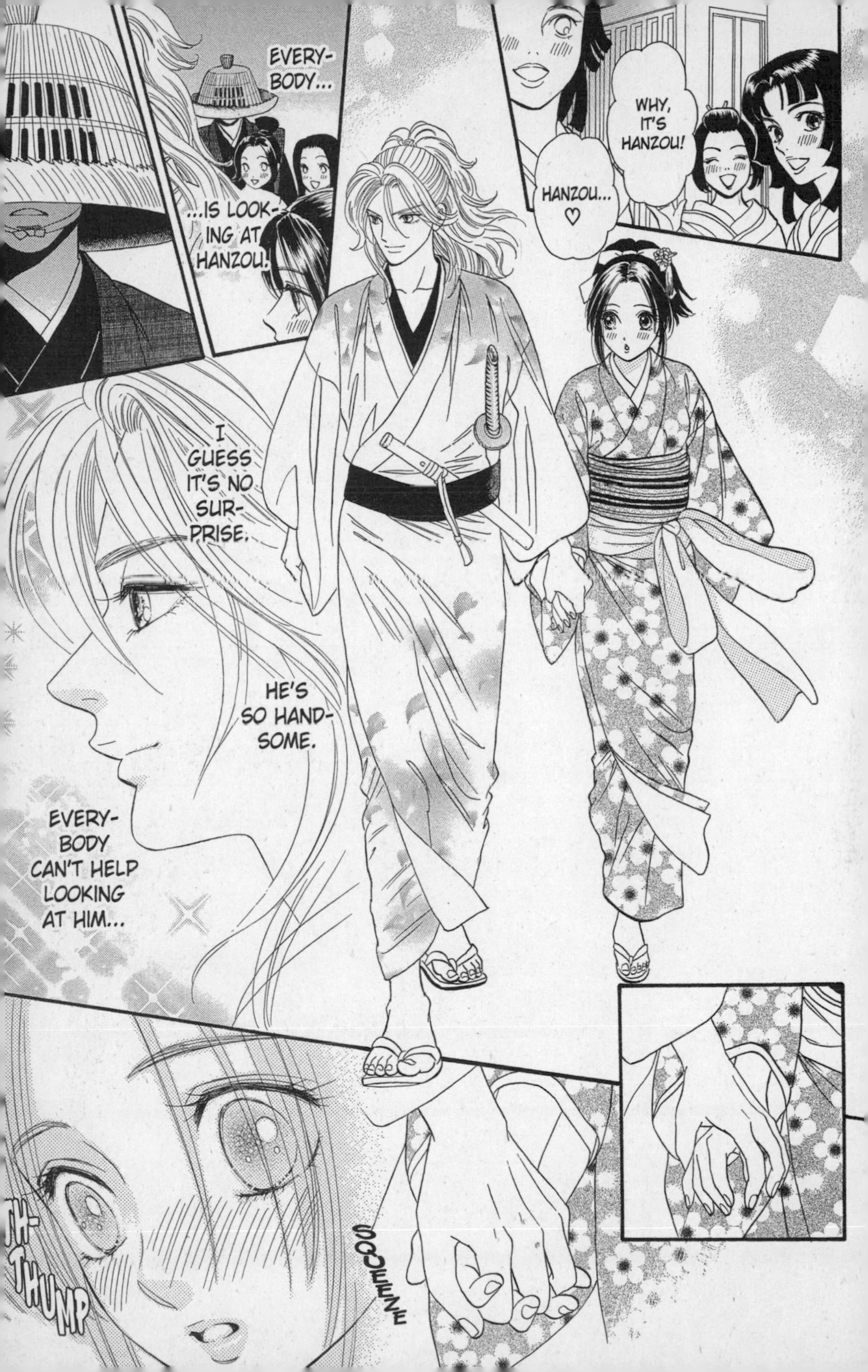
WHY, IT'S HANZOU!
HANZOU... ♡
EVERY-BODY...
...IS LOOK-ING AT HANZOU!
I GUESS IT'S NO SUR-PRISE.
HE'S SO HAND-SOME.
EVERY-BODY CAN'T HELP LOOKING AT HIM...
SQUEEZE
TH-THUMP

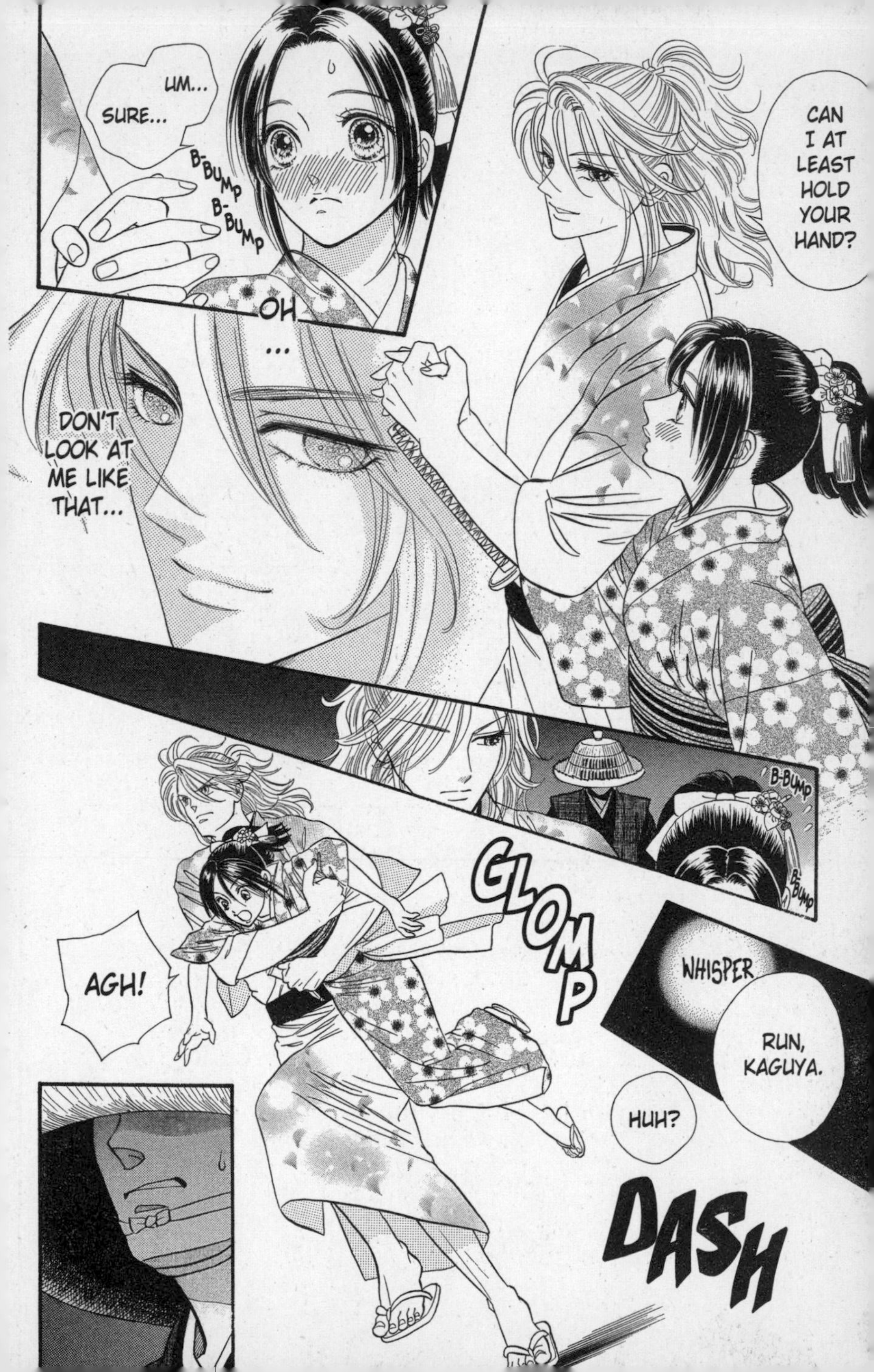
CAN I AT LEAST HOLD YOUR HAND?
UM... SURE...
B-BUMP B-BUMP
OH ...
DON'T LOOK AT ME LIKE THAT...
B-BUMP
B-BUMP
WHISPER
RUN, KAGUYA.
HUH?
GLOMP
AGH!
DASH

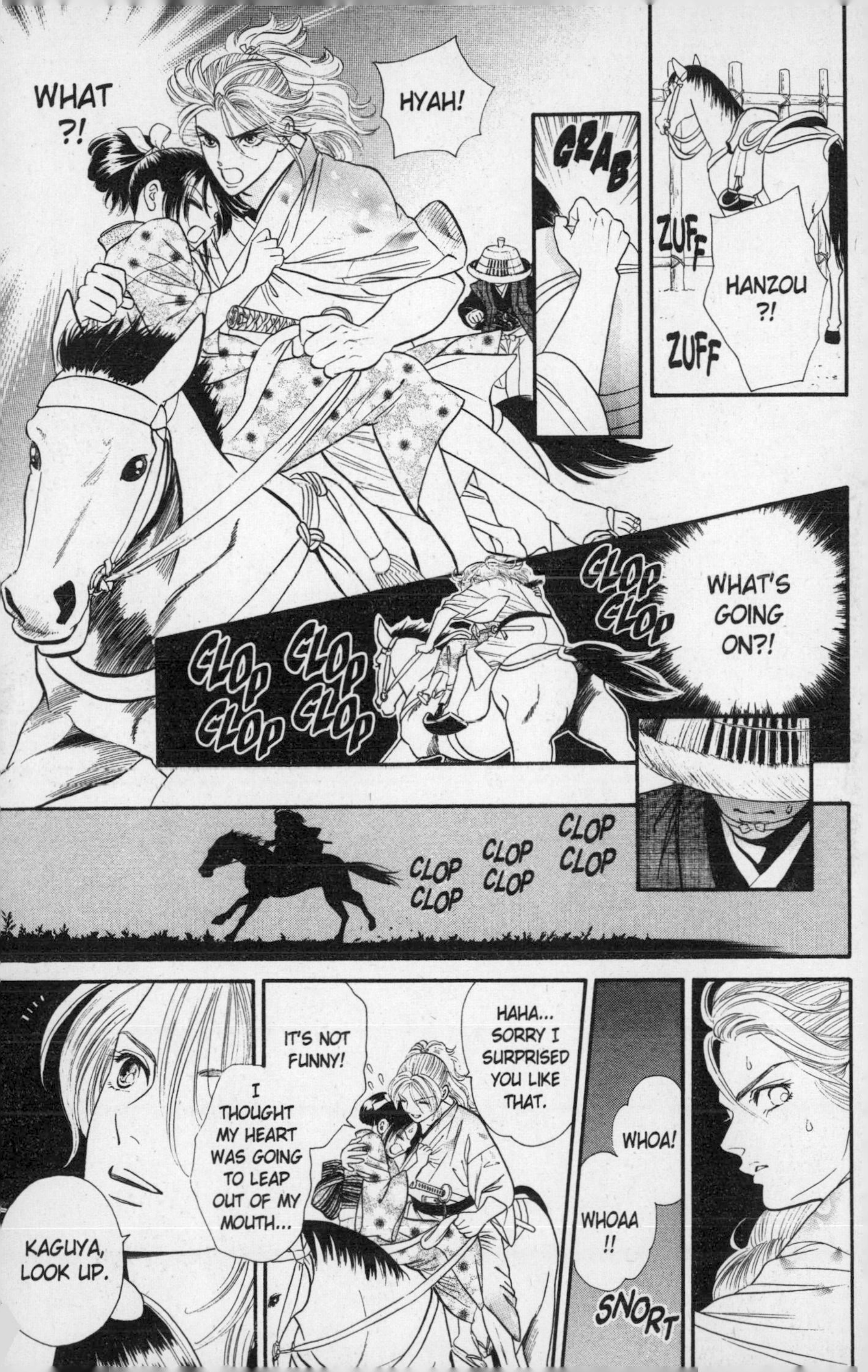
ZUFF
ZUFF
HANZOU?!
GRAB
HYAH!
WHAT?!
WHAT'S GOING ON?!
CLOP CLOP
CLOP CLOP CLOP CLOP
CLOP CLOP
CLOP CLOP
CLOP CLOP
CLOP CLOP
WHOA!
WHOAA!!
SNORT
HAHA... SORRY I SURPRISED YOU LIKE THAT.
IT'S NOT FUNNY!
I THOUGHT MY HEART WAS GOING TO LEAP OUT OF MY MOUTH...
KAGUYA, LOOK UP.

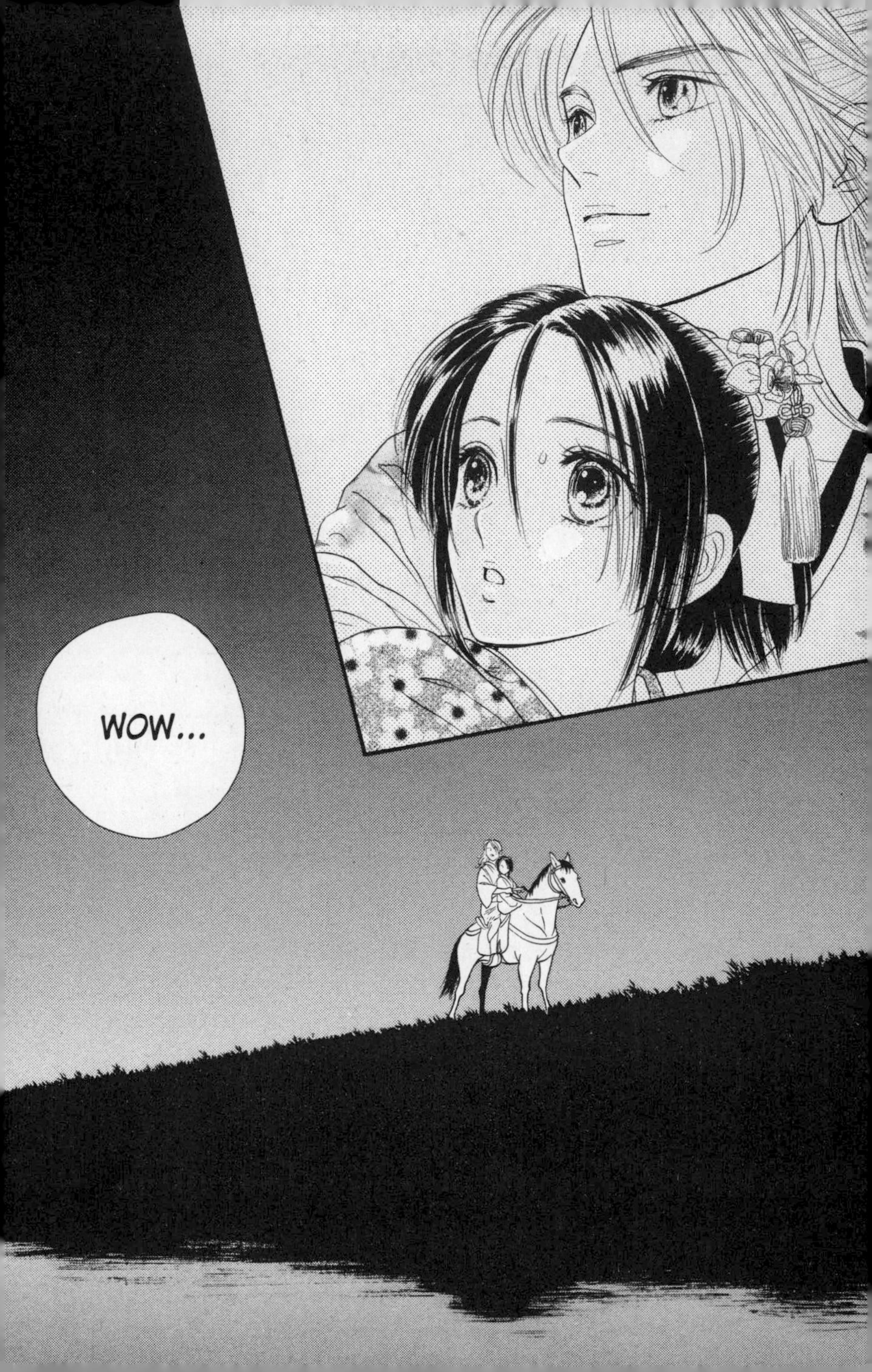
WOW...

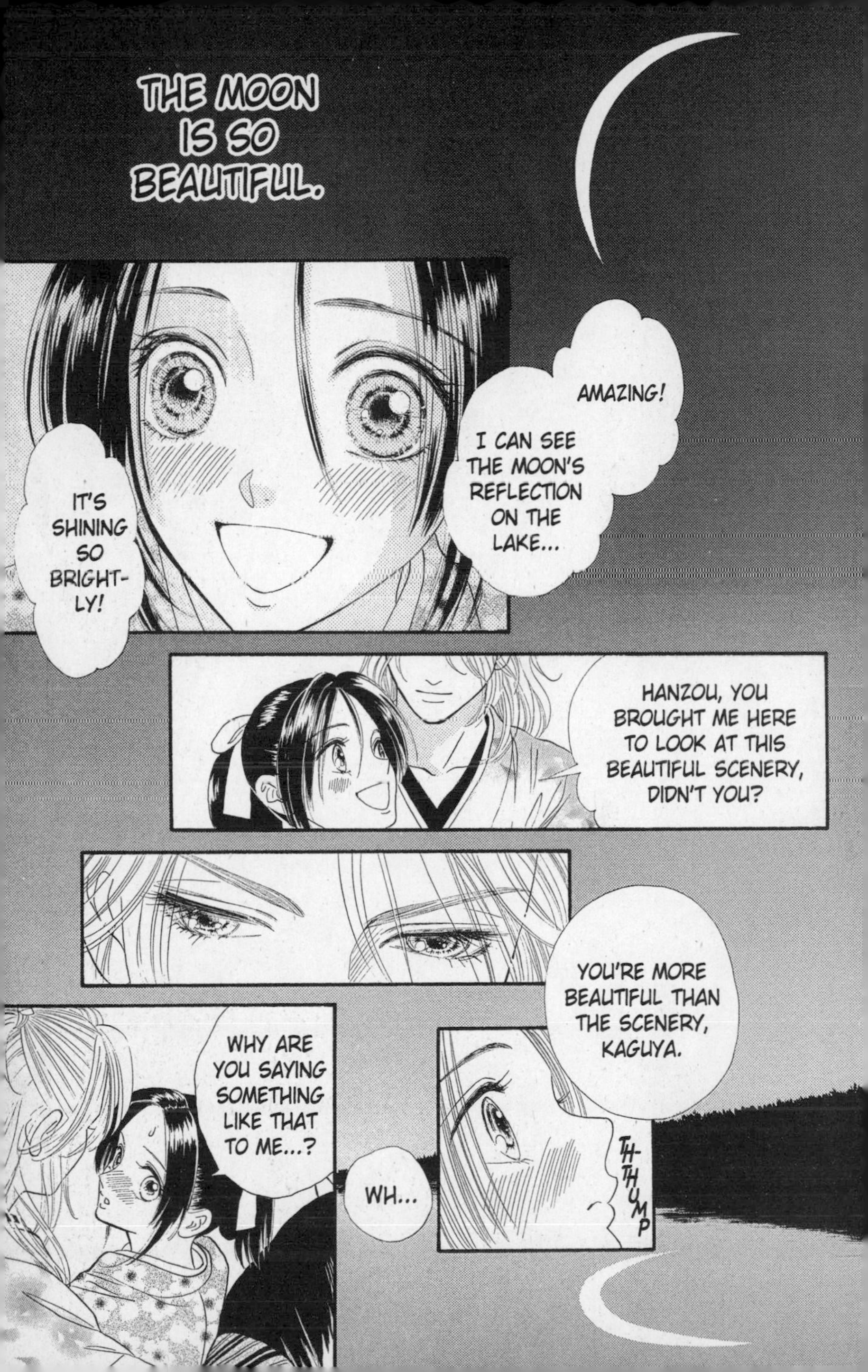
THE MOON IS SO BEAUTIFUL.
AMAZING!
I CAN SEE THE MOON'S REFLECTION ON THE LAKE...
IT'S SHINING SO BRIGHTLY!
HANZOU, YOU BROUGHT ME HERE TO LOOK AT THIS BEAUTIFUL SCENERY, DIDN'T YOU?
YOU'RE MORE BEAUTIFUL THAN THE SCENERY, KAGUYA.
TH-THUMP
WH...
WHY ARE YOU SAYING SOMETHING LIKE THAT TO ME...?

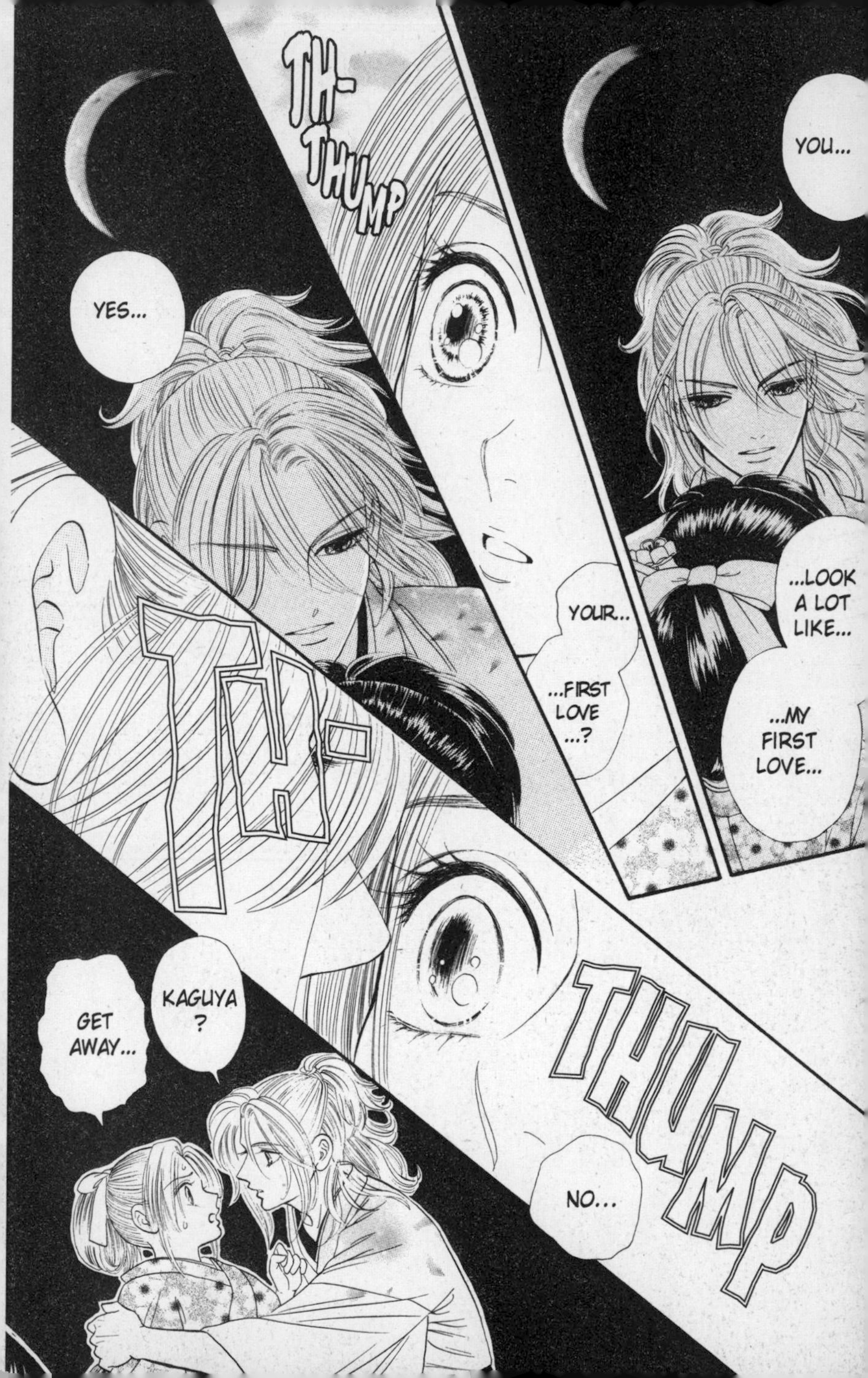
YOU...
...LOOK A LOT LIKE...
...MY FIRST LOVE...
TH-THUMP
YOUR...
...FIRST LOVE ...?
YES...
TH-
THUMP
NO...
KAGUYA ?
GET AWAY...

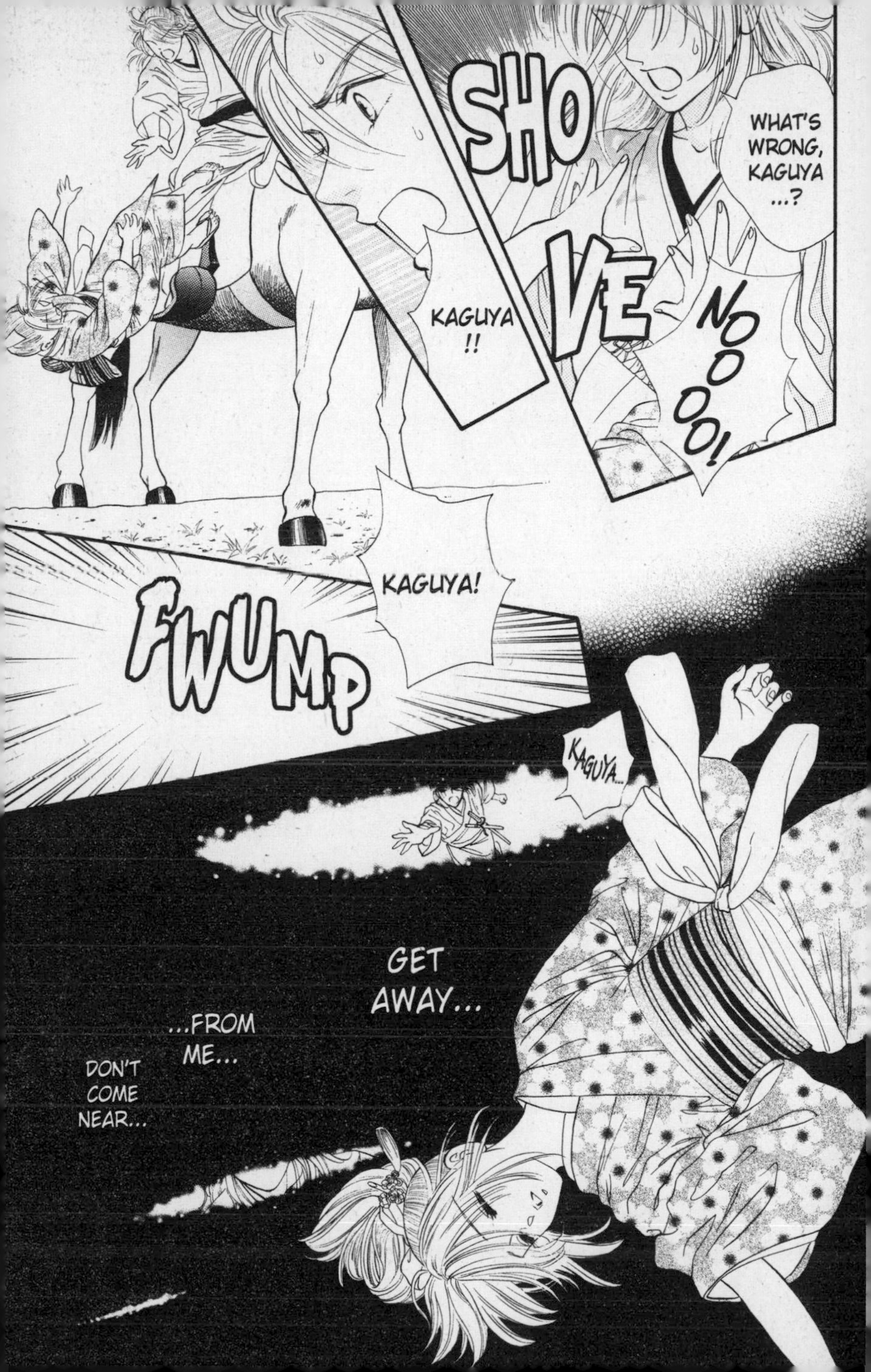
WHAT'S WRONG, KAGUYA ...?
SHOVE
NOOOOO!
KAGUYA !!
KAGUYA!
FWUMP
KAGUYA...
GET AWAY...
...FROM ME...
DON'T COME NEAR...

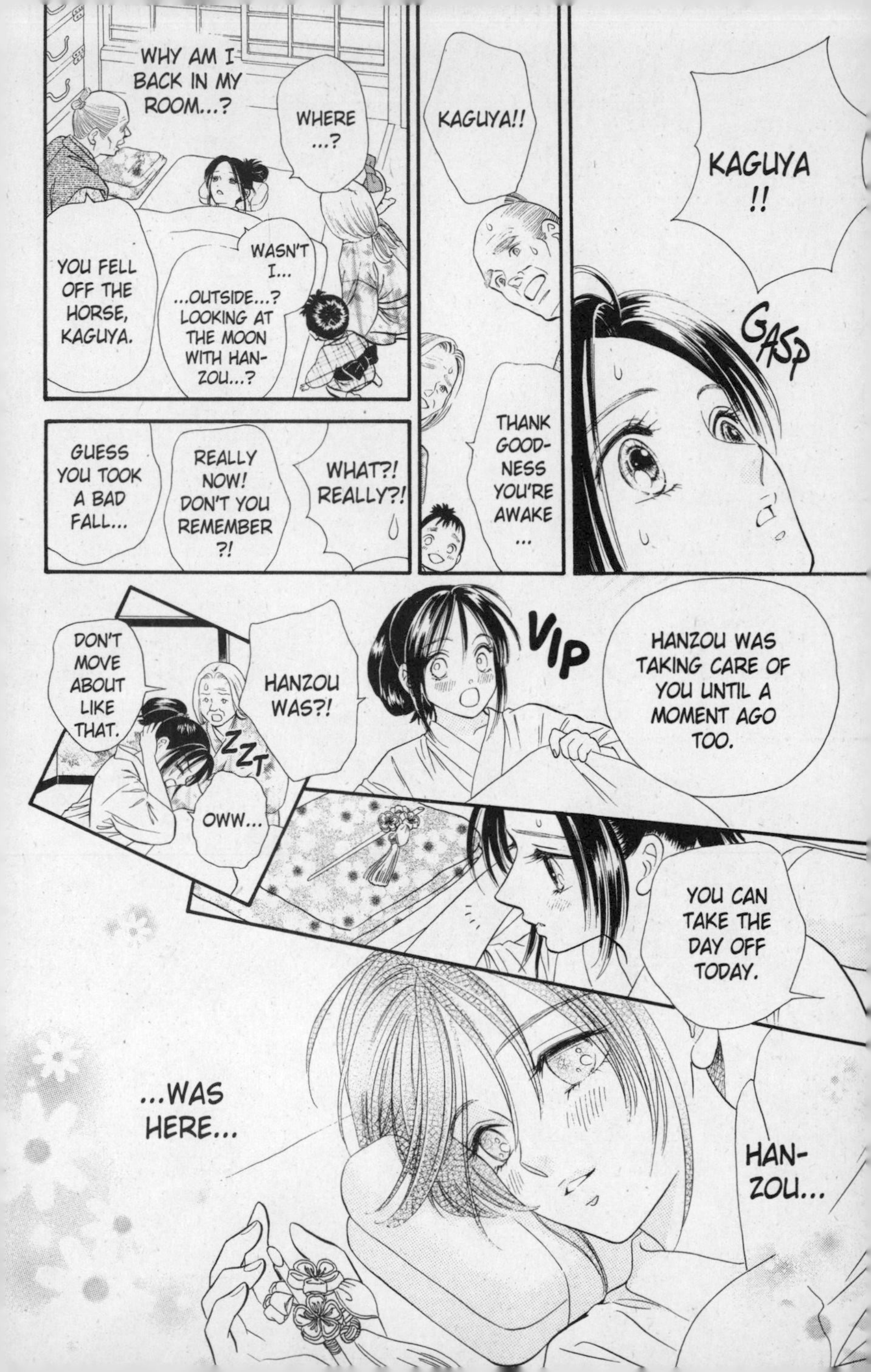
KAGUYA !!
GASP
KAGUYA!!
THANK GOODNESS YOU'RE AWAKE ...
WHERE ...?
WHY AM I BACK IN MY ROOM...?
WASN'T I... ...OUTSIDE...? LOOKING AT THE MOON WITH HAN-ZOU...?
YOU FELL OFF THE HORSE, KAGUYA.
WHAT?! REALLY?!
REALLY NOW! DON'T YOU REMEMBER ?!
GUESS YOU TOOK A BAD FALL...
HANZOU WAS TAKING CARE OF YOU UNTIL A MOMENT AGO TOO.
VIP
HANZOU WAS?!
DON'T MOVE ABOUT LIKE THAT.
ZZT
OWW...
YOU CAN TAKE THE DAY OFF TODAY.
HAN-ZOU...
...WAS HERE...

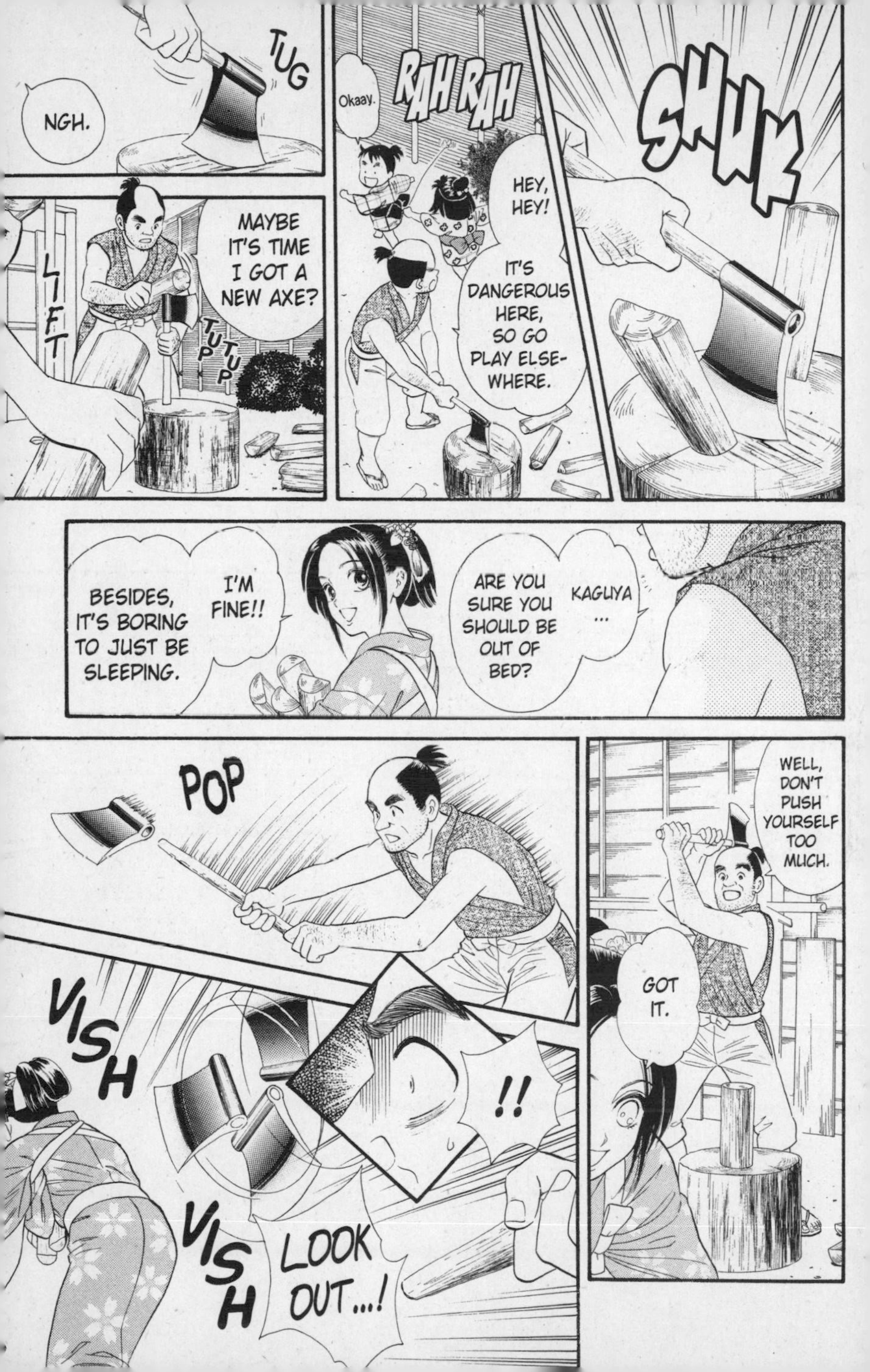
SHUK
HEY, HEY!
IT'S DANGEROUS HERE, SO GO PLAY ELSE-WHERE.
RAH RAH
Okaay.
TUG
NGH.
MAYBE IT'S TIME I GOT A NEW AXE?
LIFT
TUP TUP
KAGUYA...
ARE YOU SURE YOU SHOULD BE OUT OF BED?
I'M FINE!!
BESIDES, IT'S BORING TO JUST BE SLEEPING.
WELL, DON'T PUSH YOURSELF TOO MUCH.
GOT IT.
POP
!!
VISH
VISH
LOOK OUT...!

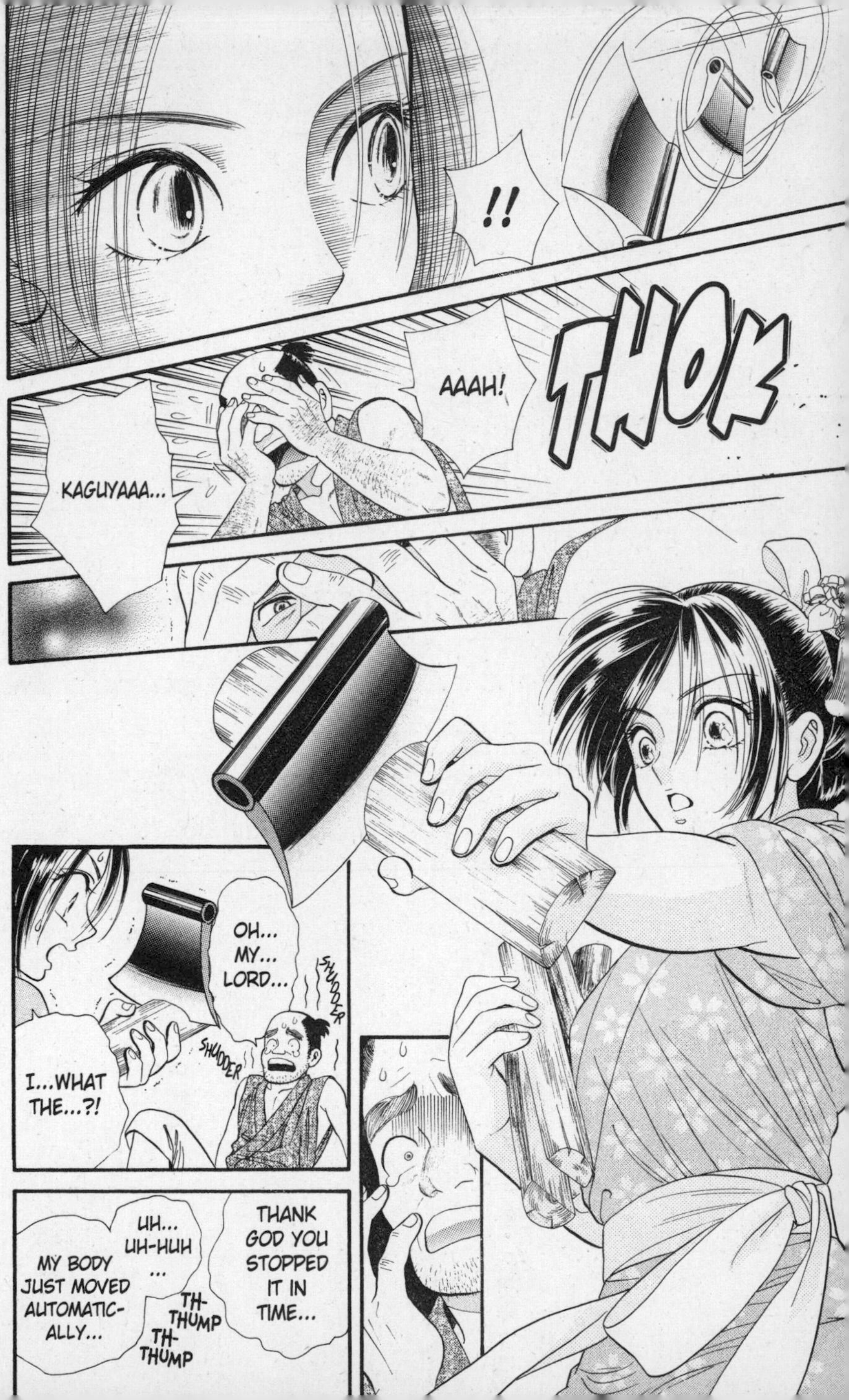
!!
THOK
AAAH!
KAGUYAAA...
OH... MY... LORD...
SHUDDER
SHUDDER
I...WHAT THE...?!
THANK GOD YOU STOPPED IT IN TIME...
UH... UH-HUH...
MY BODY JUST MOVED AUTOMATIC-ALLY...
TH-THUMP
TH-THUMP

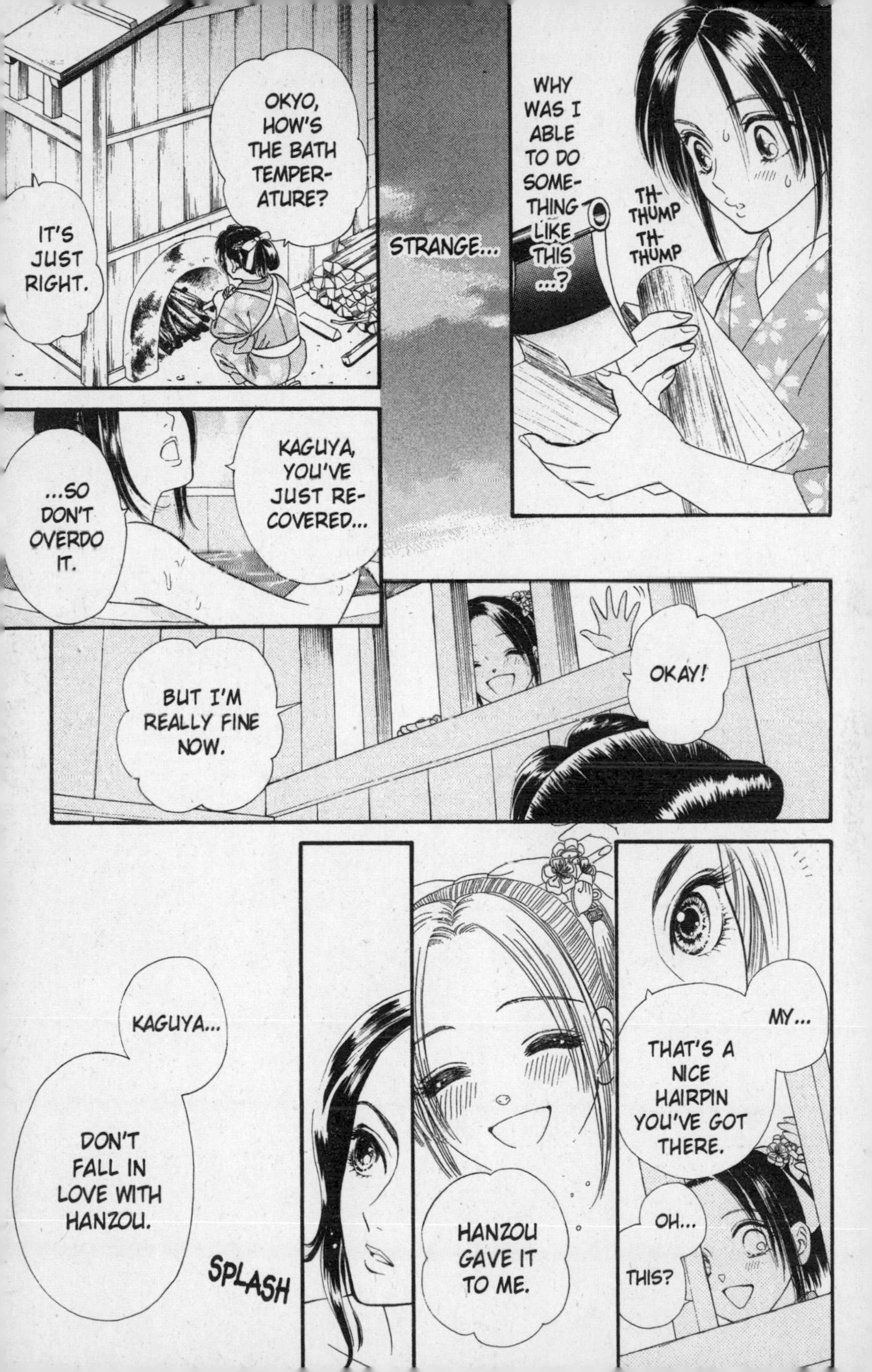
WHY WAS I ABLE TO DO SOMETHING LIKE THIS ...?
TH-THUMP TH-THUMP
STRANGE...
OKYO, HOW'S THE BATH TEMPER-ATURE?
IT'S JUST RIGHT.
KAGUYA, YOU'VE JUST RE-COVERED...
...SO DON'T OVERDO IT.
OKAY!
BUT I'M REALLY FINE NOW.
MY...
THAT'S A NICE HAIRPIN YOU'VE GOT THERE.
OH... THIS?
HANZOU GAVE IT TO ME.
KAGUYA...
DON'T FALL IN LOVE WITH HANZOU.
SPLASH

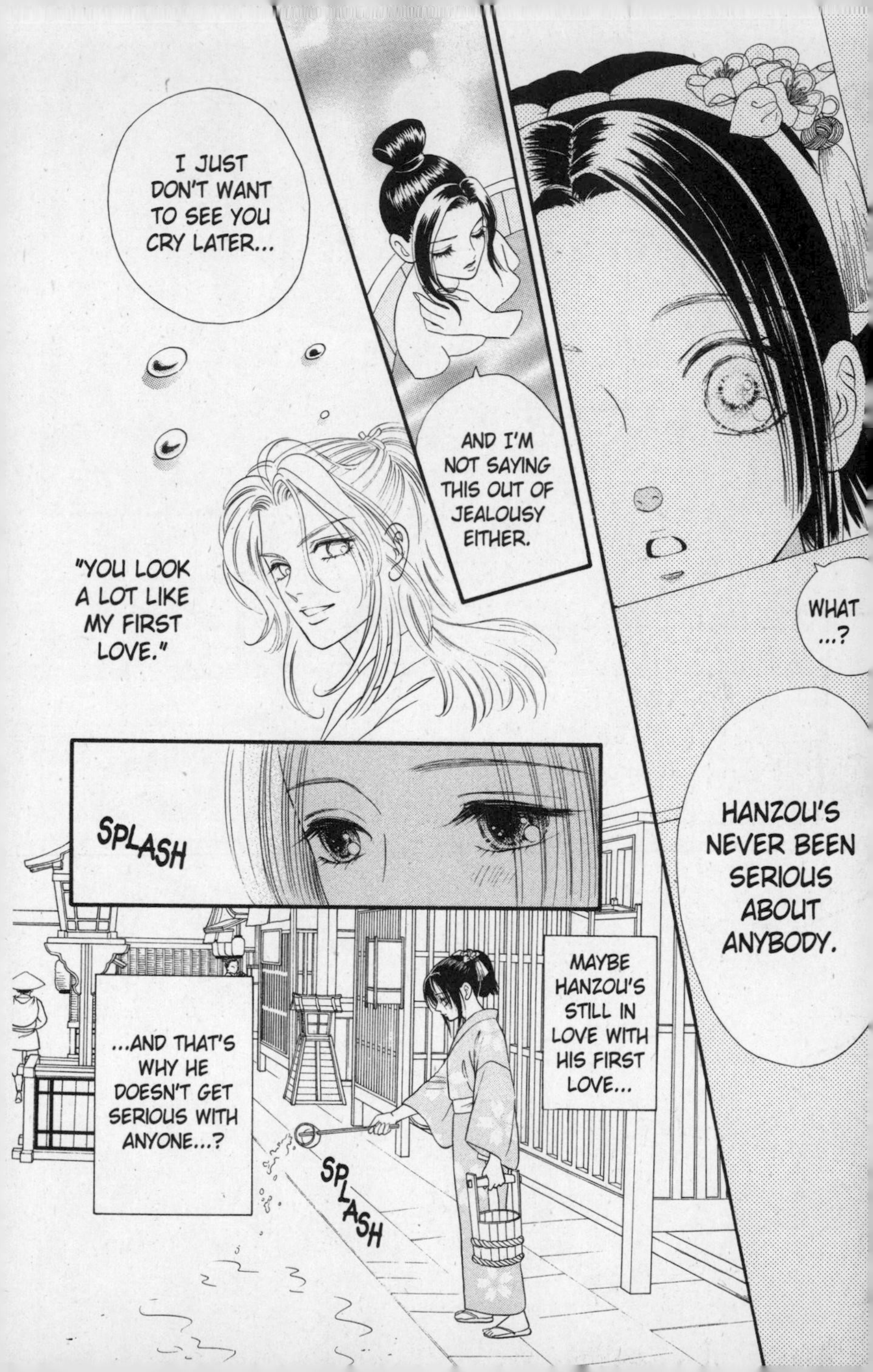
WHAT ...?
HANZOU'S NEVER BEEN SERIOUS ABOUT ANYBODY.
AND I'M NOT SAYING THIS OUT OF JEALOUSY EITHER.
I JUST DON'T WANT TO SEE YOU CRY LATER...
"YOU LOOK A LOT LIKE MY FIRST LOVE."
SPLASH
MAYBE HANZOU'S STILL IN LOVE WITH HIS FIRST LOVE...
...AND THAT'S WHY HE DOESN'T GET SERIOUS WITH ANYONE...?
SPLASH

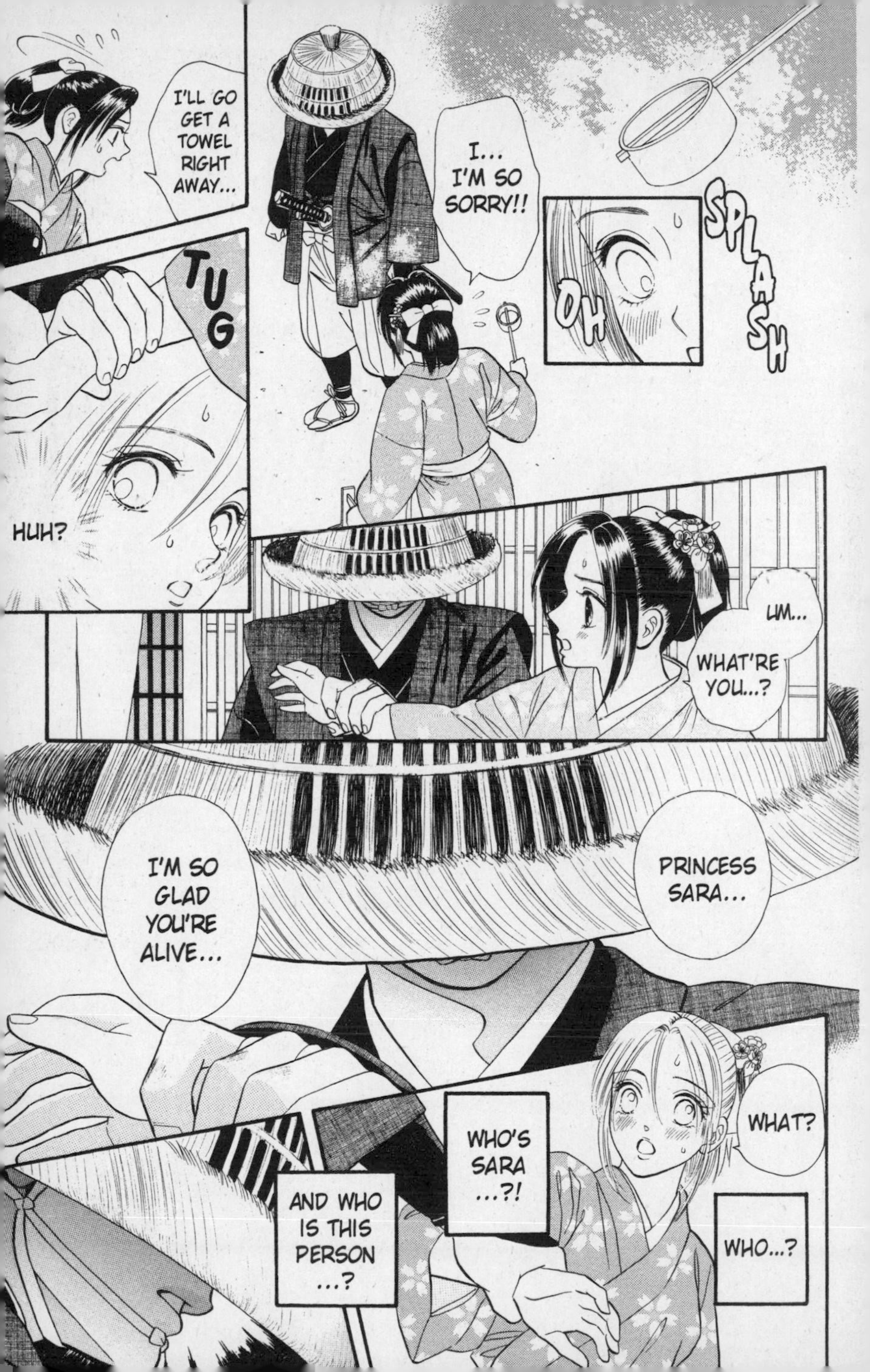
SPLASH
OH
I... I'M SO SORRY!!
I'LL GO GET A TOWEL RIGHT AWAY...
TUG
HUH?
UM...
WHAT'RE YOU...?
PRINCESS SARA...
I'M SO GLAD YOU'RE ALIVE...
WHAT?
WHO...?
WHO'S SARA ...?!
AND WHO IS THIS PERSON ...?

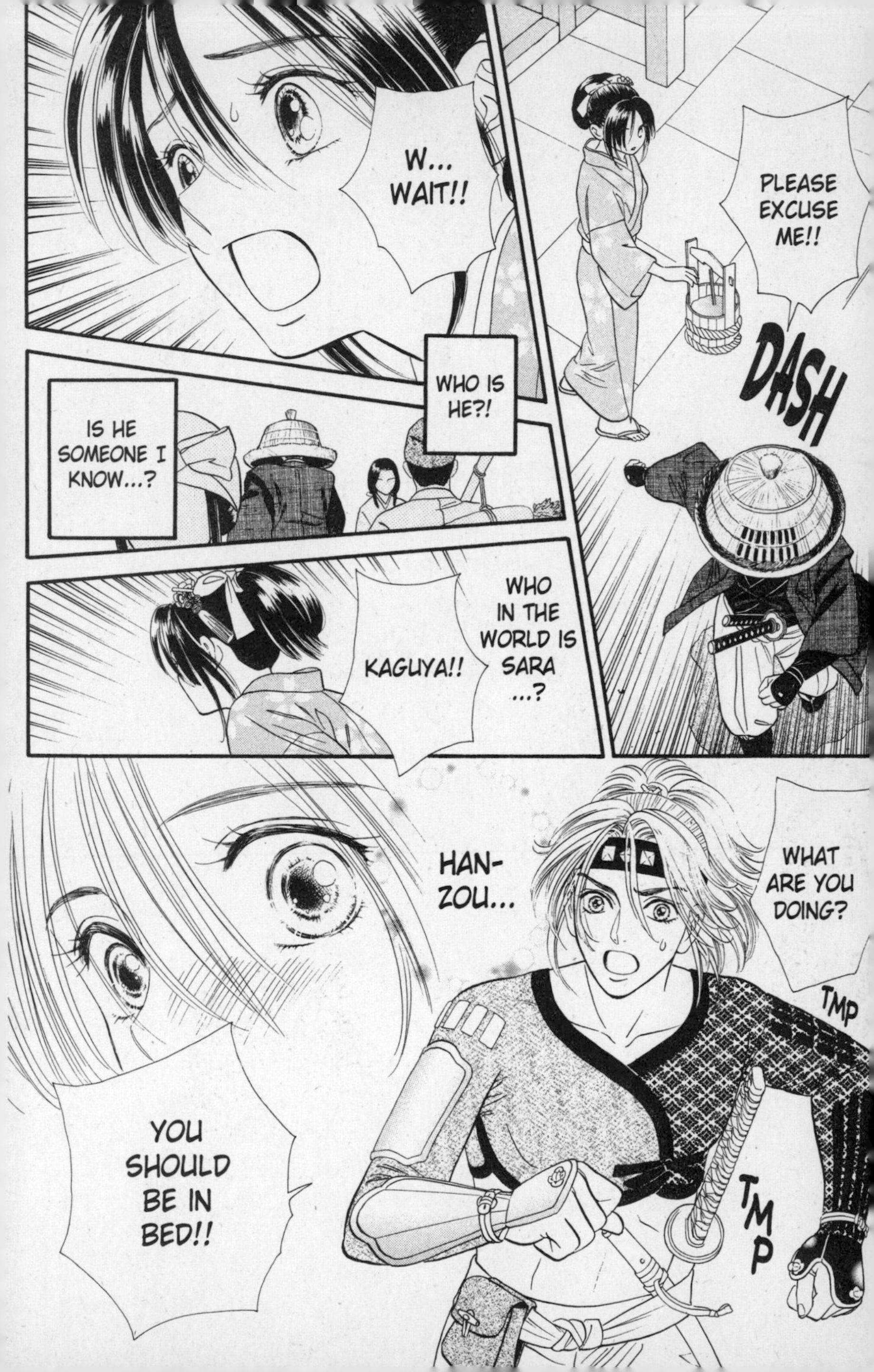
PLEASE EXCUSE ME!!
DASH
W... WAIT!!
WHO IS HE?!
IS HE SOMEONE I KNOW...?
WHO IN THE WORLD IS SARA ...?
KAGUYA!!
WHAT ARE YOU DOING?
TMP
HAN-ZOU...
TMP
YOU SHOULD BE IN BED!!

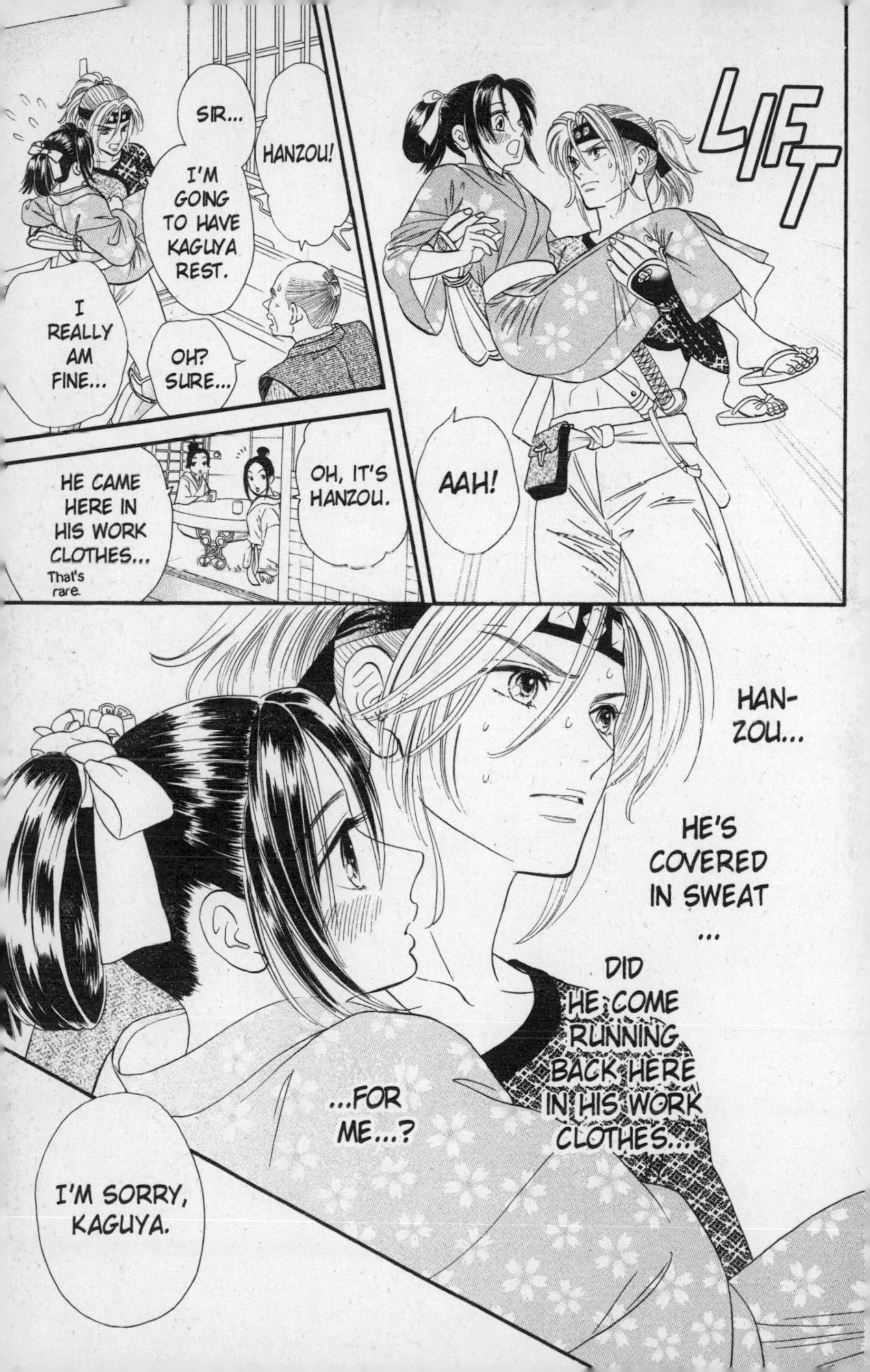
LIFT
AAH!
HANZOU!
SIR... I'M GOING TO HAVE KAGUYA REST.
OH? SURE...
I REALLY AM FINE...
OH, IT'S HANZOU.
HE CAME HERE IN HIS WORK CLOTHES...
That's rare.
HAN-ZOU...
HE'S COVERED IN SWEAT ...
DID HE COME RUNNING BACK HERE IN HIS WORK CLOTHES...
...FOR ME...?
I'M SORRY, KAGUYA.

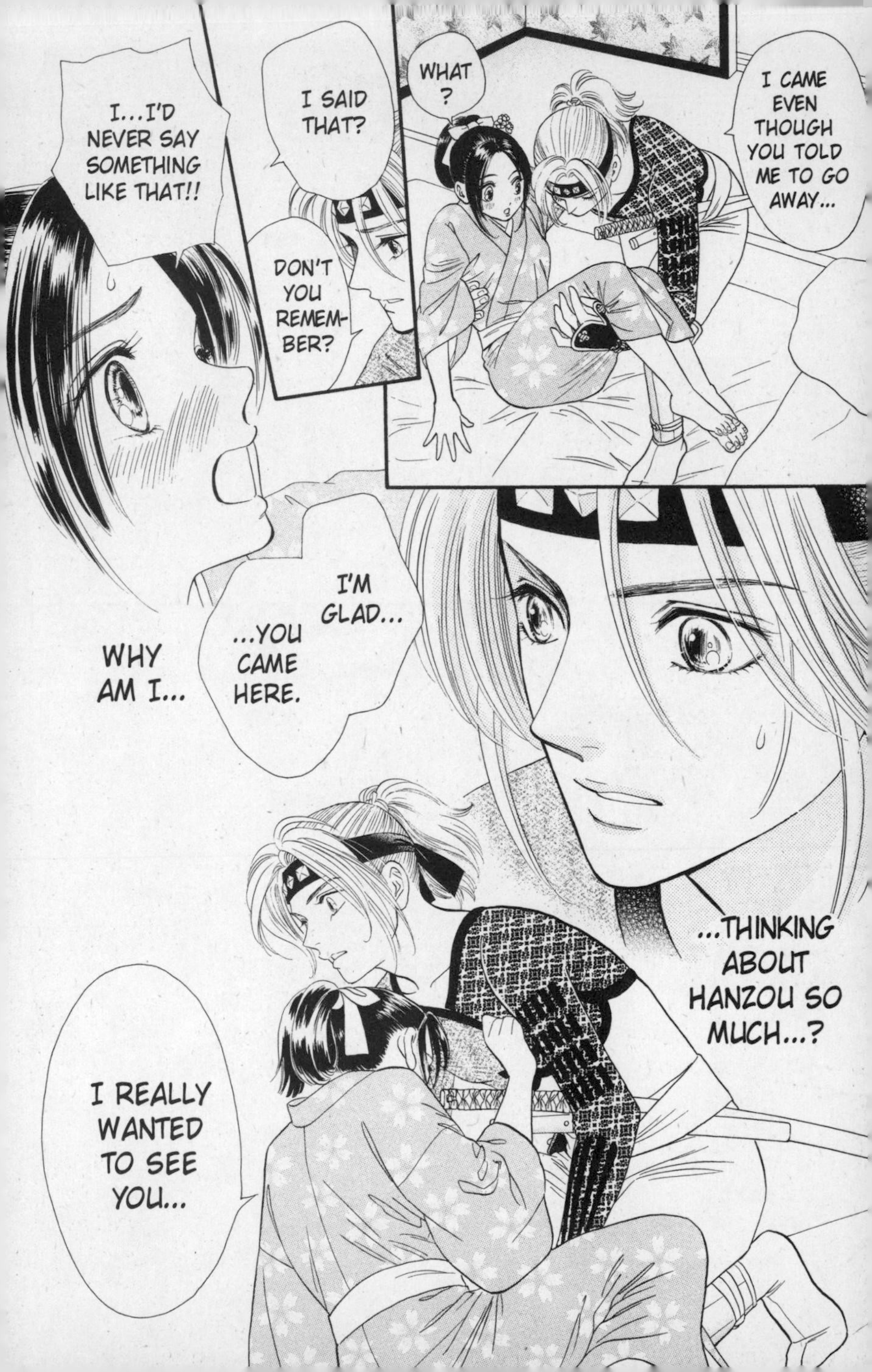
I CAME EVEN THOUGH YOU TOLD ME TO GO AWAY...
WHAT?
I SAID THAT?
DON'T YOU REMEM-BER?
I...I'D NEVER SAY SOMETHING LIKE THAT!!
I'M GLAD...
...YOU CAME HERE.
WHY AM I...
...THINKING ABOUT HANZOU SO MUCH...?
I REALLY WANTED TO SEE YOU...

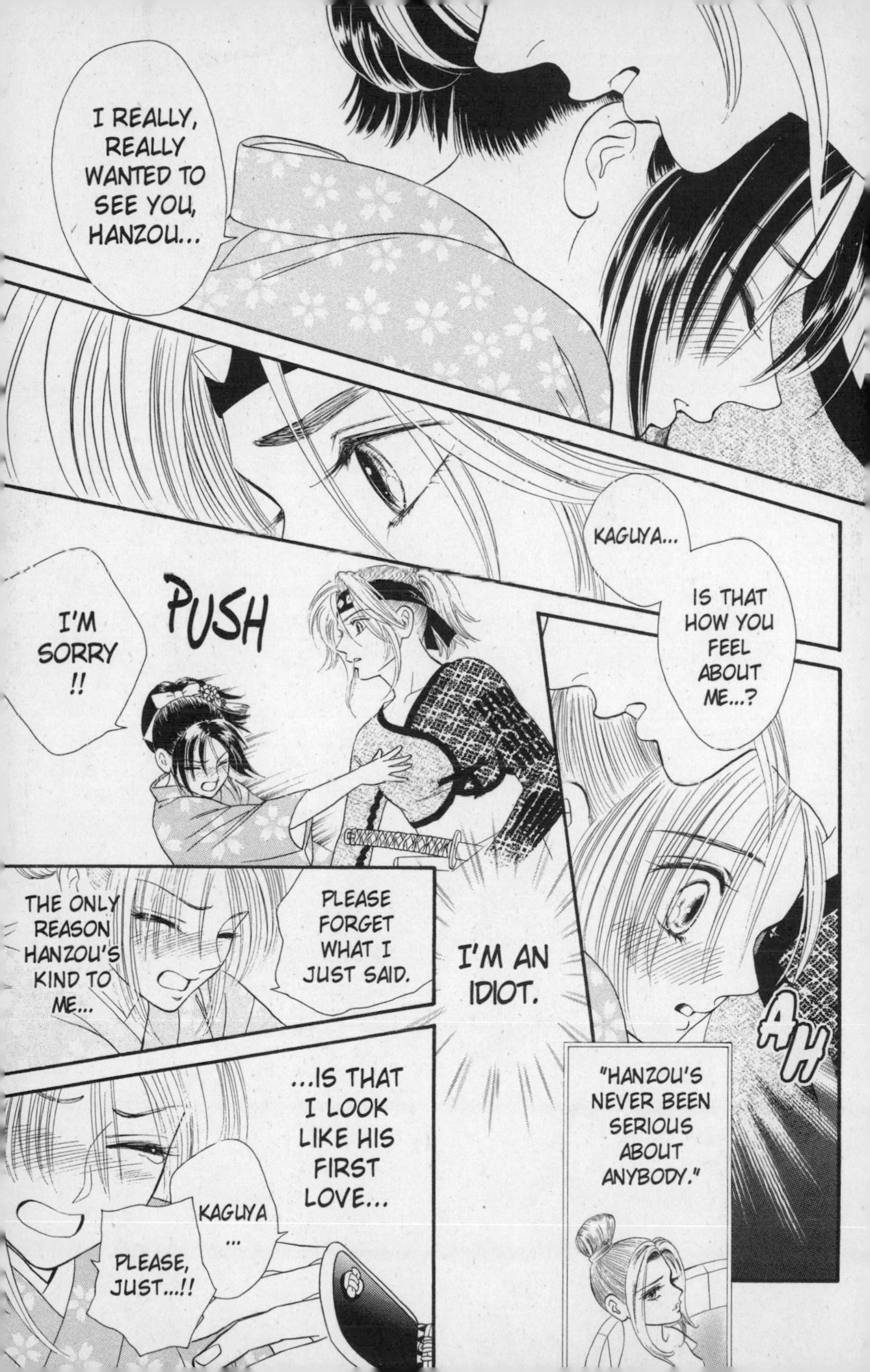
I REALLY, REALLY WANTED TO SEE YOU, HANZOU...
KAGUYA...
IS THAT HOW YOU FEEL ABOUT ME...?
AH
PUSH
I'M SORRY !!
I'M AN IDIOT.
PLEASE FORGET WHAT I JUST SAID.
THE ONLY REASON HANZOU'S KIND TO ME...
"HANZOU'S NEVER BEEN SERIOUS ABOUT ANYBODY."
...IS THAT I LOOK LIKE HIS FIRST LOVE...
KAGUYA ...
PLEASE, JUST...!!

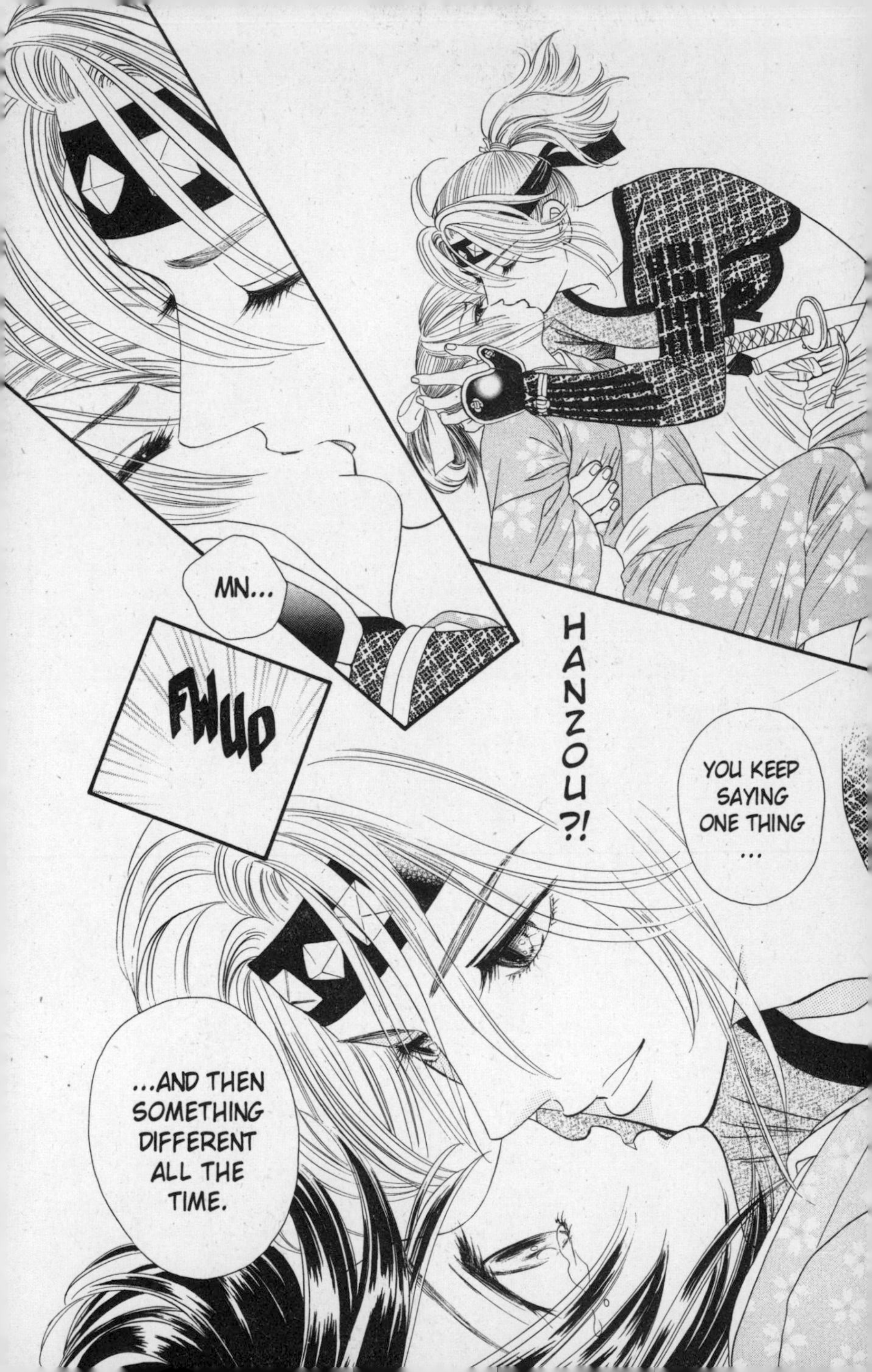
MN...
FWUP
HANZOU?!
YOU KEEP SAYING ONE THING ...
...AND THEN SOMETHING DIFFERENT ALL THE TIME.

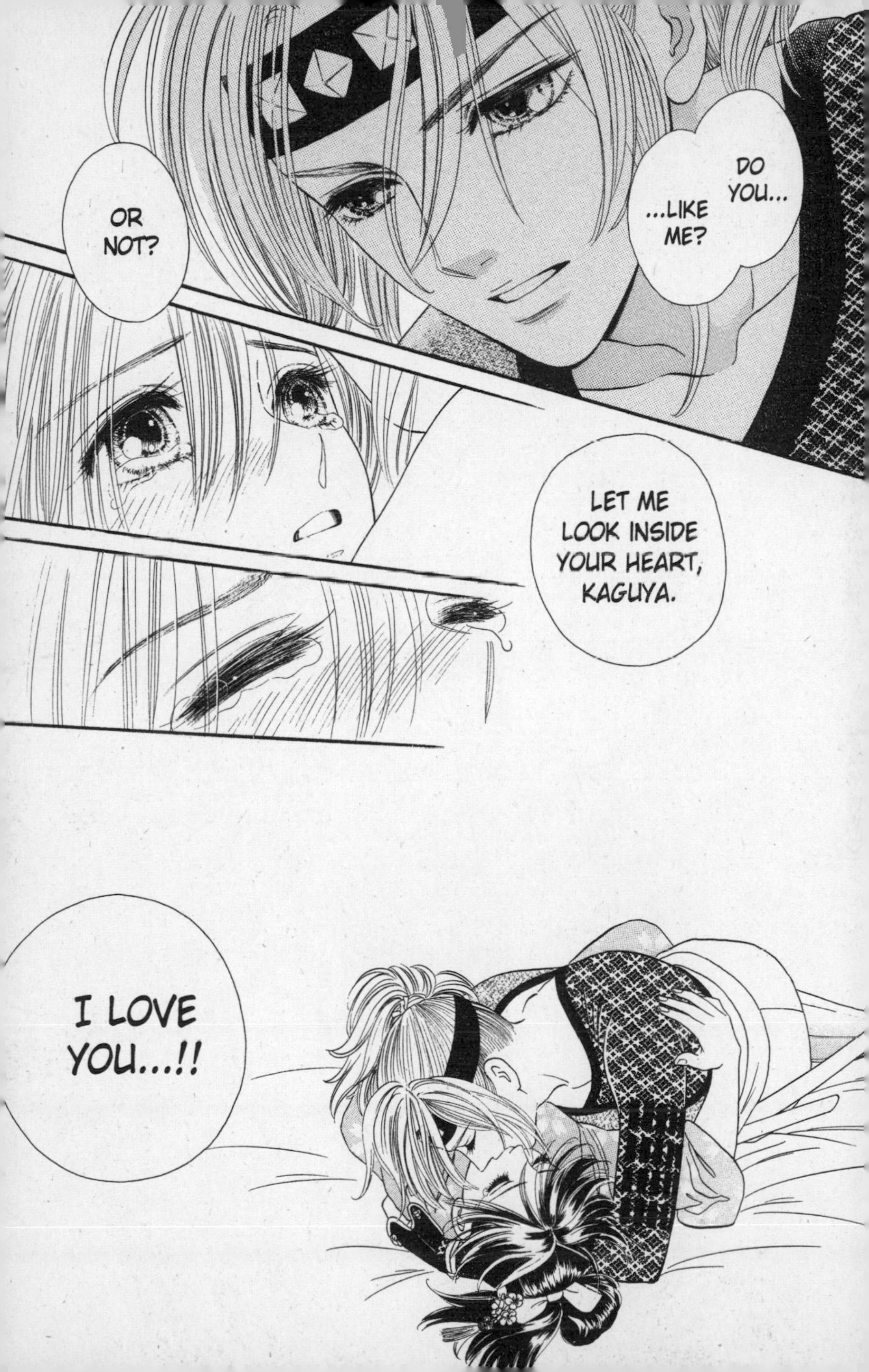
DO YOU...
...LIKE ME?
OR NOT?
LET ME LOOK INSIDE YOUR HEART, KAGUYA.
I LOVE YOU...!!

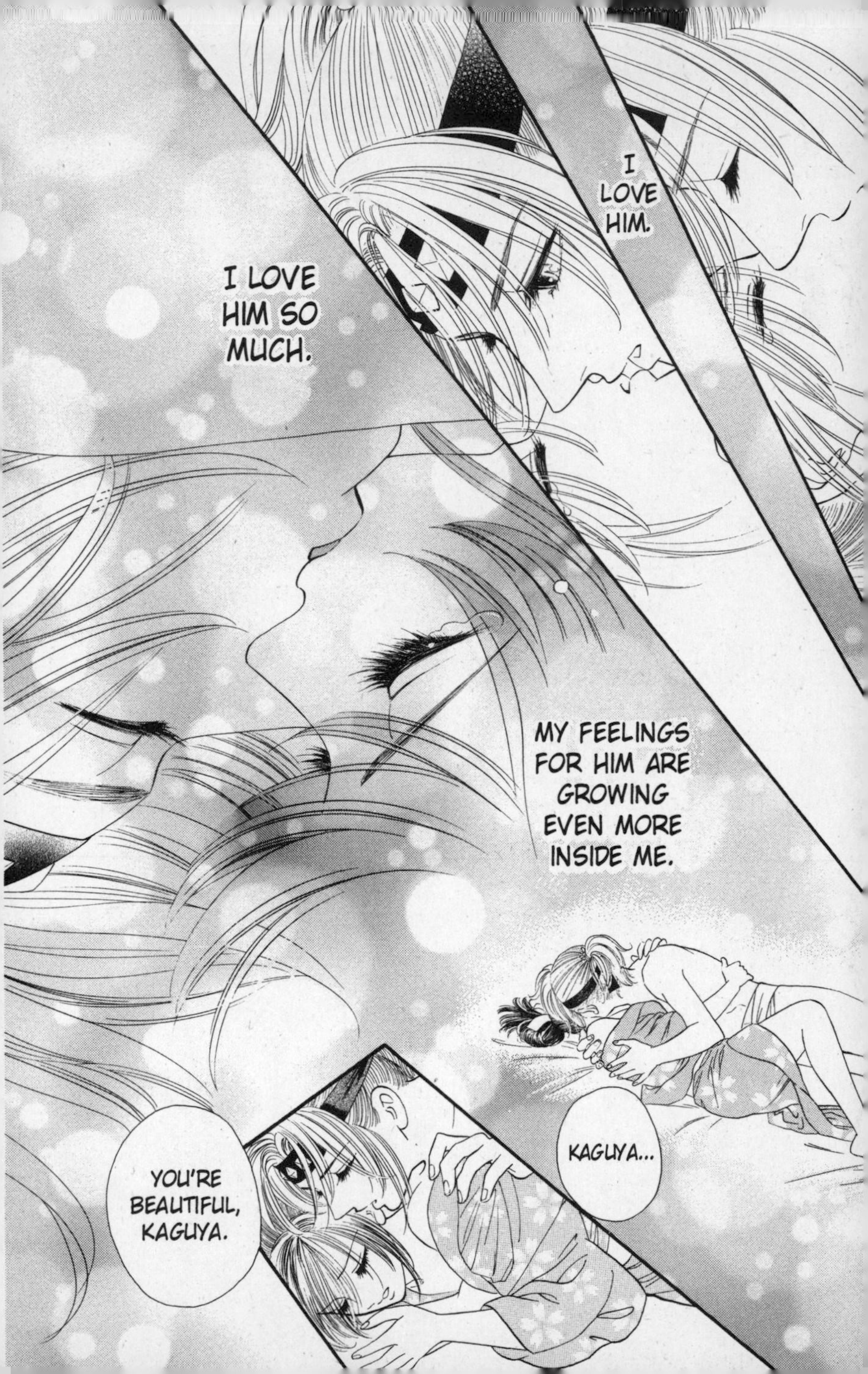
I LOVE HIM.
I LOVE HIM SO MUCH.
MY FEELINGS FOR HIM ARE GROWING EVEN MORE INSIDE ME.
KAGUYA...
YOU'RE BEAUTIFUL, KAGUYA.

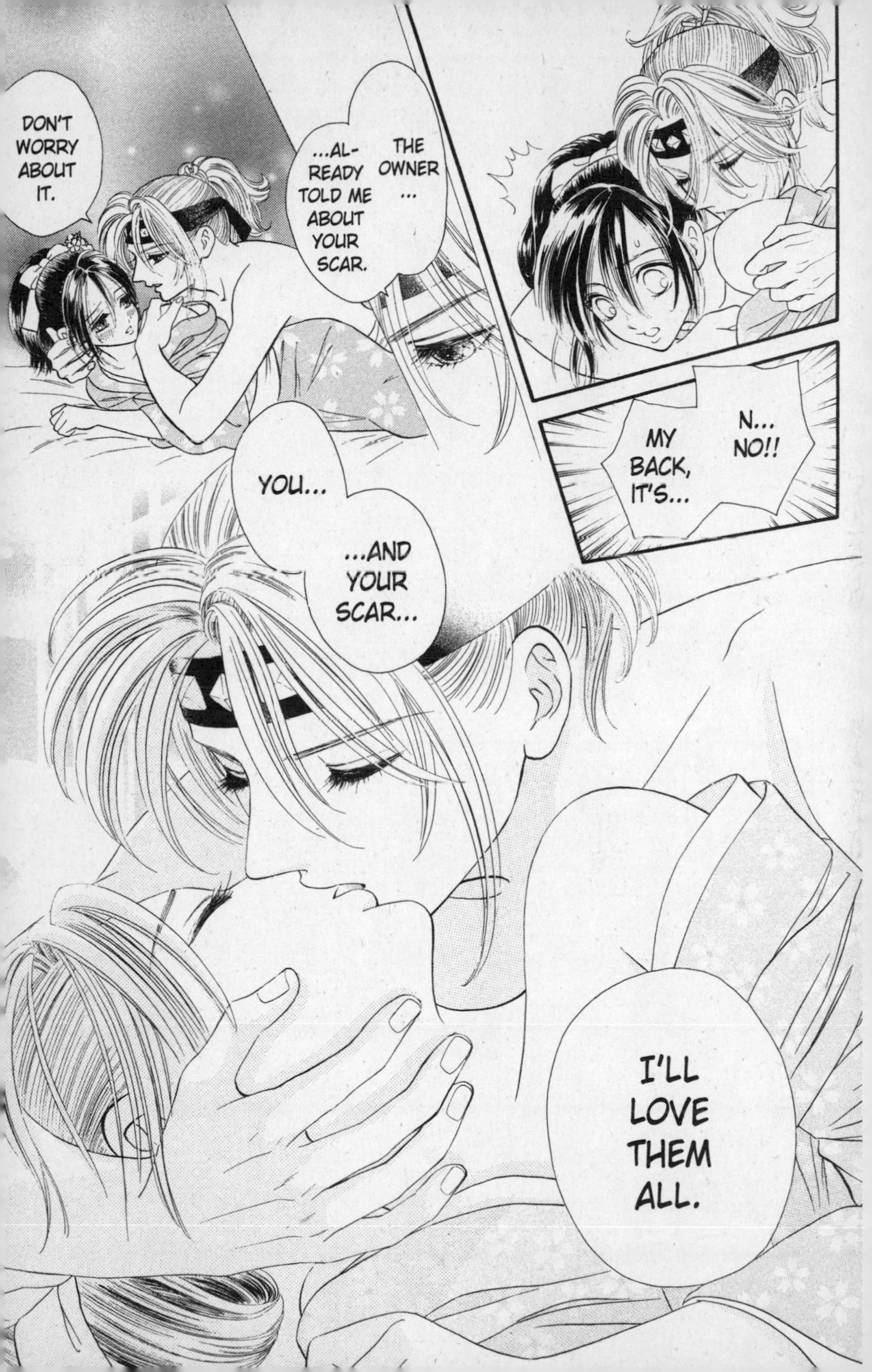
N... NO!!
MY BACK, IT'S...
DON'T WORRY ABOUT IT.
THE OWNER... ...AL-READY TOLD ME ABOUT YOUR SCAR.
YOU...
...AND YOUR SCAR...
I'LL LOVE THEM ALL.

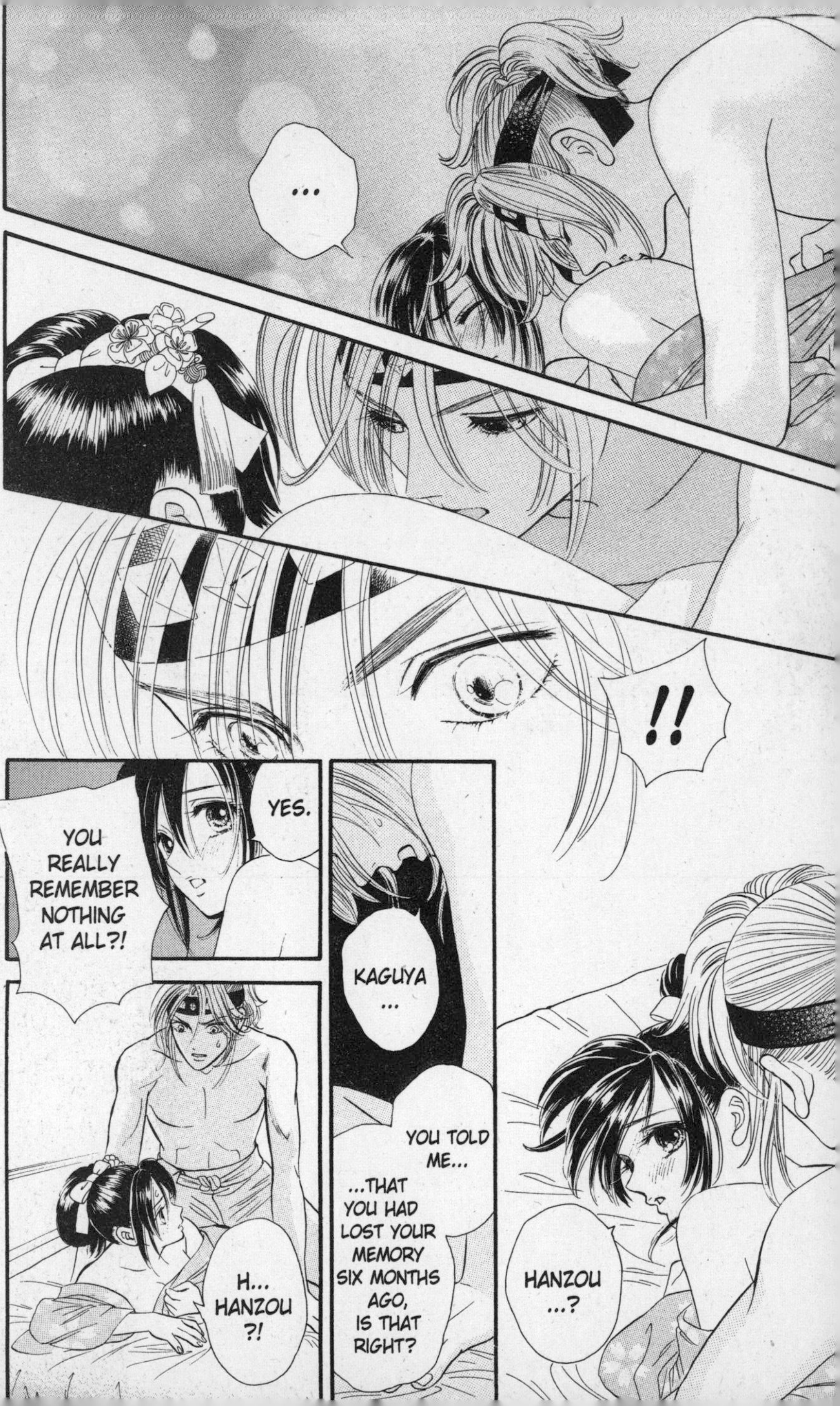
...
!!
HANZOU ...?
KAGUYA ...
YOU TOLD ME...
...THAT YOU HAD LOST YOUR MEMORY SIX MONTHS AGO, IS THAT RIGHT?
YES.
YOU REALLY REMEMBER NOTHING AT ALL?!
H... HANZOU ?!

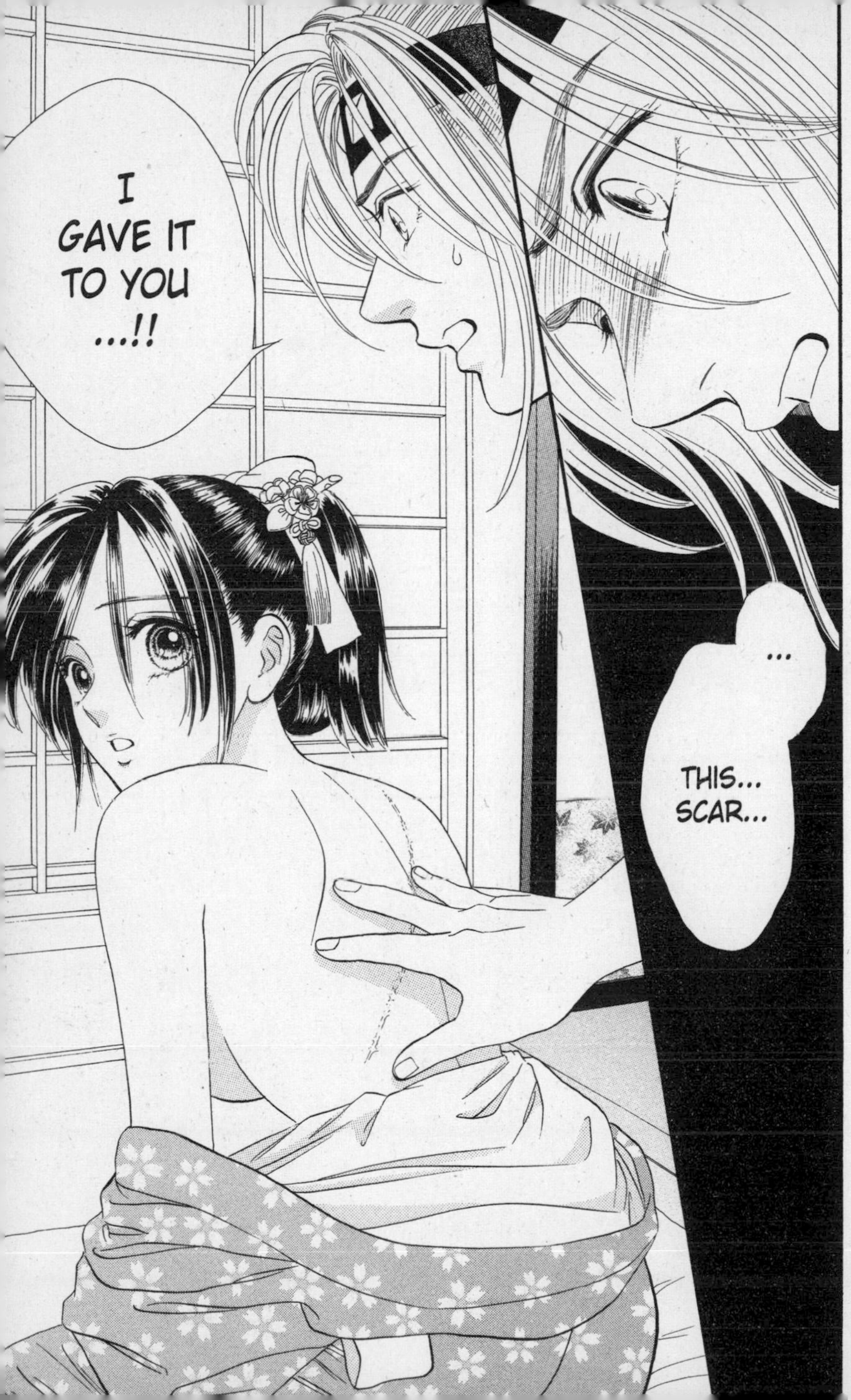
I GAVE IT TO YOU ...!!
...
THIS... SCAR...

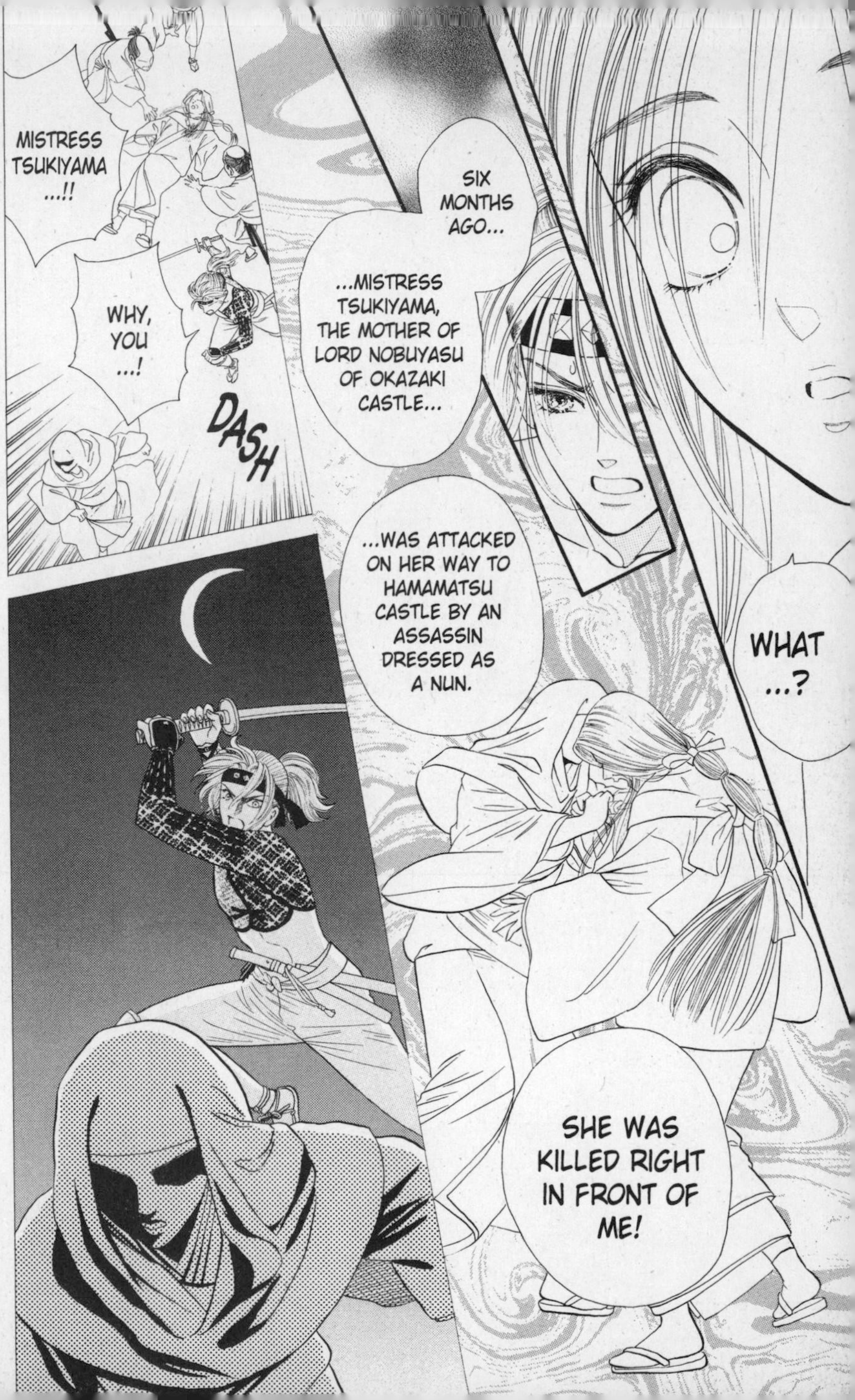
WHAT ...?
SIX MONTHS AGO...
...MISTRESS TSUKIYAMA, THE MOTHER OF LORD NOBUYASU OF OKAZAKI CASTLE...
...WAS ATTACKED ON HER WAY TO HAMAMATSU CASTLE BY AN ASSASSIN DRESSED AS A NUN.
SHE WAS KILLED RIGHT IN FRONT OF ME!
MISTRESS TSUKIYAMA ...!!
WHY, YOU ...!
DASH

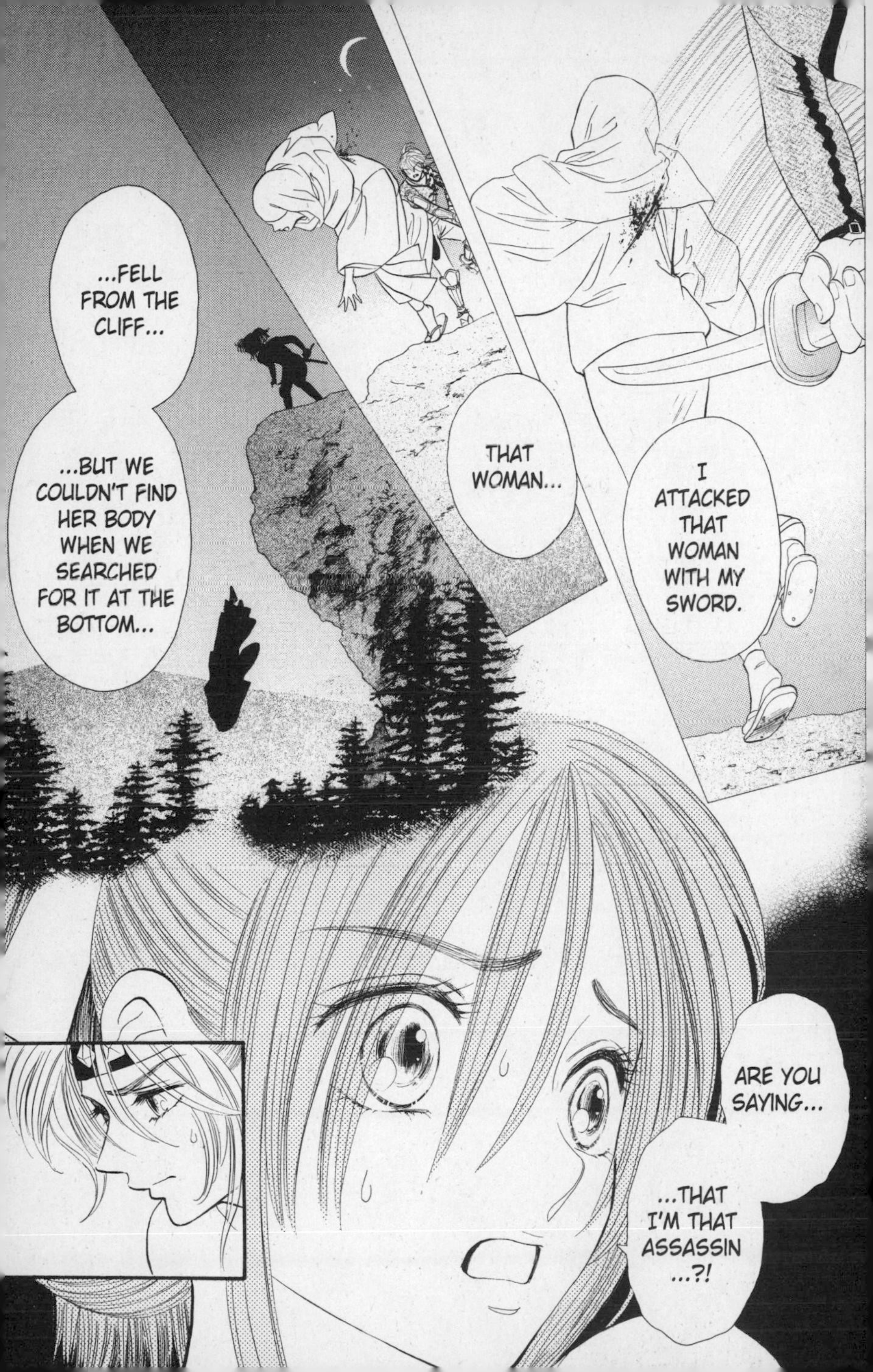
I ATTACKED THAT WOMAN WITH MY SWORD.
THAT WOMAN...
...FELL FROM THE CLIFF...
...BUT WE COULDN'T FIND HER BODY WHEN WE SEARCHED FOR IT AT THE BOTTOM...
ARE YOU SAYING...
...THAT I'M THAT ASSASSIN ...?!

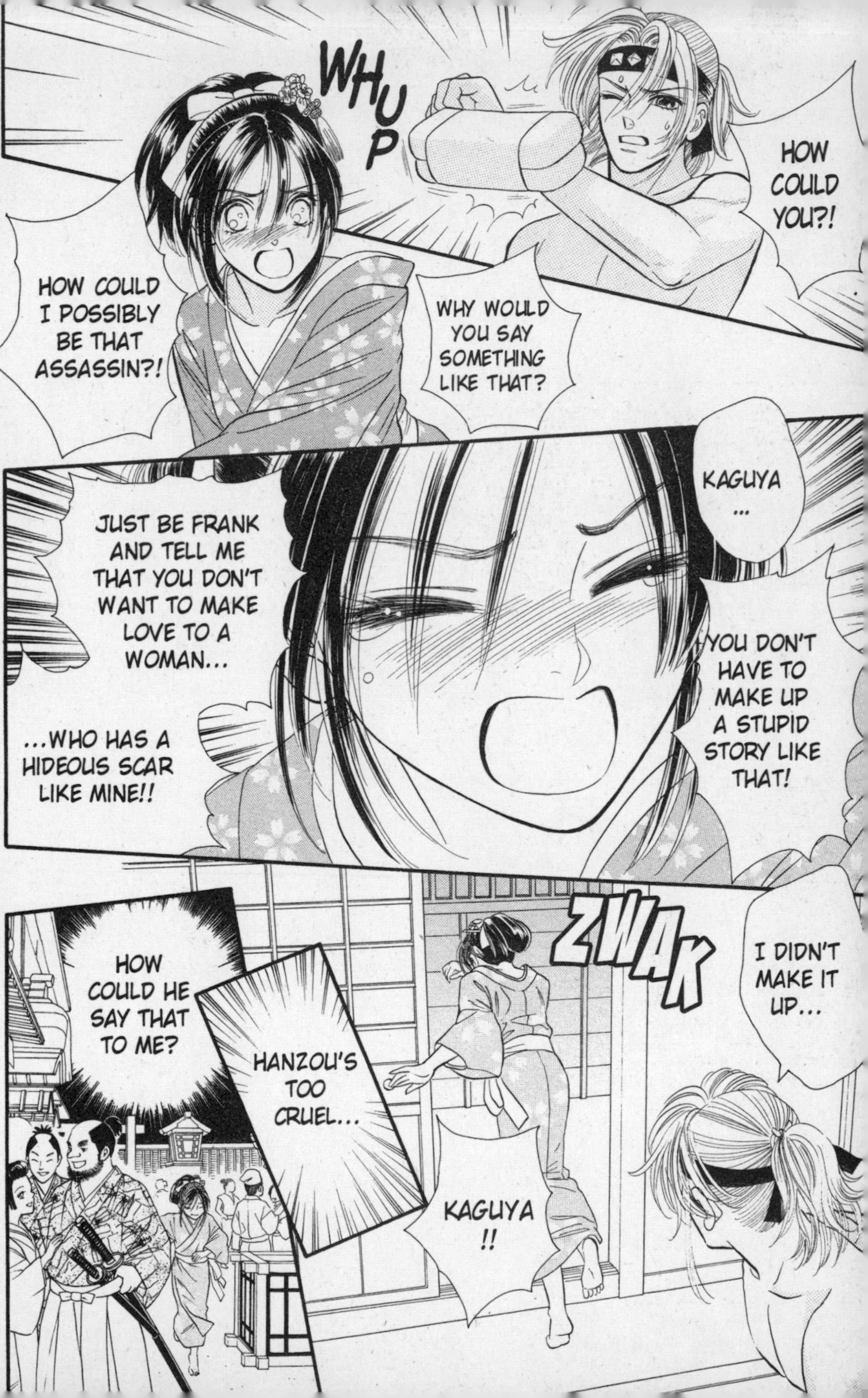
HOW COULD YOU?!
WHUP
WHY WOULD YOU SAY SOMETHING LIKE THAT?
HOW COULD I POSSIBLY BE THAT ASSASSIN?!
KAGUYA ...
YOU DON'T HAVE TO MAKE UP A STUPID STORY LIKE THAT!
JUST BE FRANK AND TELL ME THAT YOU DON'T WANT TO MAKE LOVE TO A WOMAN...
...WHO HAS A HIDEOUS SCAR LIKE MINE!!
I DIDN'T MAKE IT UP...
ZWAK
KAGUYA !!
HOW COULD HE SAY THAT TO ME?
HANZOU'S TOO CRUEL...

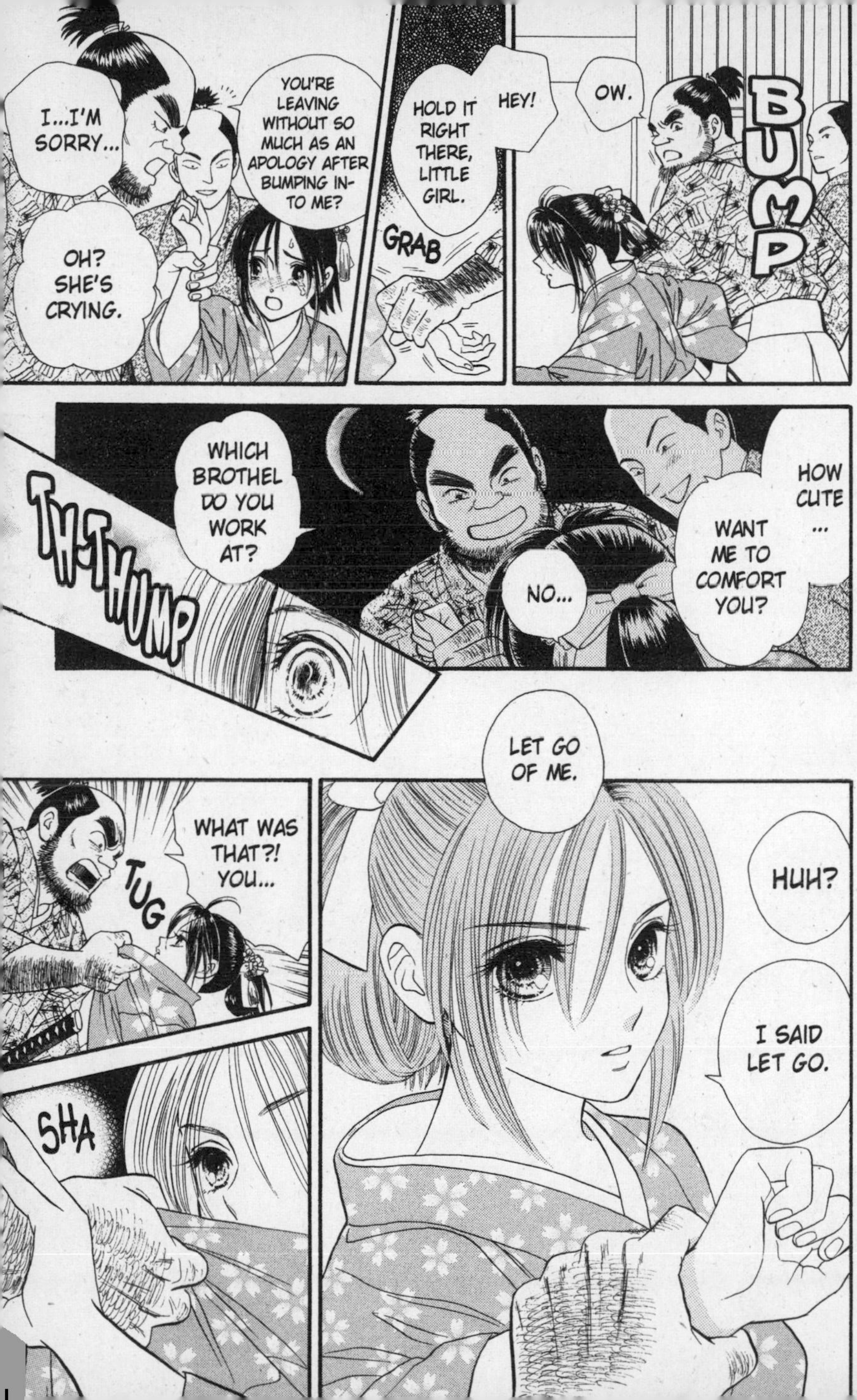
BUMP
OW.
HEY!
HOLD IT RIGHT THERE, LITTLE GIRL.
GRAB
YOU'RE LEAVING WITHOUT SO MUCH AS AN APOLOGY AFTER BUMPING IN-TO ME?
I...I'M SORRY...
OH? SHE'S CRYING.
HOW CUTE...
WANT ME TO COMFORT YOU?
NO...
WHICH BROTHEL DO YOU WORK AT?
TH-THUMP
LET GO OF ME.
HUH?
I SAID LET GO.
WHAT WAS THAT?! YOU...
TUG
SHA

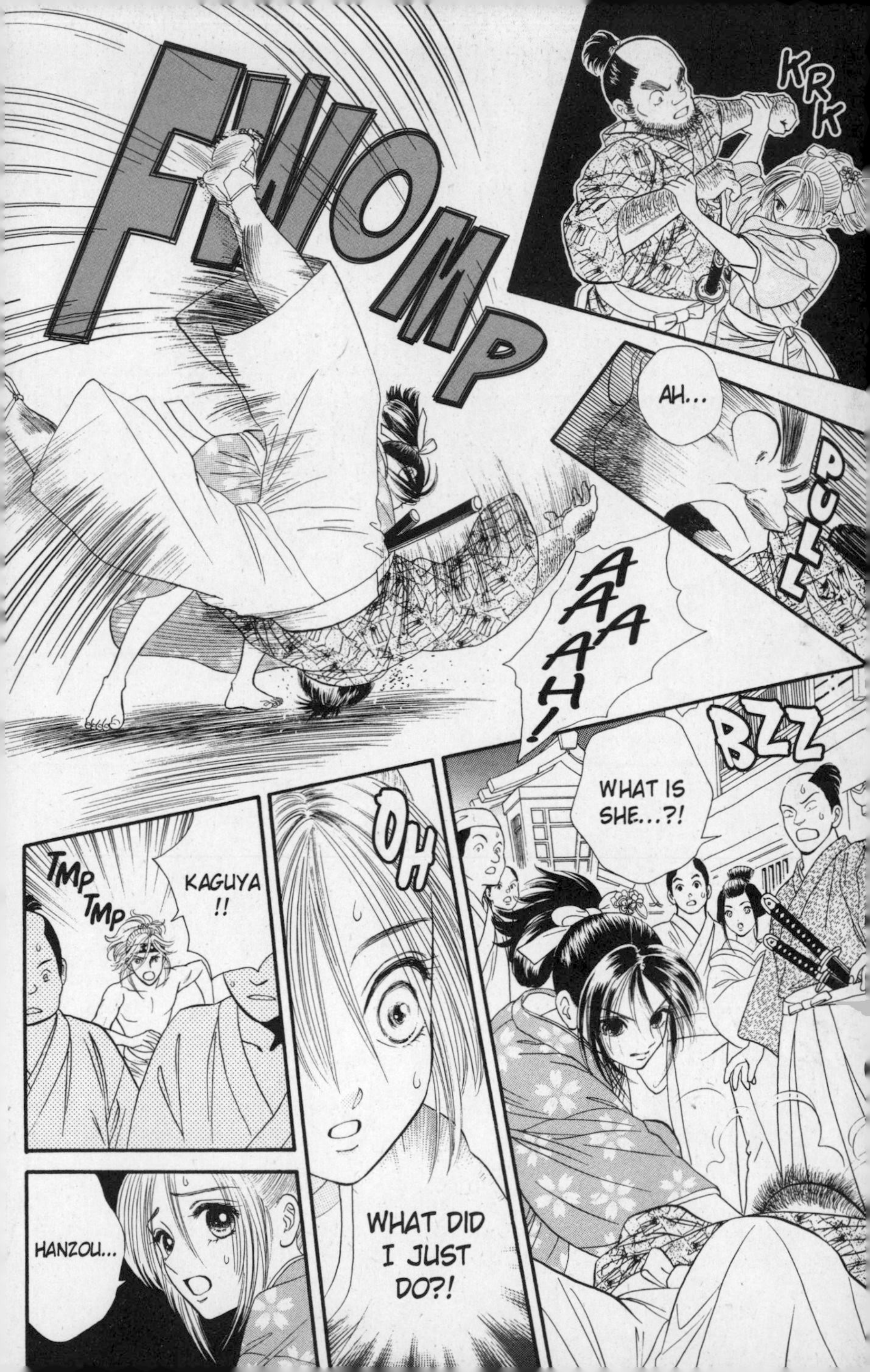
KRK
AH...
PULL
FWOMP
AAAAH!
BZZ
WHAT IS SHE...?!
OH
WHAT DID I JUST DO?!
TMP TMP
KAGUYA !!
HANZOU...

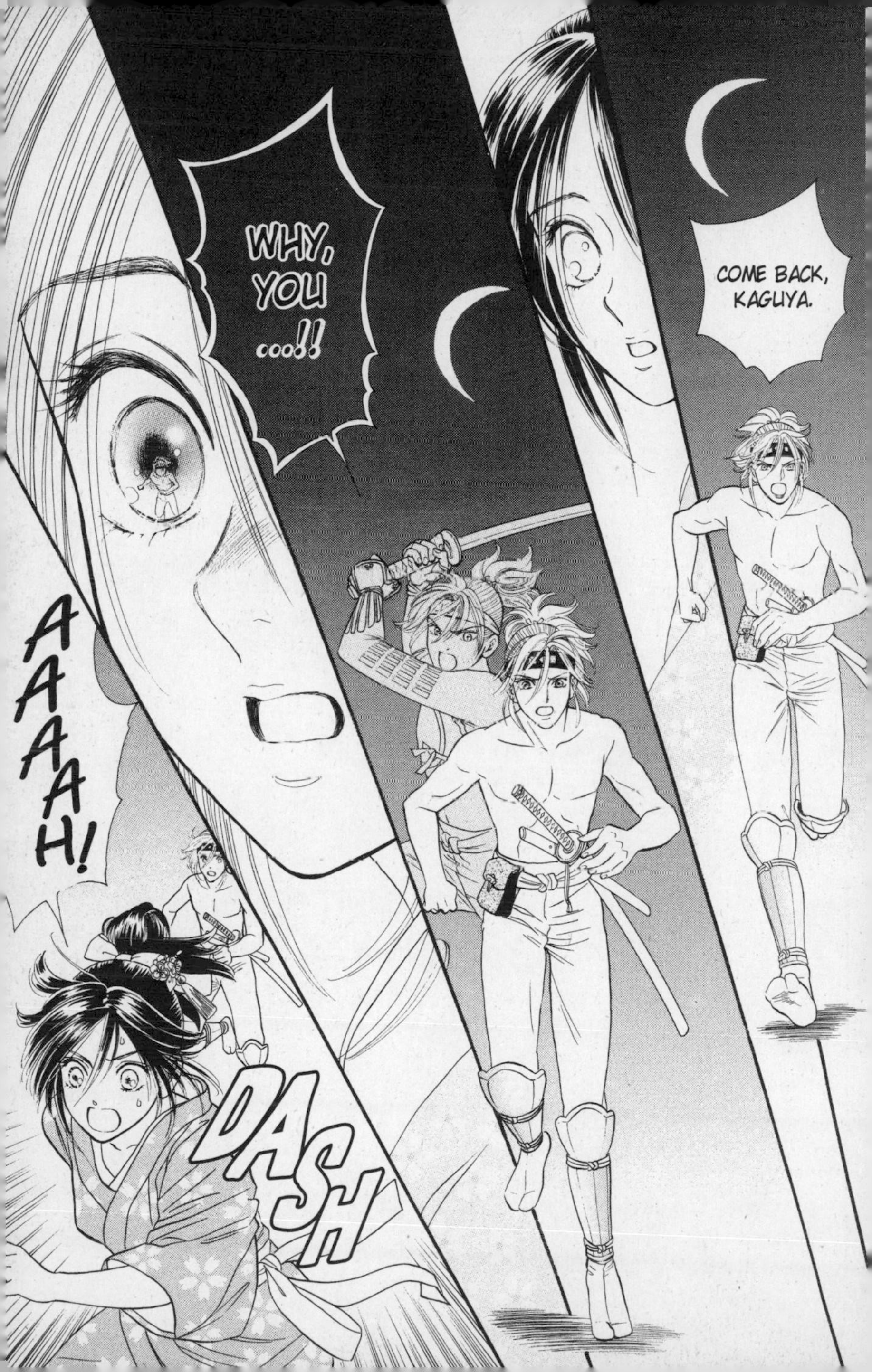
COME BACK, KAGUYA.
WHY, YOU ...!!
AAAAAH!
DASH

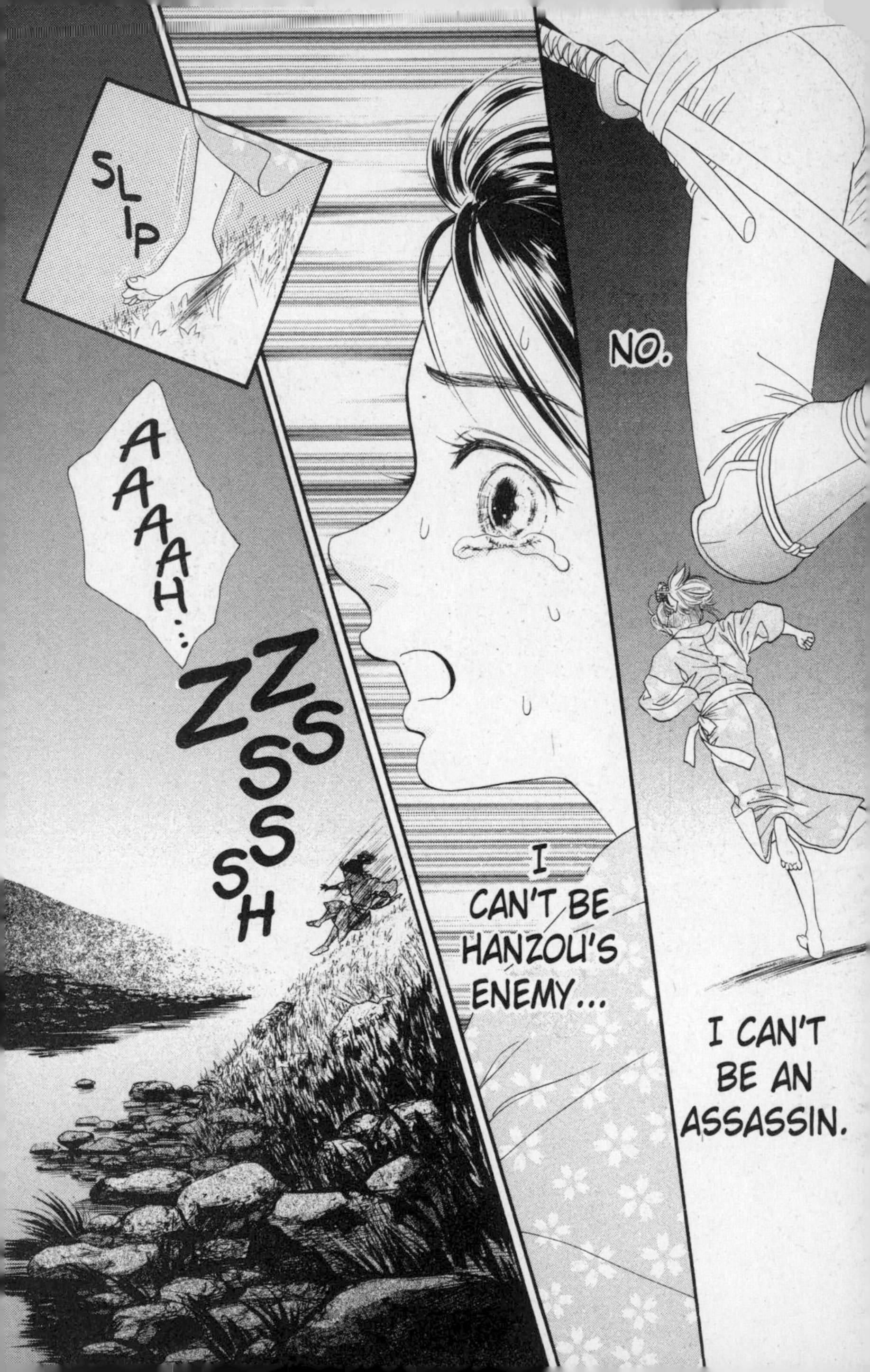
NO.
I CAN'T BE AN ASSASSIN.
I CAN'T BE HANZOU'S ENEMY...
SLIP
AAAAH...
ZZSSSSH

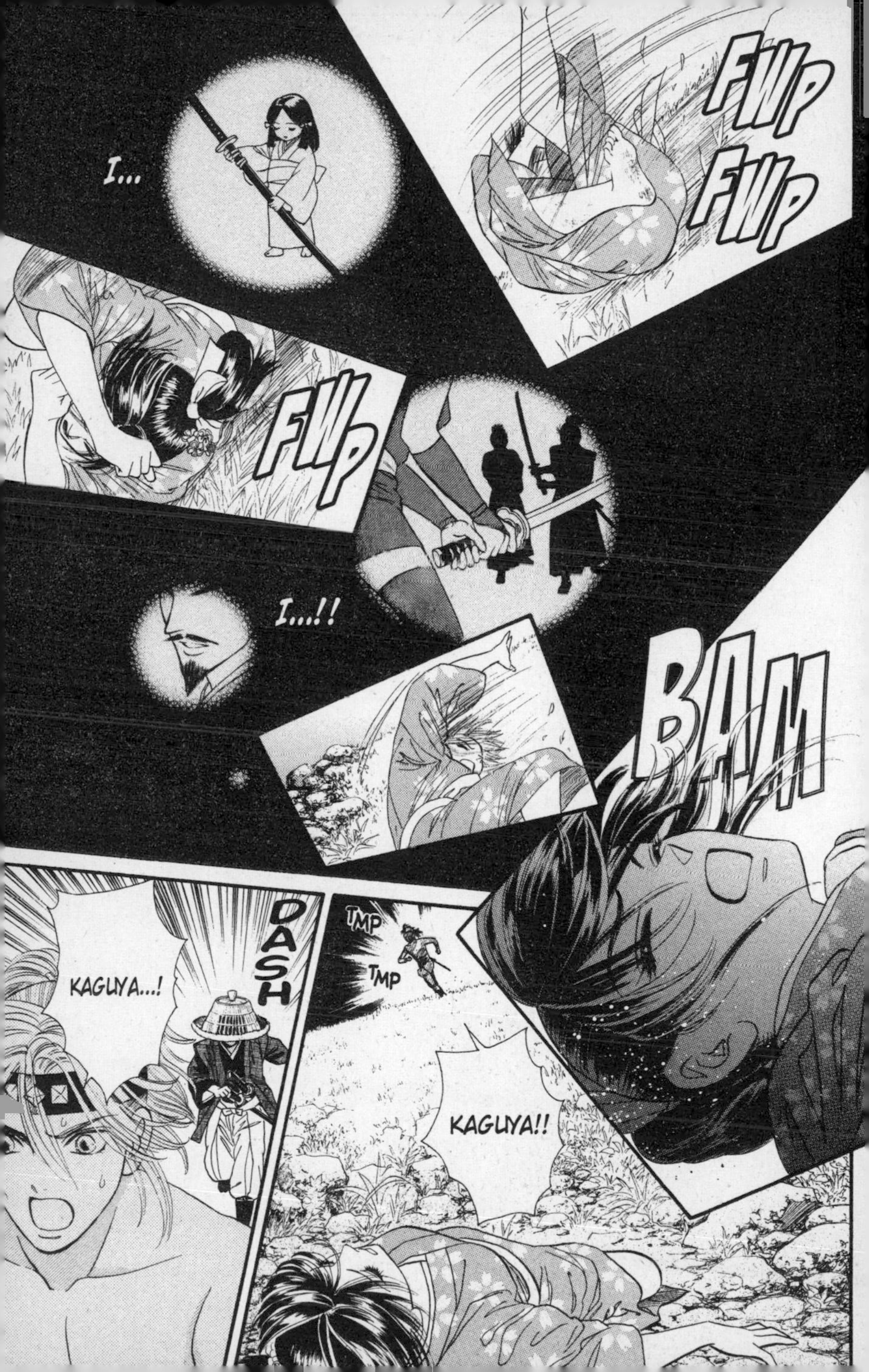
FWP
FWP
I...
FWP
I...!!
BAM
TMP
TMP
KAGUYA!!
DASH
KAGUYA...!

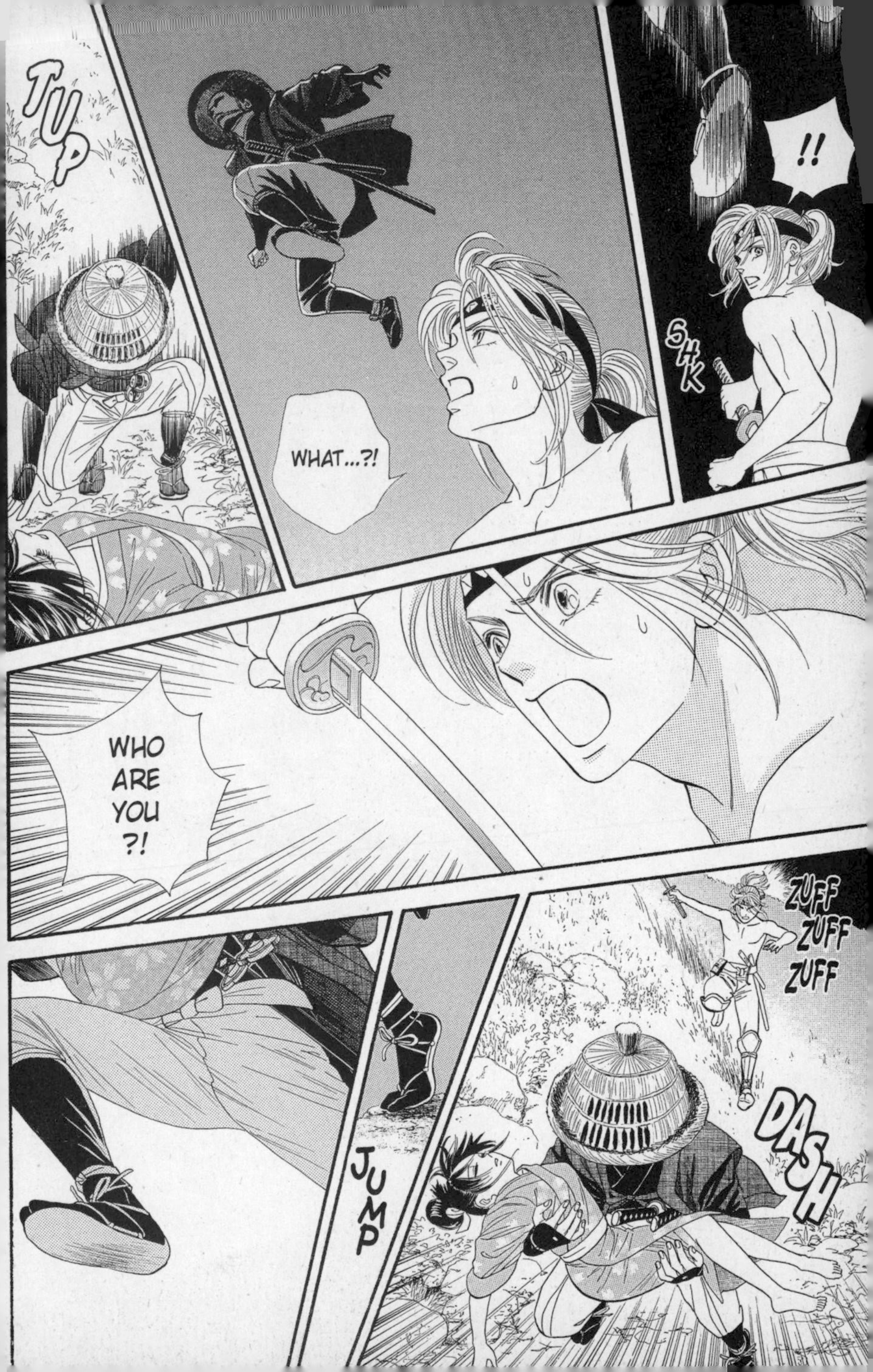
!!
SHK
WHAT...?!
TUP
WHO ARE YOU ?!
ZUFF ZUFF ZUFF
DASH
JUMP

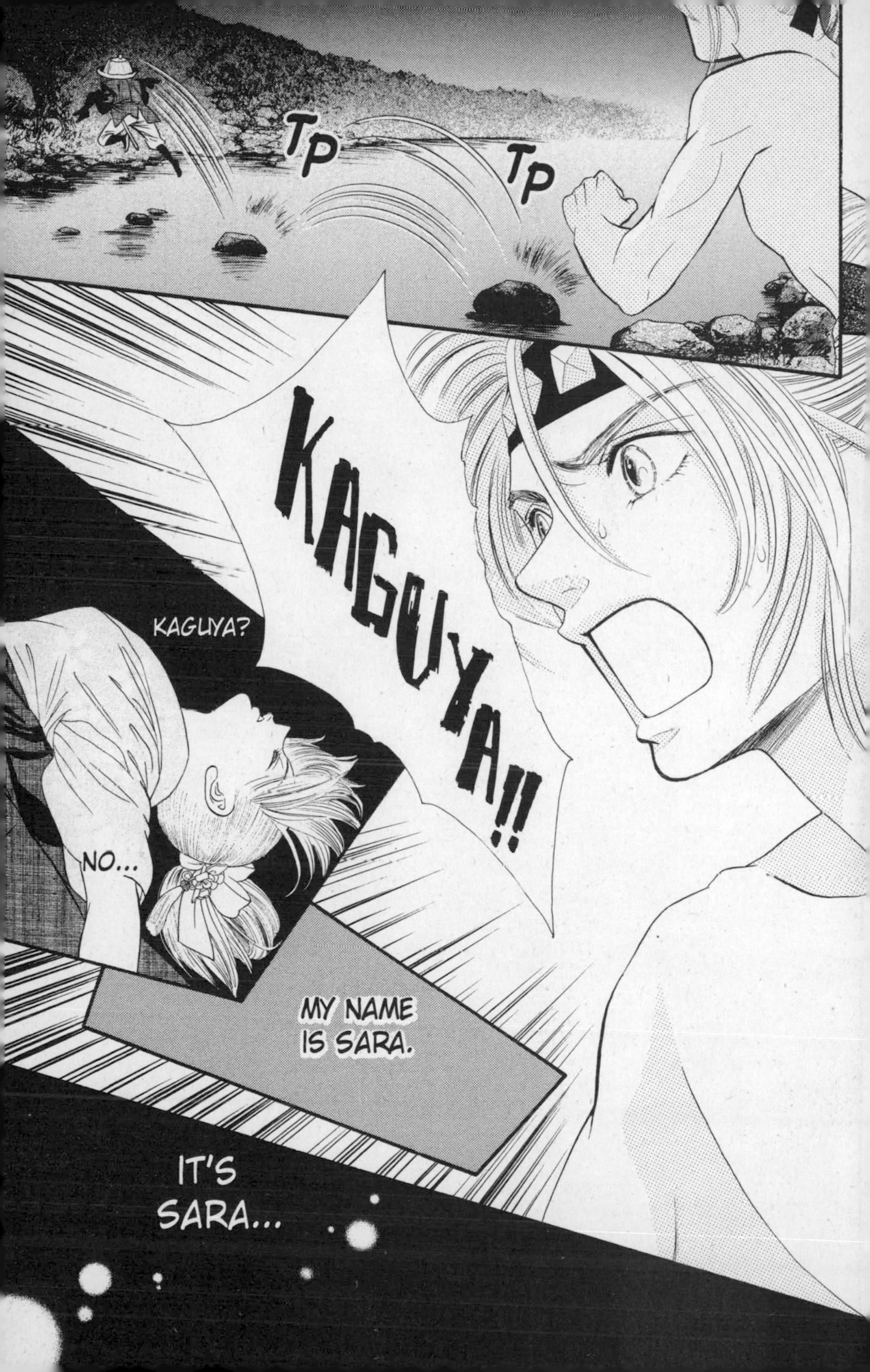
TP
TP
KAGUYA!!
KAGUYA?
NO...
MY NAME IS SARA.
IT'S SARA...

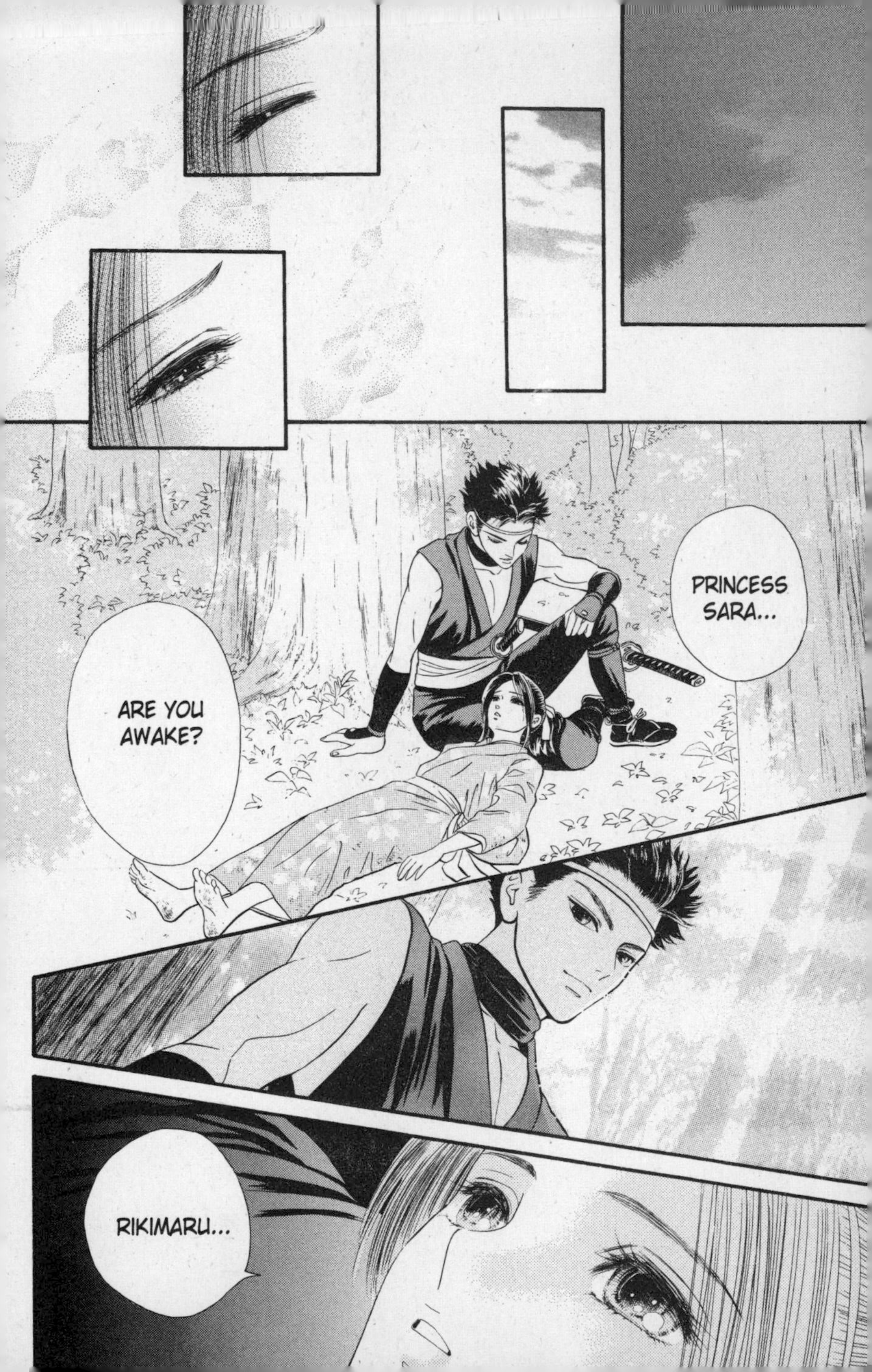
PRINCESS SARA...
ARE YOU AWAKE?
RIKIMARU...

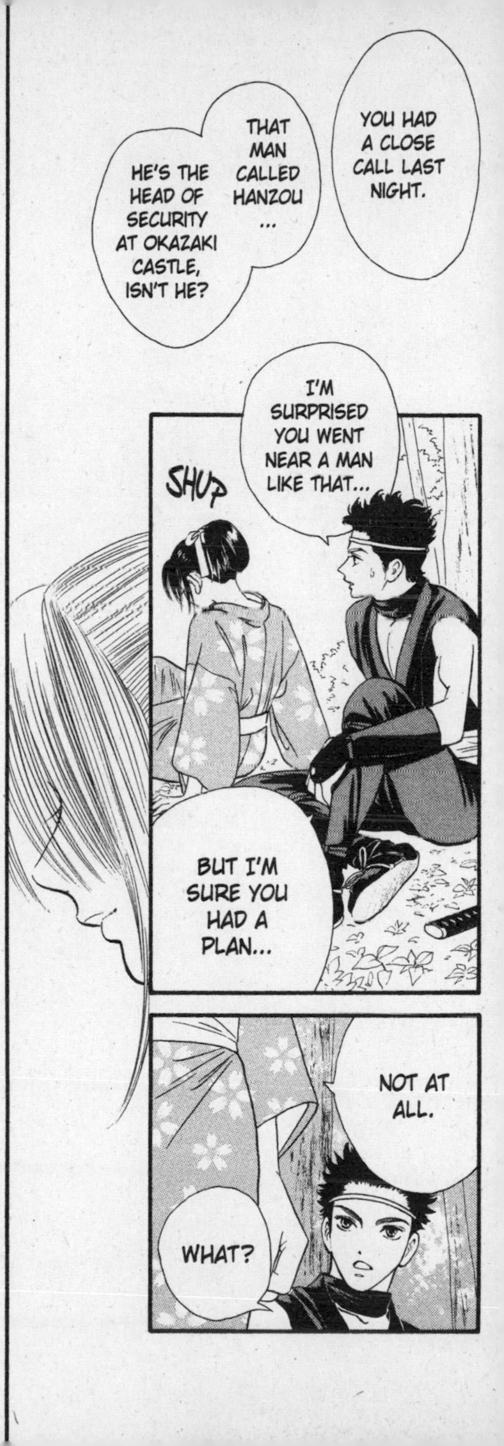
YOU HAD A CLOSE CALL LAST NIGHT.
THAT MAN CALLED HANZOU ...
HE'S THE HEAD OF SECURITY AT OKAZAKI CASTLE, ISN'T HE?
I'M SURPRISED YOU WENT NEAR A MAN LIKE THAT...
SHUP
BUT I'M SURE YOU HAD A PLAN...
NOT AT ALL.
WHAT?
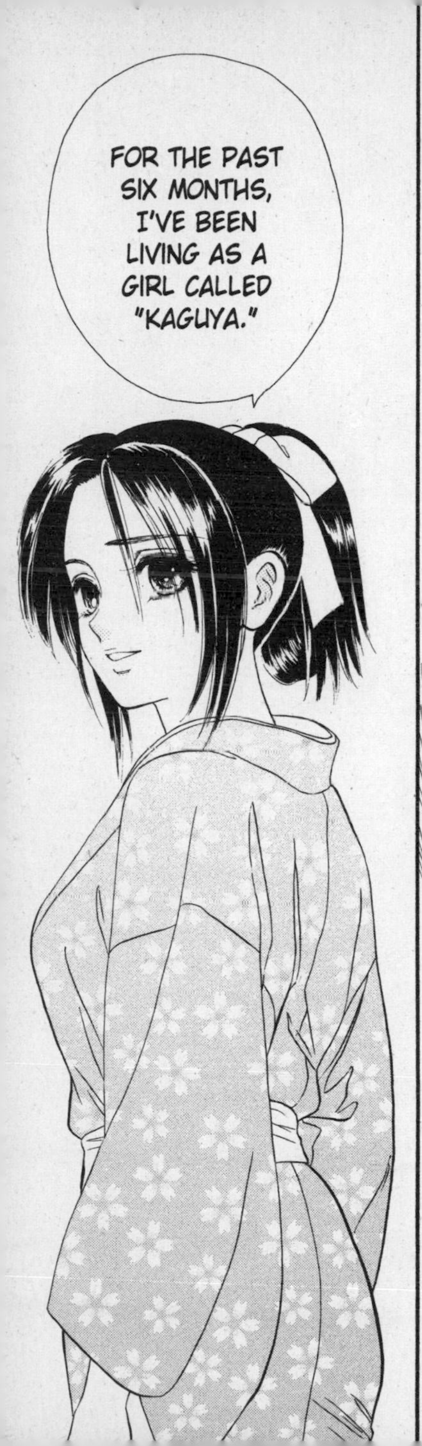
FOR THE PAST SIX MONTHS, I'VE BEEN LIVING AS A GIRL CALLED "KAGUYA."

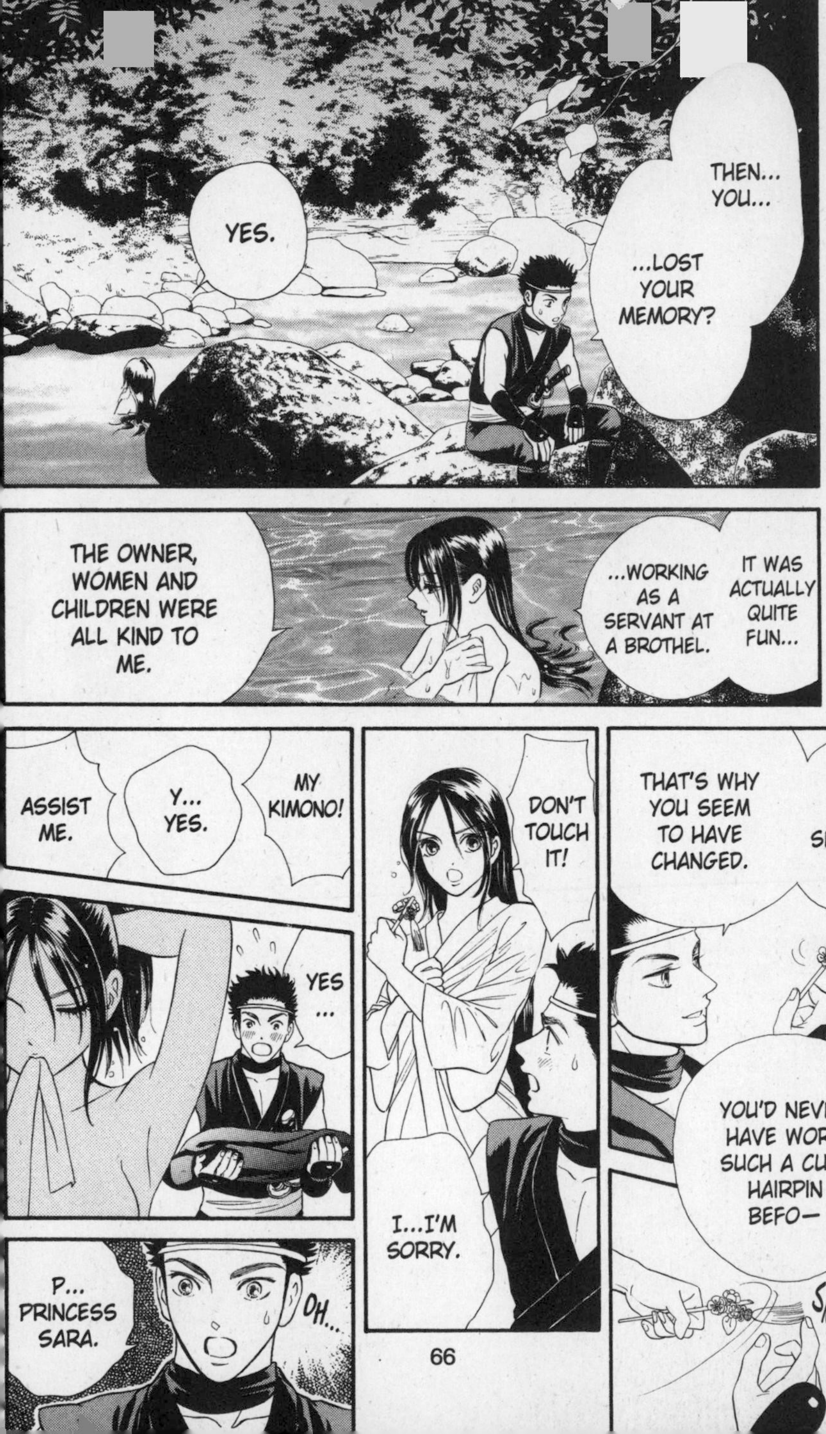
THEN... YOU...
...LOST YOUR MEMORY?
YES.
IT WAS ACTUALLY QUITE FUN...
...WORKING AS A SERVANT AT A BROTHEL.
THE OWNER, WOMEN AND CHILDREN WERE ALL KIND TO ME.
I SEE.
THAT'S WHY YOU SEEM TO HAVE CHANGED.
YOU'D NEVER HAVE WORN SUCH A CUTE HAIRPIN BEFO—
SNATCH
DON'T TOUCH IT!
I...I'M SORRY.
MY KIMONO!
Y... YES.
ASSIST ME.
YES ...
OH...
P... PRINCESS SARA.

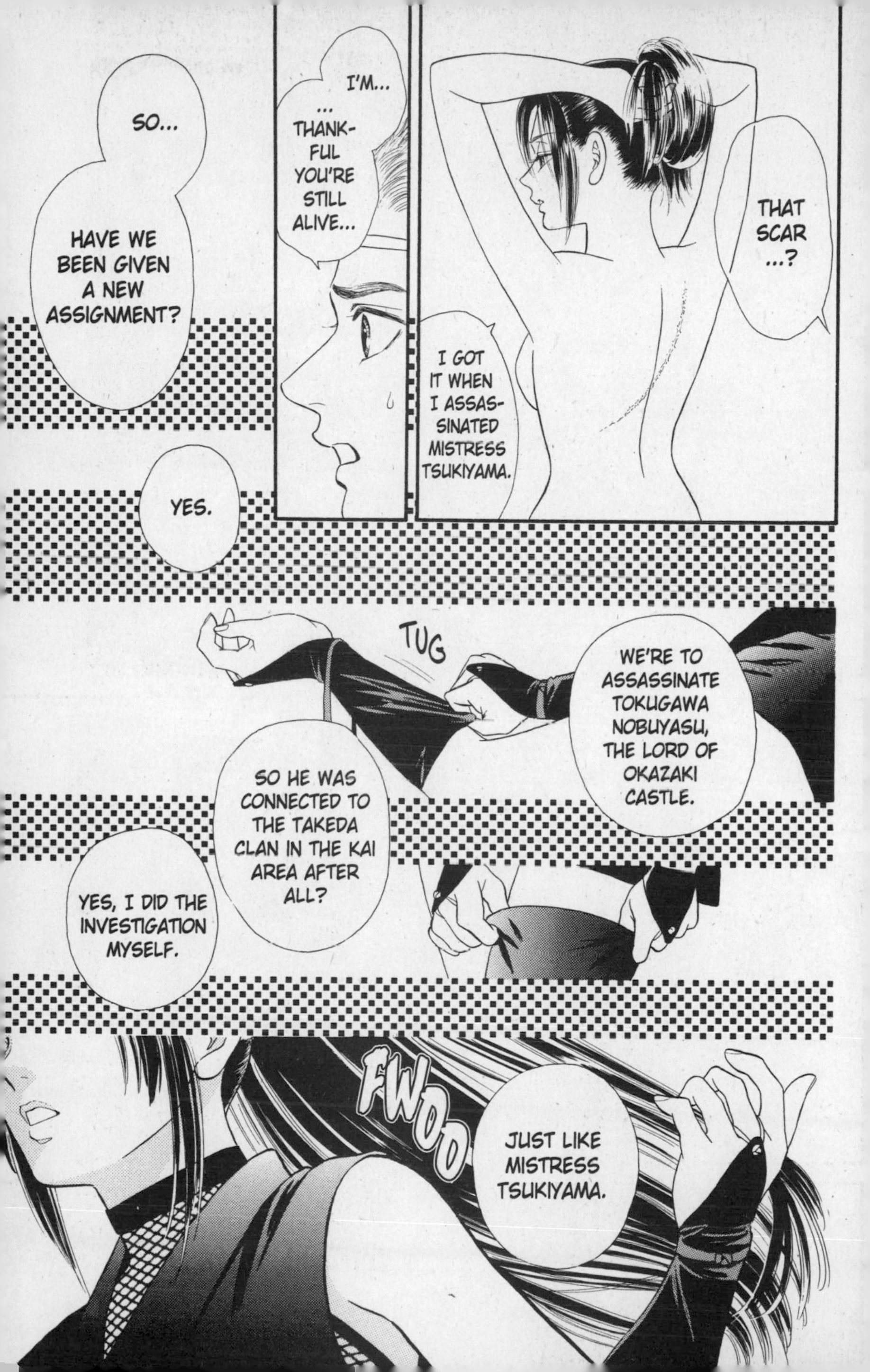
THAT SCAR ...?
I GOT IT WHEN I ASSASSINATED MISTRESS TSUKIYAMA.
I'M... ... THANKFUL YOU'RE STILL ALIVE...
SO... HAVE WE BEEN GIVEN A NEW ASSIGNMENT?
YES.
TUG
WE'RE TO ASSASSINATE TOKUGAWA NOBUYASU, THE LORD OF OKAZAKI CASTLE.
SO HE WAS CONNECTED TO THE TAKEDA CLAN IN THE KAI AREA AFTER ALL?
YES, I DID THE INVESTIGATION MYSELF.
FWOO
JUST LIKE MISTRESS TSUKIYAMA.

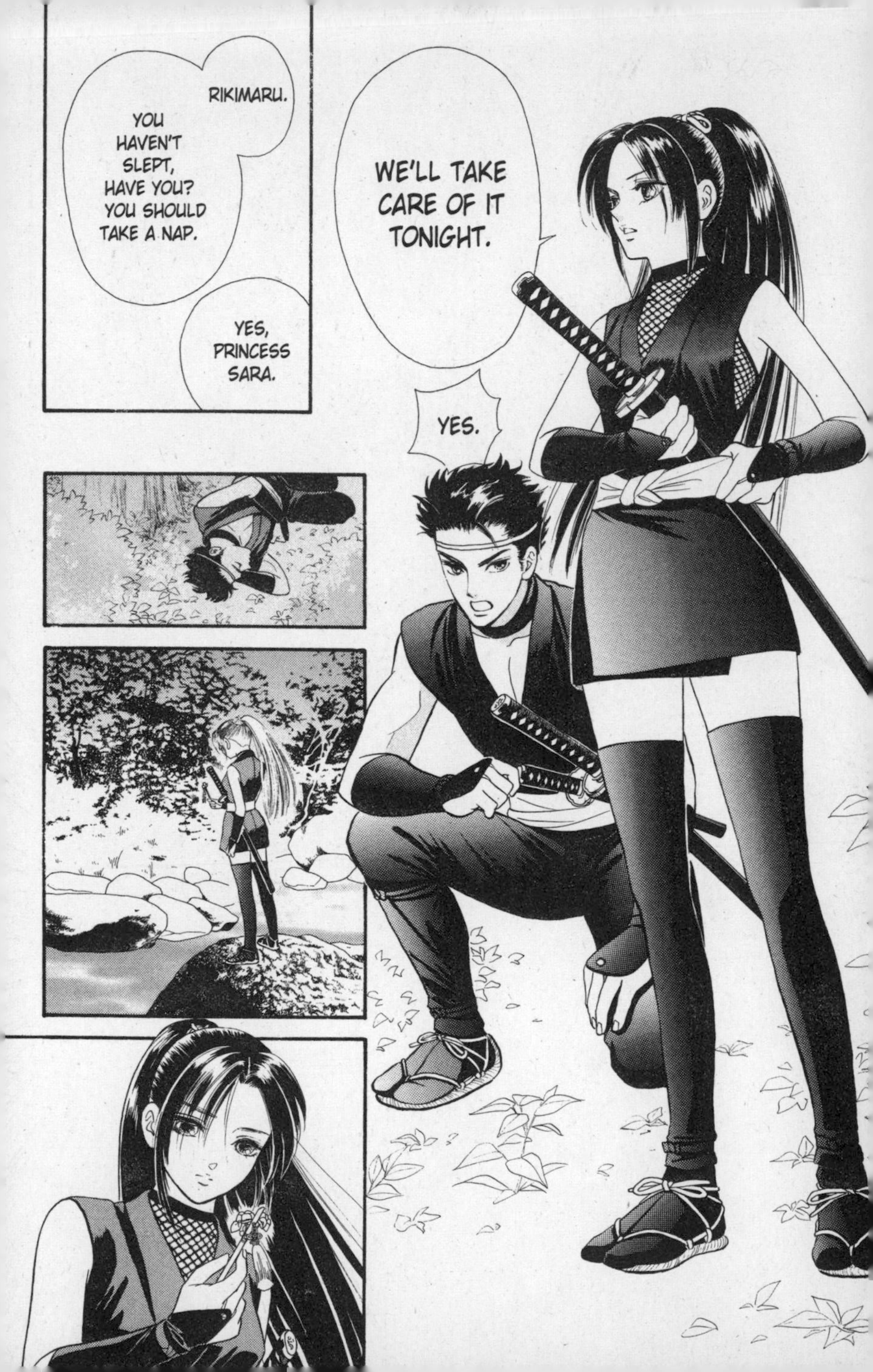
WE'LL TAKE CARE OF IT TONIGHT.
YES.
RIKIMARU.
YOU HAVEN'T SLEPT, HAVE YOU? YOU SHOULD TAKE A NAP.
YES, PRINCESS SARA.

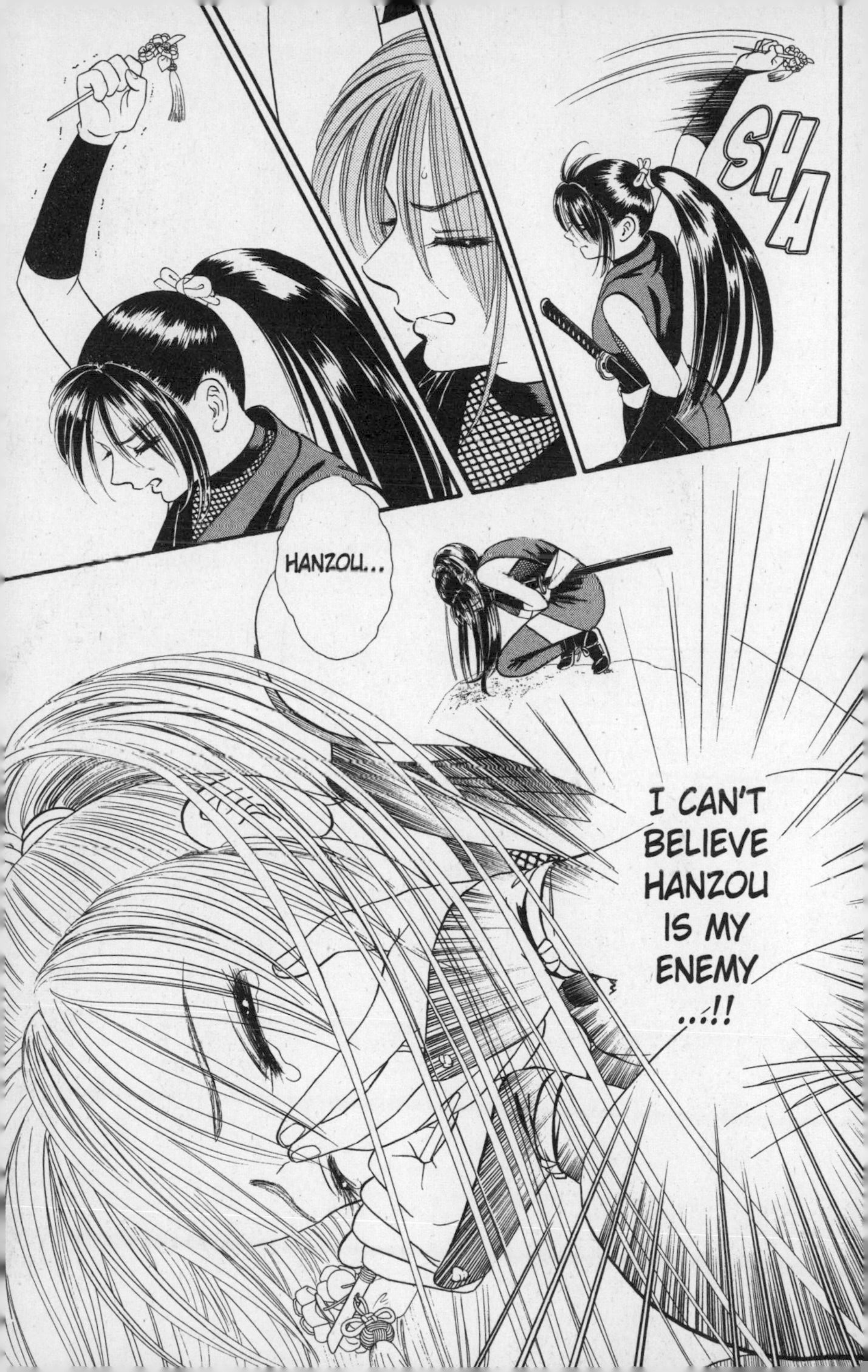
SHA
HANZOU...
I CAN'T BELIEVE HANZOU IS MY ENEMY ...!!

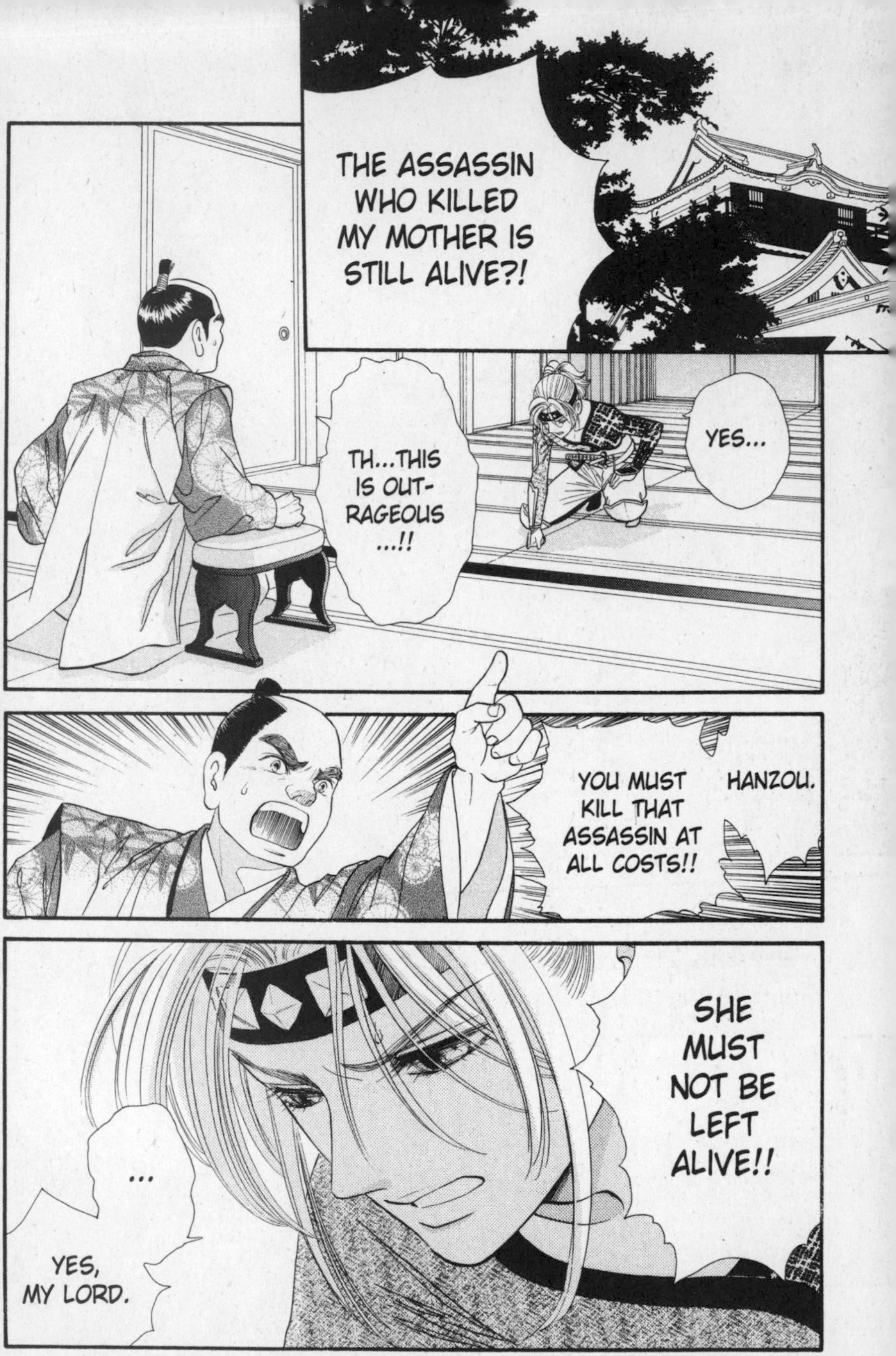
THE ASSASSIN WHO KILLED MY MOTHER IS STILL ALIVE?!
YES...
TH...THIS IS OUT-RAGEOUS ...!!
HANZOU.
YOU MUST KILL THAT ASSASSIN AT ALL COSTS!!
SHE MUST NOT BE LEFT ALIVE!!
...
YES, MY LORD.

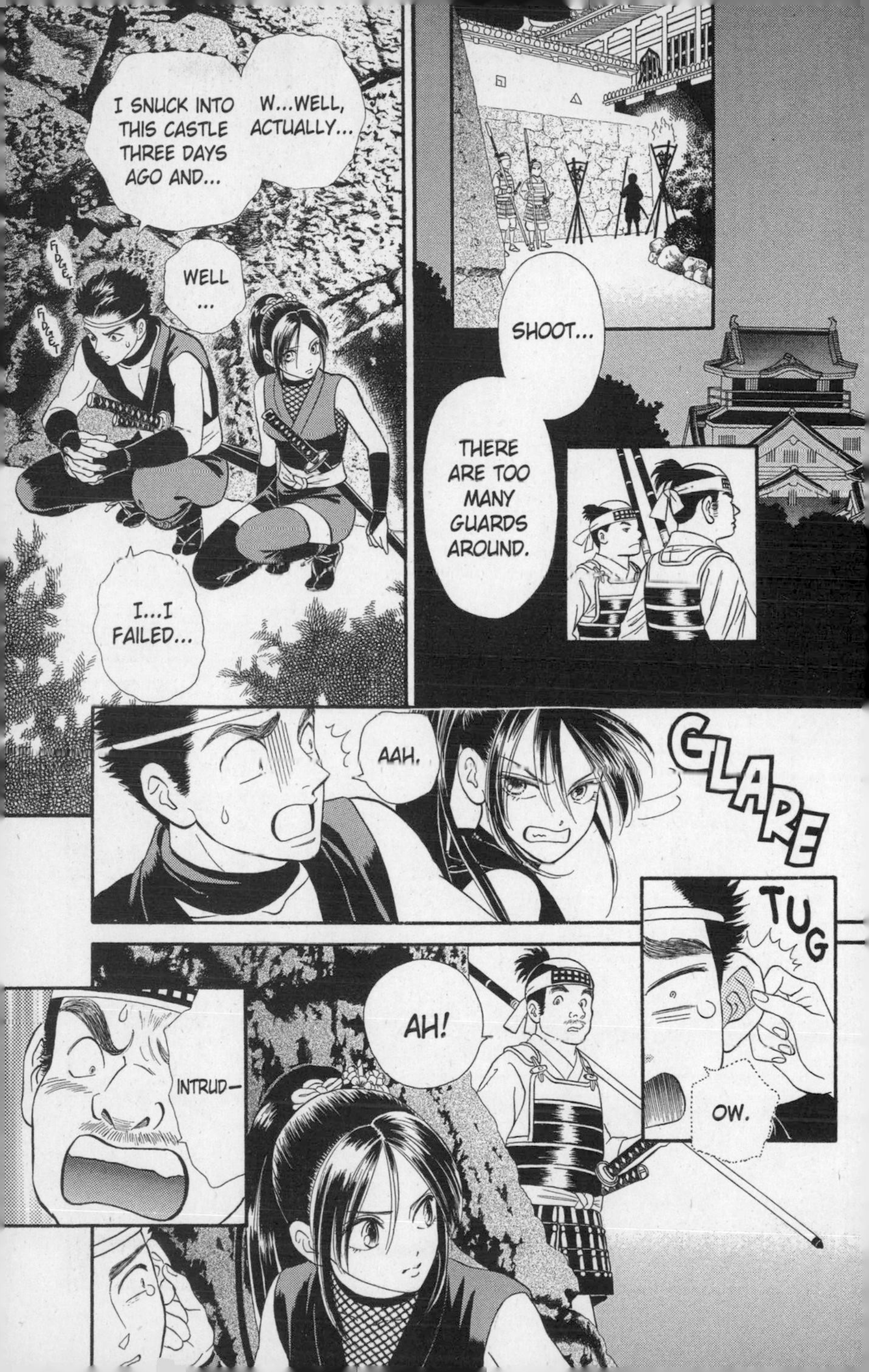
SHOOT...
THERE ARE TOO MANY GUARDS AROUND.
W...WELL, ACTUALLY...
I SNUCK INTO THIS CASTLE THREE DAYS AGO AND...
FIDGET
FIDGET
WELL ...
I...I FAILED...
GLARE
AAH.
TUG
OW.
AH!
INTRUD—

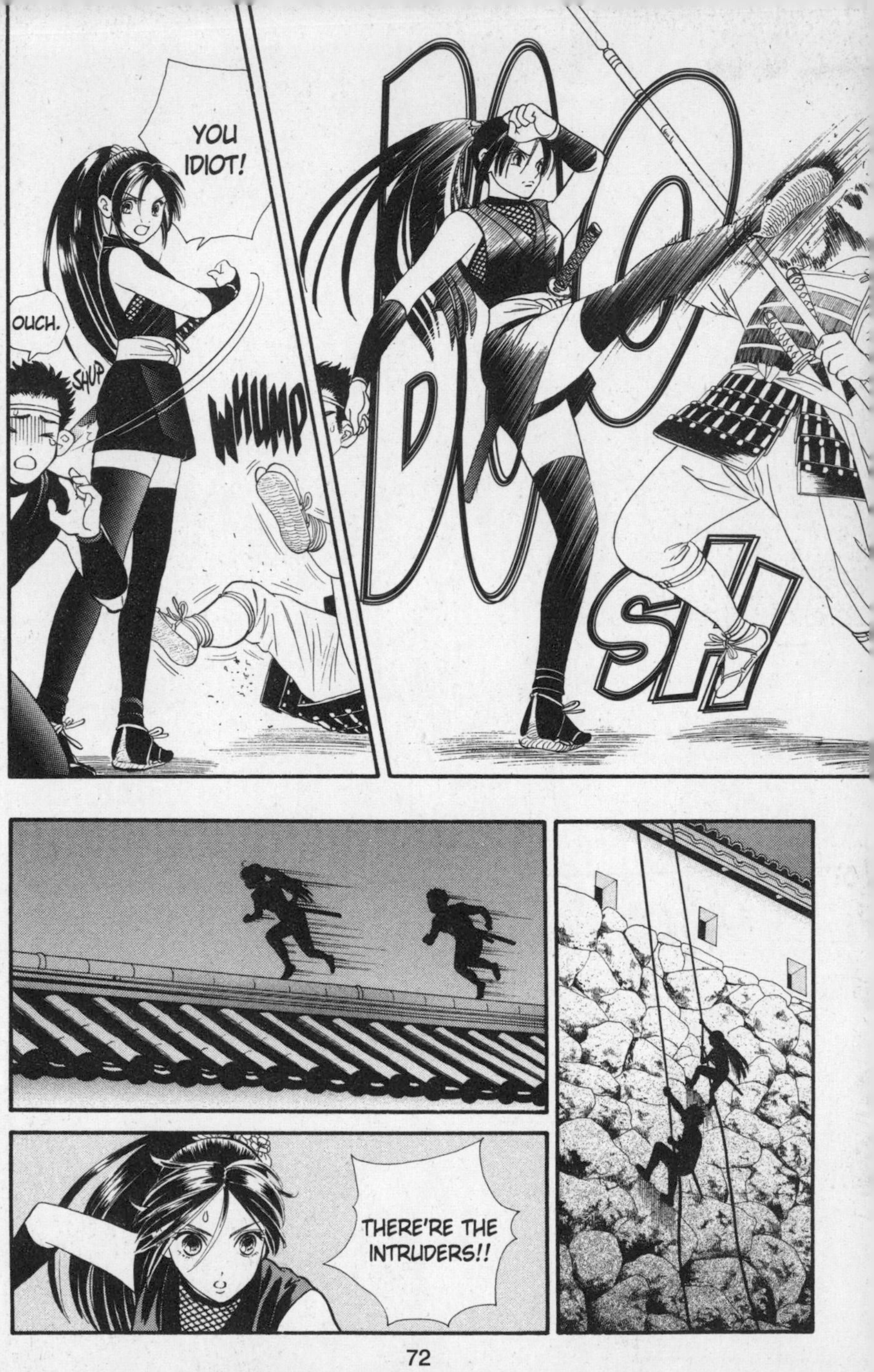
DOOSH
YOU IDIOT!
OUCH.
SHUP
WHUMP
THERE'RE THE INTRUDERS!!

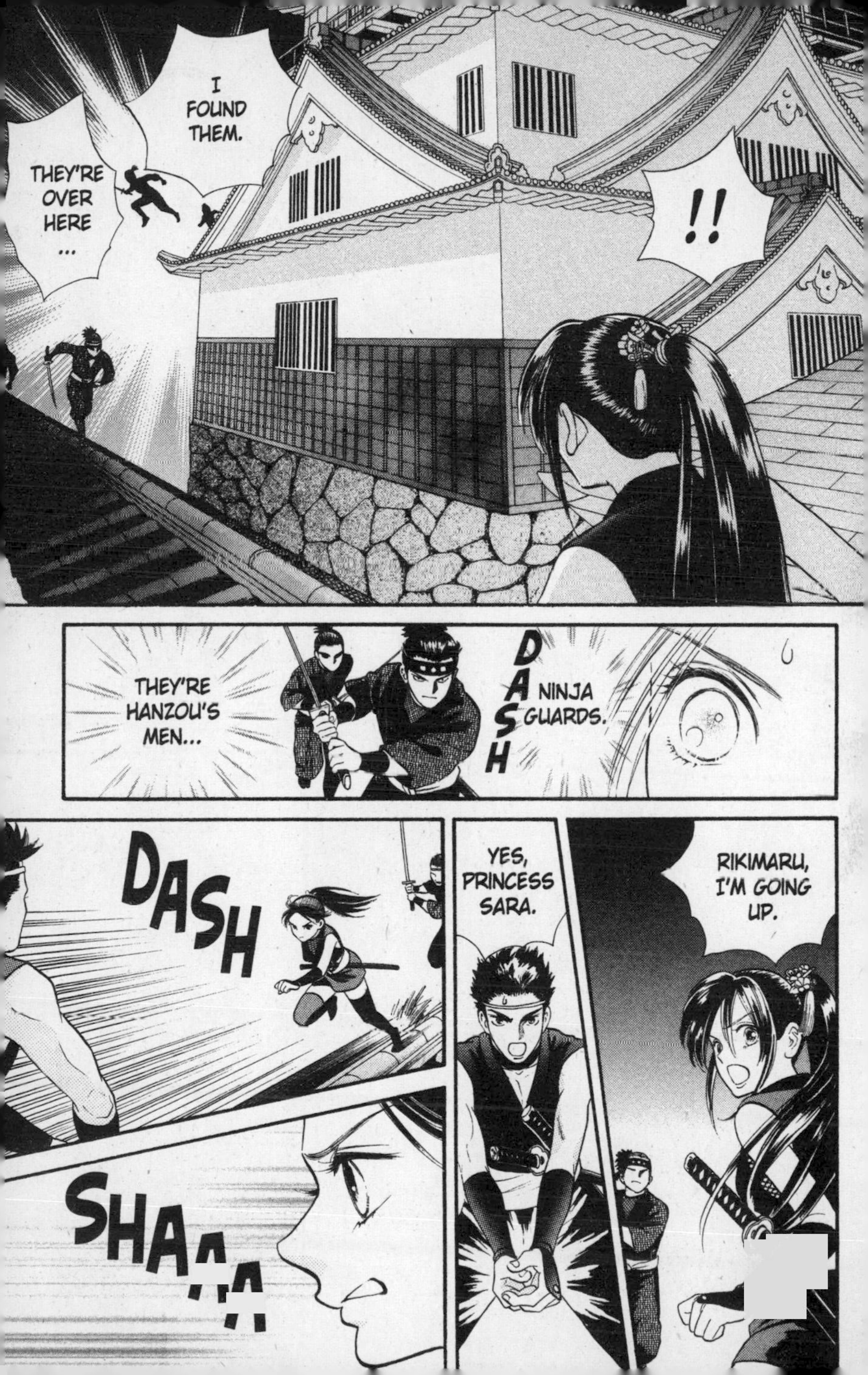
I FOUND THEM.
THEY'RE OVER HERE ...
!!
NINJA GUARDS.
DASH
THEY'RE HANZOU'S MEN...
RIKIMARU, I'M GOING UP.
YES, PRINCESS SARA.
DASH
SHAAA

I'M SORRY, NOBUYASU !!

GLINT

HUF

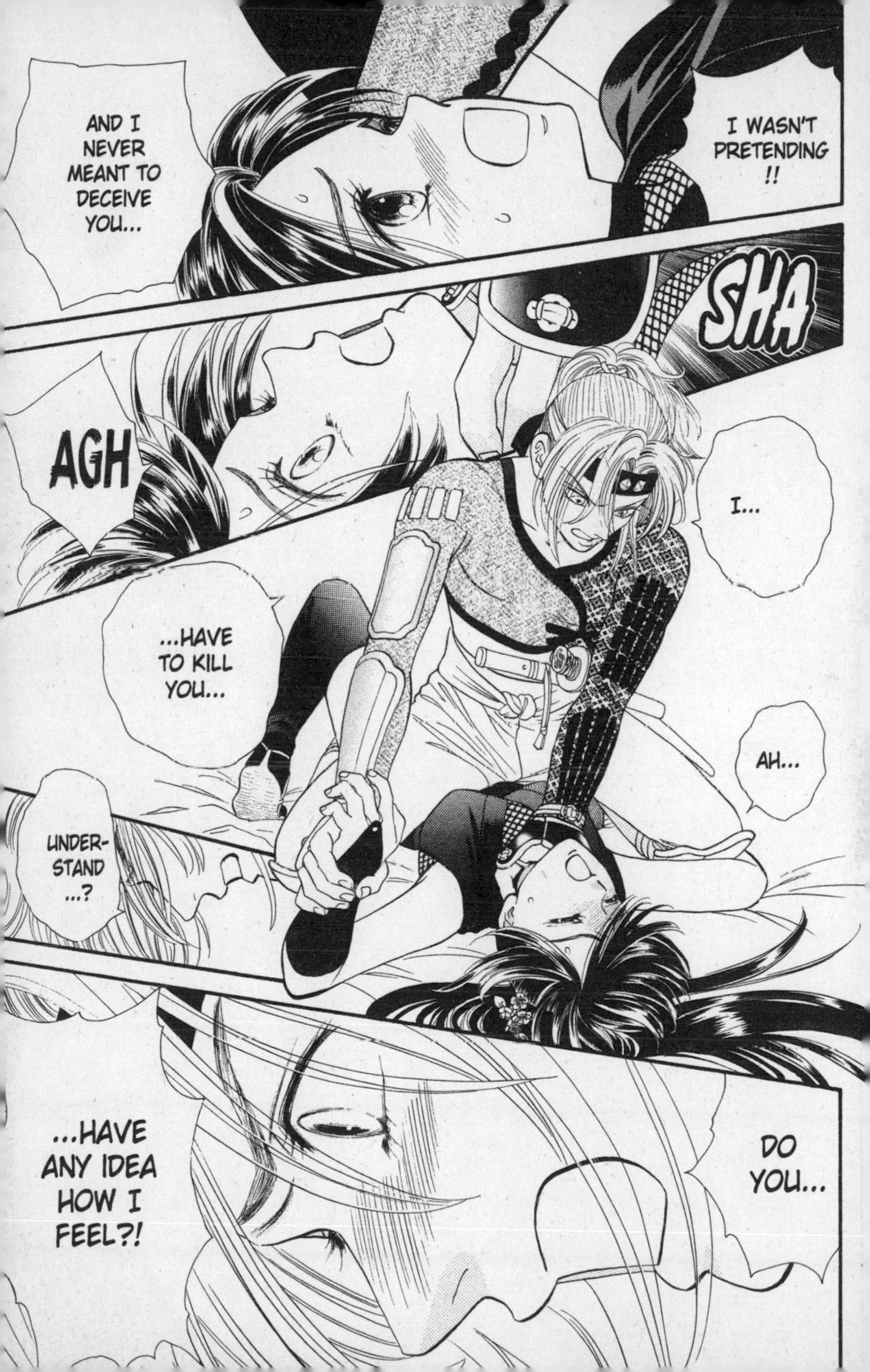
I WASN'T PRETENDING !!
AND I NEVER MEANT TO DECEIVE YOU...
SHA
AGH
I...
...HAVE TO KILL YOU...
AH...
UNDER-STAND ...?
DO YOU...
...HAVE ANY IDEA HOW I FEEL?!

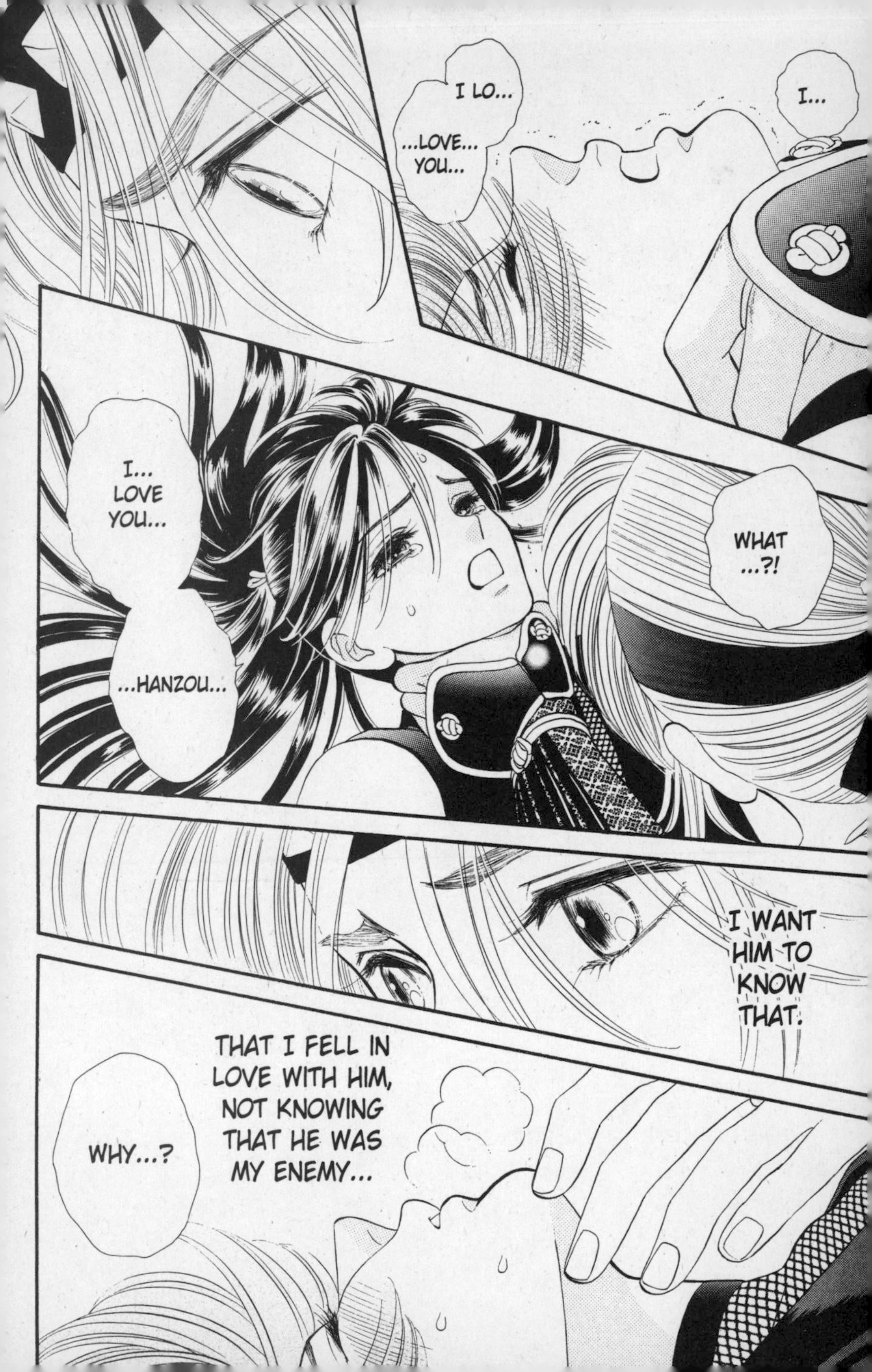
I...
I LO...
...LOVE... YOU...
WHAT ...?!
I... LOVE YOU...
...HANZOU...
I WANT HIM TO KNOW THAT.
THAT I FELL IN LOVE WITH HIM, NOT KNOWING THAT HE WAS MY ENEMY...
WHY...?

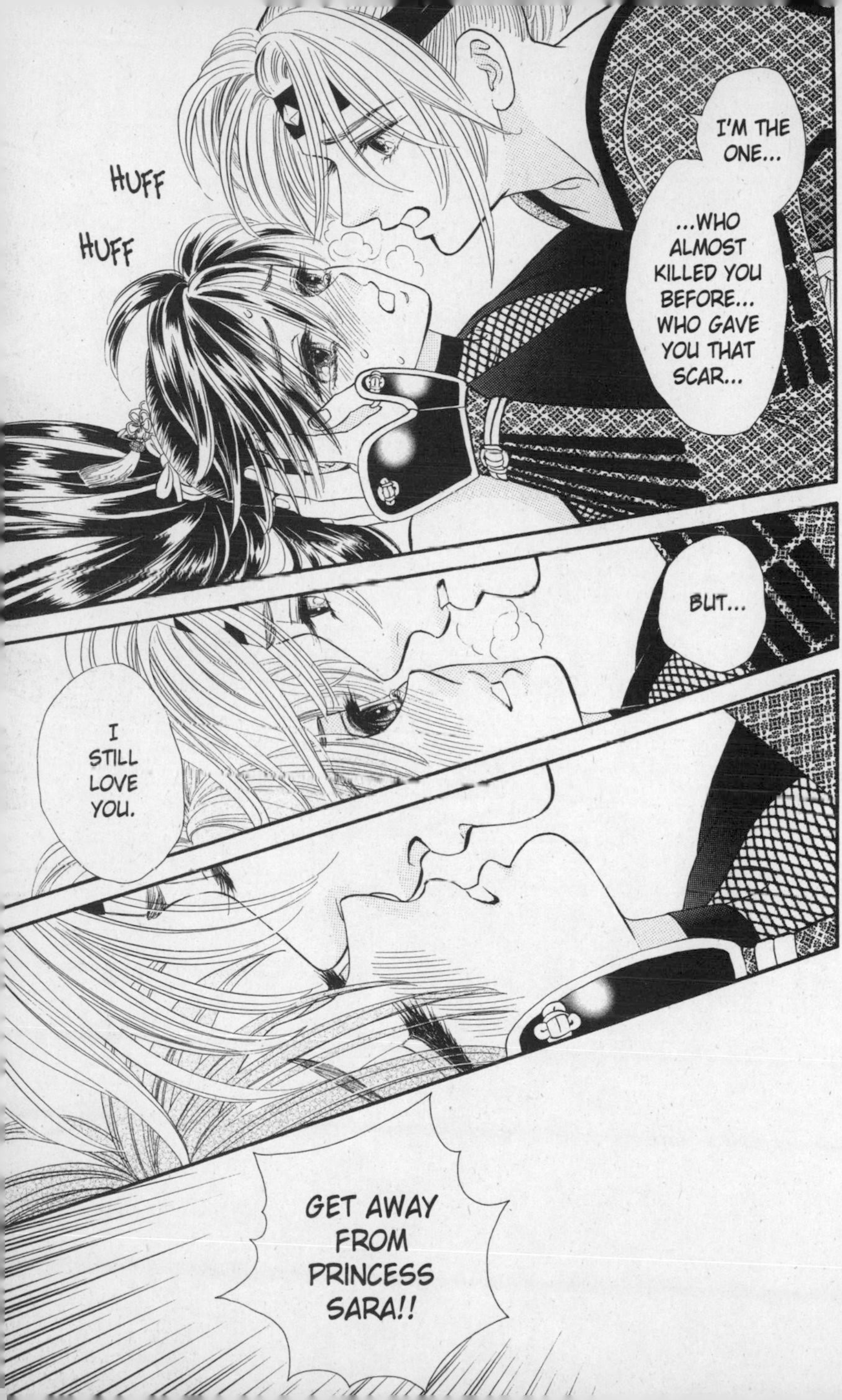
I'M THE ONE...
...WHO ALMOST KILLED YOU BEFORE... WHO GAVE YOU THAT SCAR...
HUFF
HUFF
BUT...
I STILL LOVE YOU.
GET AWAY FROM PRINCESS SARA!!

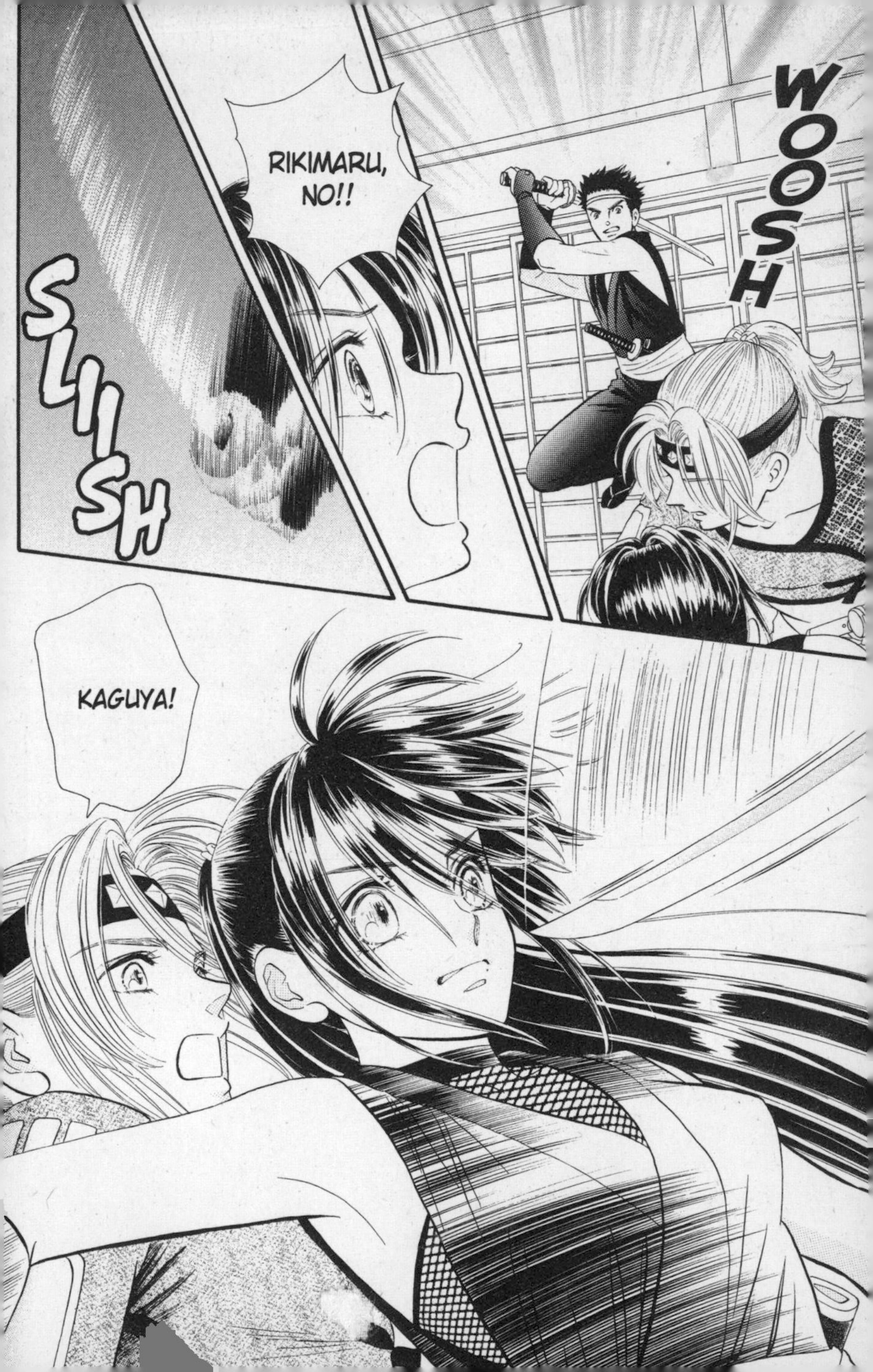
WOOSH
RIKIMARU, NO!!
SLIISH
KAGUYA!

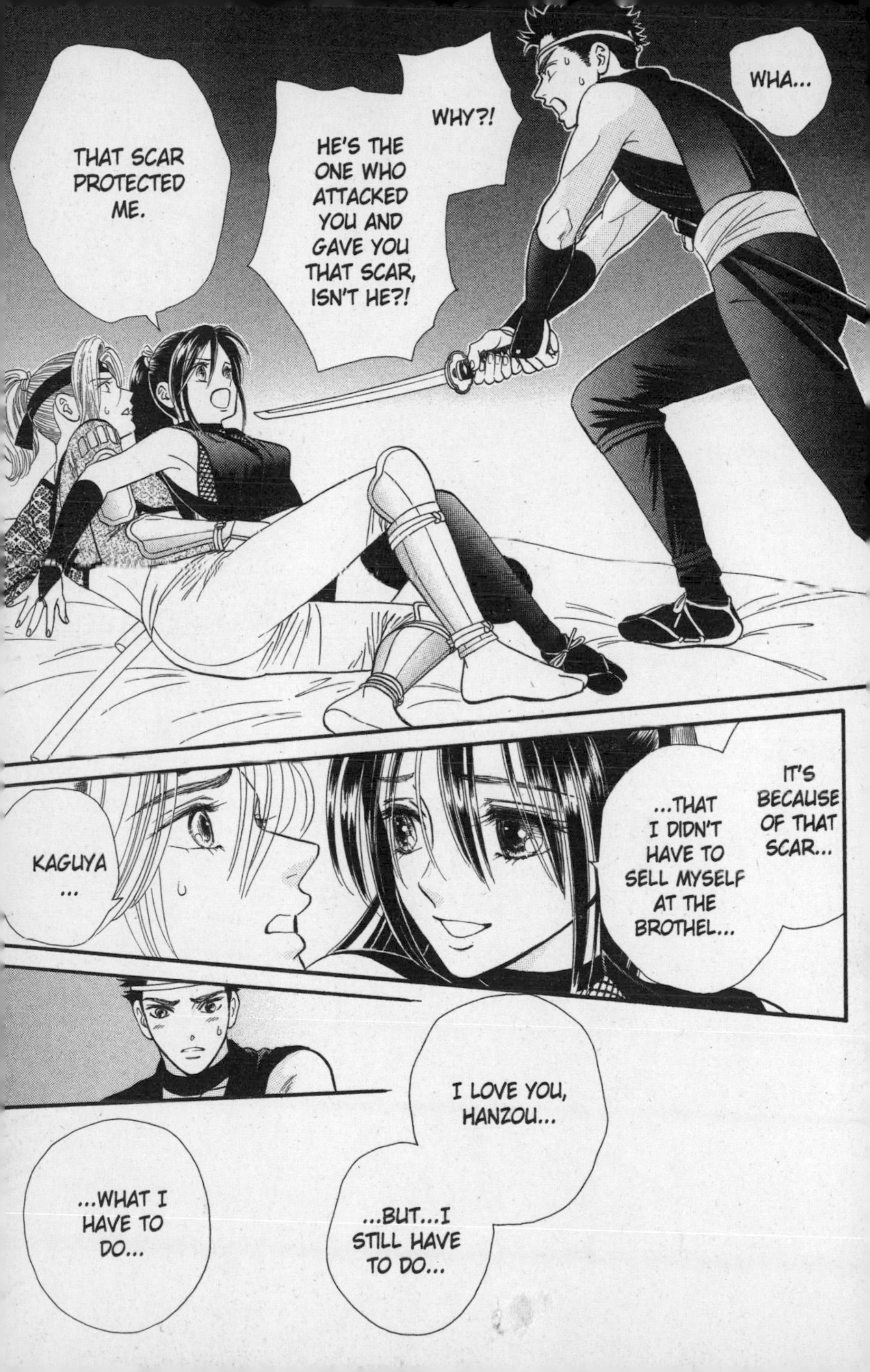
WHA...
WHY?!
HE'S THE ONE WHO ATTACKED YOU AND GAVE YOU THAT SCAR, ISN'T HE?!
THAT SCAR PROTECTED ME.
IT'S BECAUSE OF THAT SCAR...
...THAT I DIDN'T HAVE TO SELL MYSELF AT THE BROTHEL...
KAGUYA ...
I LOVE YOU, HANZOU...
...BUT...I STILL HAVE TO DO...
...WHAT I HAVE TO DO...

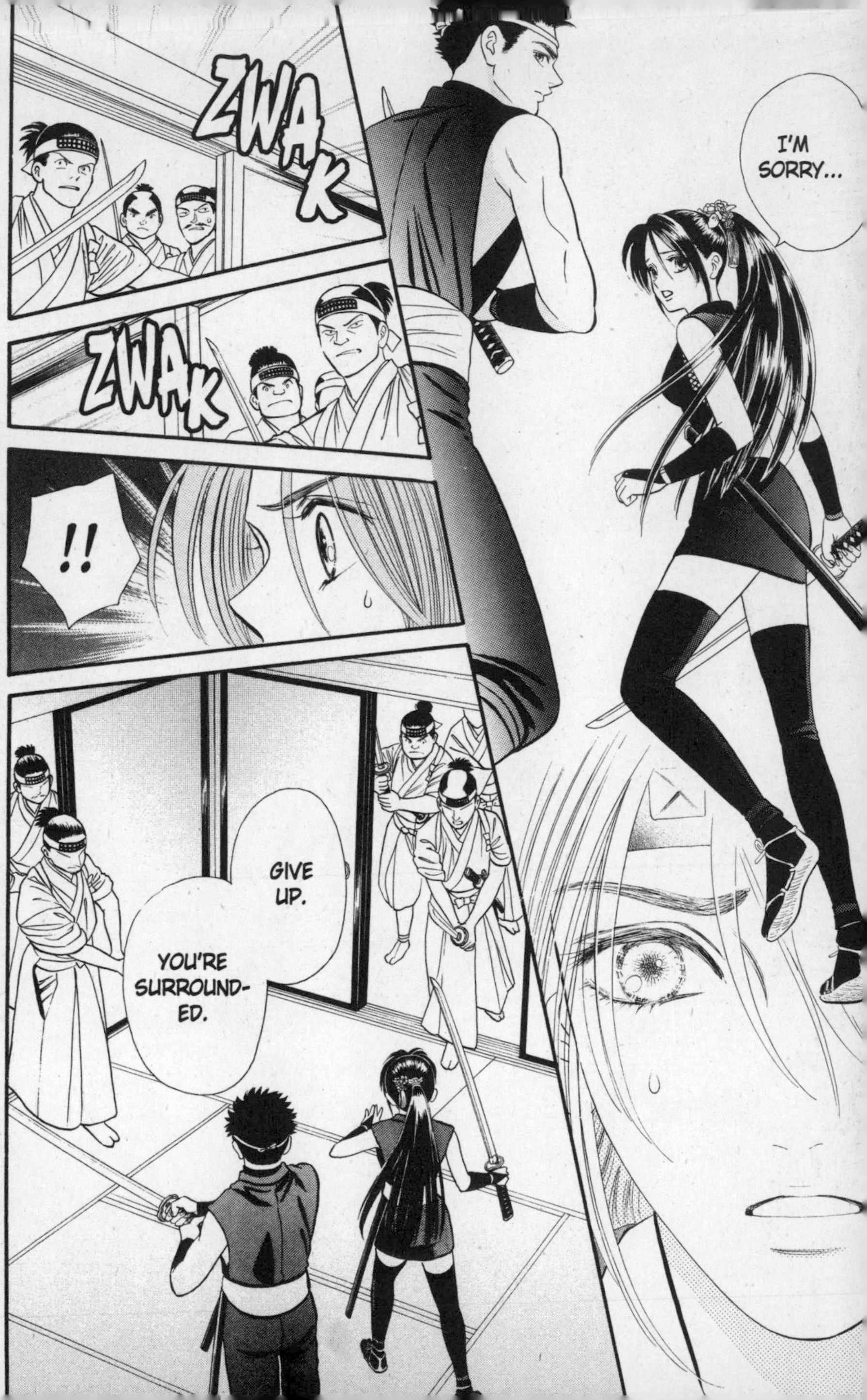
I'M SORRY...
ZWAK
ZWAK
!!
GIVE UP.
YOU'RE SURROUNDED-ED.

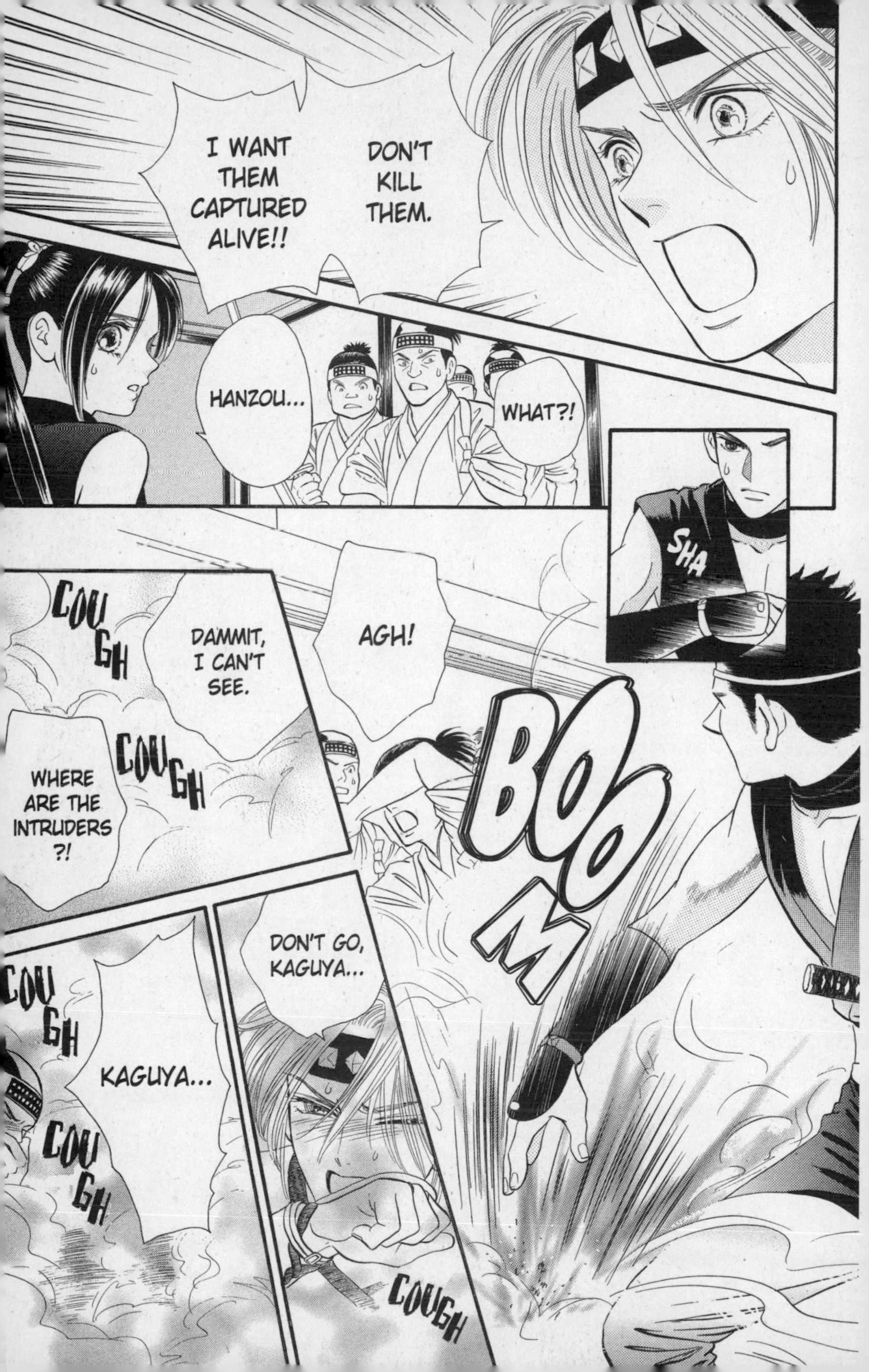
DON'T KILL THEM.
I WANT THEM CAPTURED ALIVE!!
SHA
WHAT?!
HANZOU...
BOOM
AGH!
COUGH
DAMMIT, I CAN'T SEE.
COUGH
WHERE ARE THE INTRUDERS?!
DON'T GO, KAGUYA...
COUGH
COUGH
KAGUYA...
COUGH

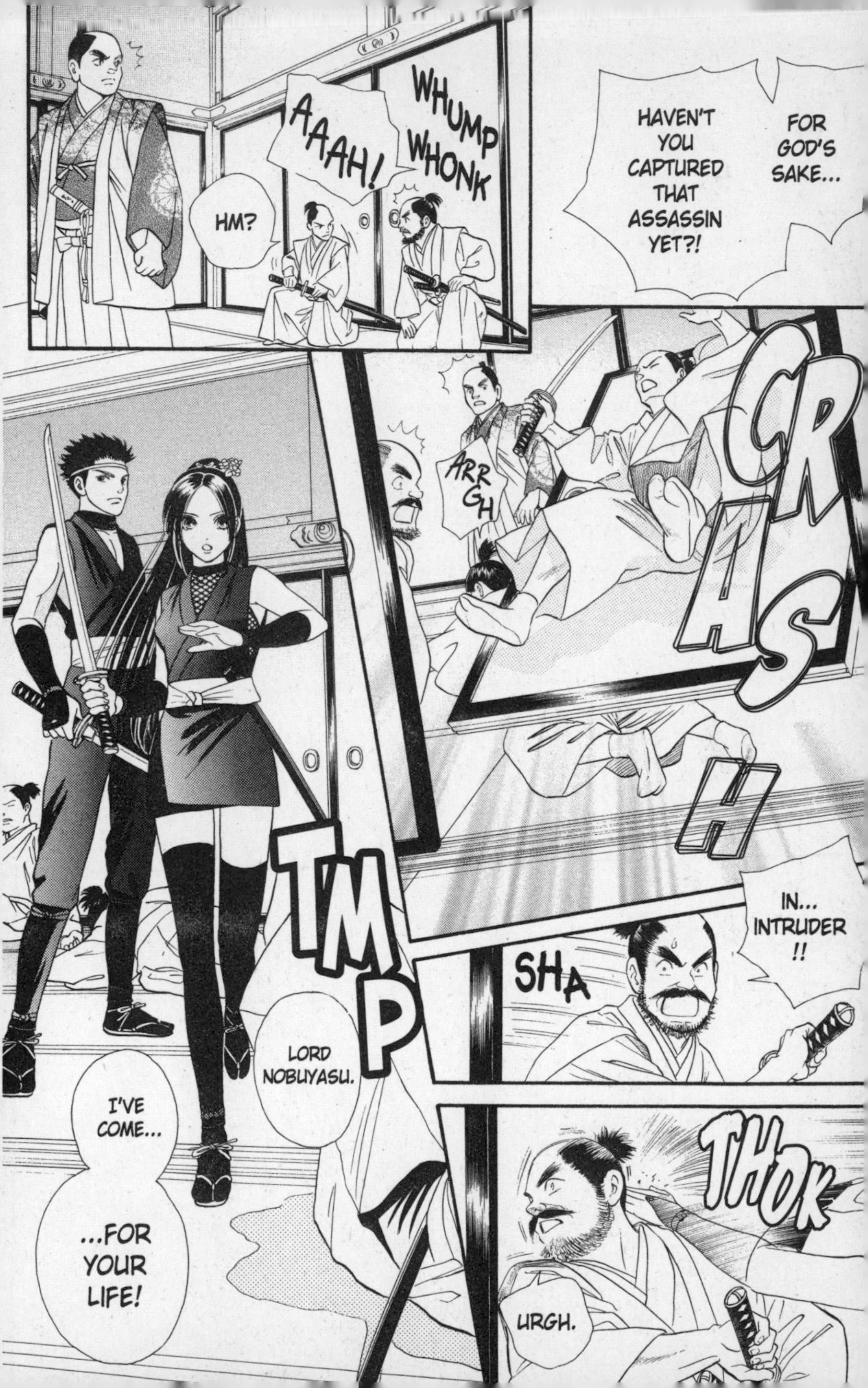
FOR GOD'S SAKE...
HAVEN'T YOU CAPTURED THAT ASSASSIN YET?!
WHUMP WHONK
AAAH!
HM?
CRASH
ARRGH
IN... INTRUDER!!
SHA
THOK
URGH.
TMP
LORD NOBUYASU.
I'VE COME...
...FOR YOUR LIFE!

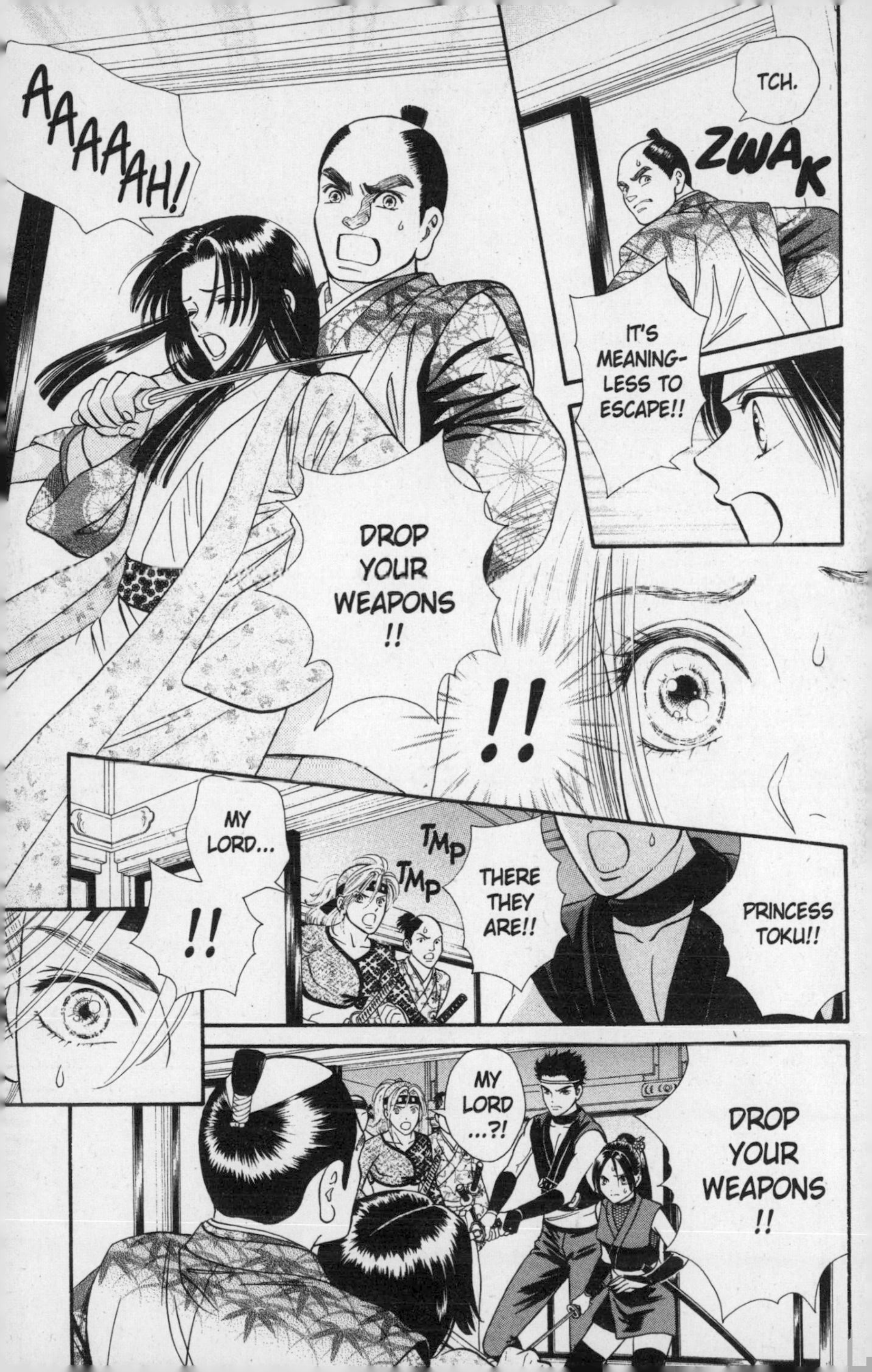
TCH.
ZWAK
IT'S MEANING-LESS TO ESCAPE!!
!!
AAAAAH!
DROP YOUR WEAPONS !!
PRINCESS TOKU!!
THERE THEY ARE!!
TMP TMP
MY LORD...
!!
DROP YOUR WEAPONS !!
MY LORD ...?!

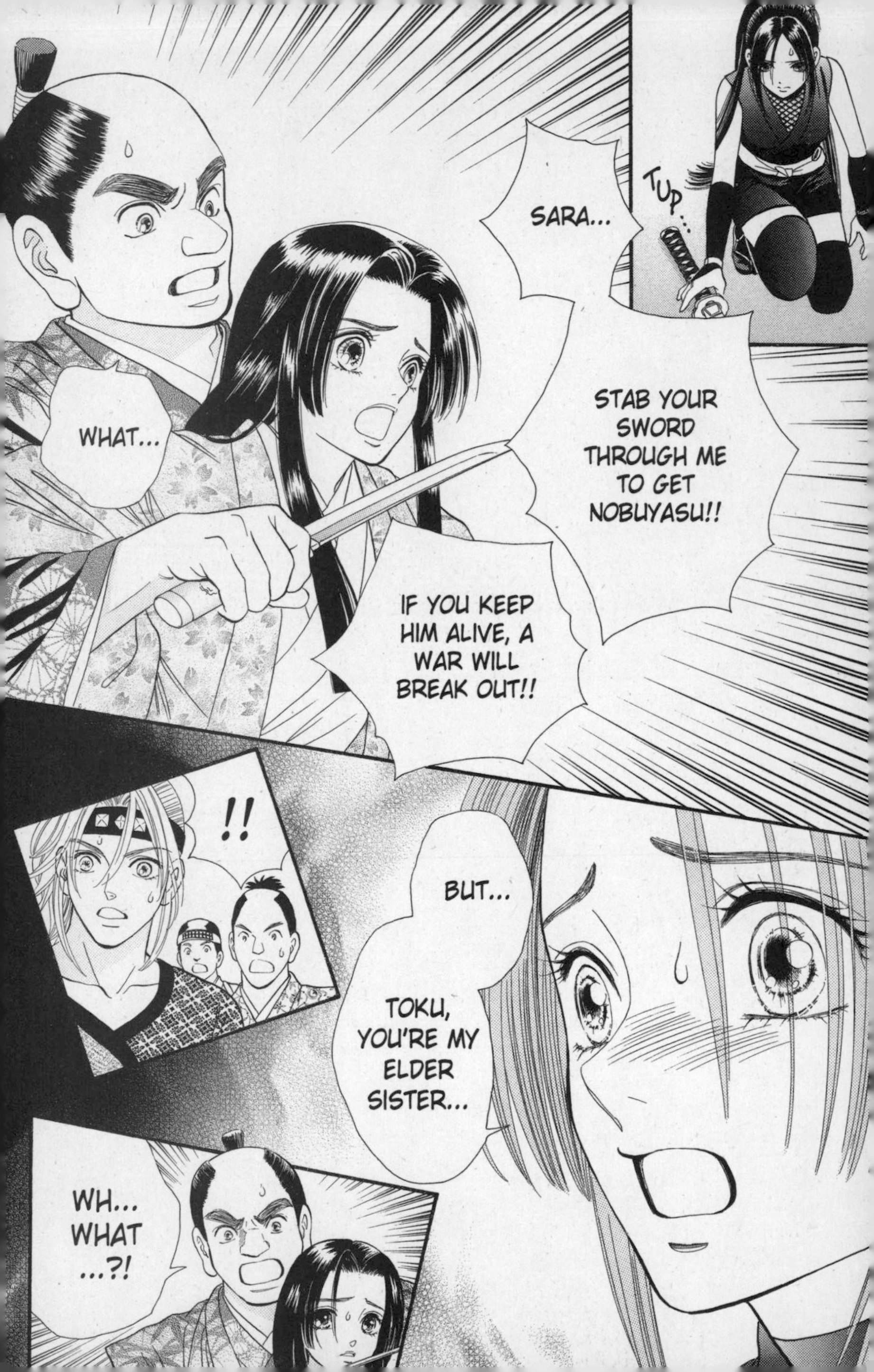
TUP...
SARA...
STAB YOUR SWORD THROUGH ME TO GET NOBUYASU!!
WHAT...
IF YOU KEEP HIM ALIVE, A WAR WILL BREAK OUT!!
BUT...
TOKU, YOU'RE MY ELDER SISTER...
!!
WH... WHAT ...?!

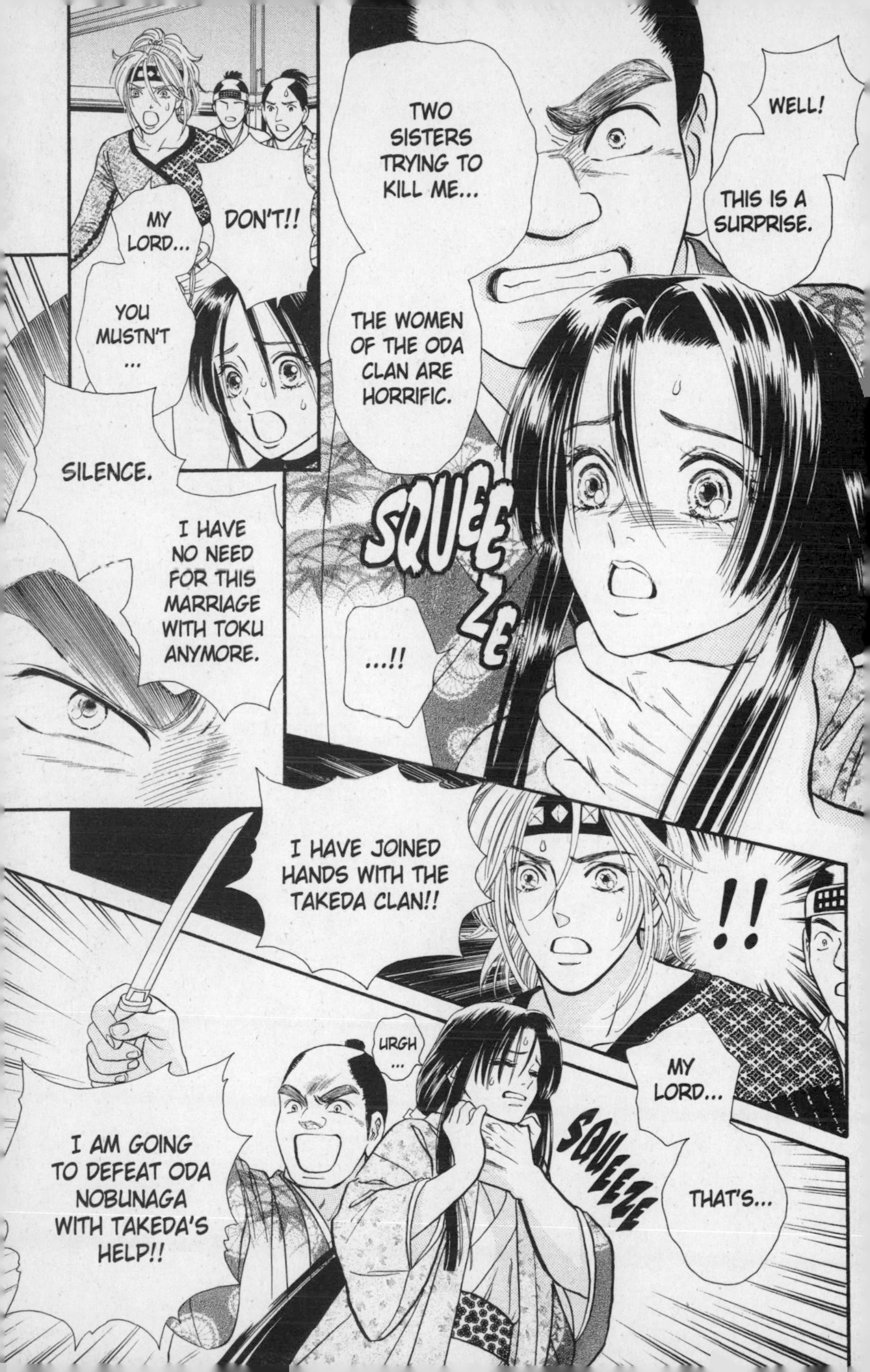
WELL!
THIS IS A SURPRISE.
TWO SISTERS TRYING TO KILL ME...
THE WOMEN OF THE ODA CLAN ARE HORRIFIC.
SQUEEZE
...!!
DON'T!!
MY LORD...
YOU MUSTN'T ...
SILENCE.
I HAVE NO NEED FOR THIS MARRIAGE WITH TOKU ANYMORE.
I HAVE JOINED HANDS WITH THE TAKEDA CLAN!!
!!
MY LORD...
THAT'S...
SQUEEZE
URGH ...
I AM GOING TO DEFEAT ODA NOBUNAGA WITH TAKEDA'S HELP!!

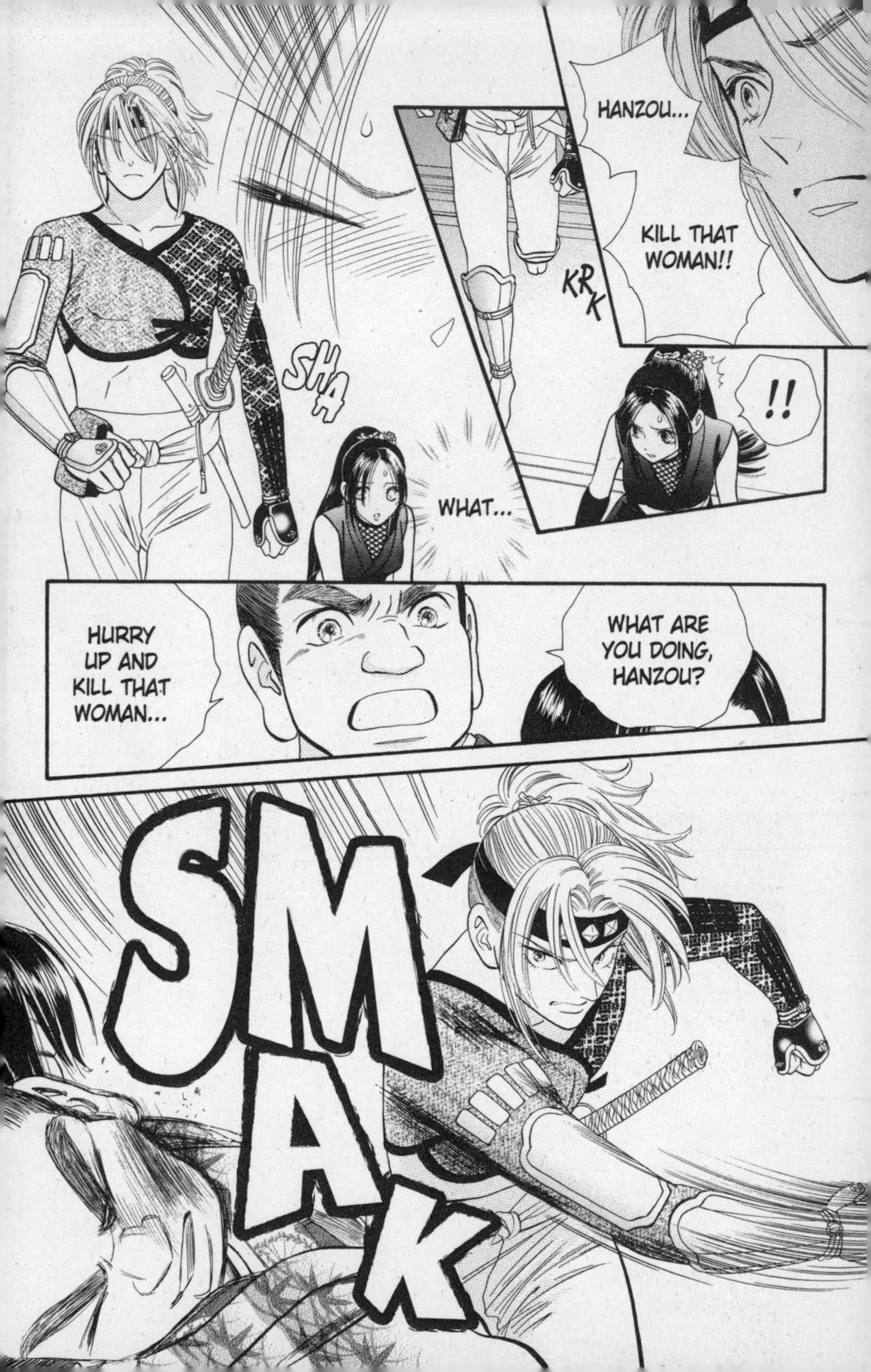

HANZOU...
KILL THAT WOMAN!!
KRK
!!
SHA
WHAT...
WHAT ARE YOU DOING, HANZOU?
HURRY UP AND KILL THAT WOMAN...
SMAK

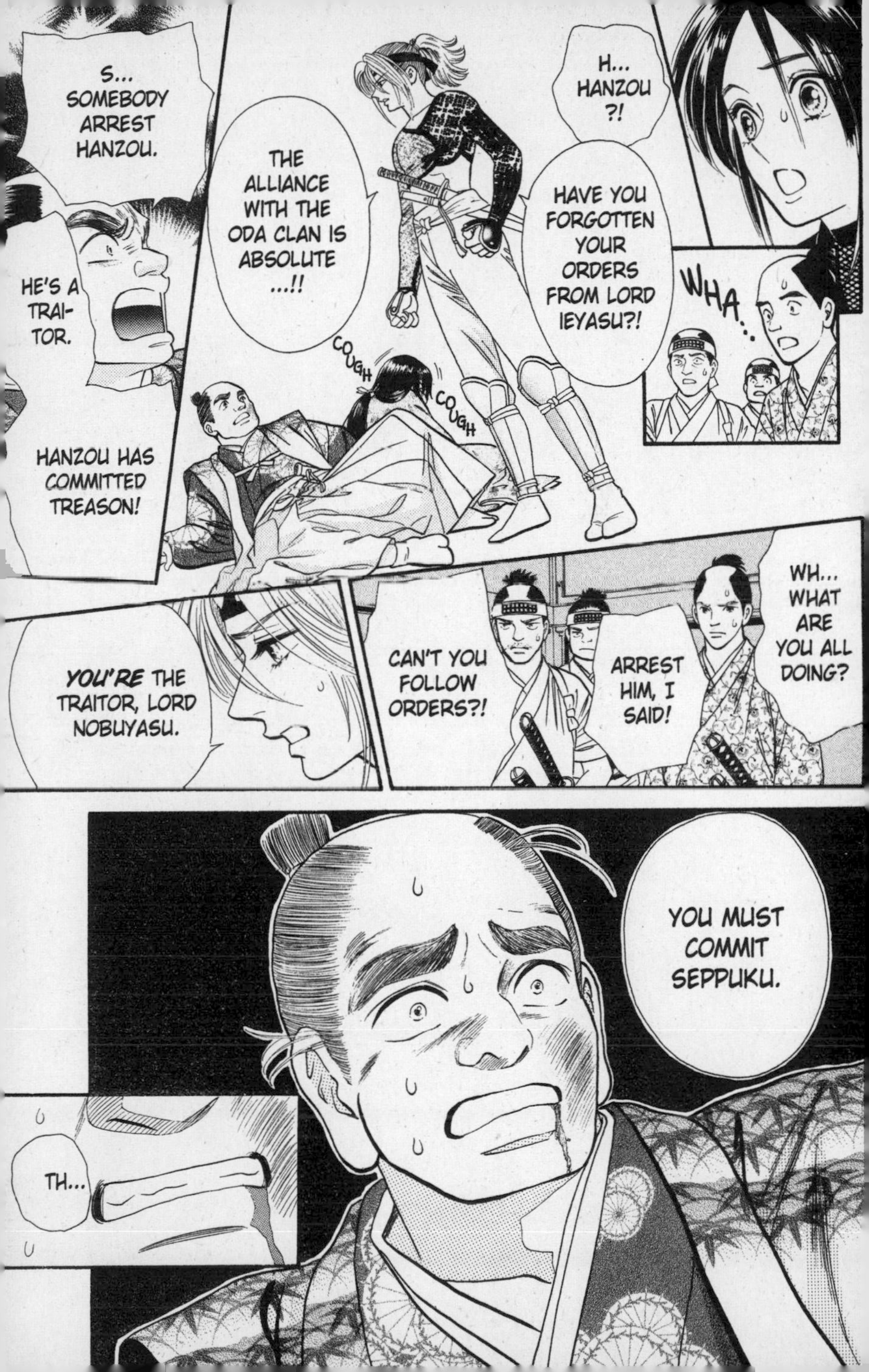
H... HANZOU ?!
WHA...
HAVE YOU FORGOTTEN YOUR ORDERS FROM LORD IEYASU?!
THE ALLIANCE WITH THE ODA CLAN IS ABSOLUTE ...!!
COUGH
COUGH
S... SOMEBODY ARREST HANZOU.
HE'S A TRAI-TOR.
HANZOU HAS COMMITTED TREASON!
WH... WHAT ARE YOU ALL DOING?
ARREST HIM, I SAID!
CAN'T YOU FOLLOW ORDERS?!
YOU'RE THE TRAITOR, LORD NOBUYASU.
YOU MUST COMMIT SEPPUKU.
TH...

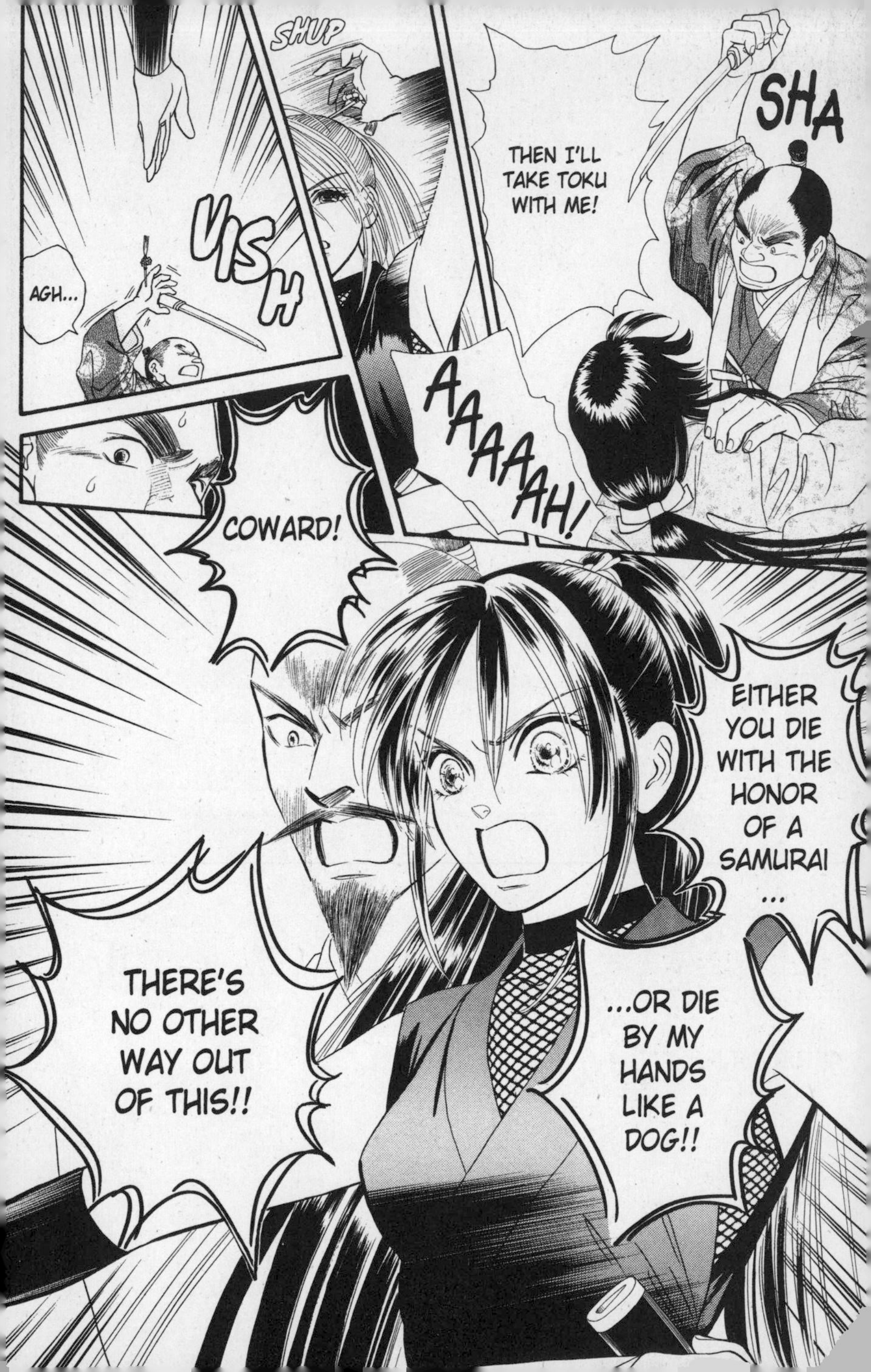
SHA
THEN I'LL TAKE TOKU WITH ME!
AAAAAAH!
SHUP
VISH
AGH...
COWARD!
EITHER YOU DIE WITH THE HONOR OF A SAMURAI ...
...OR DIE BY MY HANDS LIKE A DOG!!
THERE'S NO OTHER WAY OUT OF THIS!!

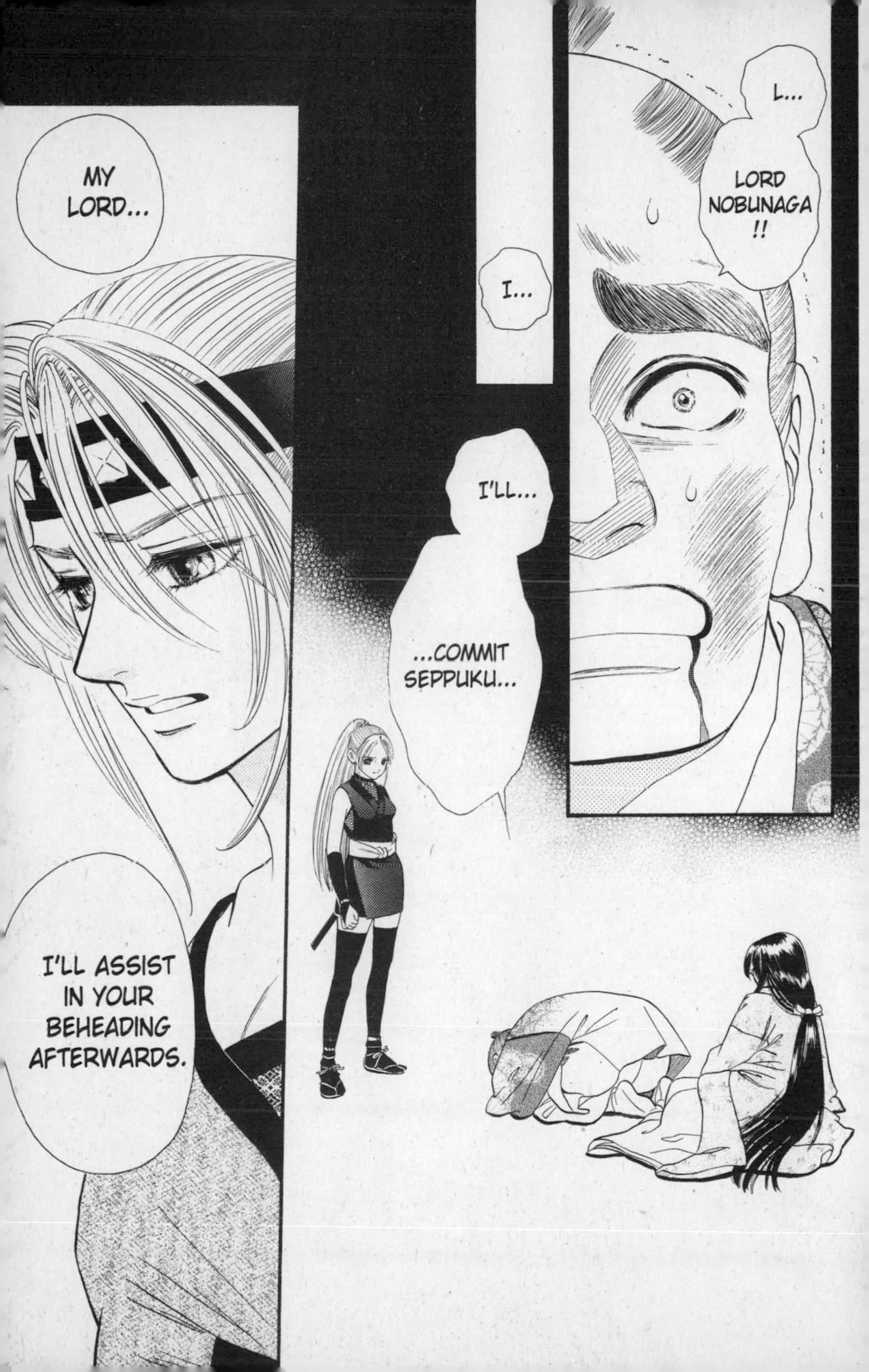
L...
LORD NOBUNAGA!!
I...
I'LL...
...COMMIT SEPPUKU...
MY LORD...
I'LL ASSIST IN YOUR BEHEADING AFTERWARDS.

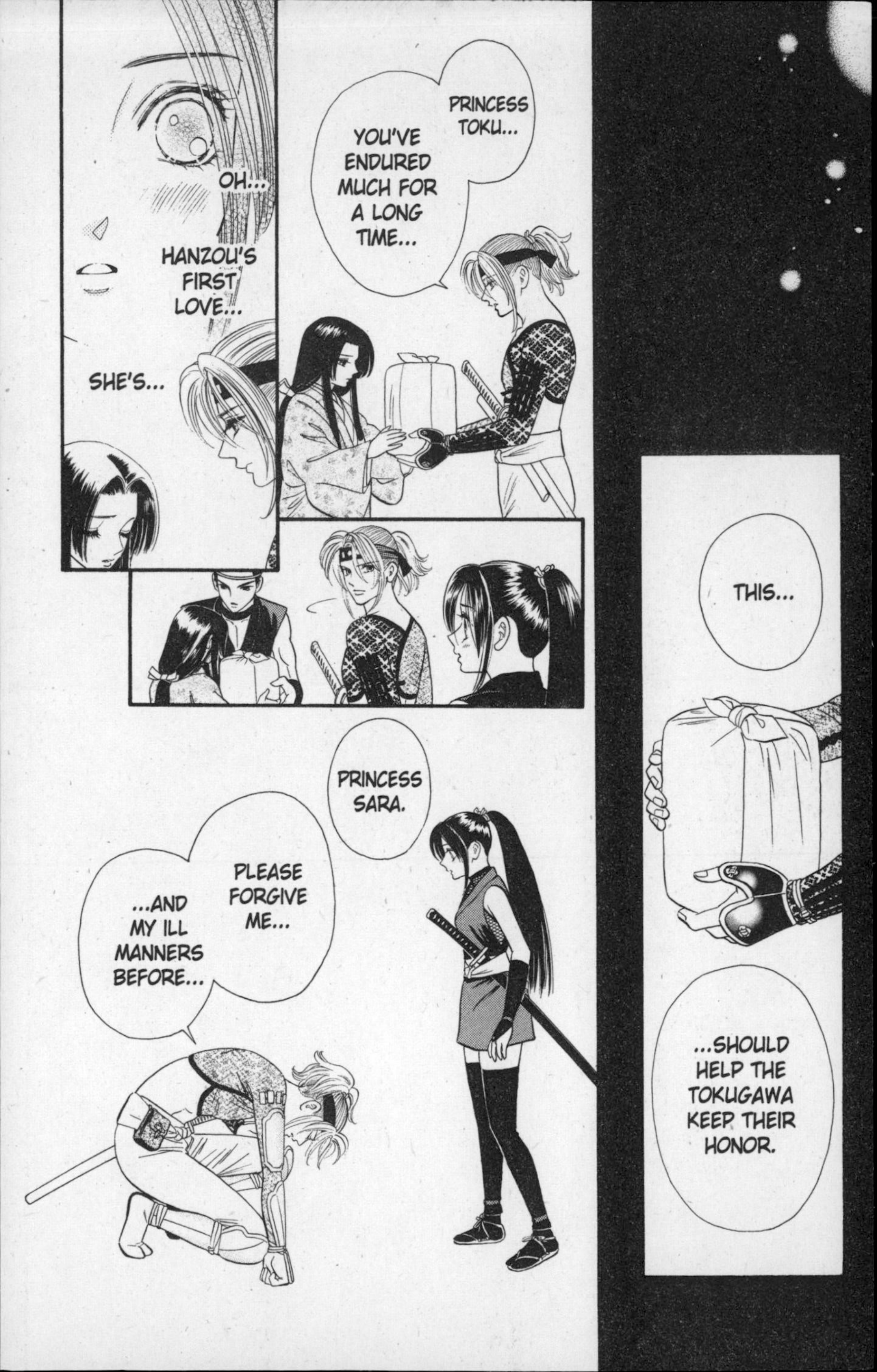
THIS...
...SHOULD HELP THE TOKUGAWA KEEP THEIR HONOR.
PRINCESS TOKU...
YOU'VE ENDURED MUCH FOR A LONG TIME...
OH...
HANZOU'S FIRST LOVE...
SHE'S...
PRINCESS SARA.
PLEASE FORGIVE ME...
...AND MY ILL MANNERS BEFORE...

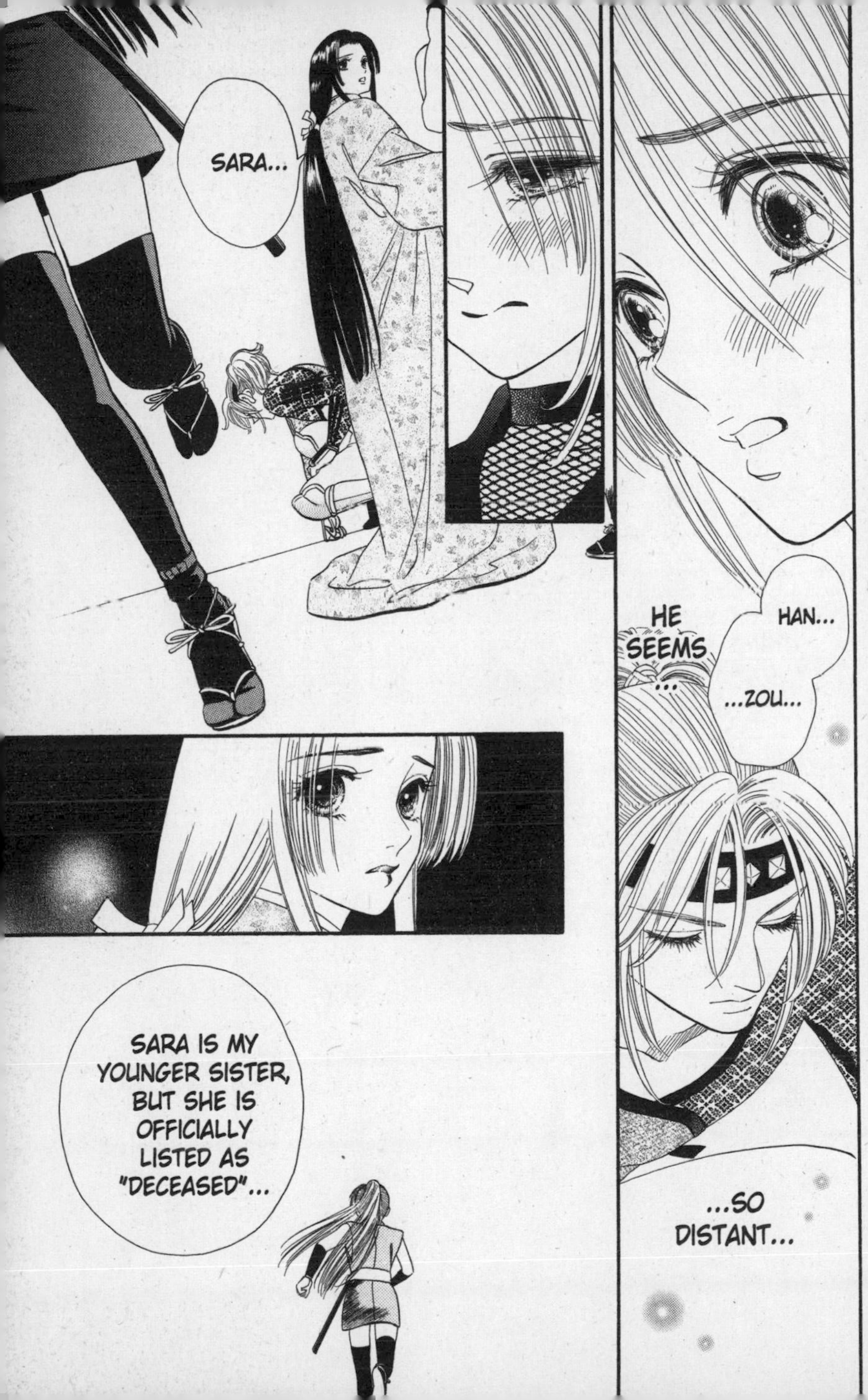
HAN... ...ZOU...
HE SEEMS ...
...SO DISTANT...
SARA...
SARA IS MY YOUNGER SISTER, BUT SHE IS OFFICIALLY LISTED AS "DECEASED"...

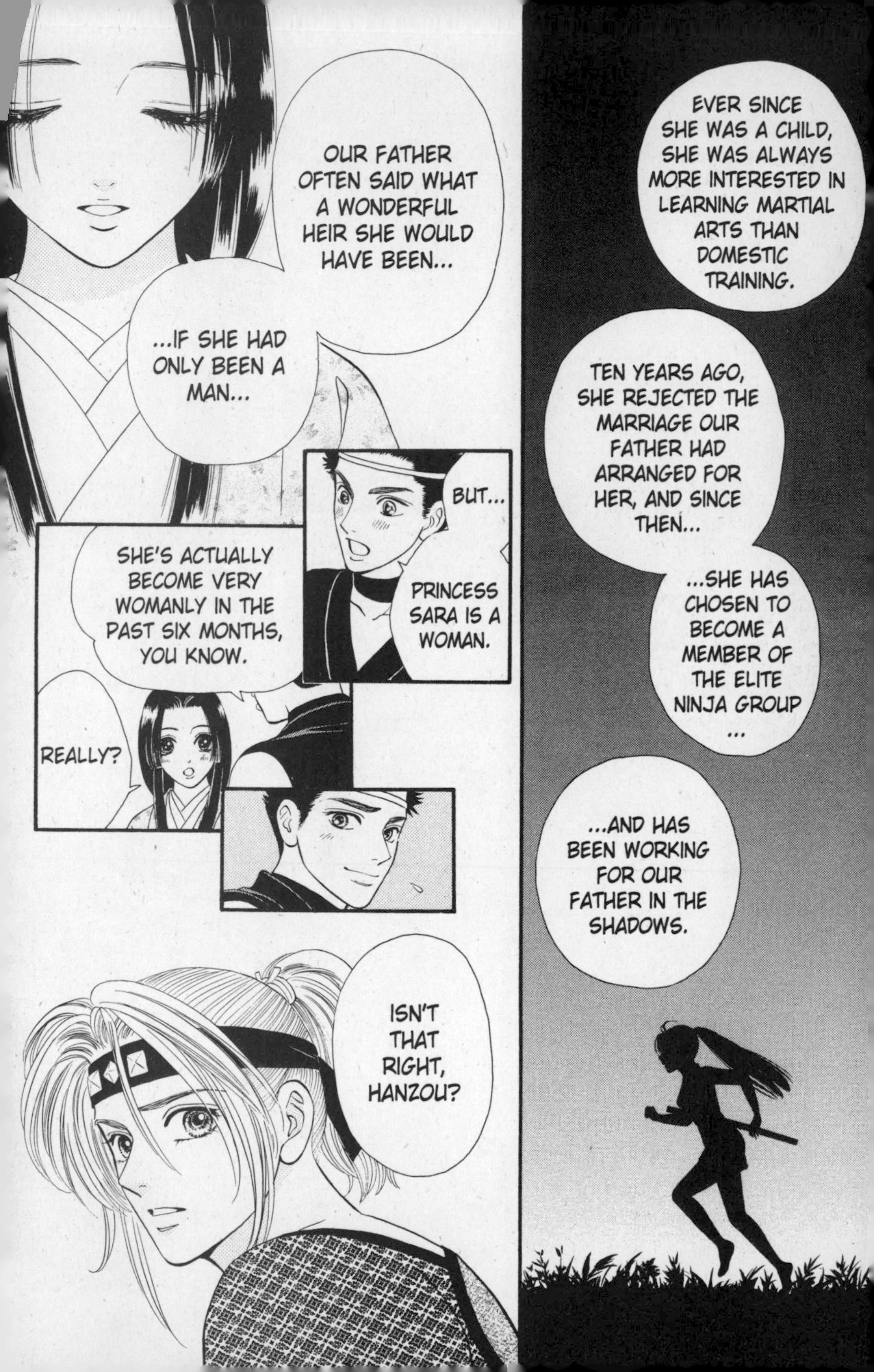
EVER SINCE SHE WAS A CHILD, SHE WAS ALWAYS MORE INTERESTED IN LEARNING MARTIAL ARTS THAN DOMESTIC TRAINING.
TEN YEARS AGO, SHE REJECTED THE MARRIAGE OUR FATHER HAD ARRANGED FOR HER, AND SINCE THEN...
...SHE HAS CHOSEN TO BECOME A MEMBER OF THE ELITE NINJA GROUP ...
...AND HAS BEEN WORKING FOR OUR FATHER IN THE SHADOWS.
OUR FATHER OFTEN SAID WHAT A WONDERFUL HEIR SHE WOULD HAVE BEEN...
...IF SHE HAD ONLY BEEN A MAN...
BUT...
PRINCESS SARA IS A WOMAN.
SHE'S ACTUALLY BECOME VERY WOMANLY IN THE PAST SIX MONTHS, YOU KNOW.
REALLY?
ISN'T THAT RIGHT, HANZOU?

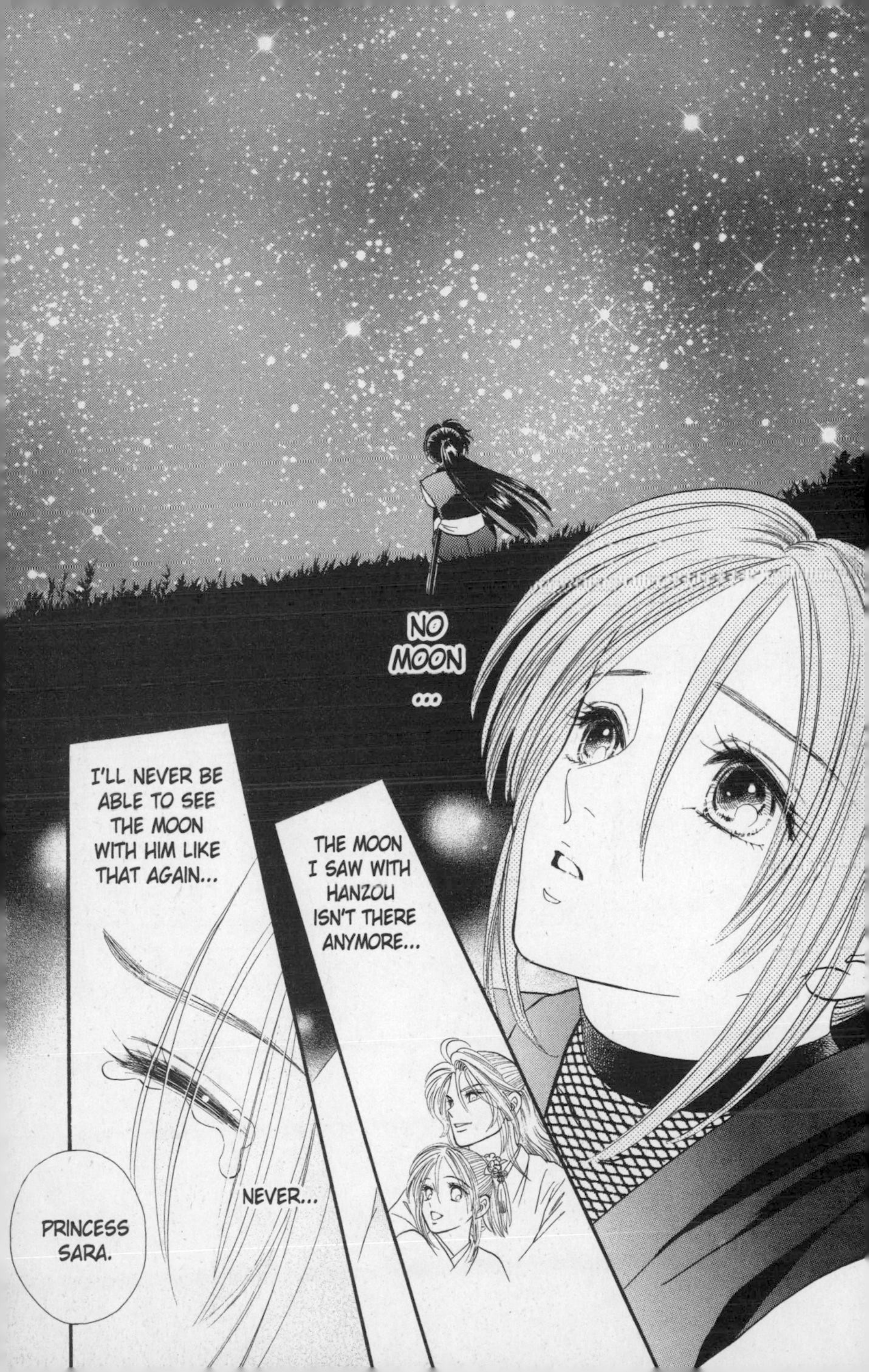
NO MOON...
THE MOON I SAW WITH HANZOU ISN'T THERE ANYMORE...
I'LL NEVER BE ABLE TO SEE THE MOON WITH HIM LIKE THAT AGAIN...
NEVER...
PRINCESS SARA.

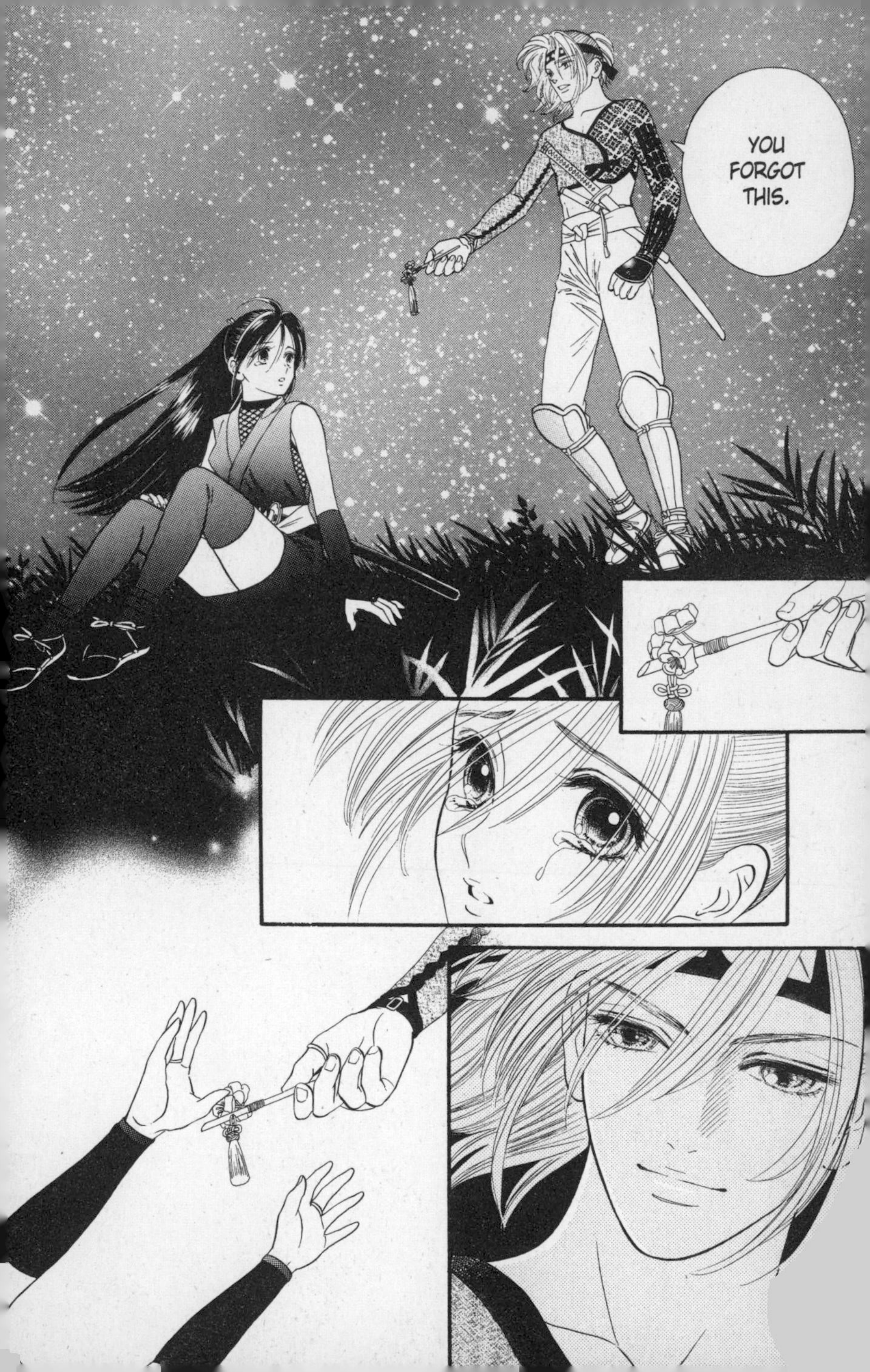
YOU FORGOT THIS.

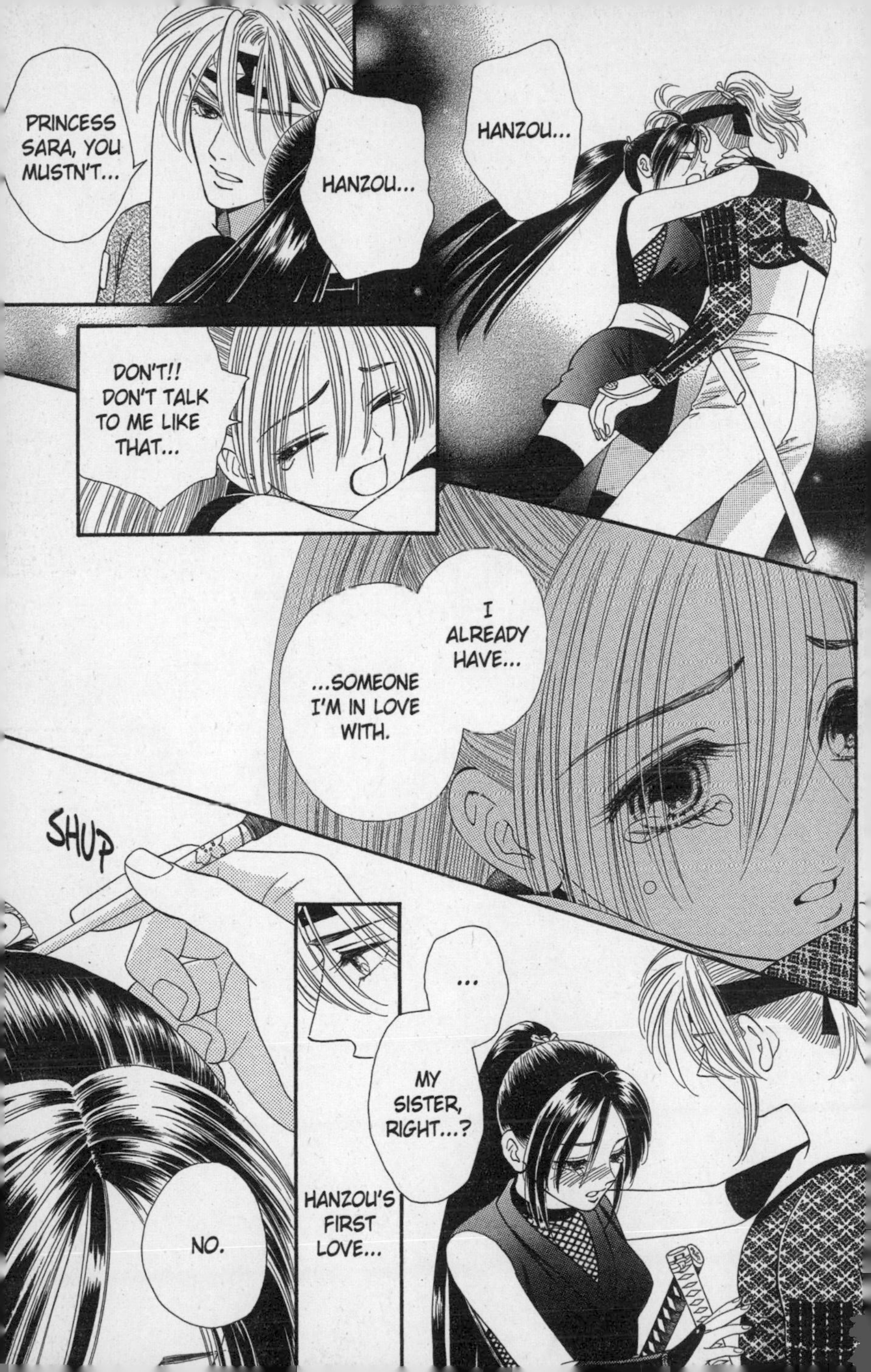
HANZOU...
HANZOU...
PRINCESS SARA, YOU MUSTN'T...
DON'T!! DON'T TALK TO ME LIKE THAT...
I ALREADY HAVE...
...SOMEONE I'M IN LOVE WITH.
...
MY SISTER, RIGHT...?
HANZOU'S FIRST LOVE...
SHUP
NO.

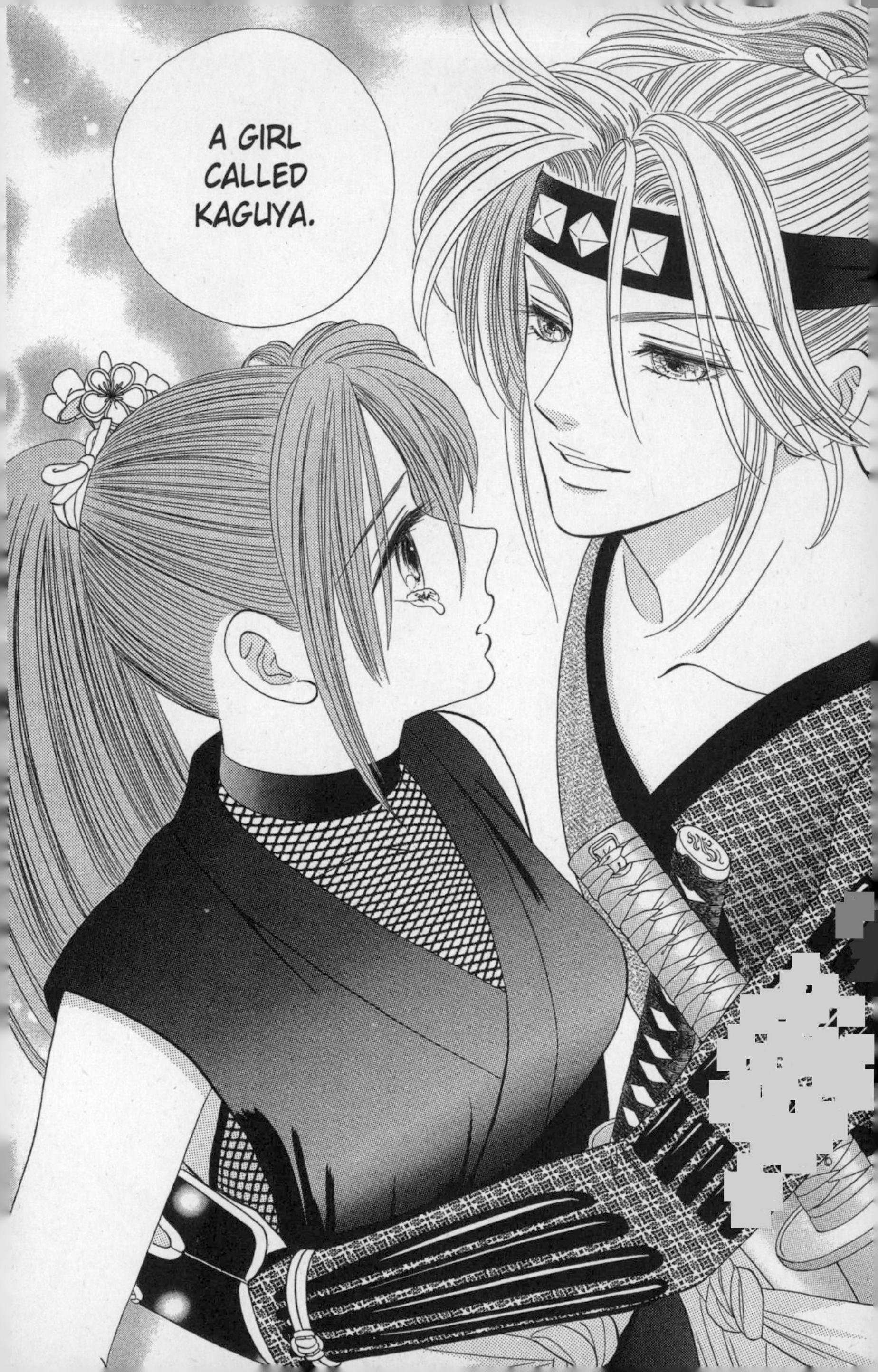
A GIRL CALLED KAGUYA.

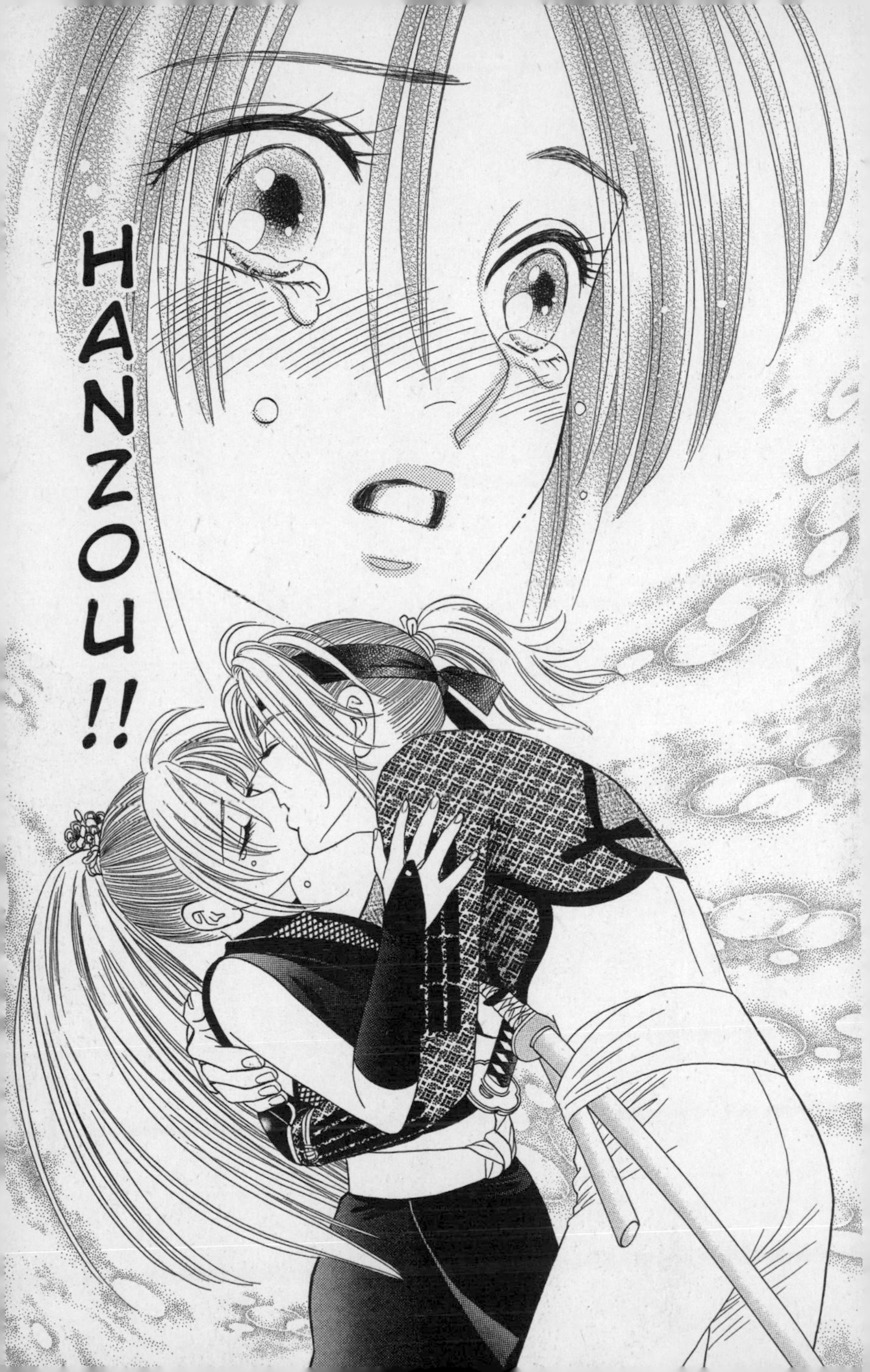
HANZOU!!

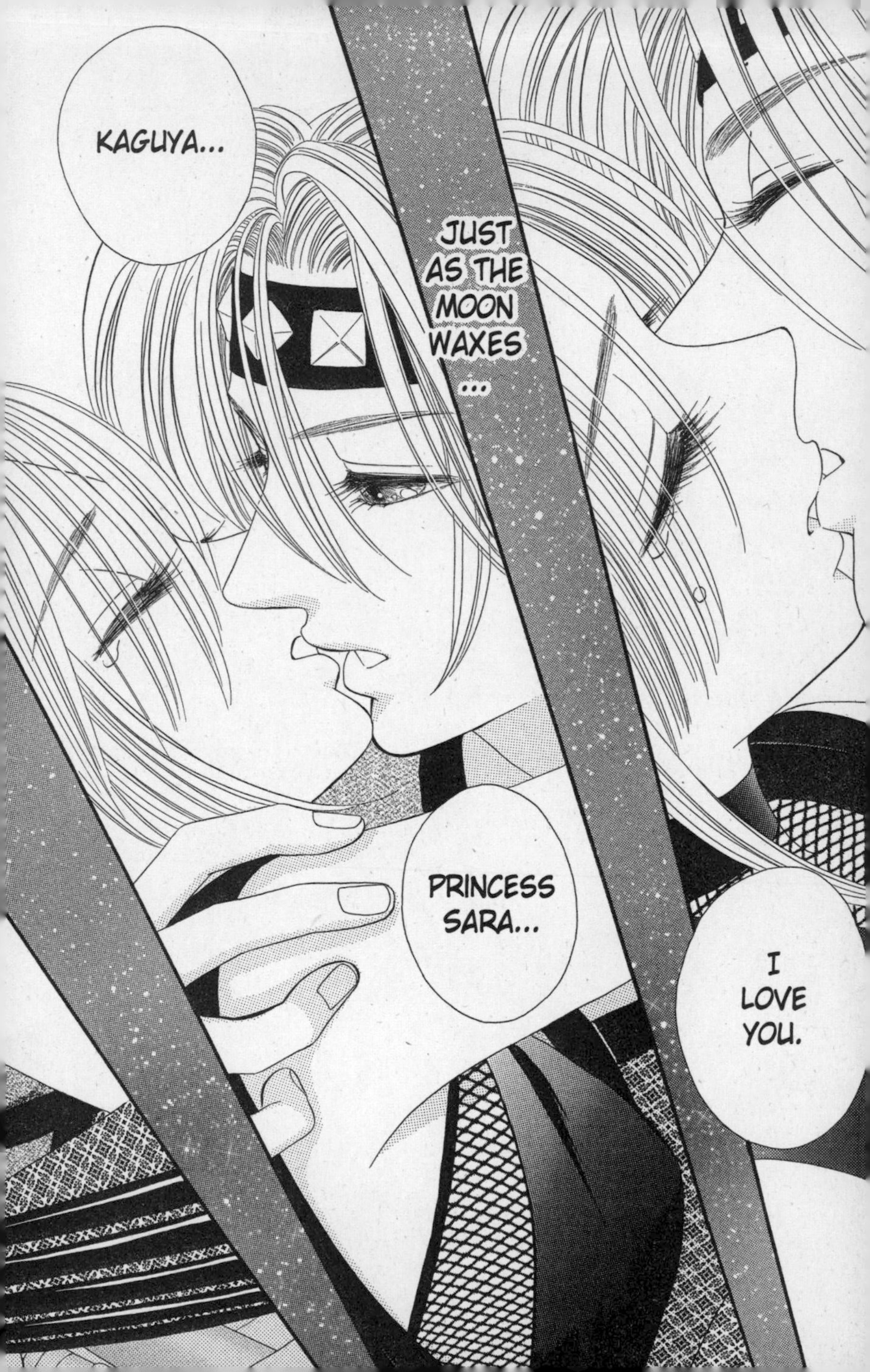
KAGUYA...
JUST AS THE MOON WAXES...
PRINCESS SARA...
I LOVE YOU.

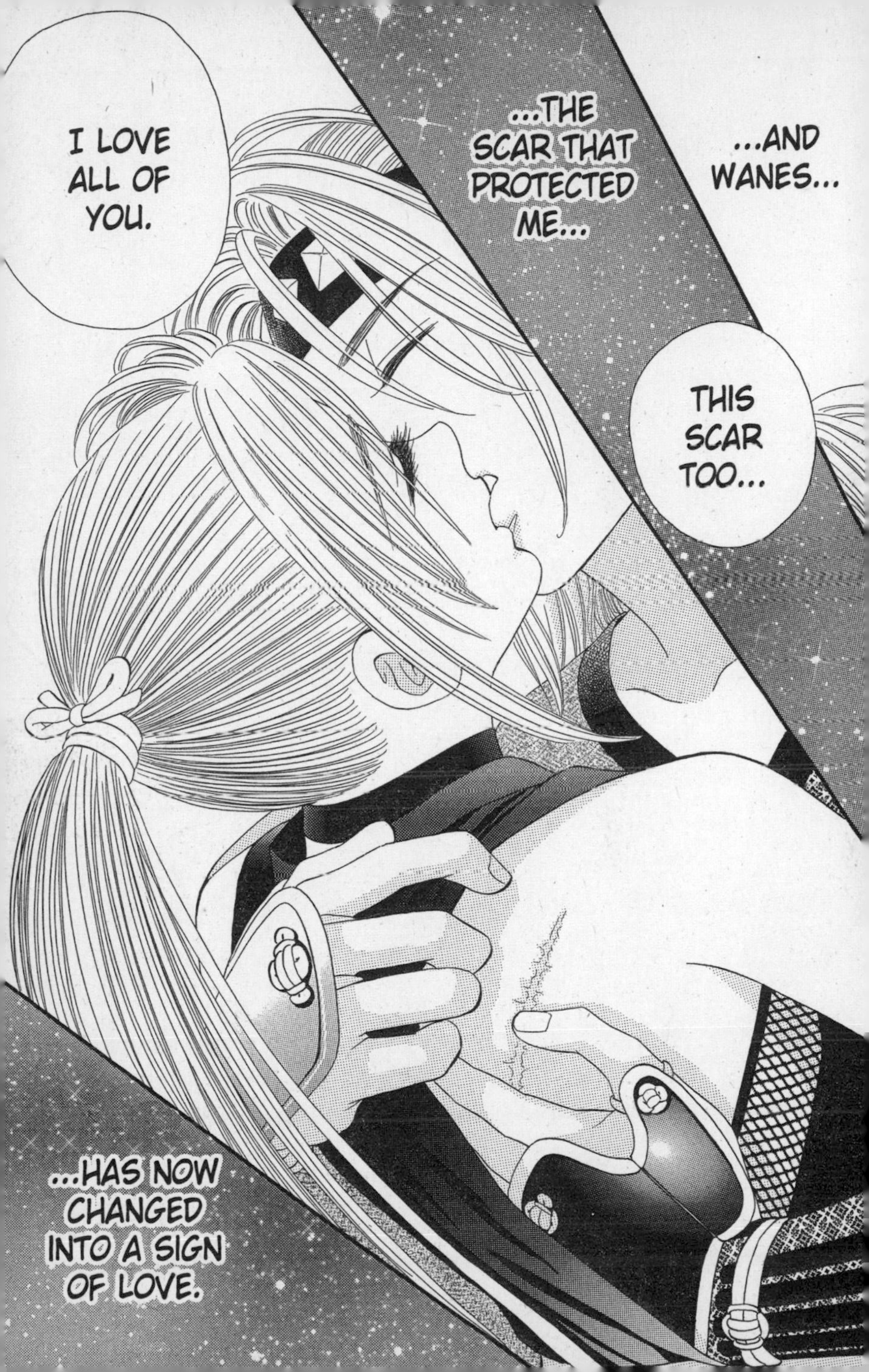
...AND WANES...
...THE SCAR THAT PROTECTED ME...
I LOVE ALL OF YOU.
THIS SCAR TOO...
...HAS NOW CHANGED INTO A SIGN OF LOVE.

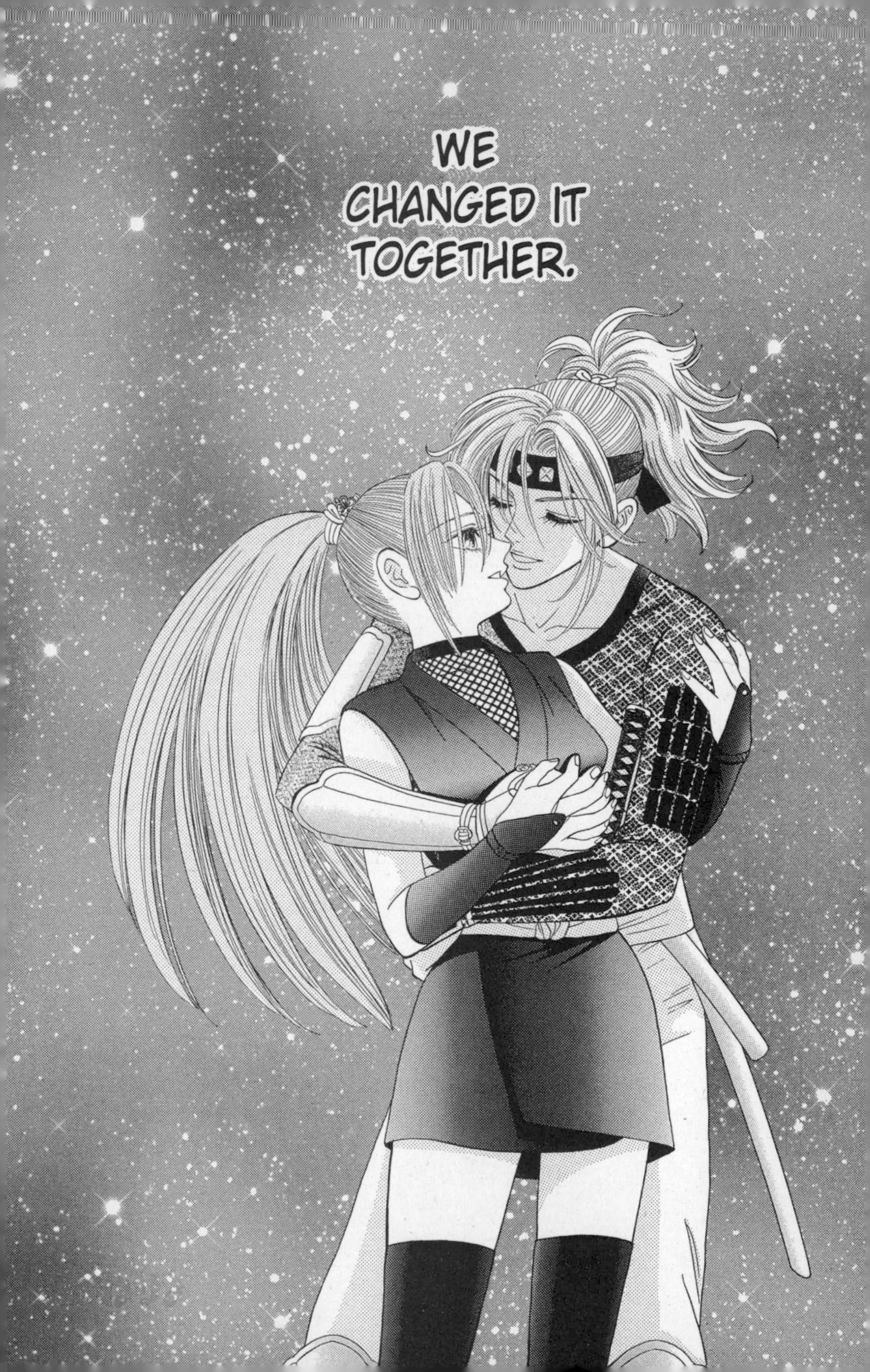
WE CHANGED IT TOGETHER.

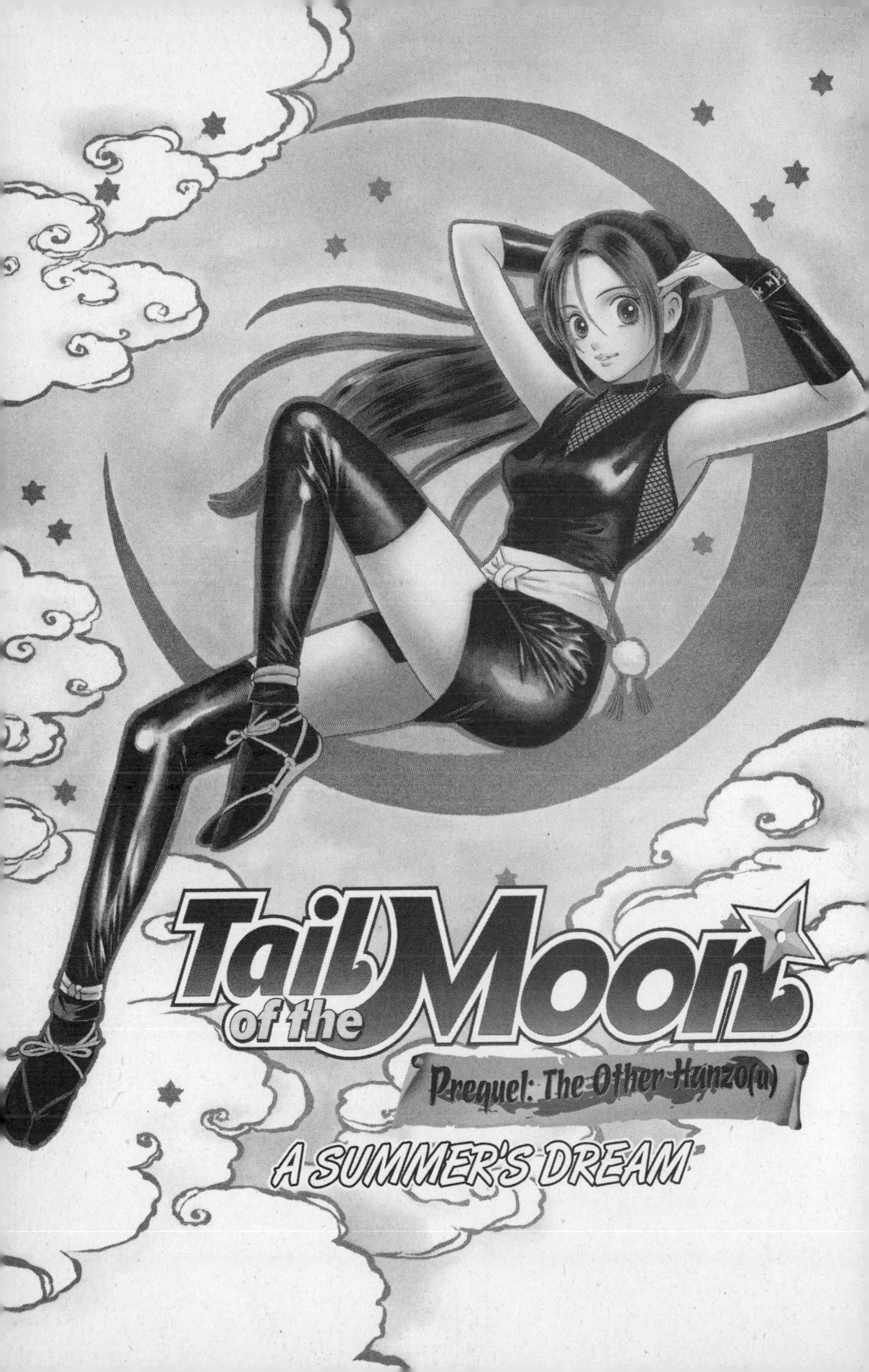
Tail of the Moon
Prequel: The Other Hanzo(u)
A SUMMER'S DREAM

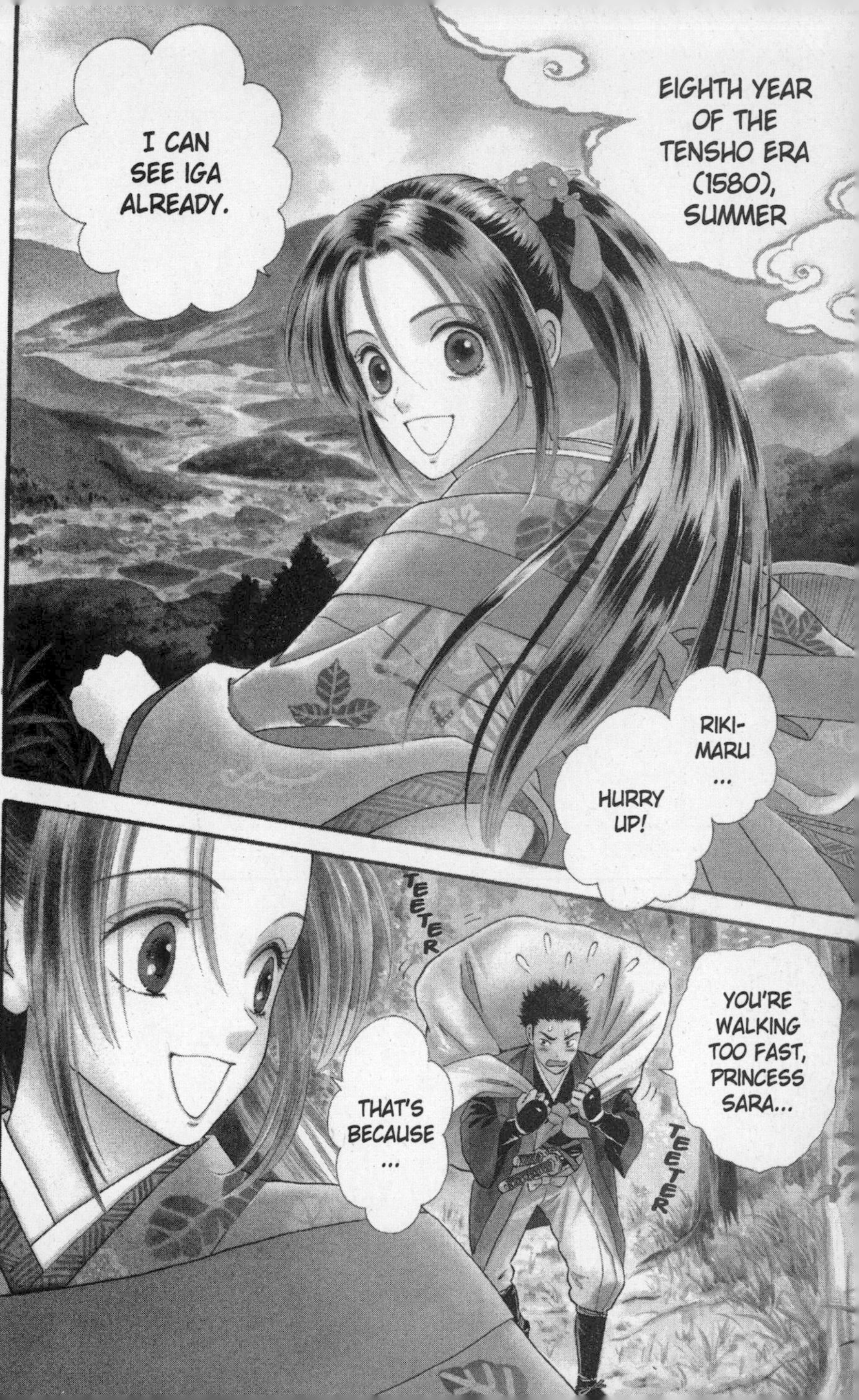
EIGHTH YEAR OF THE TENSHO ERA (1580), SUMMER
I CAN SEE IGA ALREADY.
RIKI-MARU ... HURRY UP!
TEETER
YOU'RE WALKING TOO FAST, PRINCESS SARA...
TEETER
THAT'S BECAUSE ...

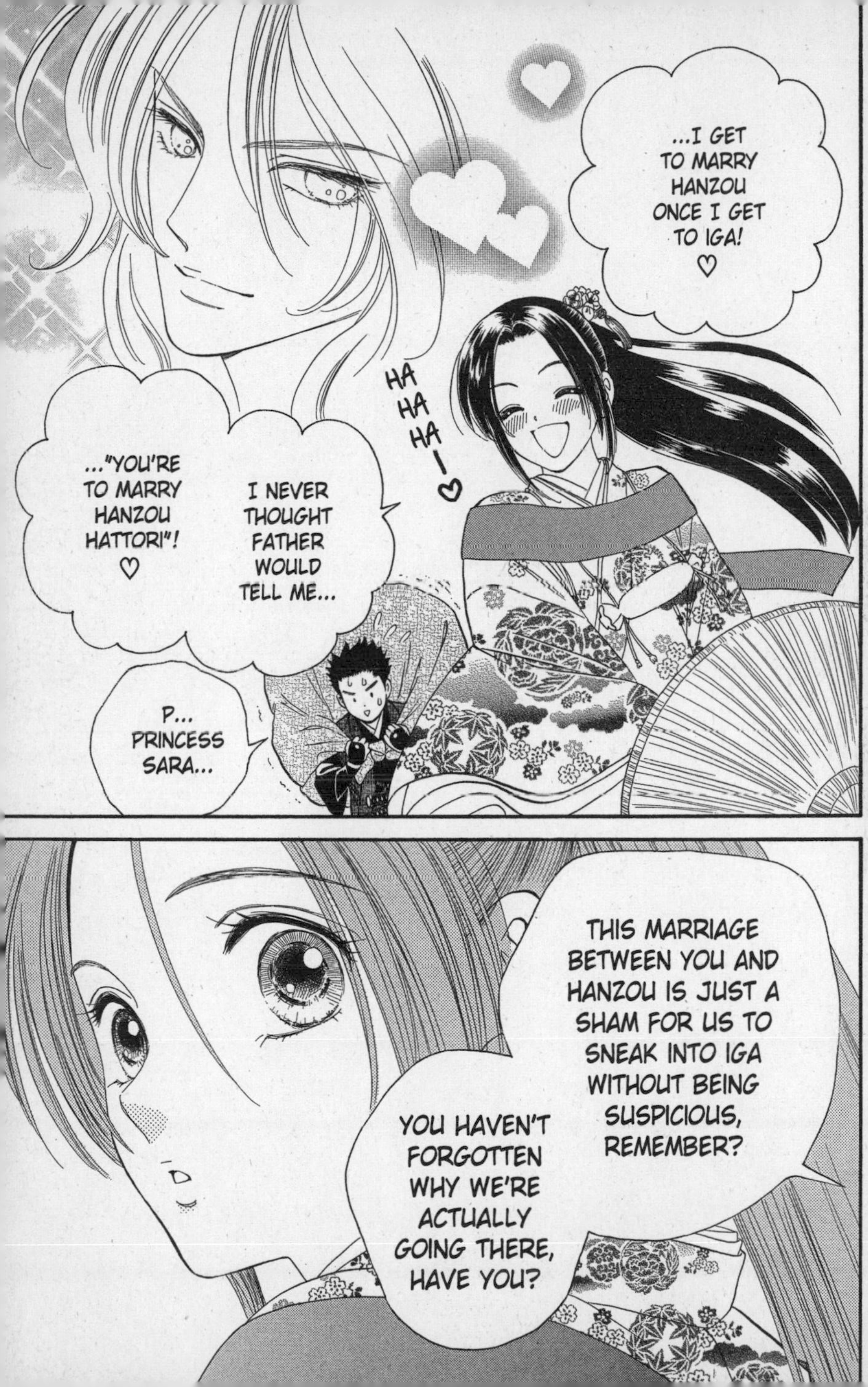
...I GET TO MARRY HANZOU ONCE I GET TO IGA! ♡
HA HA HA! ♡
I NEVER THOUGHT FATHER WOULD TELL ME...
..."YOU'RE TO MARRY HANZOU HATTORI"! ♡
P... PRINCESS SARA...
THIS MARRIAGE BETWEEN YOU AND HANZOU IS JUST A SHAM FOR US TO SNEAK INTO IGA WITHOUT BEING SUSPICIOUS, REMEMBER?
YOU HAVEN'T FORGOTTEN WHY WE'RE ACTUALLY GOING THERE, HAVE YOU?

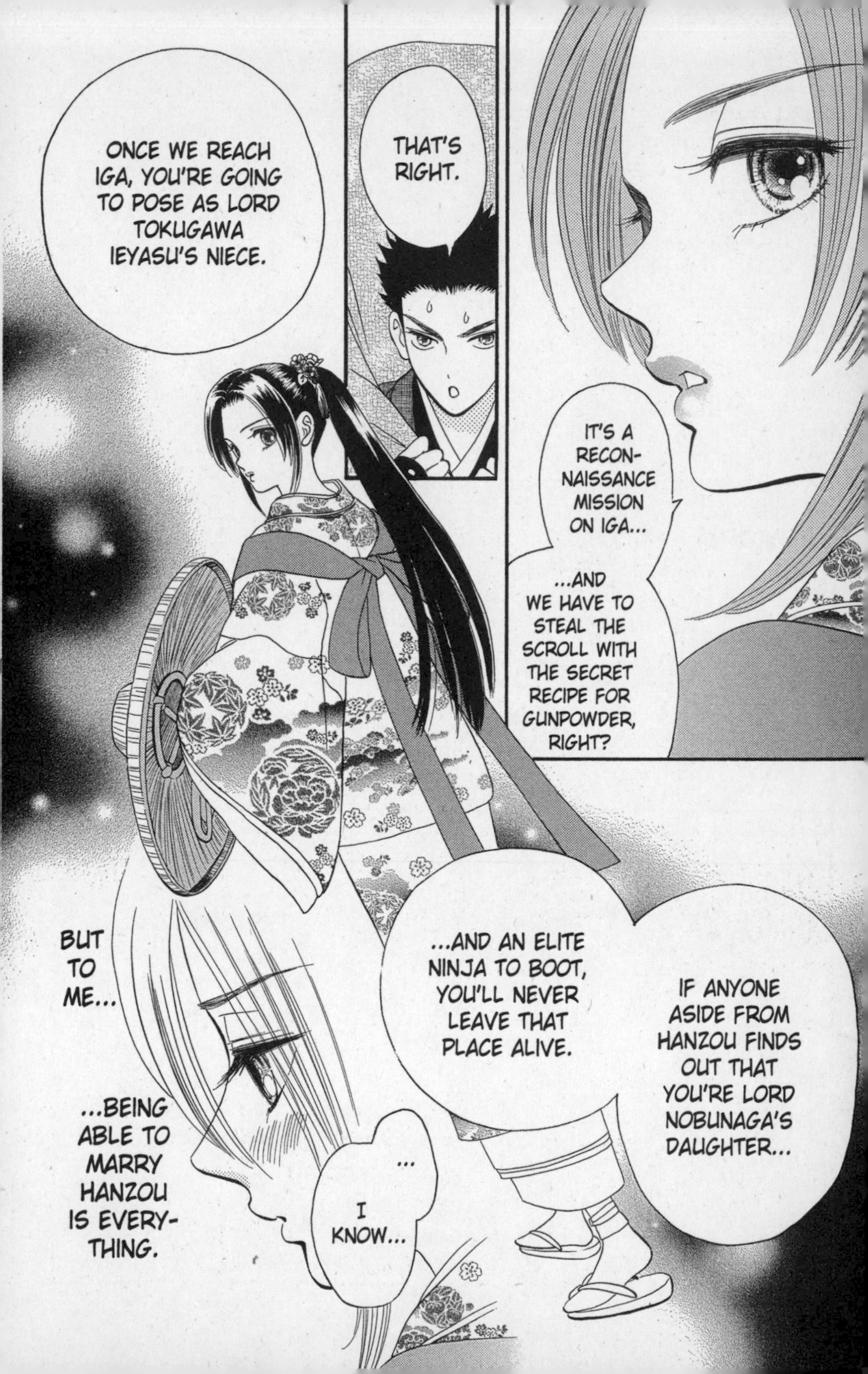
IT'S A RECONNAISSANCE MISSION ON IGA...
...AND WE HAVE TO STEAL THE SCROLL WITH THE SECRET RECIPE FOR GUNPOWDER, RIGHT?
THAT'S RIGHT.
ONCE WE REACH IGA, YOU'RE GOING TO POSE AS LORD TOKUGAWA IEYASU'S NIECE.
IF ANYONE ASIDE FROM HANZOU FINDS OUT THAT YOU'RE LORD NOBUNAGA'S DAUGHTER...
...AND AN ELITE NINJA TO BOOT, YOU'LL NEVER LEAVE THAT PLACE ALIVE.
... I KNOW...
BUT TO ME...
...BEING ABLE TO MARRY HANZOU IS EVERYTHING.

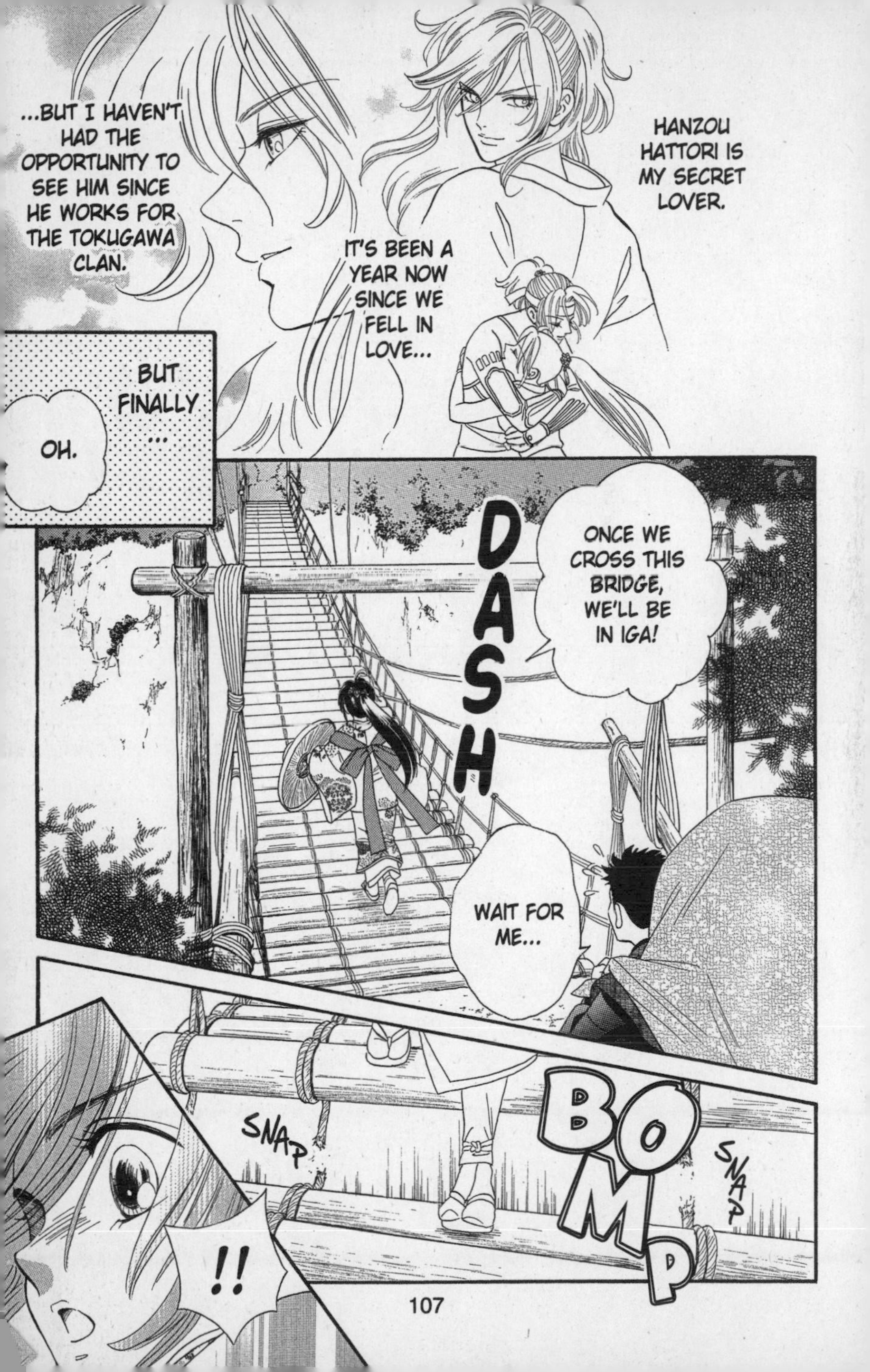
HANZOU HATTORI IS MY SECRET LOVER.
IT'S BEEN A YEAR NOW SINCE WE FELL IN LOVE...
...BUT I HAVEN'T HAD THE OPPORTUNITY TO SEE HIM SINCE HE WORKS FOR THE TOKUGAWA CLAN.
BUT FINALLY...
OH.
ONCE WE CROSS THIS BRIDGE, WE'LL BE IN IGA!
DASH
WAIT FOR ME...
BOMP
SNAP
SNAP
!!

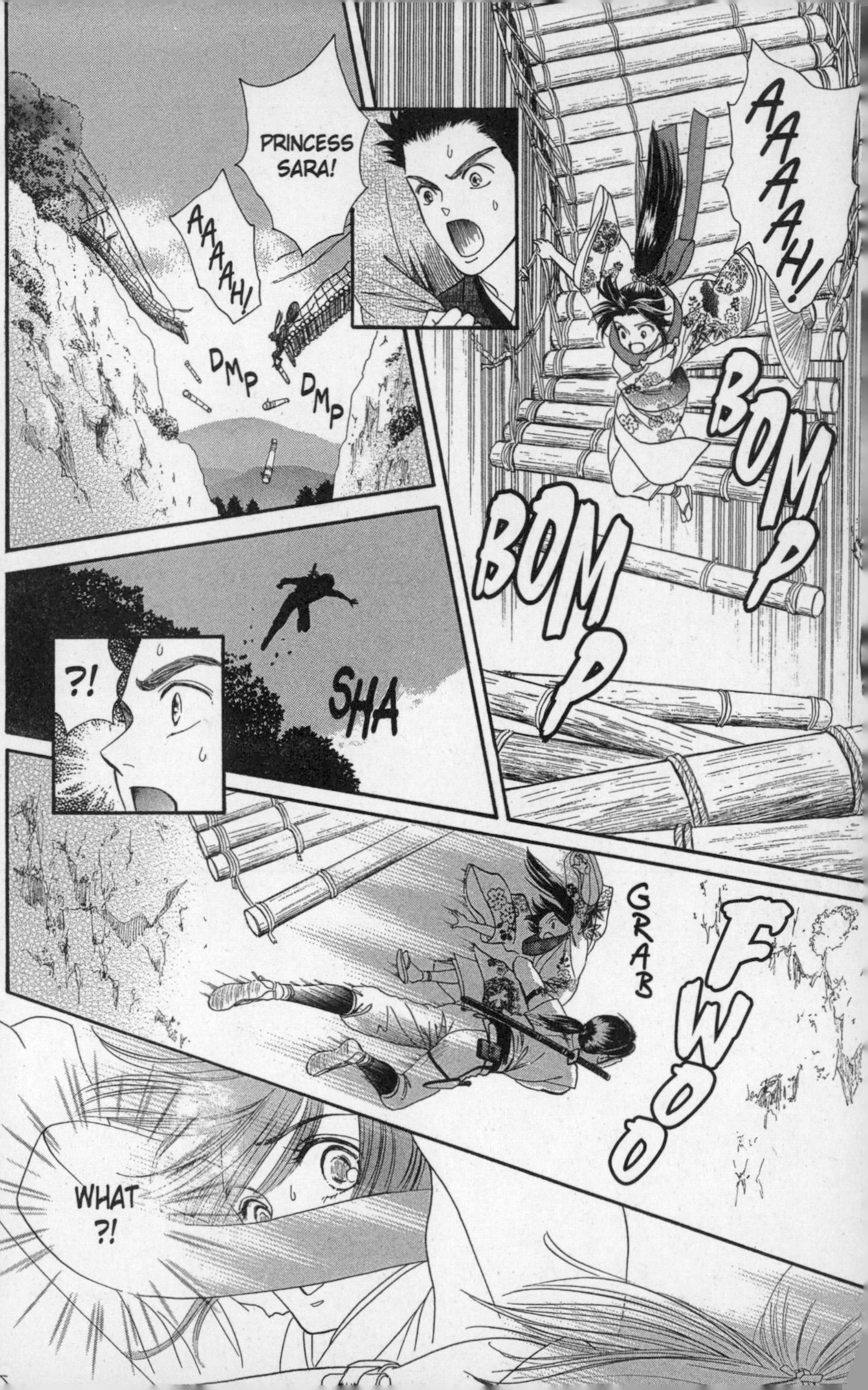
AAAAAH!
BOMP
BOMP
PRINCESS SARA!
AAAAH!
DMP
DMP
SHA
?!
GRAB
FWOOO
WHAT ?!

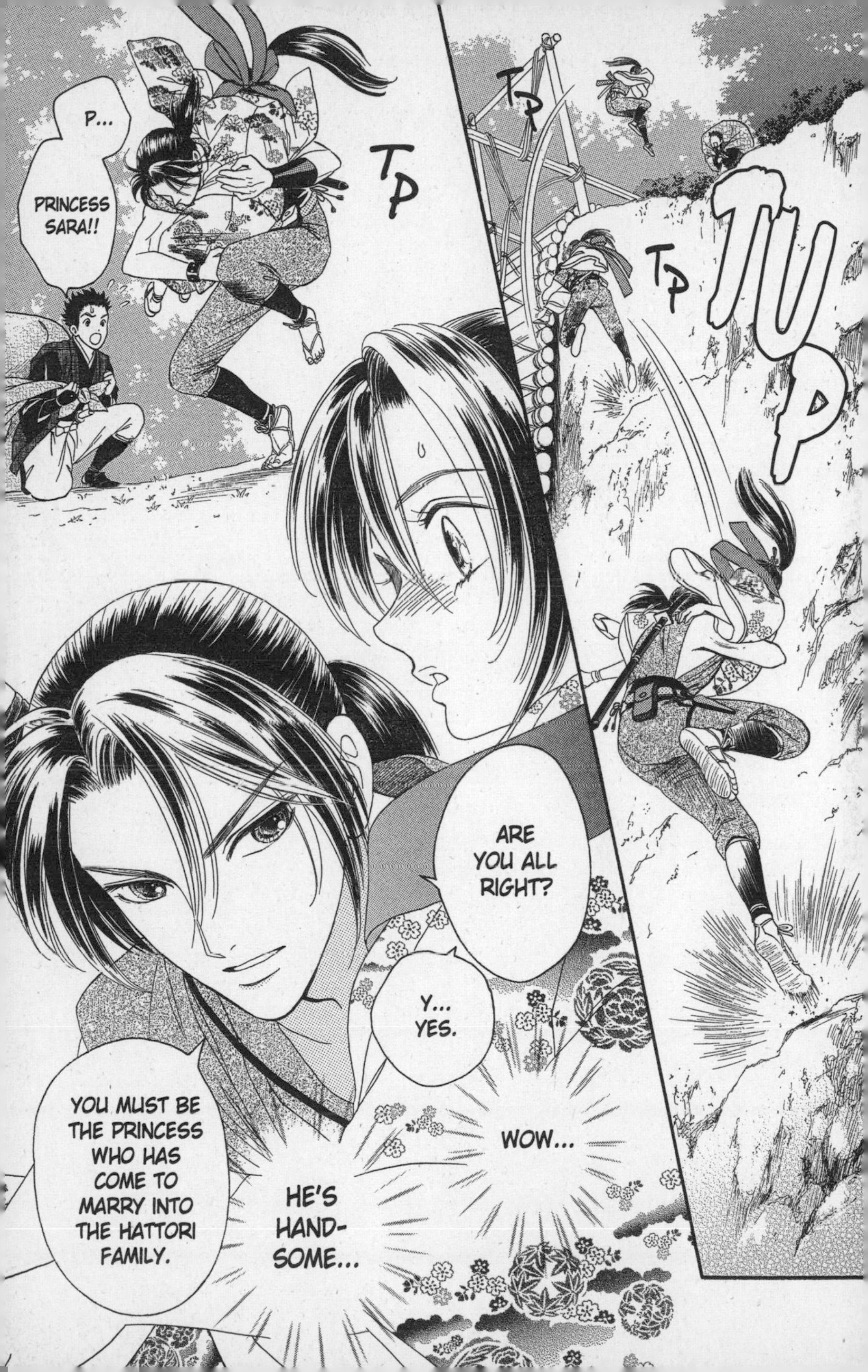

TP
TP
TUP
P...
PRINCESS SARA!!
TP
ARE YOU ALL RIGHT?
Y... YES.
YOU MUST BE THE PRINCESS WHO HAS COME TO MARRY INTO THE HATTORI FAMILY.
WOW...
HE'S HAND-SOME...

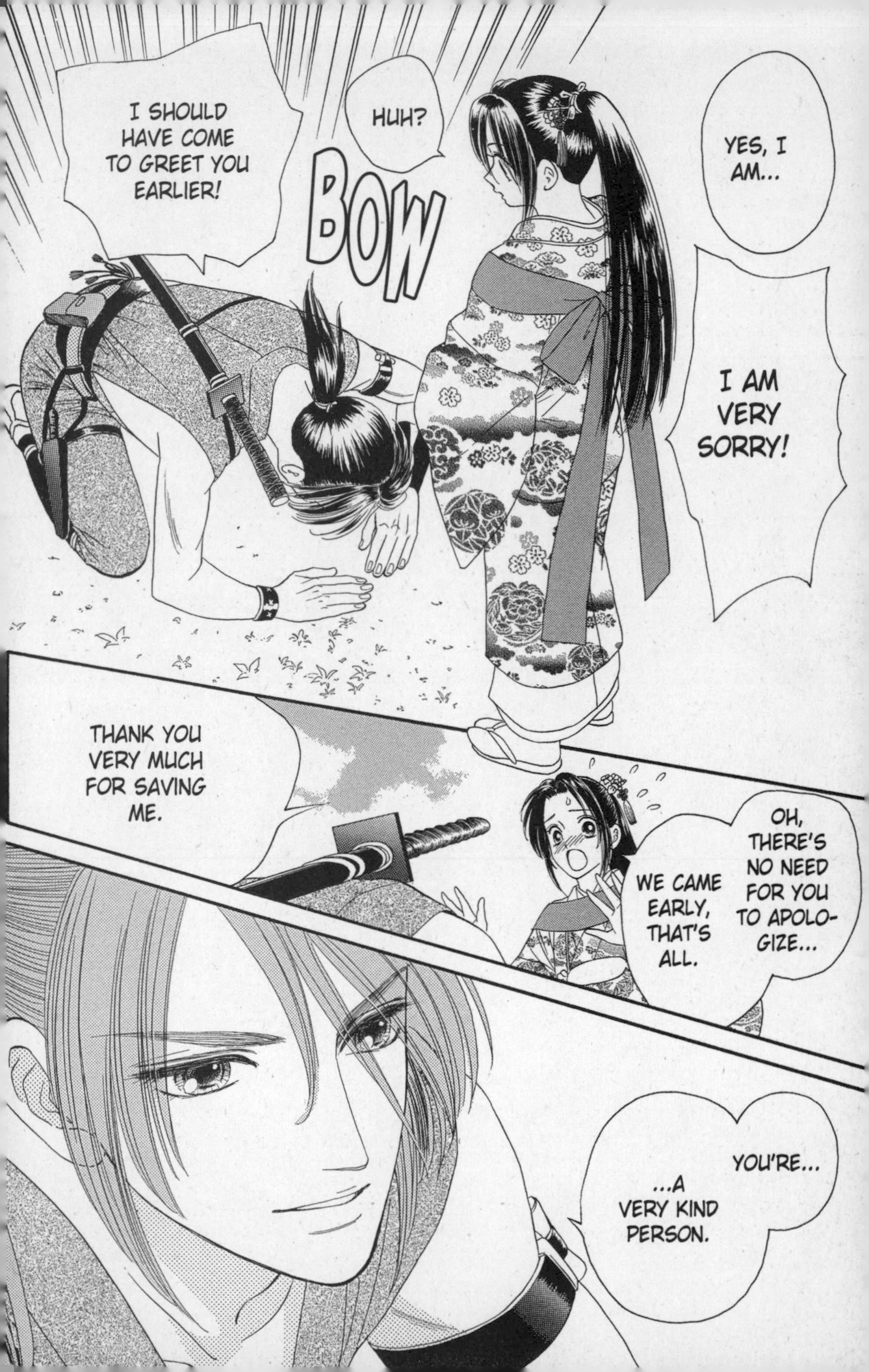
YES, I AM...
I AM VERY SORRY!
BOW
I SHOULD HAVE COME TO GREET YOU EARLIER!
HUH?
OH, THERE'S NO NEED FOR YOU TO APOLOGIZE...
WE CAME EARLY, THAT'S ALL.
THANK YOU VERY MUCH FOR SAVING ME.
YOU'RE...
...A VERY KIND PERSON.

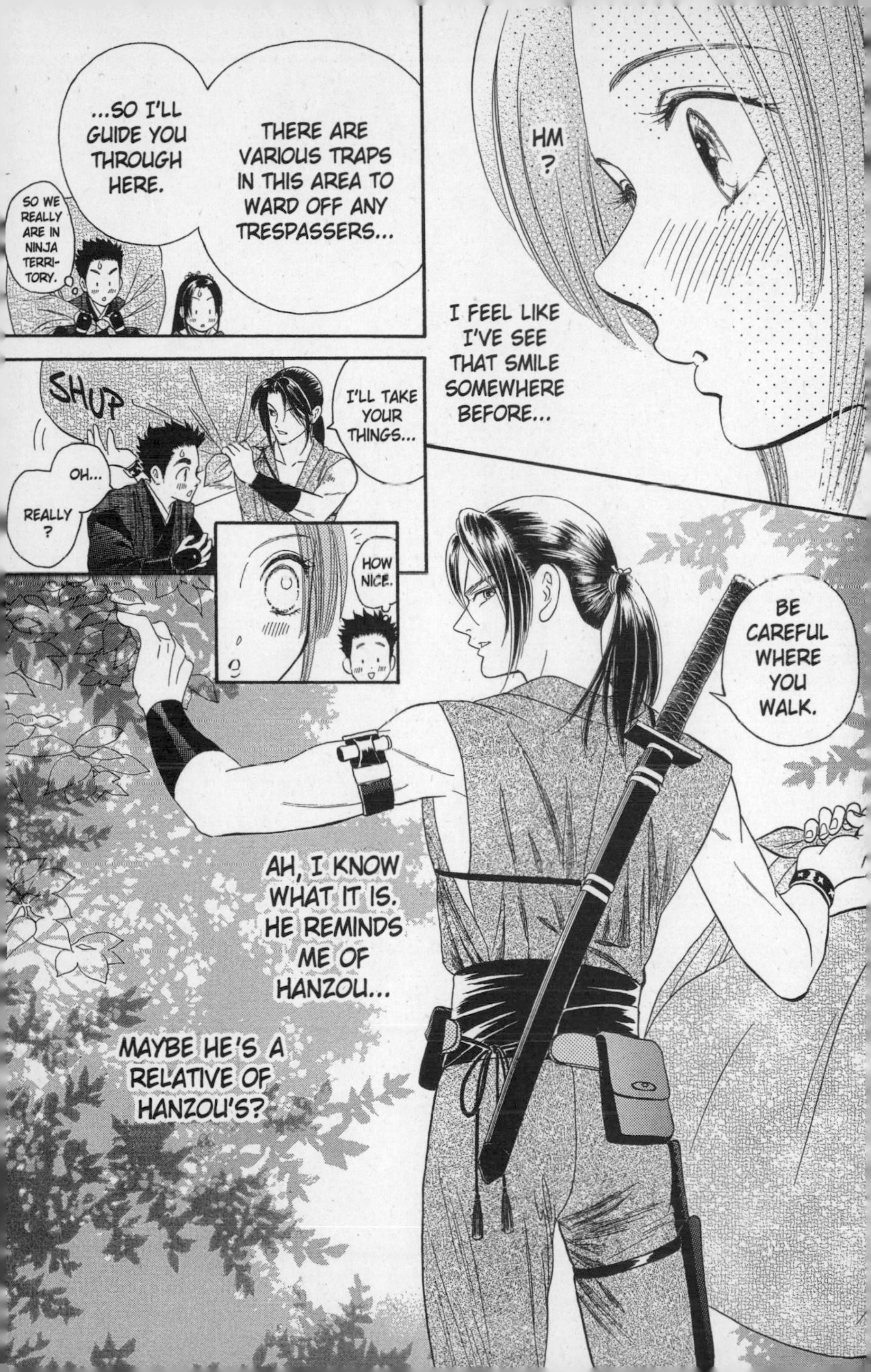
HM?
I FEEL LIKE I'VE SEE THAT SMILE SOMEWHERE BEFORE...
THERE ARE VARIOUS TRAPS IN THIS AREA TO WARD OFF ANY TRESPASSERS...
...SO I'LL GUIDE YOU THROUGH HERE.
SO WE REALLY ARE IN NINJA TERRI-TORY.
I'LL TAKE YOUR THINGS...
SHUP
OH...
REALLY?
HOW NICE.
BE CAREFUL WHERE YOU WALK.
AH, I KNOW WHAT IT IS. HE REMINDS ME OF HANZOU...
MAYBE HE'S A RELATIVE OF HANZOU'S?

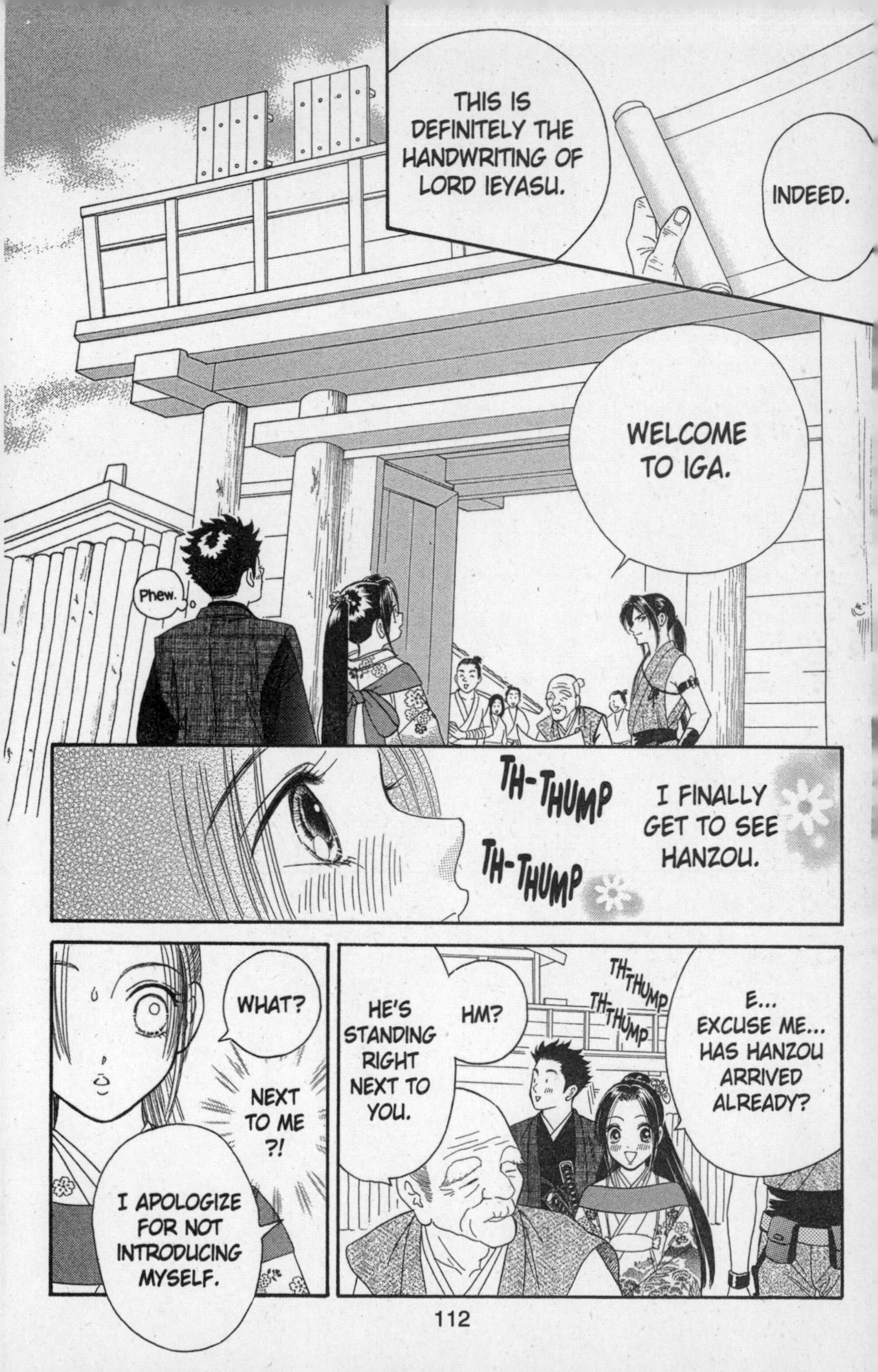
THIS IS DEFINITELY THE HANDWRITING OF LORD IEYASU.
INDEED.
WELCOME TO IGA.
Phew.
I FINALLY GET TO SEE HANZOU.
TH-THUMP
TH-THUMP
E... EXCUSE ME... HAS HANZOU ARRIVED ALREADY?
TH-THUMP
TH-THUMP
HM?
HE'S STANDING RIGHT NEXT TO YOU.
WHAT?
NEXT TO ME ?!
I APOLOGIZE FOR NOT INTRODUCING MYSELF.

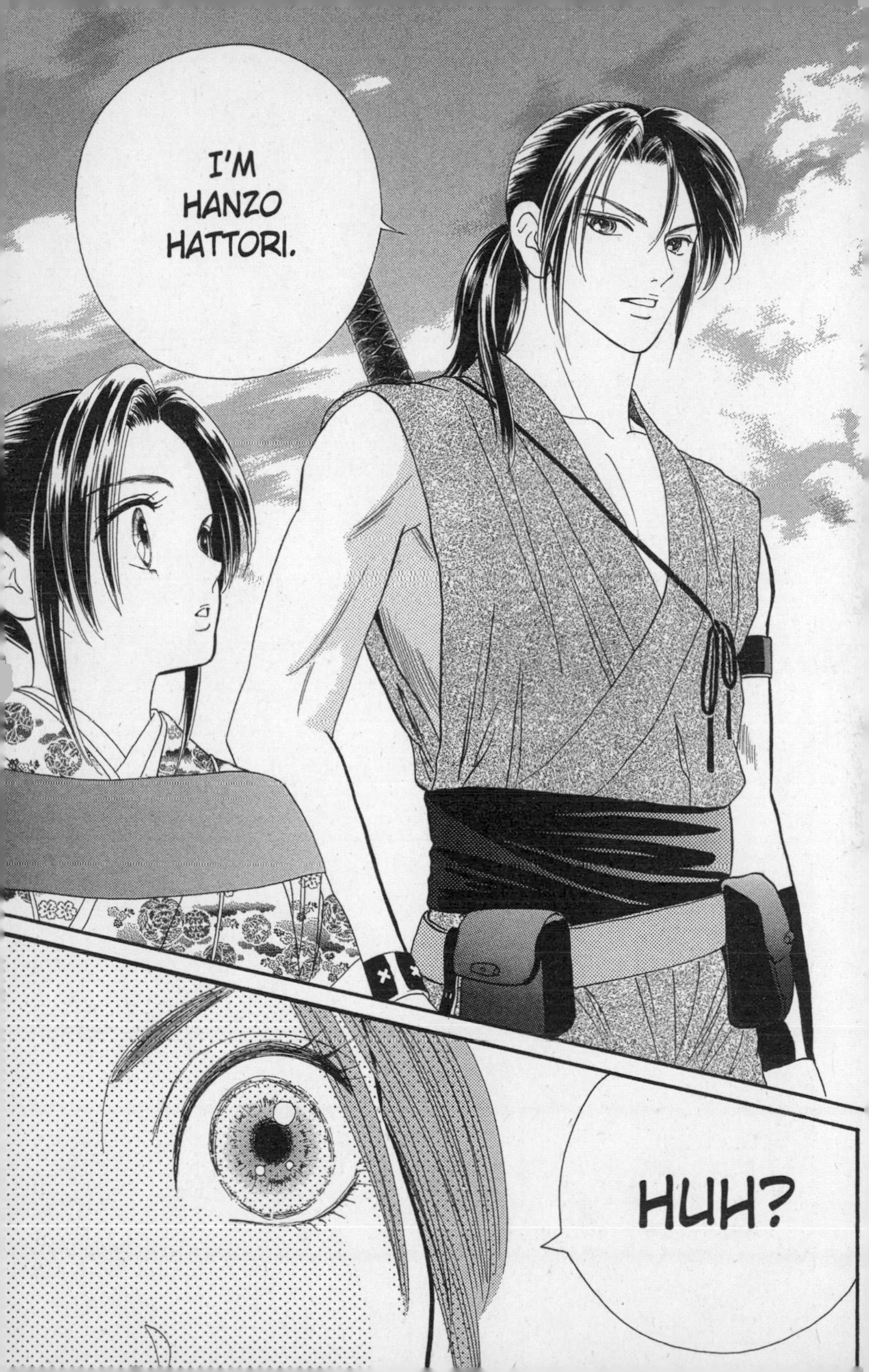
I'M HANZO HATTORI.
HUH?

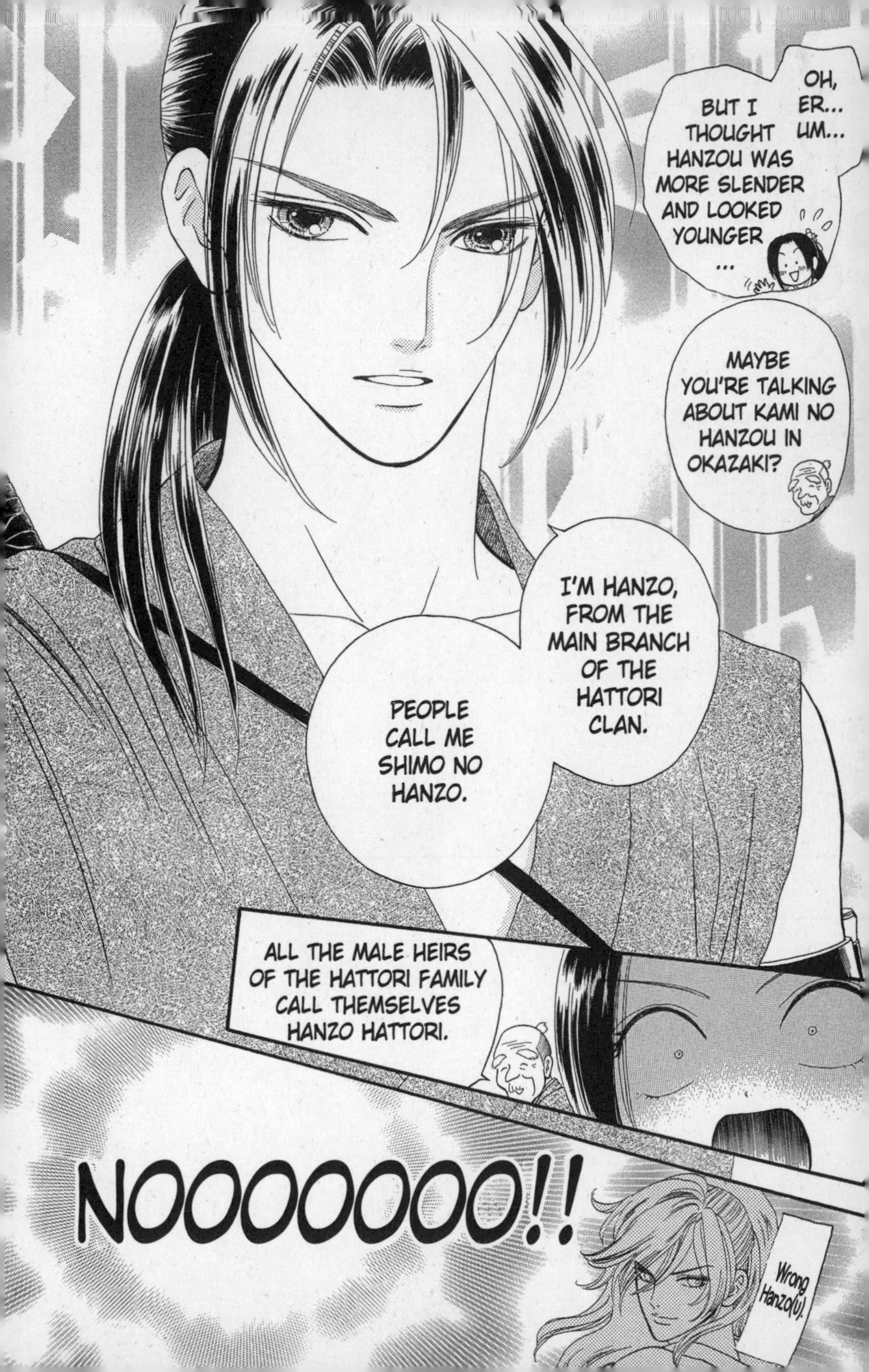
OH, ER... UM...
BUT I THOUGHT HANZOU WAS MORE SLENDER AND LOOKED YOUNGER ...
MAYBE YOU'RE TALKING ABOUT KAMI NO HANZOU IN OKAZAKI?
I'M HANZO, FROM THE MAIN BRANCH OF THE HATTORI CLAN.
PEOPLE CALL ME SHIMO NO HANZO.
ALL THE MALE HEIRS OF THE HATTORI FAMILY CALL THEMSELVES HANZO HATTORI.
NOOOOOOO!!
Wrong Hanzo(u).

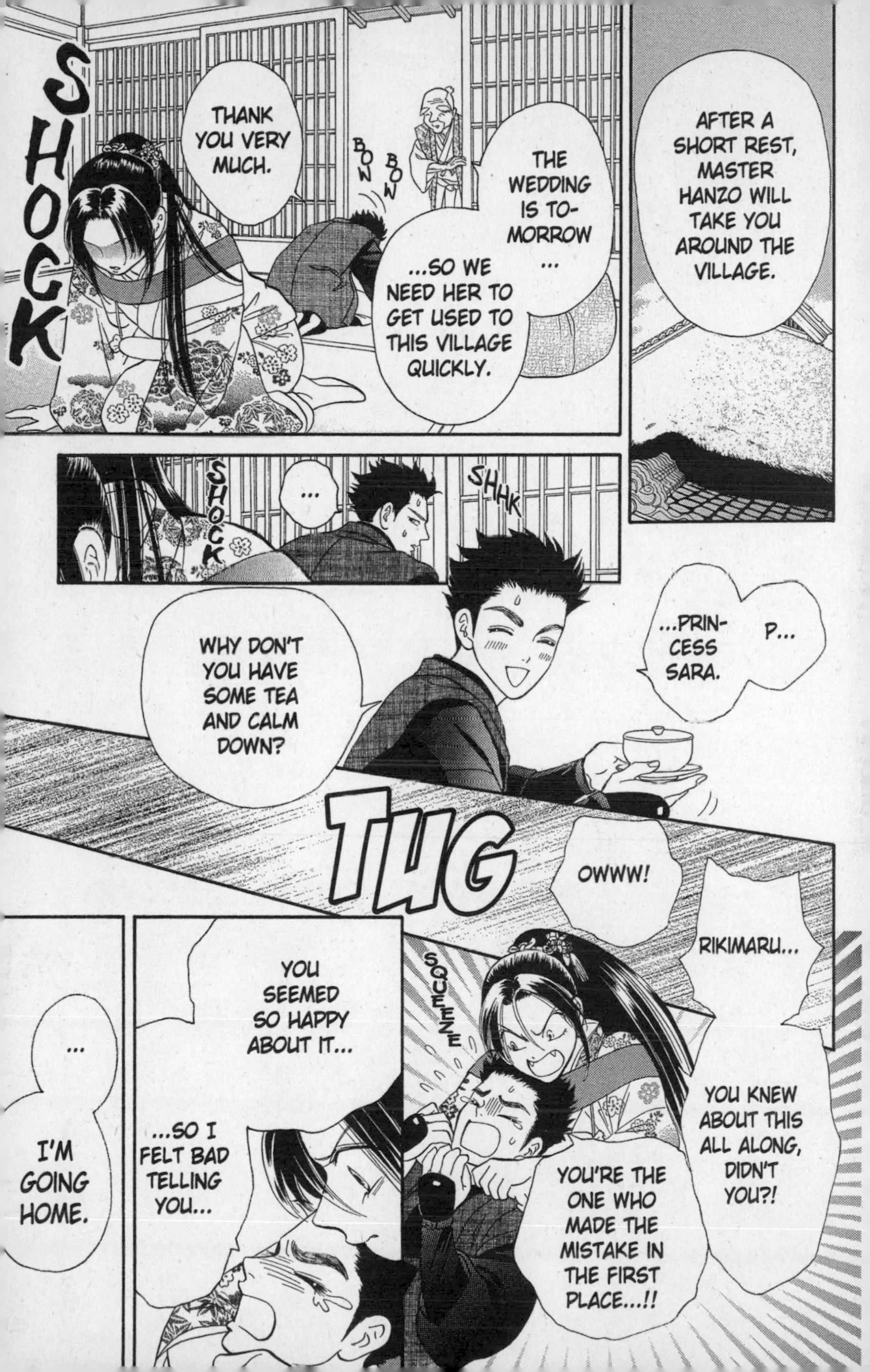
AFTER A SHORT REST, MASTER HANZO WILL TAKE YOU AROUND THE VILLAGE.
THE WEDDING IS TO-MORROW ...
...SO WE NEED HER TO GET USED TO THIS VILLAGE QUICKLY.
BOW BOW
THANK YOU VERY MUCH.
SHOCK
SHHK
...
SHOCK
P...
...PRIN-CESS SARA.
WHY DON'T YOU HAVE SOME TEA AND CALM DOWN?
TUG
OWWW!
RIKIMARU...
YOU KNEW ABOUT THIS ALL ALONG, DIDN'T YOU?!
YOU'RE THE ONE WHO MADE THE MISTAKE IN THE FIRST PLACE...!!
SQUEEZE
YOU SEEMED SO HAPPY ABOUT IT...
...SO I FELT BAD TELLING YOU...
...
I'M GOING HOME.

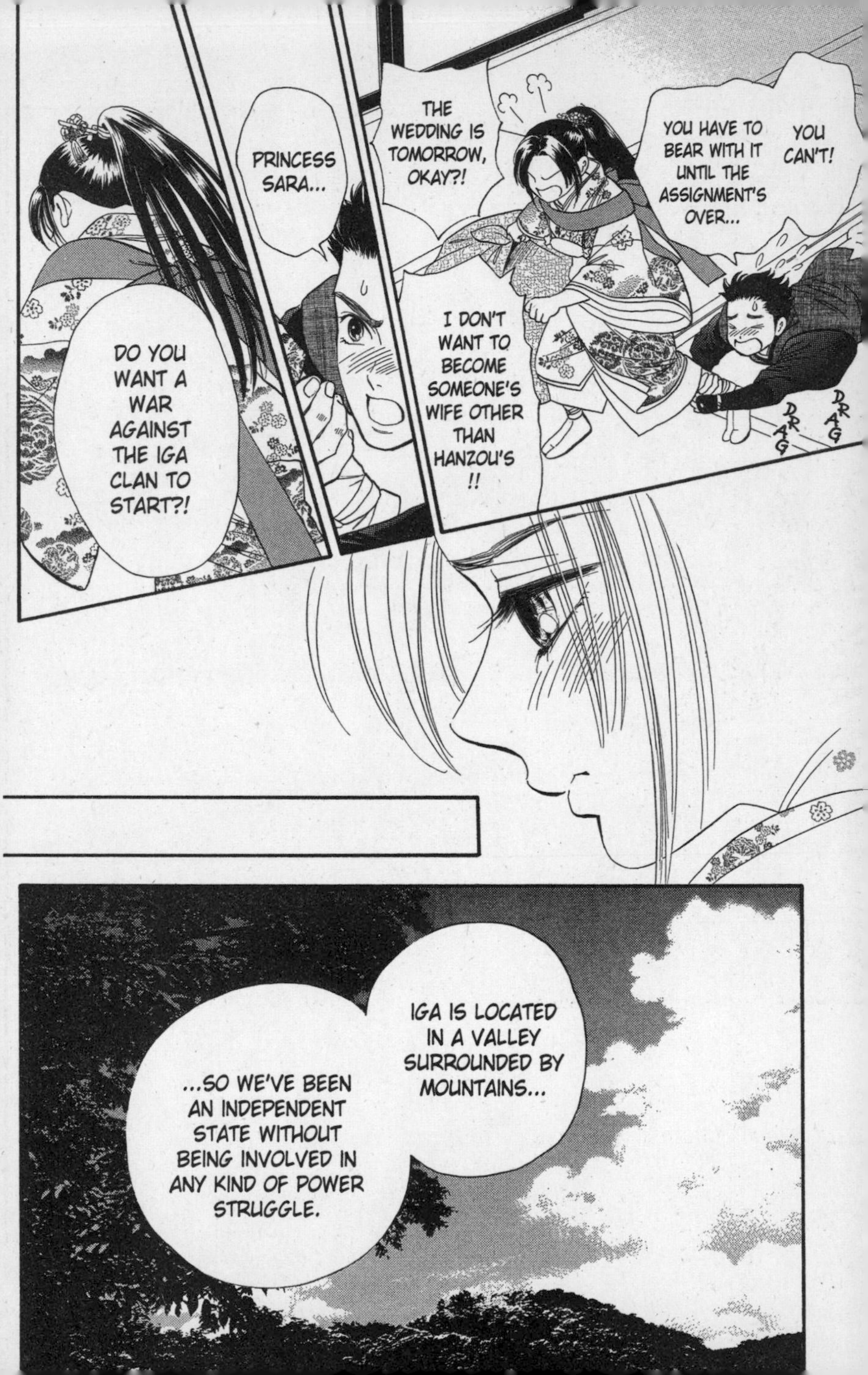
YOU CAN'T!
YOU HAVE TO BEAR WITH IT UNTIL THE ASSIGNMENT'S OVER...
THE WEDDING IS TOMORROW, OKAY?!
I DON'T WANT TO BECOME SOMEONE'S WIFE OTHER THAN HANZOU'S !!
DRAG DRAG
PRINCESS SARA...
DO YOU WANT A WAR AGAINST THE IGA CLAN TO START?!
IGA IS LOCATED IN A VALLEY SURROUNDED BY MOUNTAINS...
...SO WE'VE BEEN AN INDEPENDENT STATE WITHOUT BEING INVOLVED IN ANY KIND OF POWER STRUGGLE.

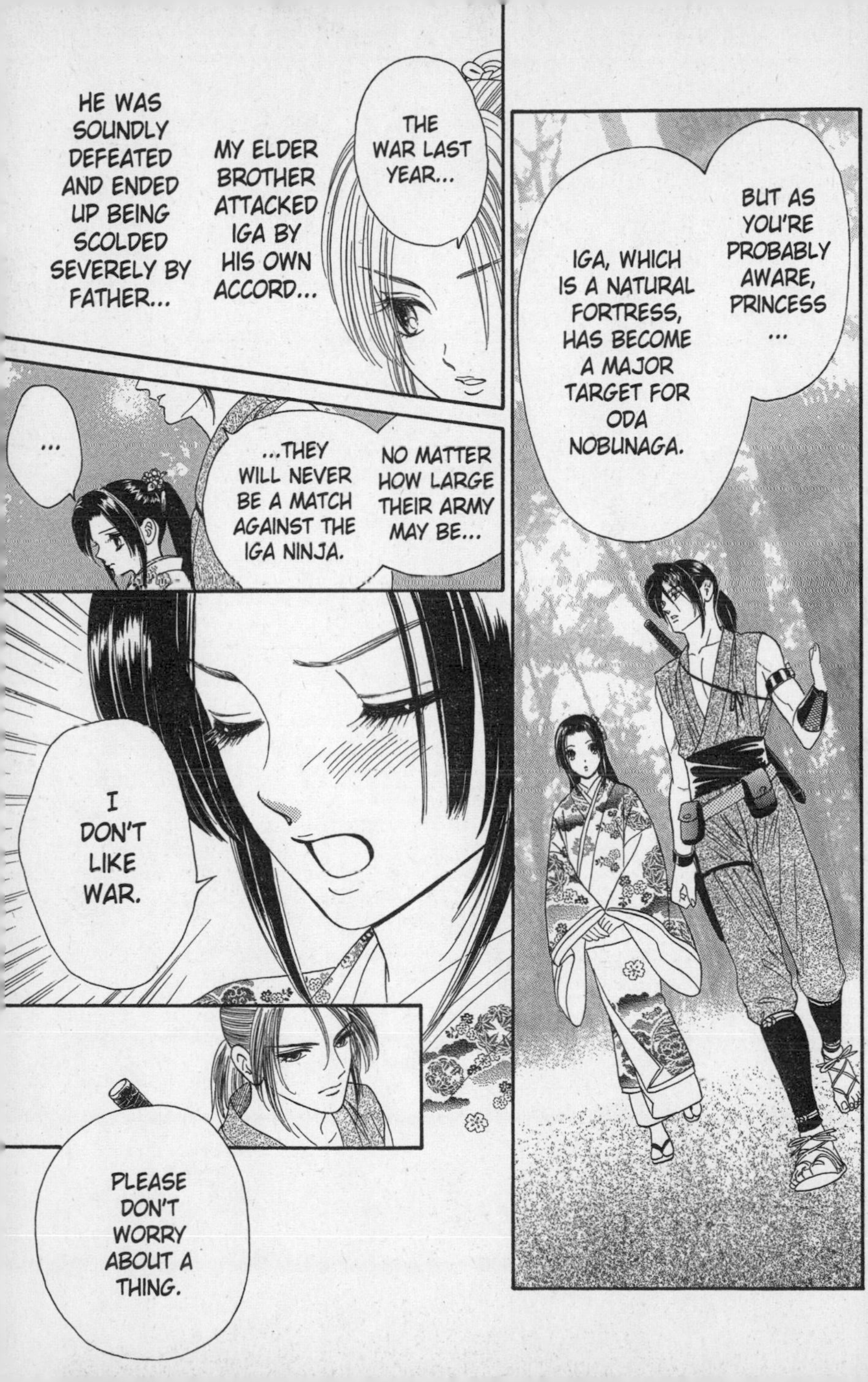
THE WAR LAST YEAR...
MY ELDER BROTHER ATTACKED IGA BY HIS OWN ACCORD...
HE WAS SOUNDLY DEFEATED AND ENDED UP BEING SCOLDED SEVERELY BY FATHER...
BUT AS YOU'RE PROBABLY AWARE, PRINCESS ...
IGA, WHICH IS A NATURAL FORTRESS, HAS BECOME A MAJOR TARGET FOR ODA NOBUNAGA.
NO MATTER HOW LARGE THEIR ARMY MAY BE...
...THEY WILL NEVER BE A MATCH AGAINST THE IGA NINJA.
...
I DON'T LIKE WAR.
PLEASE DON'T WORRY ABOUT A THING.

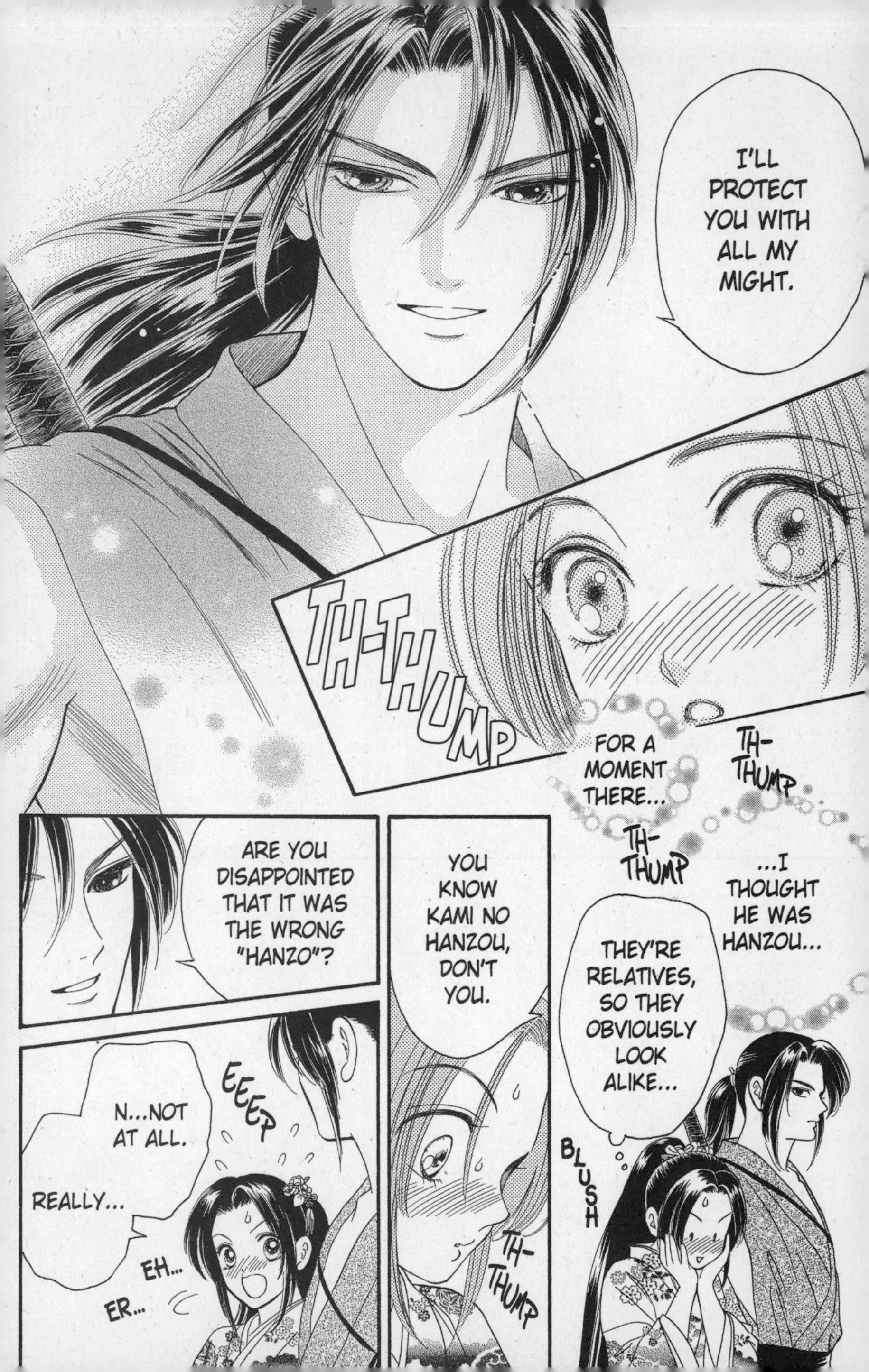
I'LL PROTECT YOU WITH ALL MY MIGHT.
TH-THUMP
FOR A MOMENT THERE...
TH-THUMP
TH-THUMP
...I THOUGHT HE WAS HANZOU...
THEY'RE RELATIVES, SO THEY OBVIOUSLY LOOK ALIKE...
BLUSH
YOU KNOW KAMI NO HANZOU, DON'T YOU.
TH-THUMP
ARE YOU DISAPPOINTED THAT IT WAS THE WRONG "HANZO"?
EEEEP
N...NOT AT ALL.
REALLY...
EH...
ER...

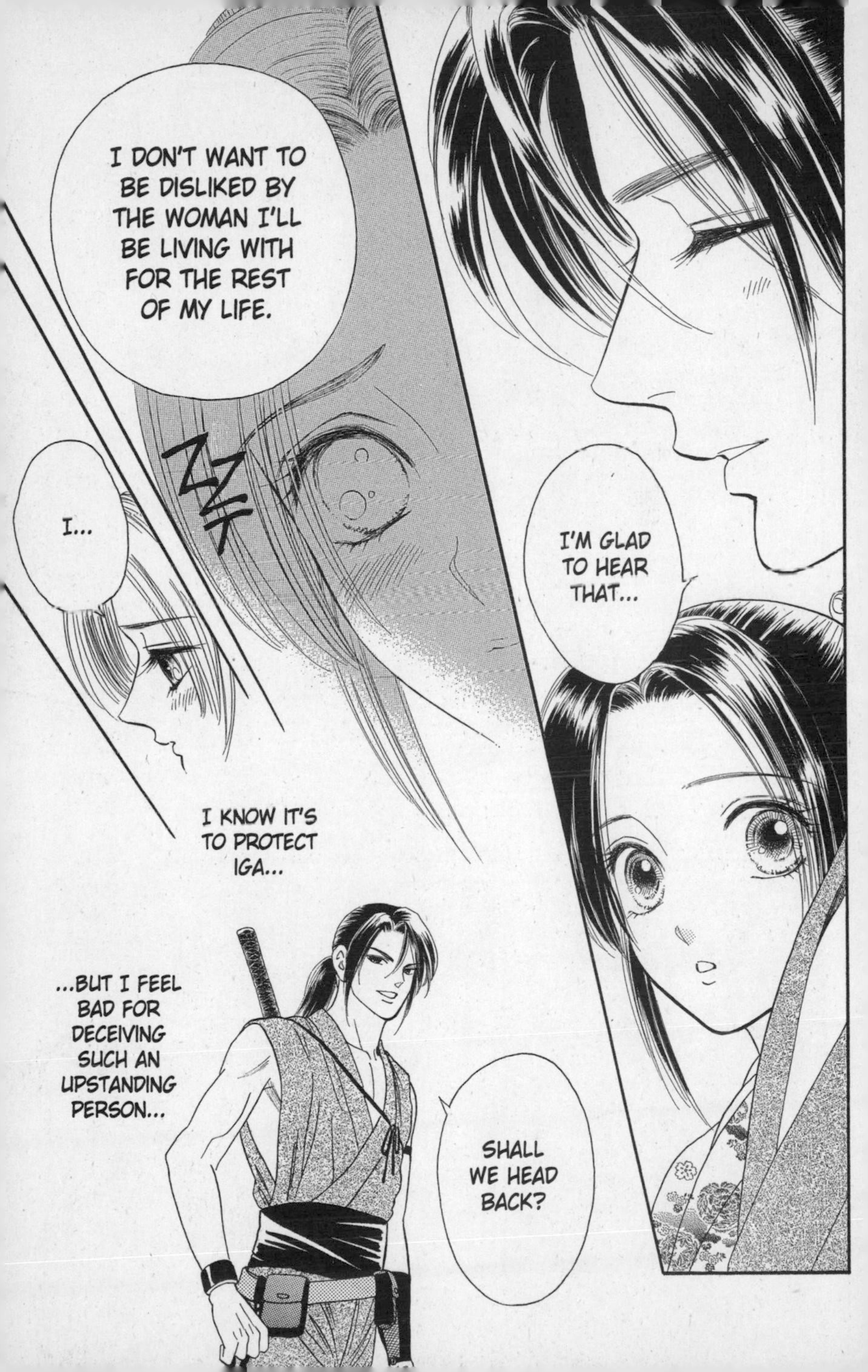
I DON'T WANT TO BE DISLIKED BY THE WOMAN I'LL BE LIVING WITH FOR THE REST OF MY LIFE.
ZZK
I...
I'M GLAD TO HEAR THAT...
I KNOW IT'S TO PROTECT IGA...
...BUT I FEEL BAD FOR DECEIVING SUCH AN UPSTANDING PERSON...
SHALL WE HEAD BACK?

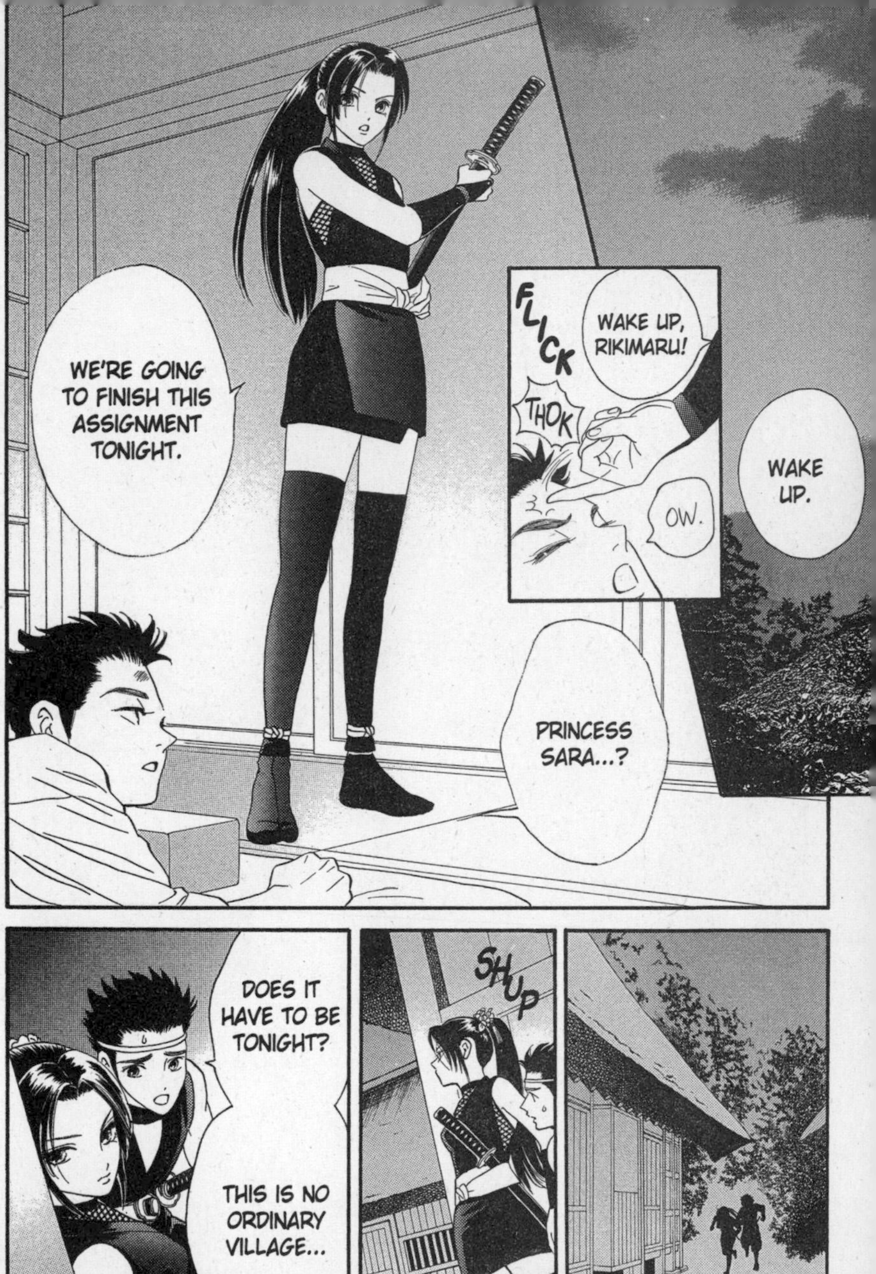
WAKE UP.
FLICK
WAKE UP, RIKIMARU!
THOK
OW.
PRINCESS SARA...?
WE'RE GOING TO FINISH THIS ASSIGNMENT TONIGHT.
SHUP
DOES IT HAVE TO BE TONIGHT?
THIS IS NO ORDINARY VILLAGE...

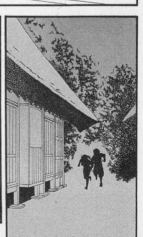

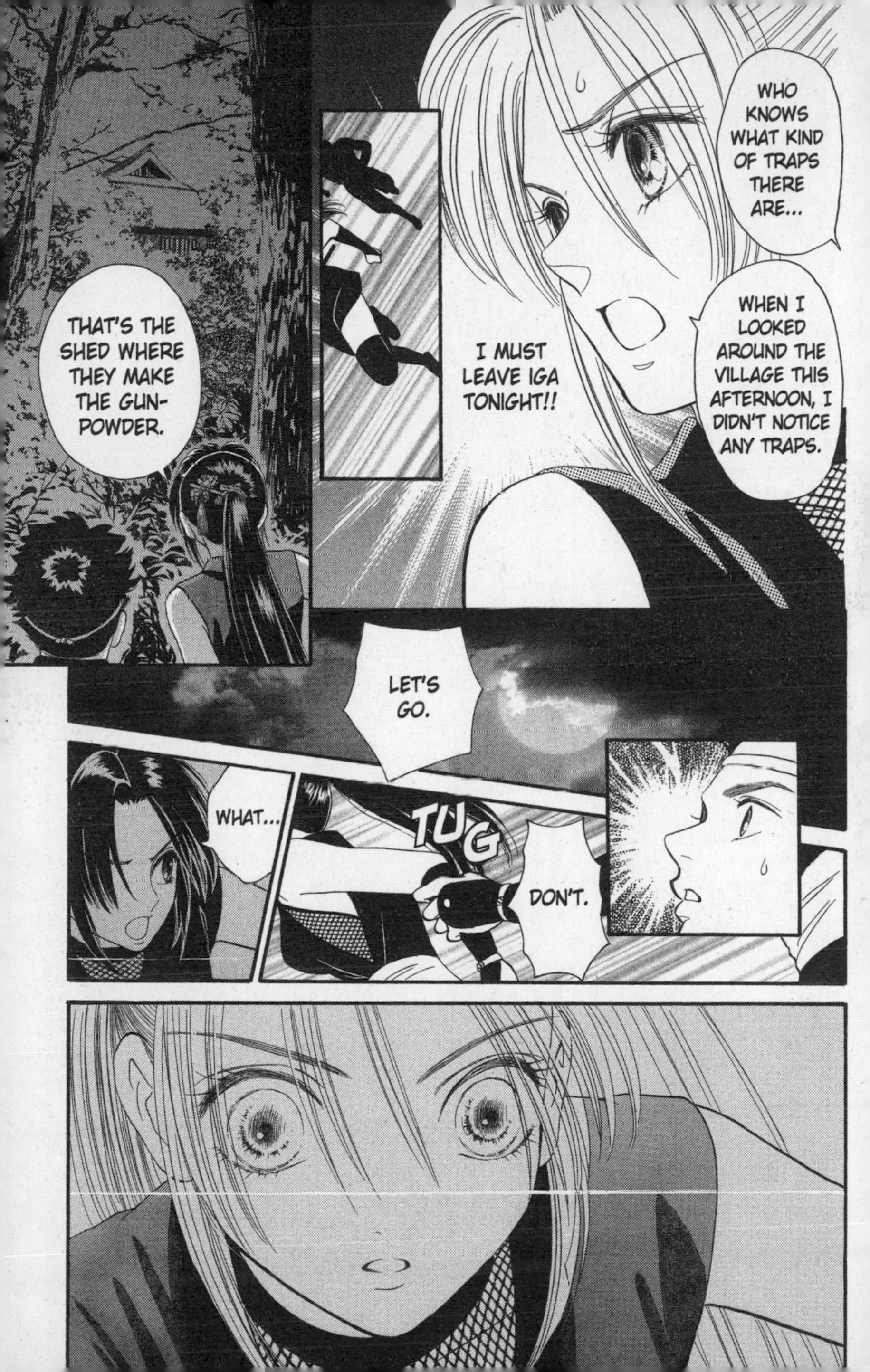
WHO KNOWS WHAT KIND OF TRAPS THERE ARE...
WHEN I LOOKED AROUND THE VILLAGE THIS AFTERNOON, I DIDN'T NOTICE ANY TRAPS.
I MUST LEAVE IGA TONIGHT!!
THAT'S THE SHED WHERE THEY MAKE THE GUN-POWDER.
LET'S GO.
TUG
DON'T.
WHAT...

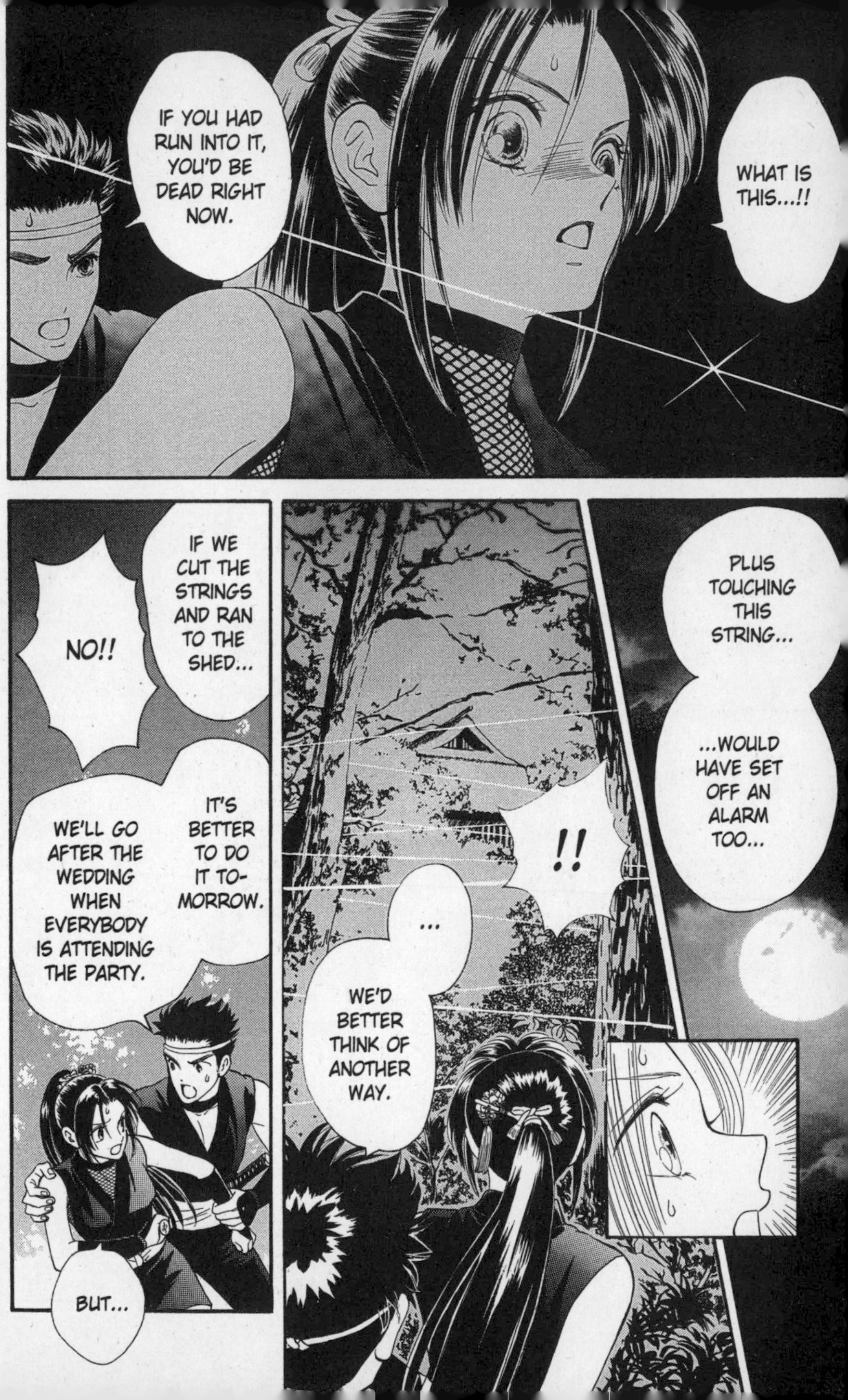
WHAT IS THIS...!!
IF YOU HAD RUN INTO IT, YOU'D BE DEAD RIGHT NOW.
PLUS TOUCHING THIS STRING...
...WOULD HAVE SET OFF AN ALARM TOO...
!!
...
WE'D BETTER THINK OF ANOTHER WAY.
IF WE CUT THE STRINGS AND RAN TO THE SHED...
NO!!
IT'S BETTER TO DO IT TO-MORROW.
WE'LL GO AFTER THE WEDDING WHEN EVERYBODY IS ATTENDING THE PARTY.
BUT...

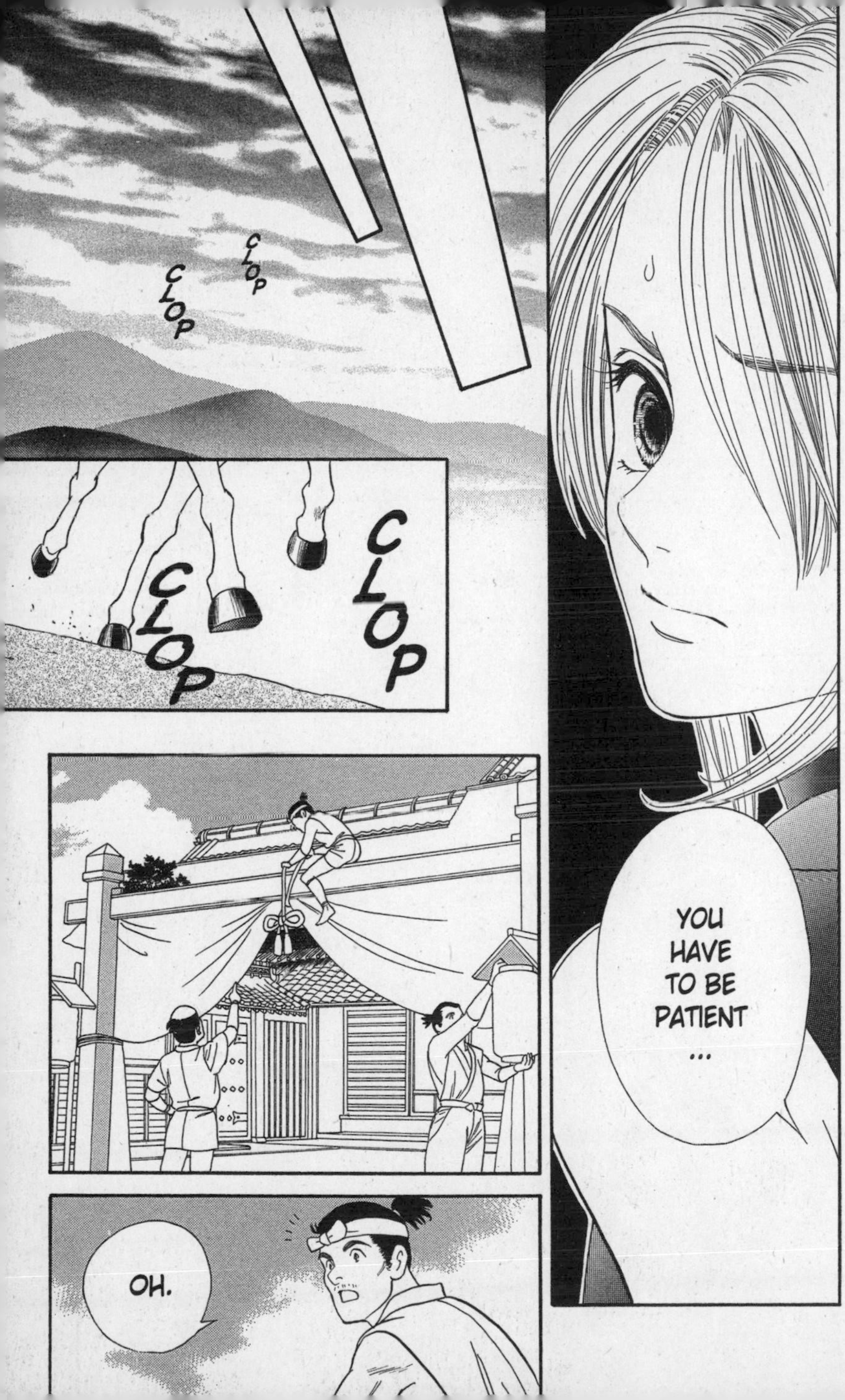
YOU HAVE TO BE PATIENT ...
CLOP
CLOP
CLOP
CLOP
OH.

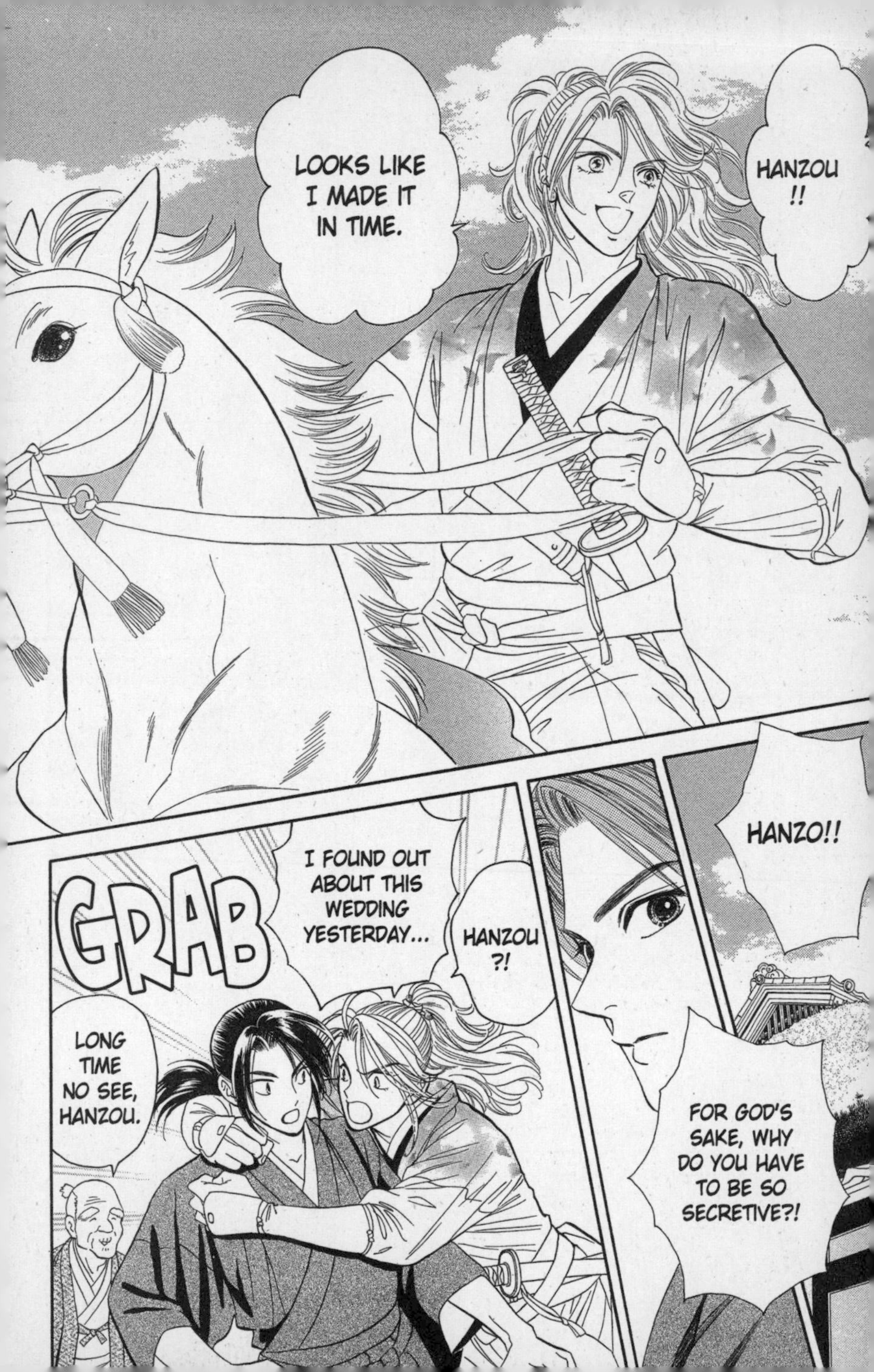
HANZOU !!
LOOKS LIKE I MADE IT IN TIME.
HANZO!!
FOR GOD'S SAKE, WHY DO YOU HAVE TO BE SO SECRETIVE?!
HANZOU ?!
I FOUND OUT ABOUT THIS WEDDING YESTERDAY...
GRAB
LONG TIME NO SEE, HANZOU.

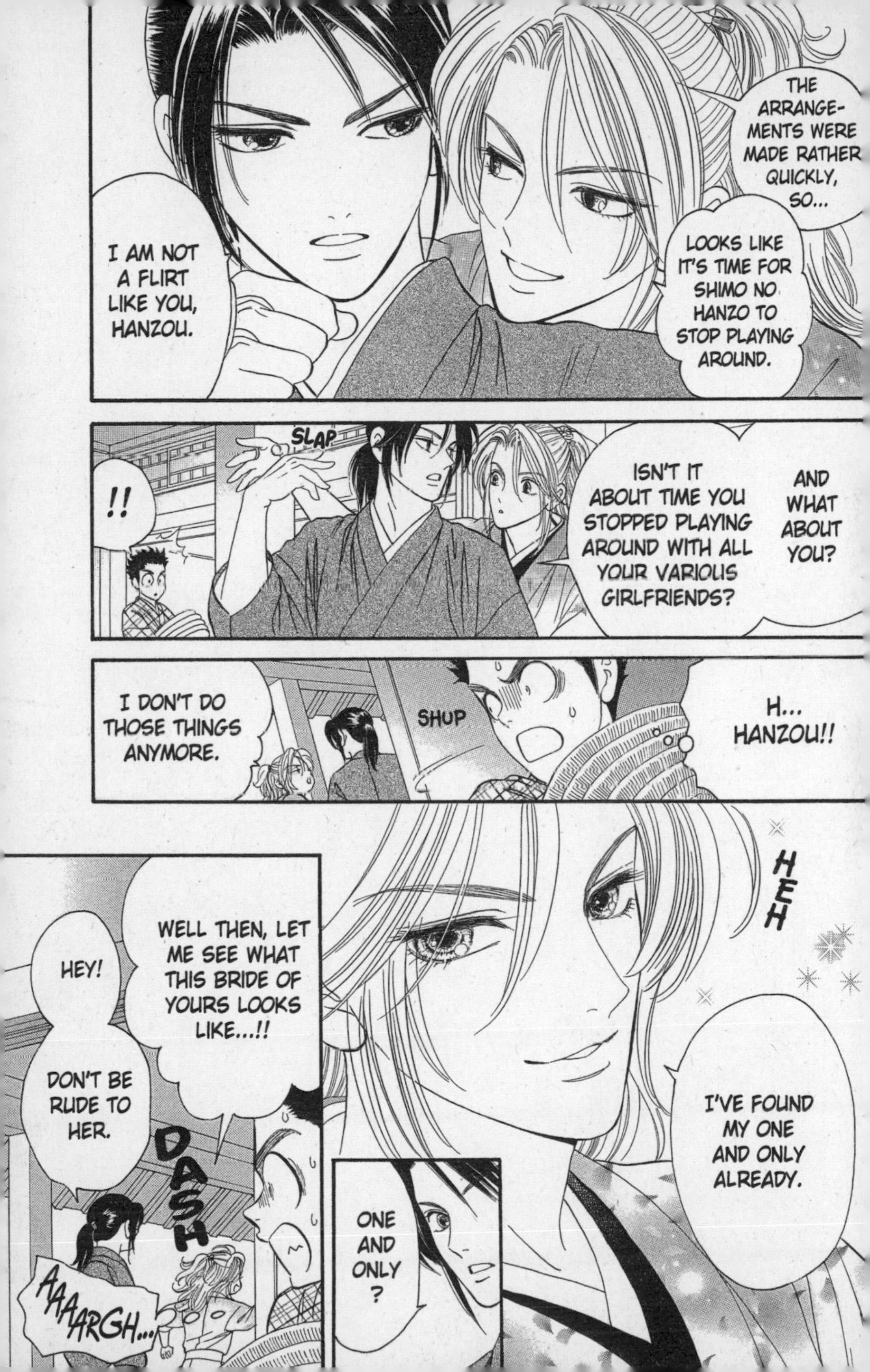
THE ARRANGEMENTS WERE MADE RATHER QUICKLY, SO...
LOOKS LIKE IT'S TIME FOR SHIMO NO HANZO TO STOP PLAYING AROUND.
I AM NOT A FLIRT LIKE YOU, HANZOU.
AND WHAT ABOUT YOU?
ISN'T IT ABOUT TIME YOU STOPPED PLAYING AROUND WITH ALL YOUR VARIOUS GIRLFRIENDS?
SLAP
!!
H... HANZOU!!
SHUP
I DON'T DO THOSE THINGS ANYMORE.
HEH
I'VE FOUND MY ONE AND ONLY ALREADY.
ONE AND ONLY ?
WELL THEN, LET ME SEE WHAT THIS BRIDE OF YOURS LOOKS LIKE...!!
HEY!
DON'T BE RUDE TO HER.
DASH
AAAARGH...

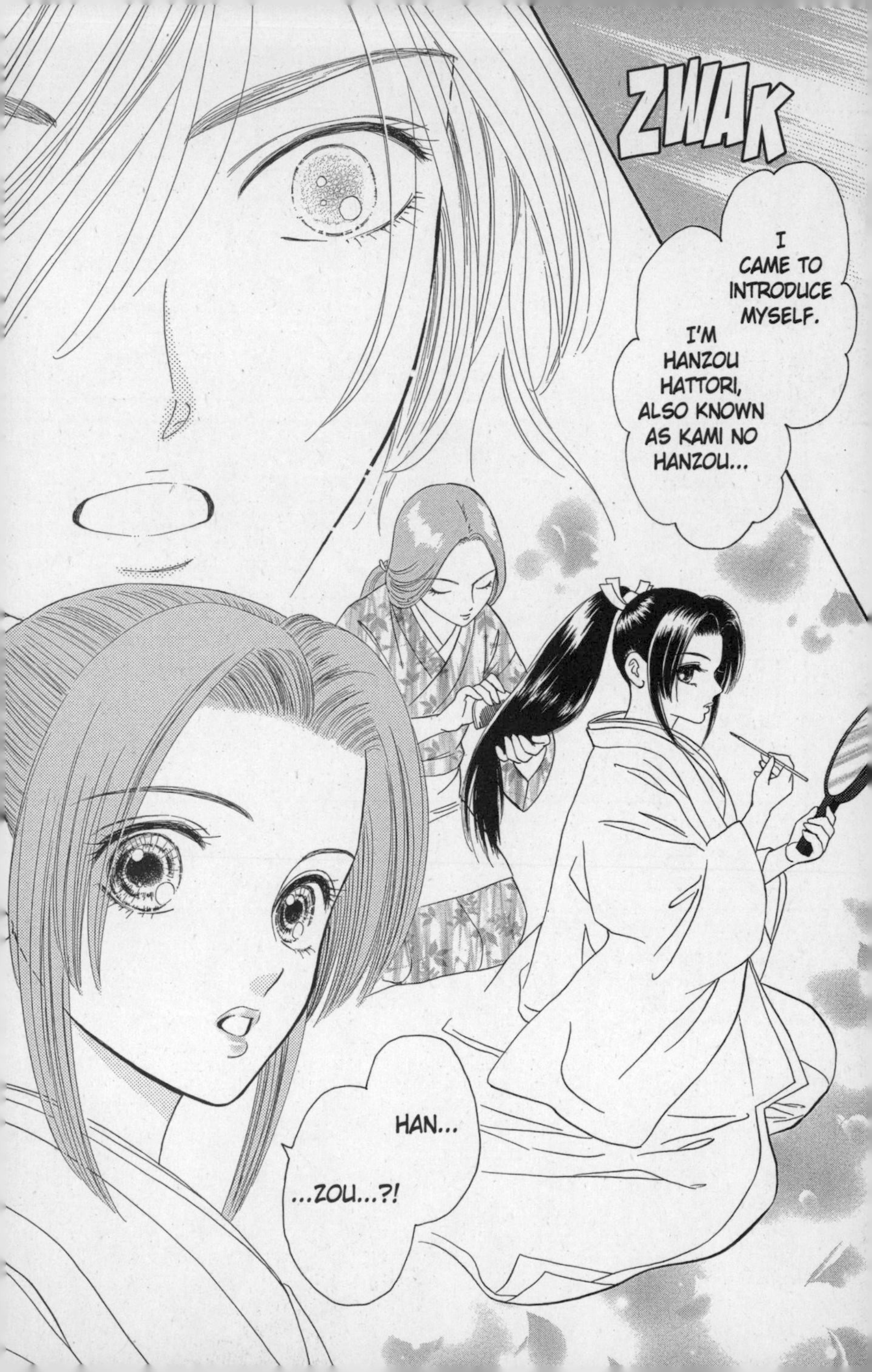
ZWAK
I CAME TO INTRODUCE MYSELF.
I'M HANZOU HATTORI, ALSO KNOWN AS KAMI NO HANZOU...
HAN...
...ZOU...?!

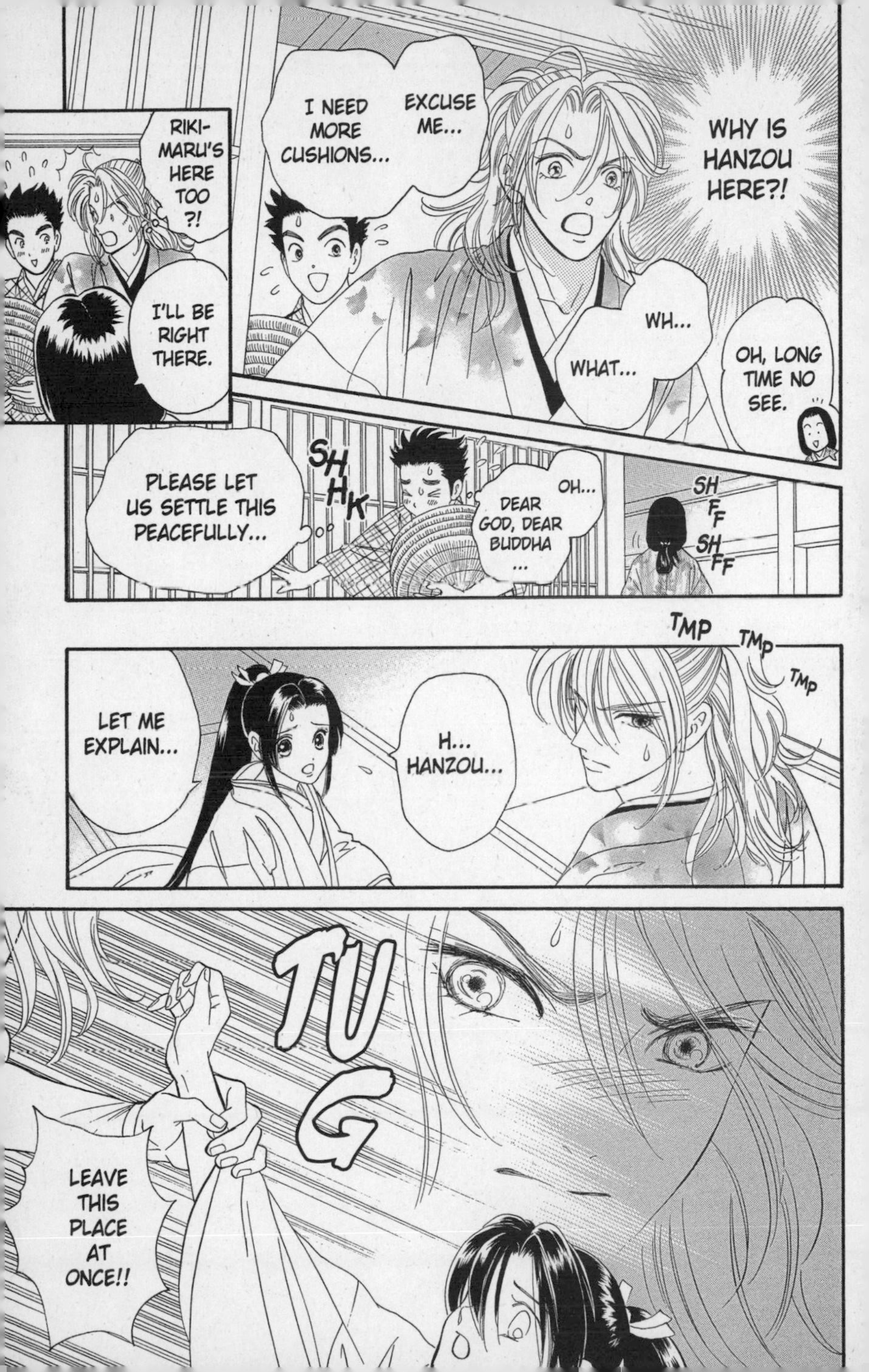

WHY IS HANZOU HERE?!
EXCUSE ME...
I NEED MORE CUSHIONS...
OH, LONG TIME NO SEE.
WH... WHAT...
RIKI-MARU'S HERE TOO?!
I'LL BE RIGHT THERE.
SH FF SH FF
OH... DEAR GOD, DEAR BUDDHA...
SHHK
PLEASE LET US SETTLE THIS PEACEFULLY...
TMP TMP TMP
H... HANZOU...
LET ME EXPLAIN...
TUG
LEAVE THIS PLACE AT ONCE!!

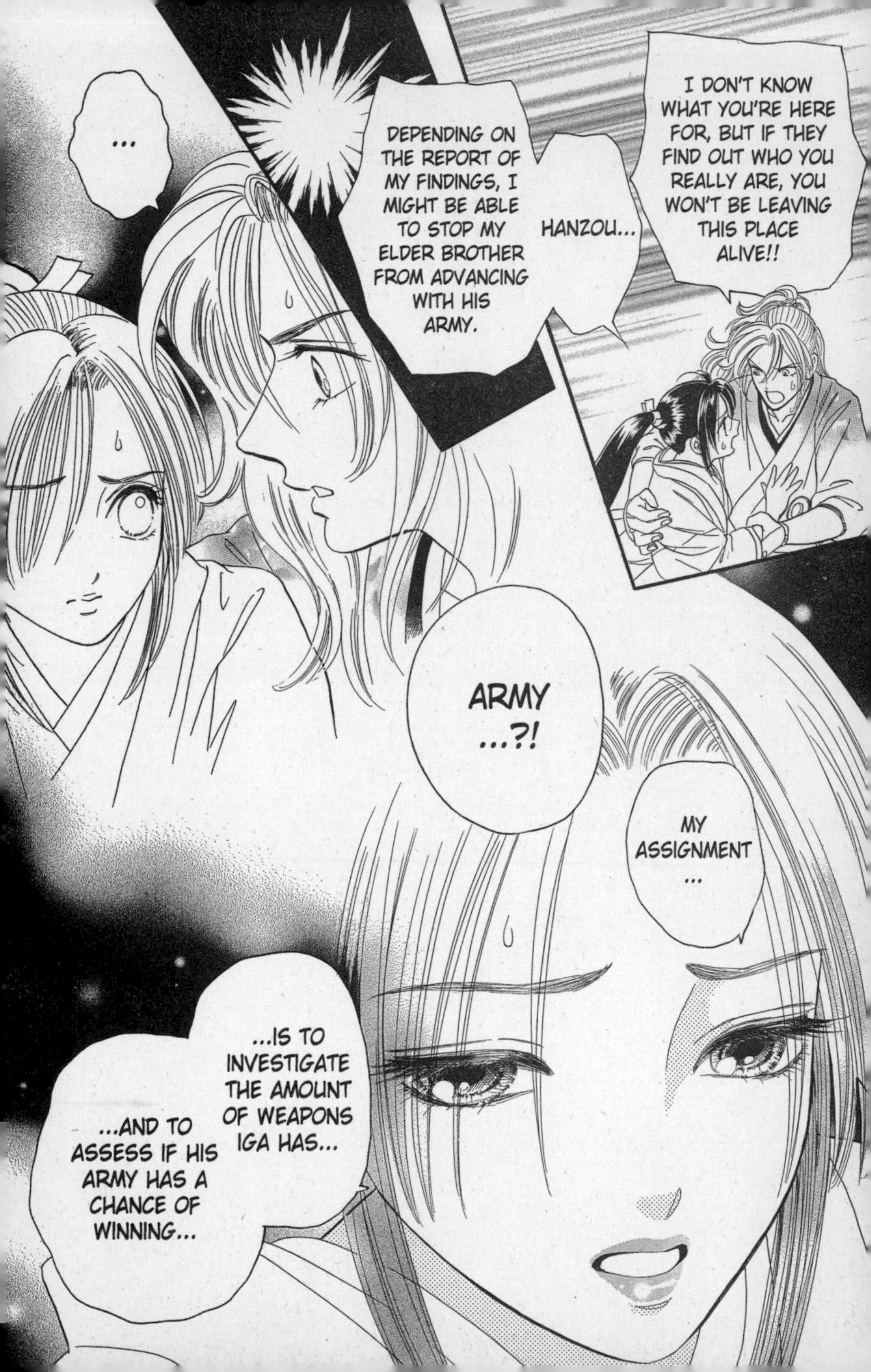
I DON'T KNOW WHAT YOU'RE HERE FOR, BUT IF THEY FIND OUT WHO YOU REALLY ARE, YOU WON'T BE LEAVING THIS PLACE ALIVE!!
HANZOU...
DEPENDING ON THE REPORT OF MY FINDINGS, I MIGHT BE ABLE TO STOP MY ELDER BROTHER FROM ADVANCING WITH HIS ARMY.
...
ARMY ...?!
MY ASSIGNMENT ...
...IS TO INVESTIGATE THE AMOUNT OF WEAPONS IGA HAS...
...AND TO ASSESS IF HIS ARMY HAS A CHANCE OF WINNING...

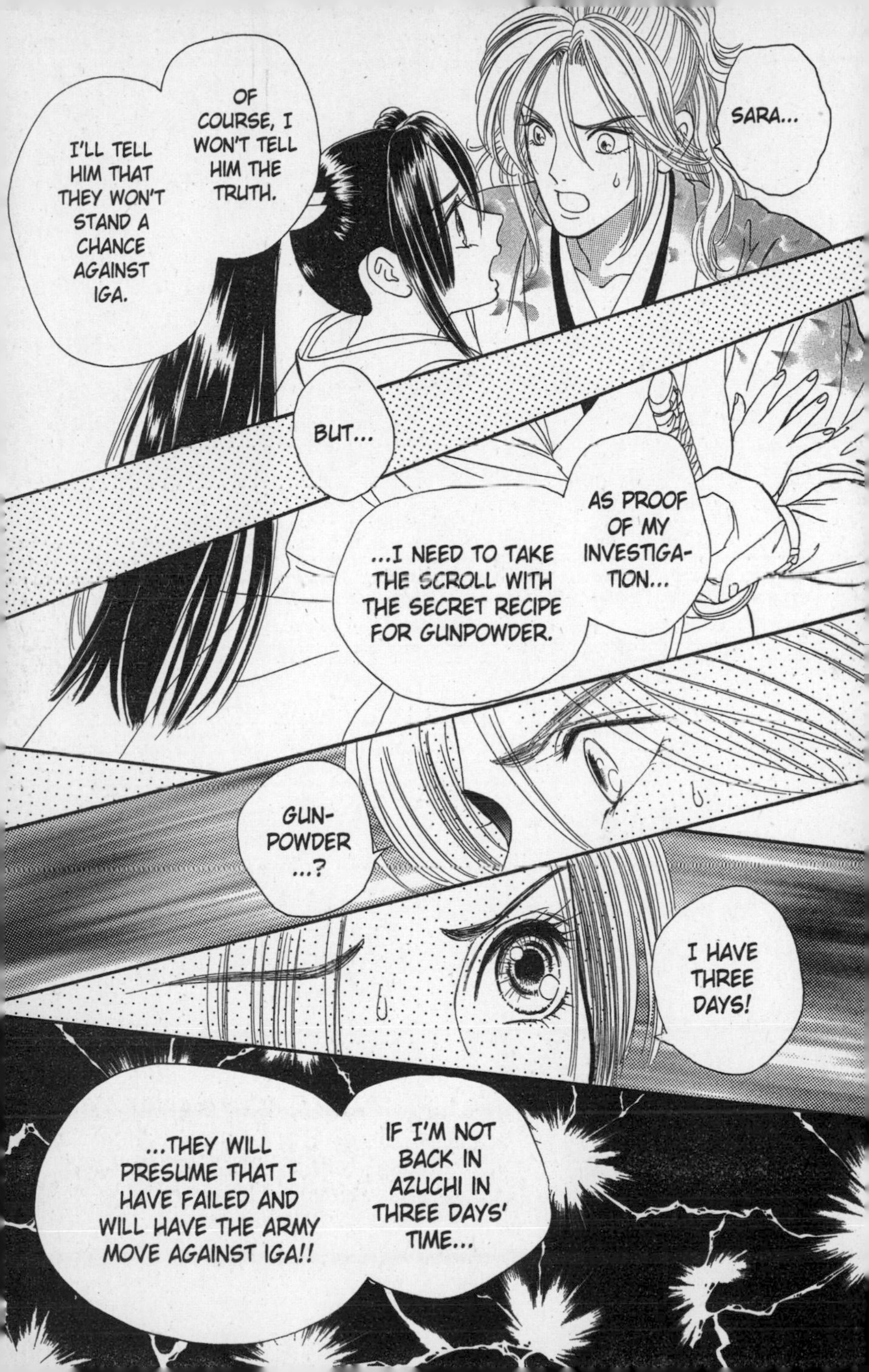
SARA...
OF COURSE, I WON'T TELL HIM THE TRUTH.
I'LL TELL HIM THAT THEY WON'T STAND A CHANCE AGAINST IGA.
BUT...
AS PROOF OF MY INVESTIGA-TION...
...I NEED TO TAKE THE SCROLL WITH THE SECRET RECIPE FOR GUNPOWDER.
GUN-POWDER ...?
I HAVE THREE DAYS!
IF I'M NOT BACK IN AZUCHI IN THREE DAYS' TIME...
...THEY WILL PRESUME THAT I HAVE FAILED AND WILL HAVE THE ARMY MOVE AGAINST IGA!!

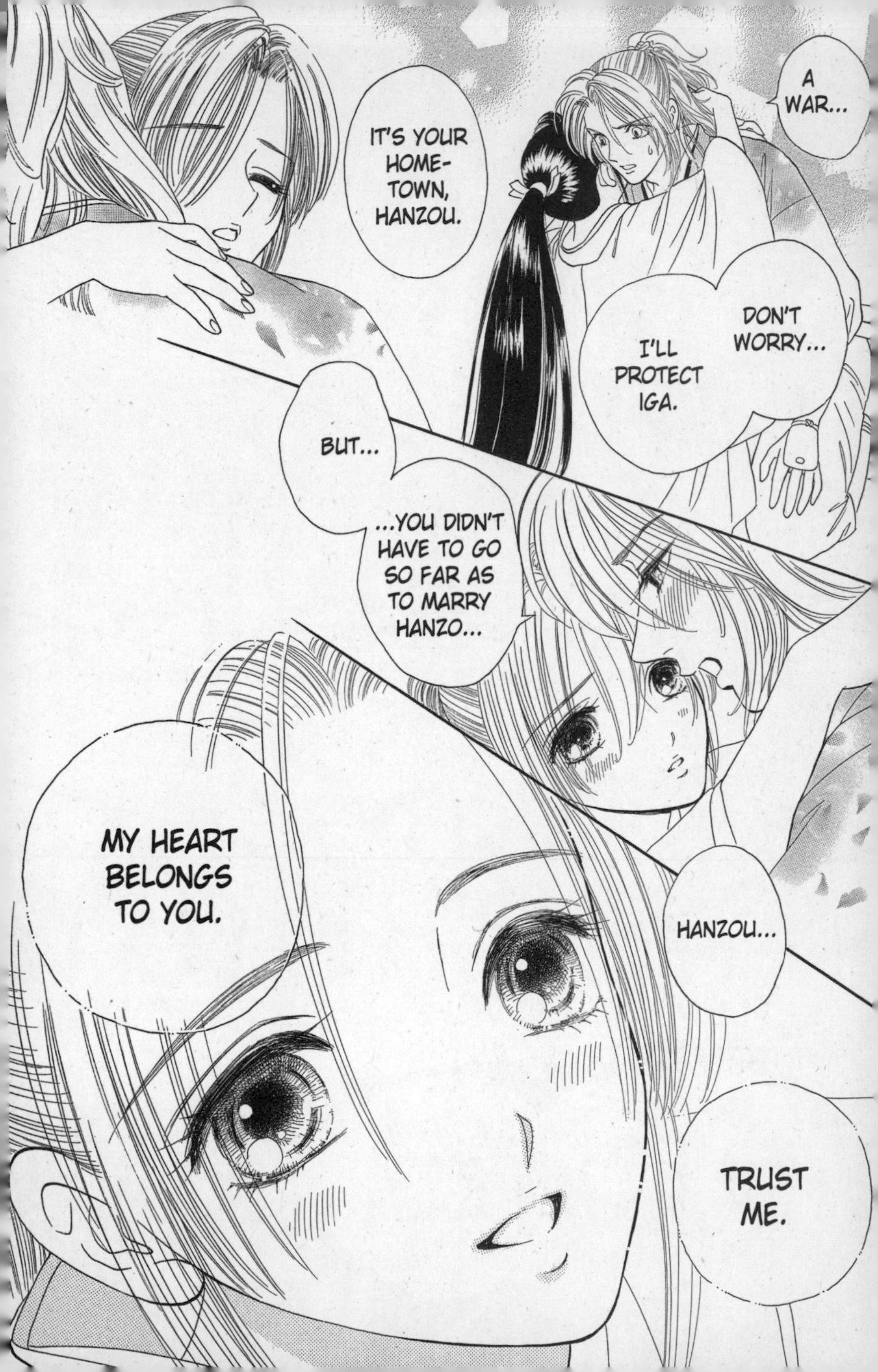
A WAR...
IT'S YOUR HOME-TOWN, HANZOU.
DON'T WORRY...
I'LL PROTECT IGA.
BUT...
...YOU DIDN'T HAVE TO GO SO FAR AS TO MARRY HANZO...
HANZOU...
TRUST ME.
MY HEART BELONGS TO YOU.

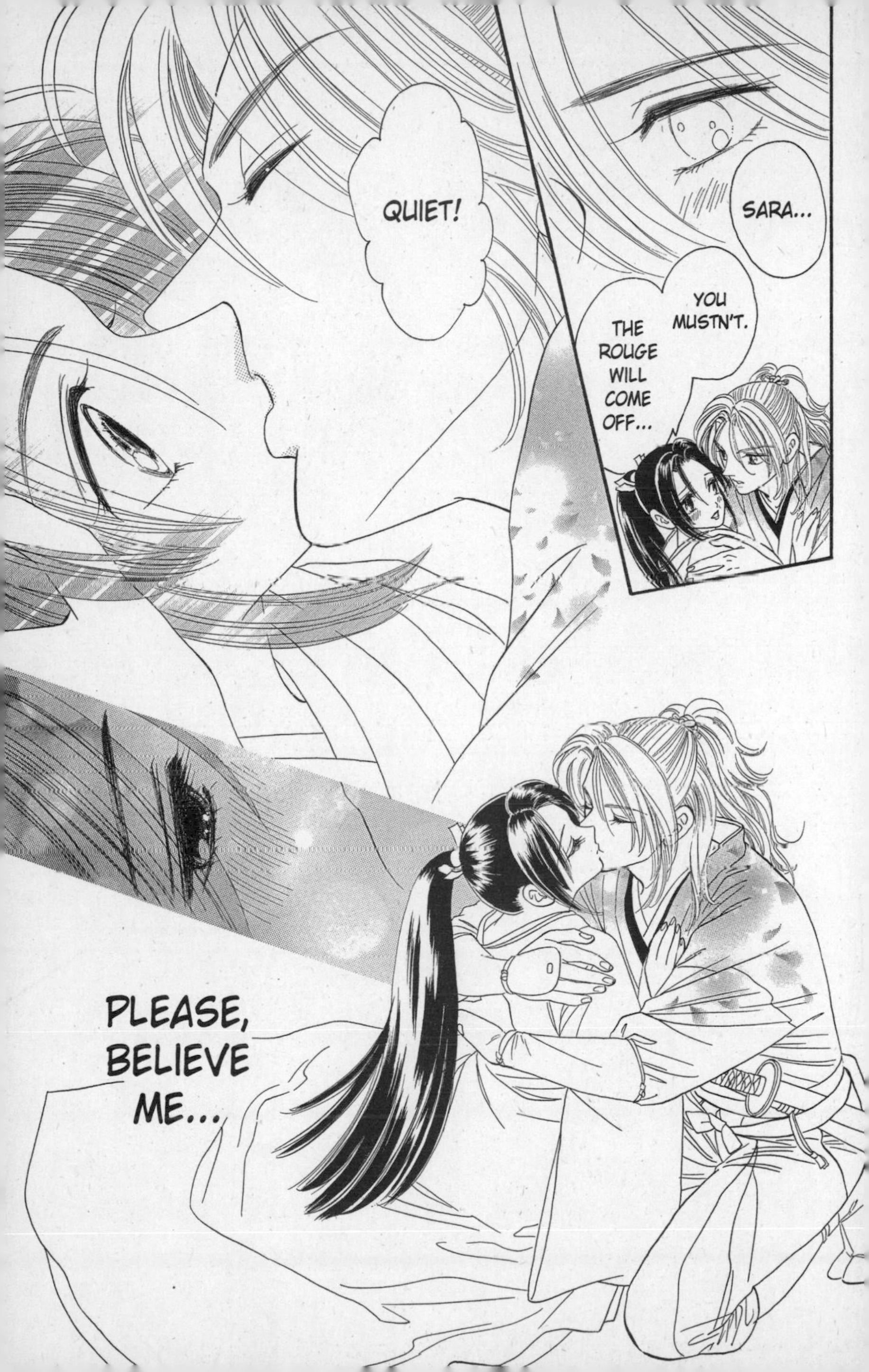
SARA...
YOU MUSTN'T.
THE ROUGE WILL COME OFF...
QUIET!
PLEASE, BELIEVE ME...

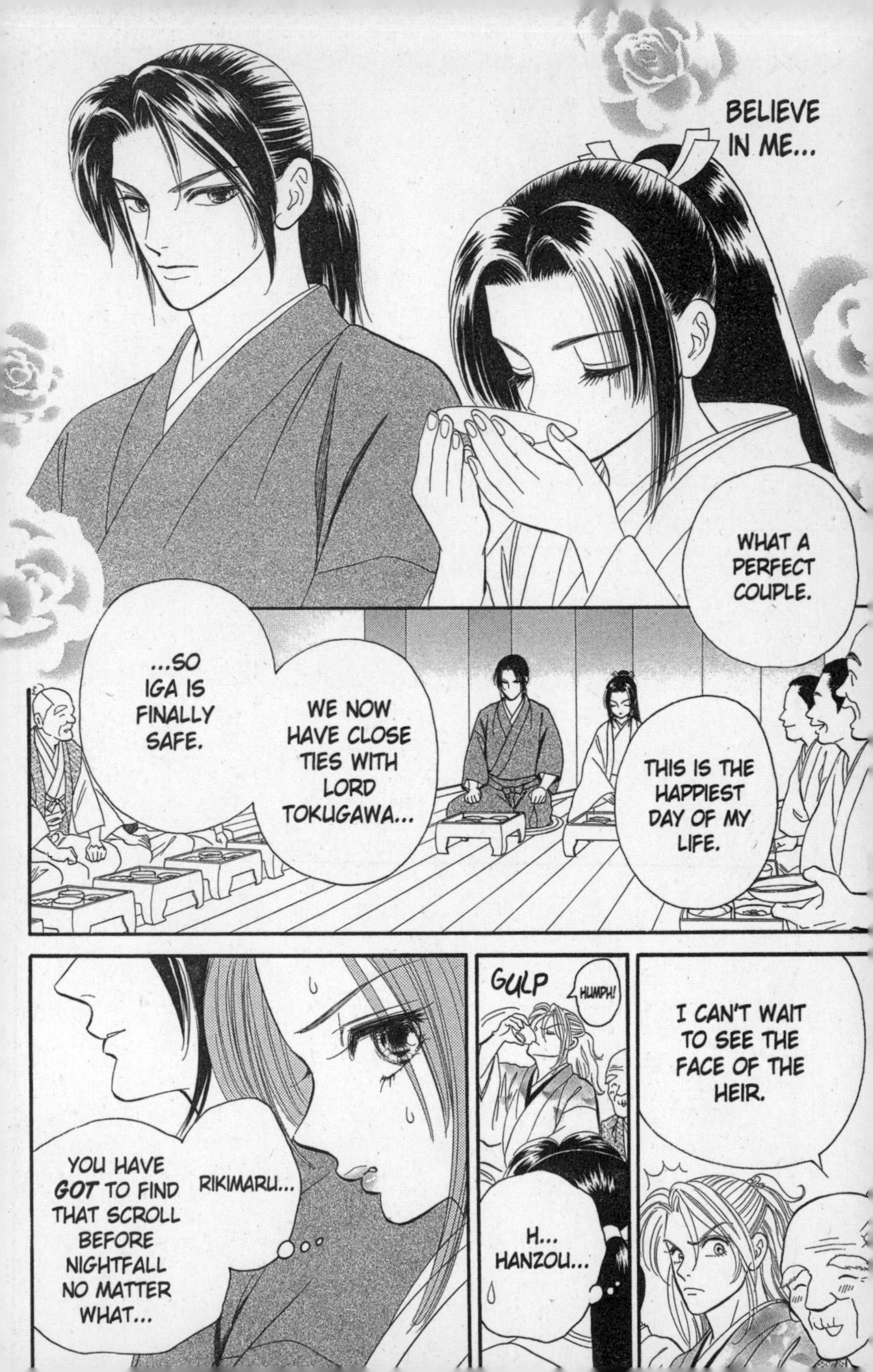
BELIEVE IN ME...
WHAT A PERFECT COUPLE.
THIS IS THE HAPPIEST DAY OF MY LIFE.
WE NOW HAVE CLOSE TIES WITH LORD TOKUGAWA...
...SO IGA IS FINALLY SAFE.
I CAN'T WAIT TO SEE THE FACE OF THE HEIR.
HUMPH!
GULP
H... HANZOU...
RIKIMARU...
YOU HAVE *GOT* TO FIND THAT SCROLL BEFORE NIGHTFALL NO MATTER WHAT...

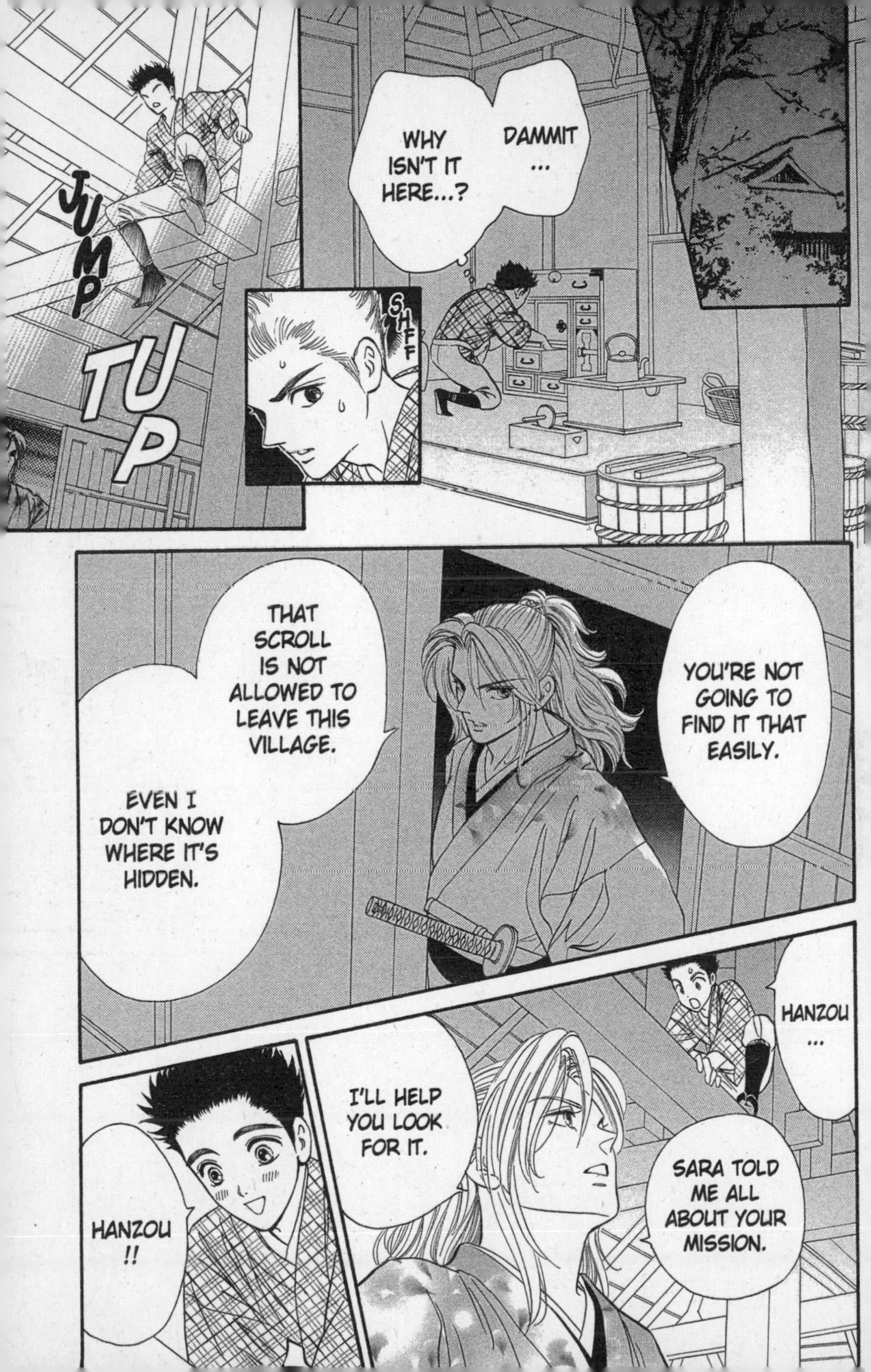
DAMMIT ...
WHY ISN'T IT HERE...?
SHFF
JUMP
TUP
YOU'RE NOT GOING TO FIND IT THAT EASILY.
THAT SCROLL IS NOT ALLOWED TO LEAVE THIS VILLAGE.
EVEN I DON'T KNOW WHERE IT'S HIDDEN.
HANZOU ...
SARA TOLD ME ALL ABOUT YOUR MISSION.
I'LL HELP YOU LOOK FOR IT.
HANZOU !!

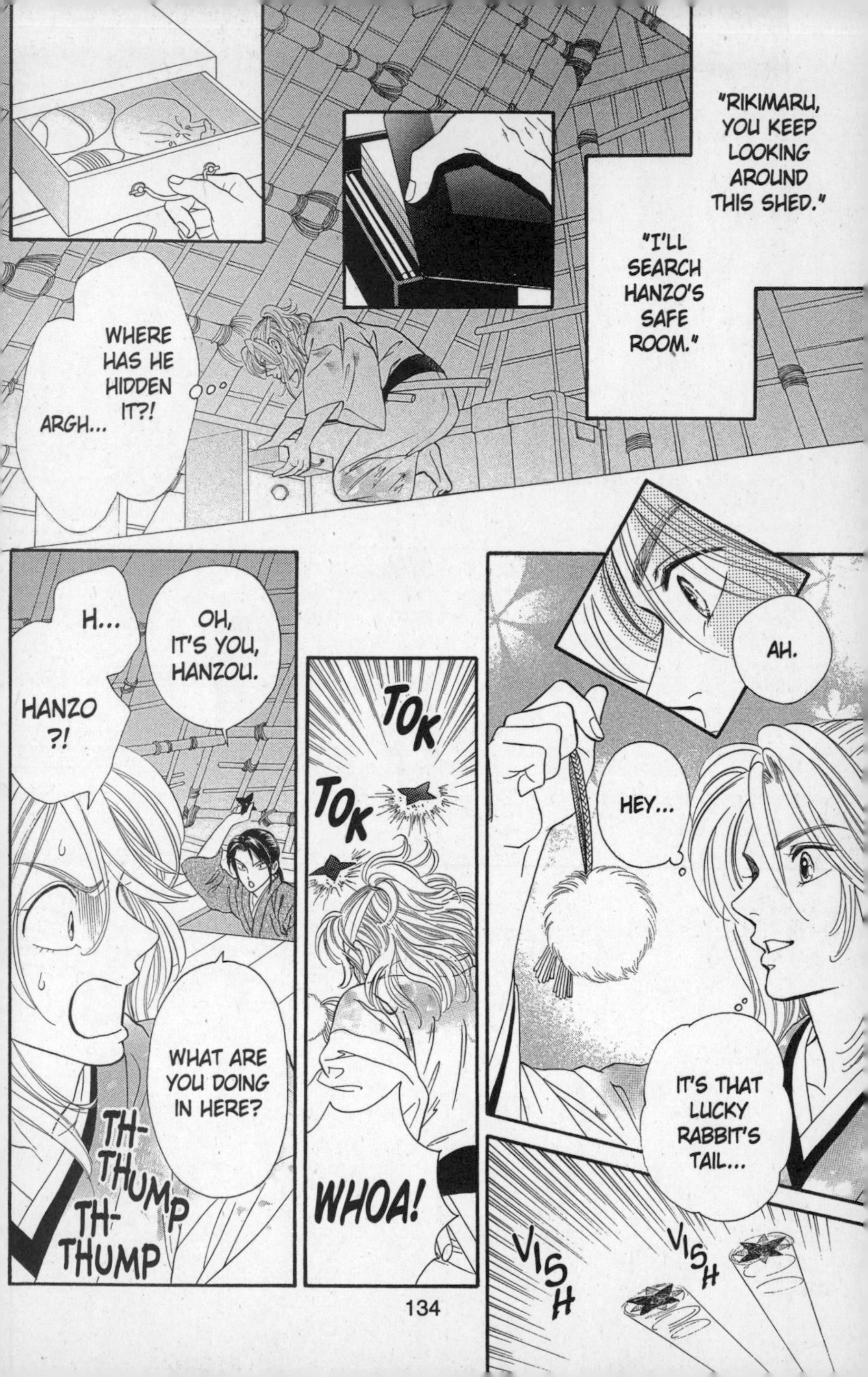
"RIKIMARU, YOU KEEP LOOKING AROUND THIS SHED."
"I'LL SEARCH HANZO'S SAFE ROOM."
WHERE HAS HE HIDDEN IT?!
ARGH...
AH.
HEY...
IT'S THAT LUCKY RABBIT'S TAIL...
VISH
VISH
TOK
TOK
WHOA!
OH, IT'S YOU, HANZOU.
H...
HANZO?!
WHAT ARE YOU DOING IN HERE?
TH-THUMP
TH-THUMP

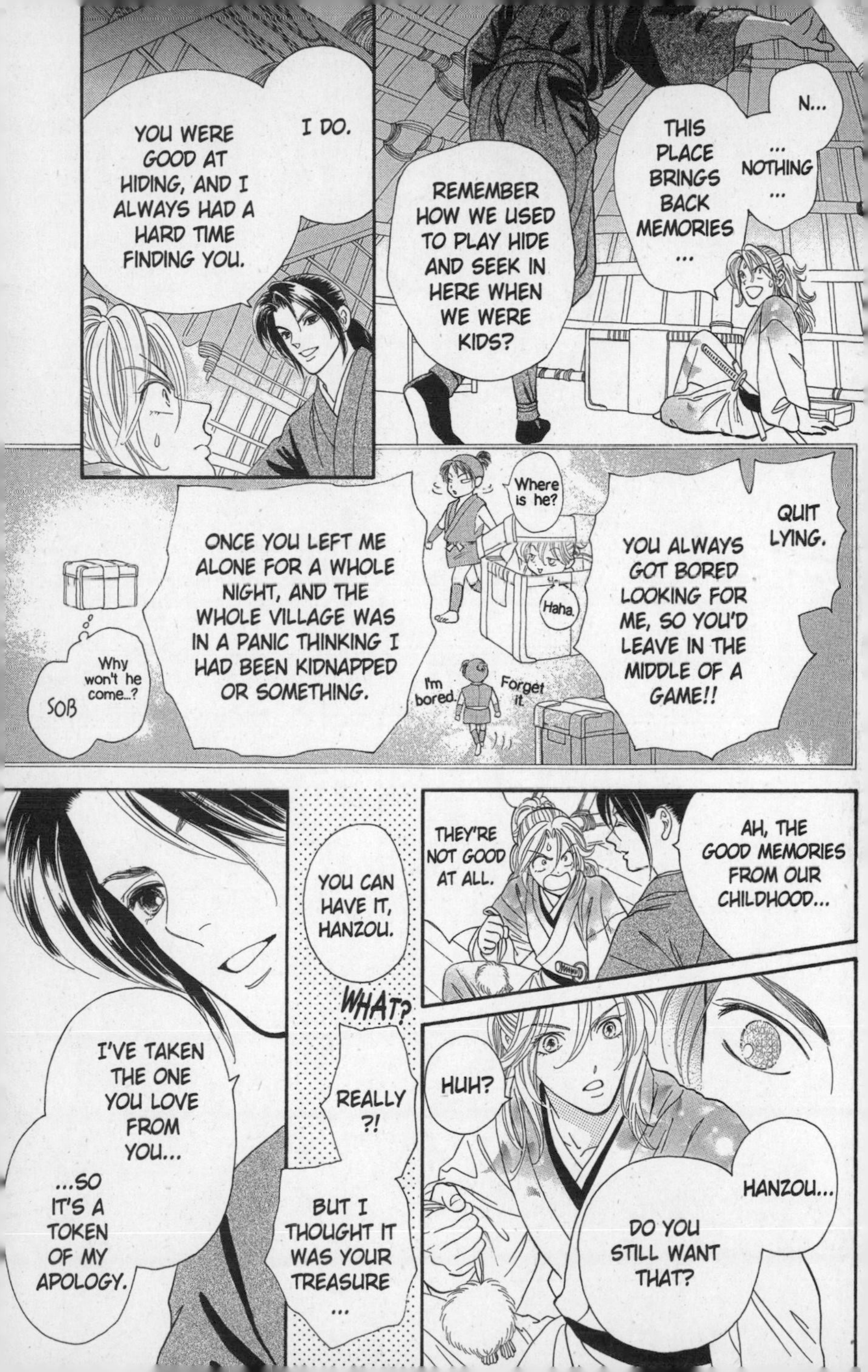
N... ...NOTHING...
THIS PLACE BRINGS BACK MEMORIES...
REMEMBER HOW WE USED TO PLAY HIDE AND SEEK IN HERE WHEN WE WERE KIDS?
I DO.
YOU WERE GOOD AT HIDING, AND I ALWAYS HAD A HARD TIME FINDING YOU.
QUIT LYING.
YOU ALWAYS GOT BORED LOOKING FOR ME, SO YOU'D LEAVE IN THE MIDDLE OF A GAME!!
Where is he?
Haha.
Forget it.
I'm bored.
ONCE YOU LEFT ME ALONE FOR A WHOLE NIGHT, AND THE WHOLE VILLAGE WAS IN A PANIC THINKING I HAD BEEN KIDNAPPED OR SOMETHING.
Why won't he come...?
SOB
AH, THE GOOD MEMORIES FROM OUR CHILDHOOD...
THEY'RE NOT GOOD AT ALL.
HANZOU...
DO YOU STILL WANT THAT?
HUH?
YOU CAN HAVE IT, HANZOU.
WHAT?
REALLY?!
BUT I THOUGHT IT WAS YOUR TREASURE...
I'VE TAKEN THE ONE YOU LOVE FROM YOU...
...SO IT'S A TOKEN OF MY APOLOGY.

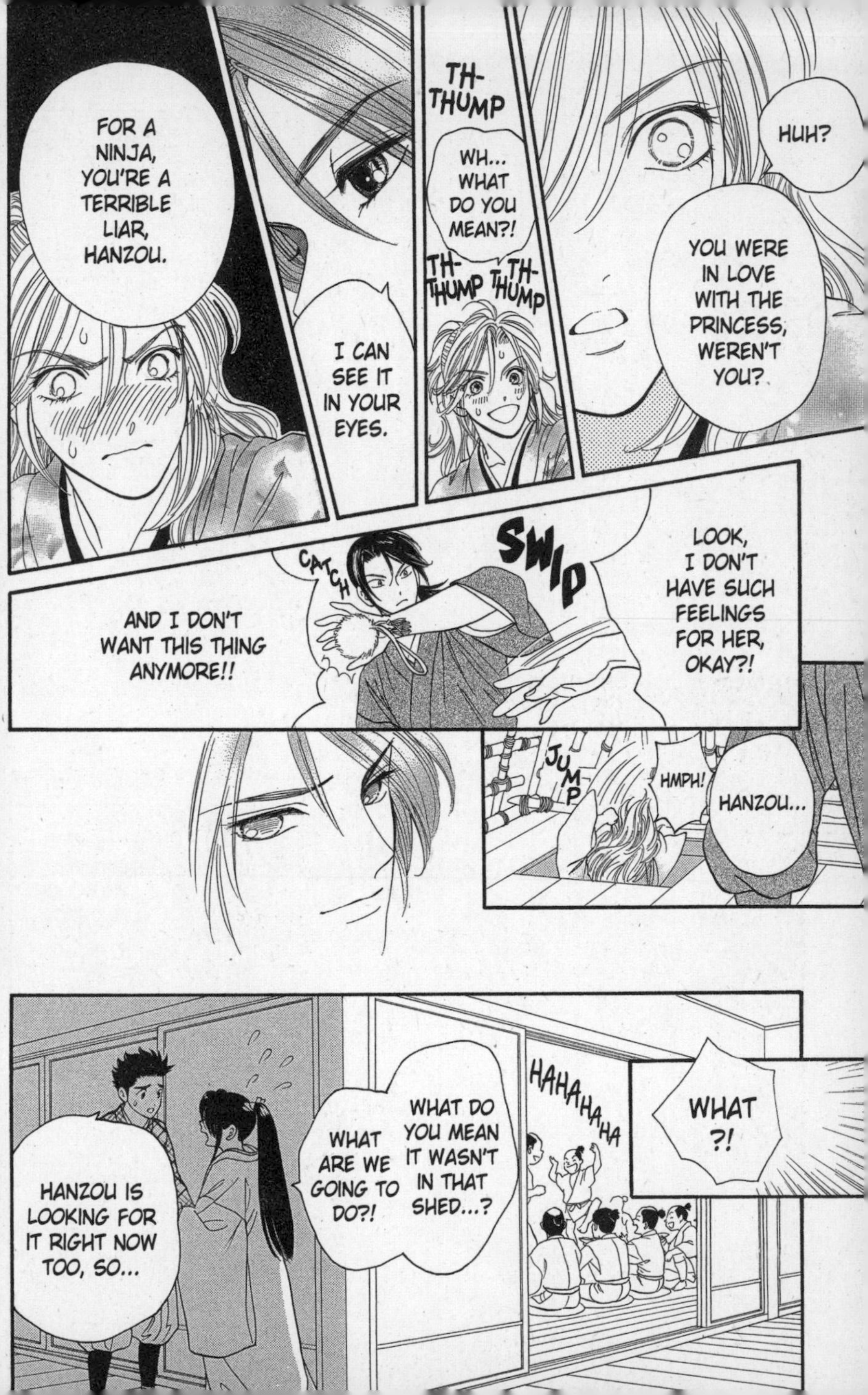
HUH?
YOU WERE IN LOVE WITH THE PRINCESS, WEREN'T YOU?
TH-THUMP
WH... WHAT DO YOU MEAN?!
TH-THUMP TH-THUMP
I CAN SEE IT IN YOUR EYES.
FOR A NINJA, YOU'RE A TERRIBLE LIAR, HANZOU.
SWIP
LOOK, I DON'T HAVE SUCH FEELINGS FOR HER, OKAY?!
CATCH
AND I DON'T WANT THIS THING ANYMORE!!
HANZOU...
HMPH!
JUMP
WHAT ?!
HAHAHAHA
WHAT DO YOU MEAN IT WASN'T IN THAT SHED...?
WHAT ARE WE GOING TO DO?!
HANZOU IS LOOKING FOR IT RIGHT NOW TOO, SO...

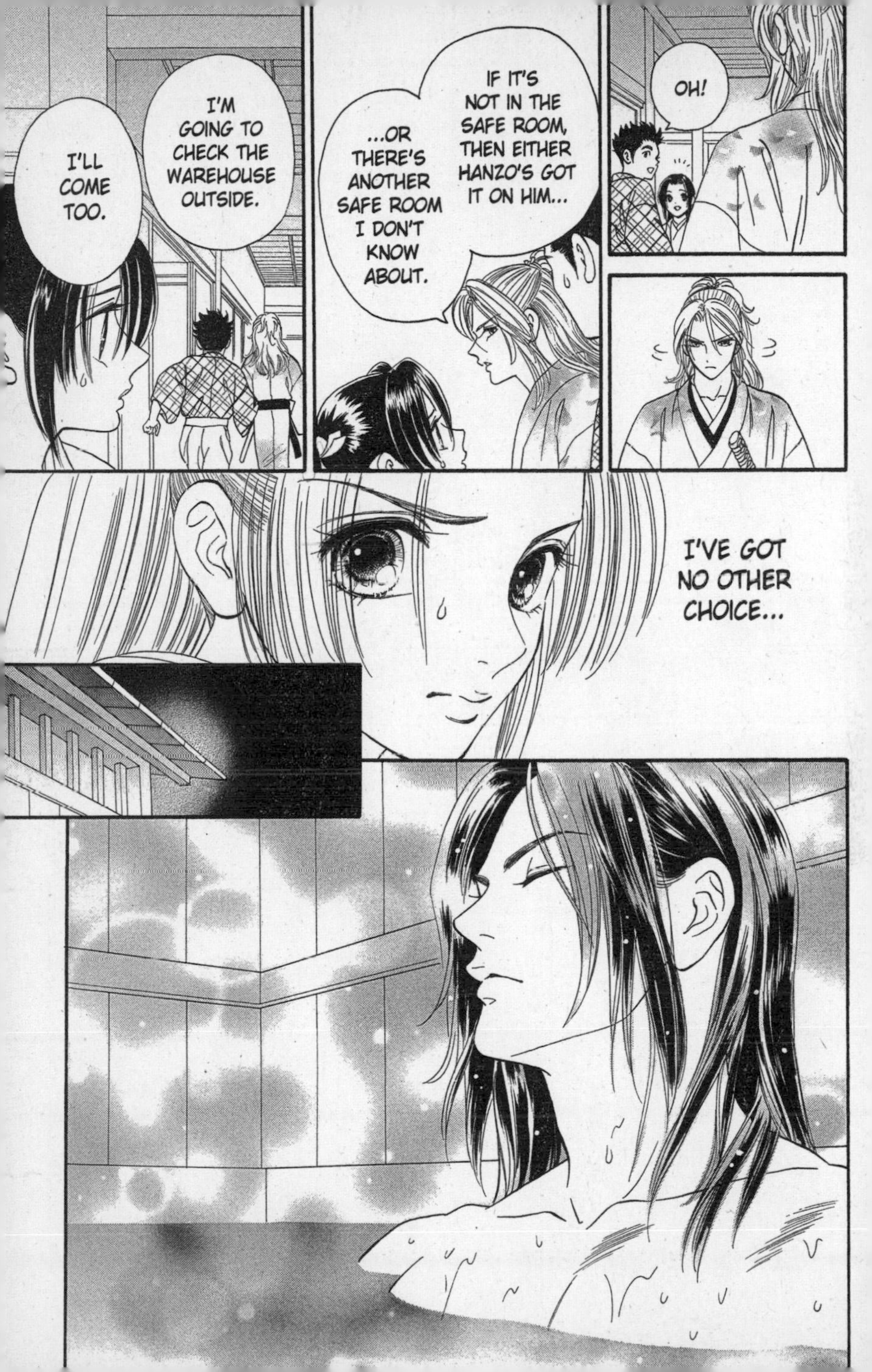
OH!
IF IT'S NOT IN THE SAFE ROOM, THEN EITHER HANZO'S GOT IT ON HIM...
...OR THERE'S ANOTHER SAFE ROOM I DON'T KNOW ABOUT.
I'M GOING TO CHECK THE WAREHOUSE OUTSIDE.
I'LL COME TOO.
I'VE GOT NO OTHER CHOICE...

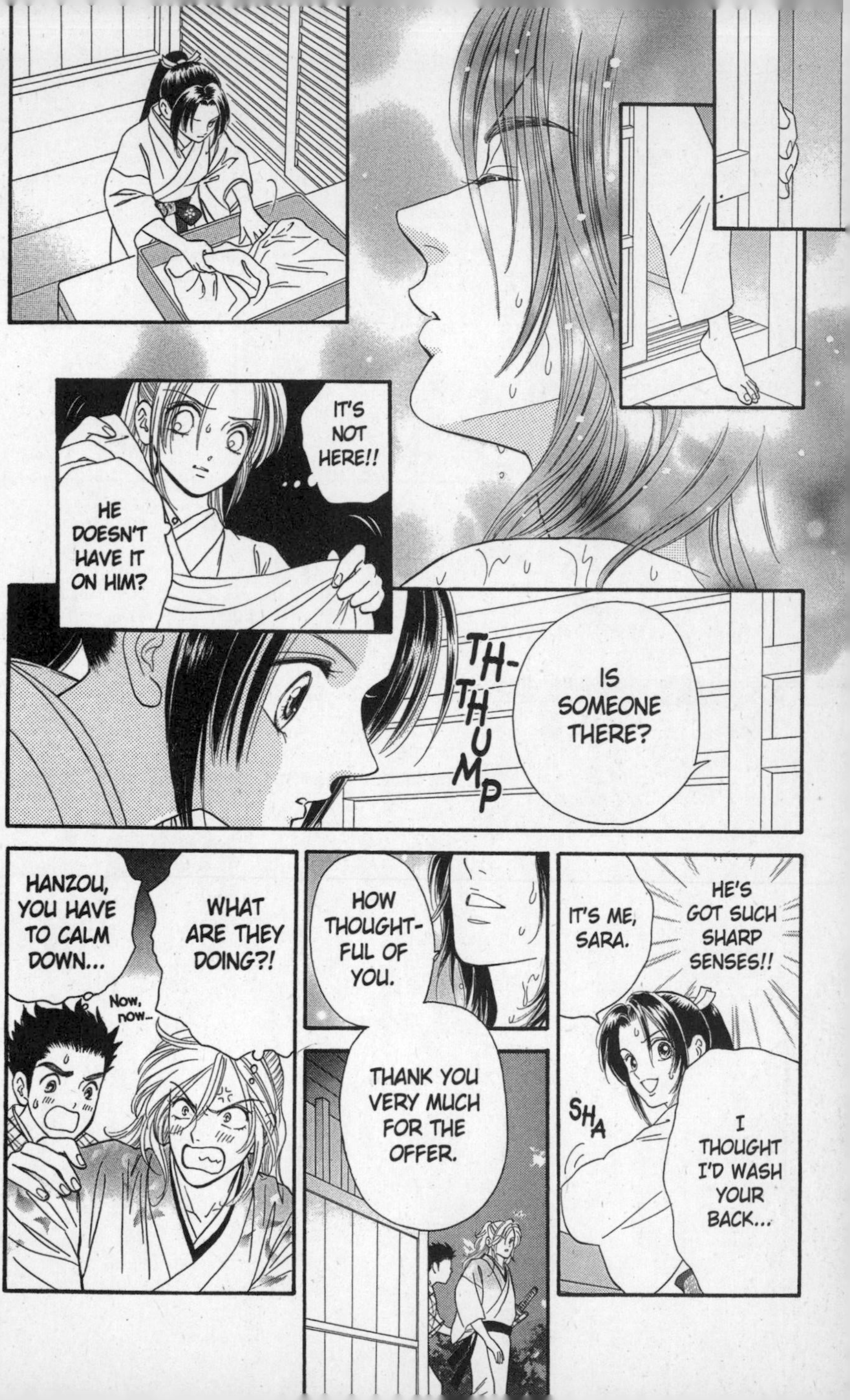
IT'S NOT HERE!!
HE DOESN'T HAVE IT ON HIM?
TH-THUMP
IS SOMEONE THERE?
HE'S GOT SUCH SHARP SENSES!!
IT'S ME, SARA.
SHA
I THOUGHT I'D WASH YOUR BACK...
HOW THOUGHTFUL OF YOU.
THANK YOU VERY MUCH FOR THE OFFER.
WHAT ARE THEY DOING?!
HANZOU, YOU HAVE TO CALM DOWN...
Now, now...

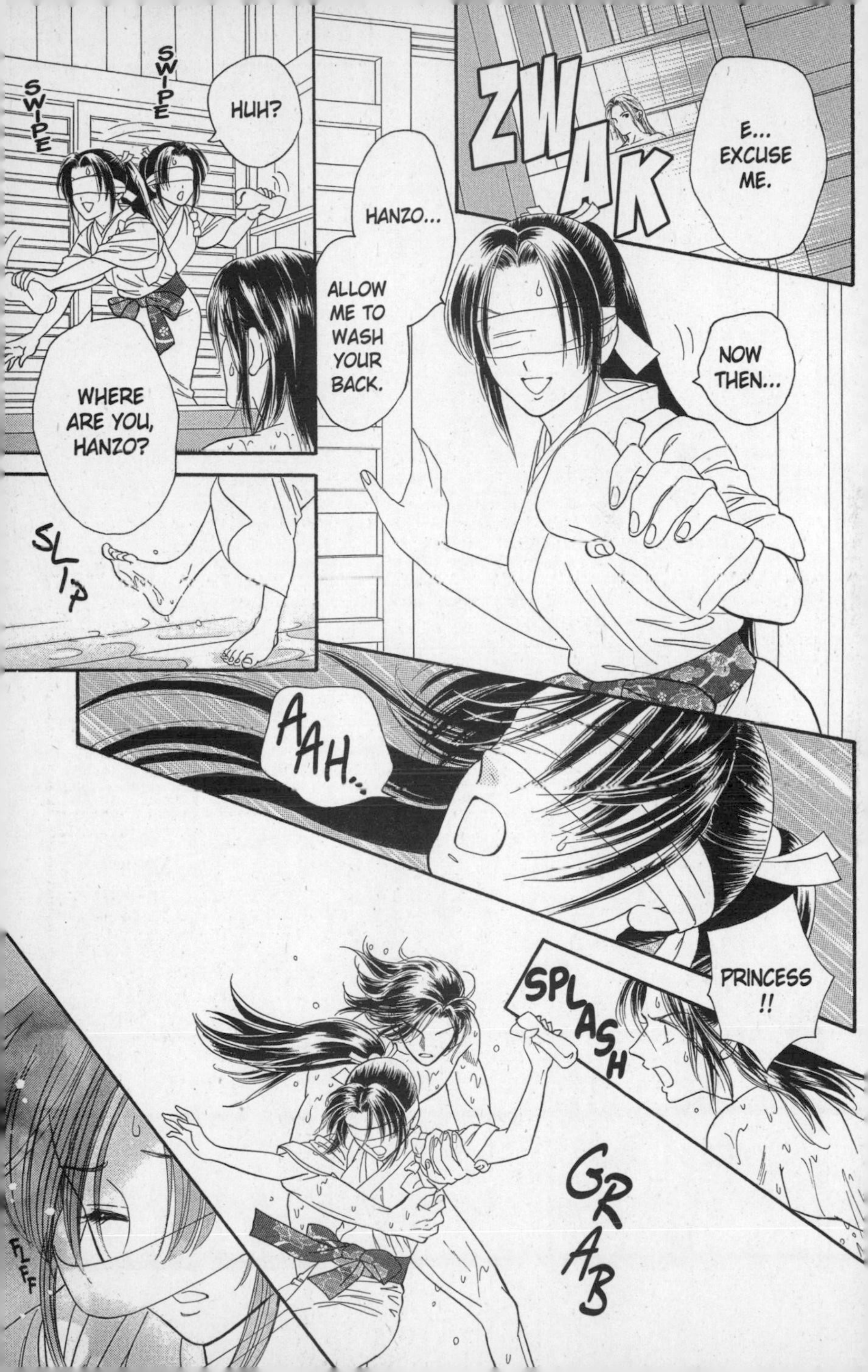
ZWAK
E... EXCUSE ME.
NOW THEN...
HANZO...
ALLOW ME TO WASH YOUR BACK.
HUH?
SWIPE
SWIPE
WHERE ARE YOU, HANZO?
SLIP
AAH...
PRINCESS !!
SPLASH
GRAB
FLEFF

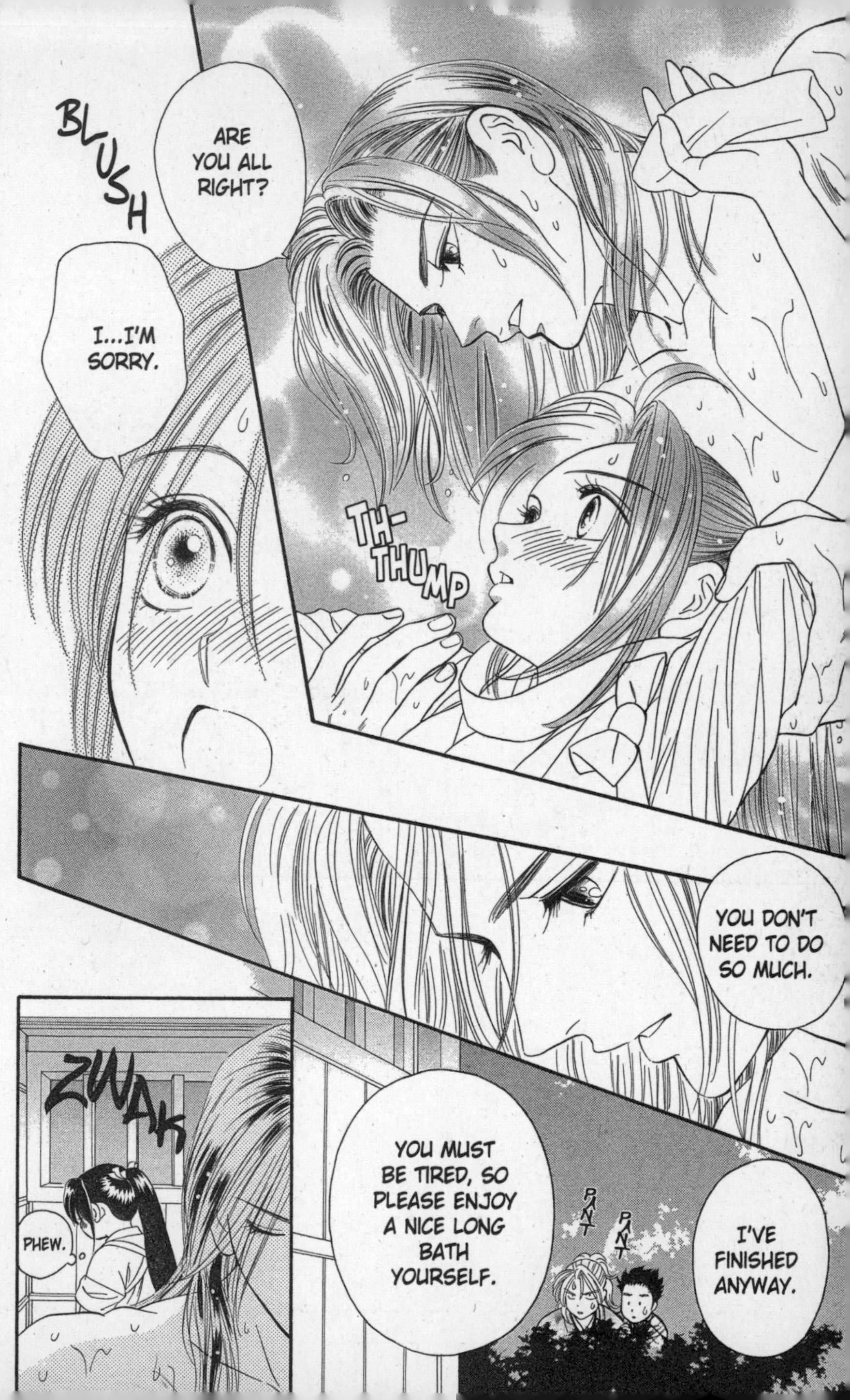
ARE YOU ALL RIGHT?
TH-THUMP
BLUSH
I...I'M SORRY.
YOU DON'T NEED TO DO SO MUCH.
I'VE FINISHED ANYWAY.
PANT PANT
YOU MUST BE TIRED, SO PLEASE ENJOY A NICE LONG BATH YOURSELF.
ZWAK
PHEW.

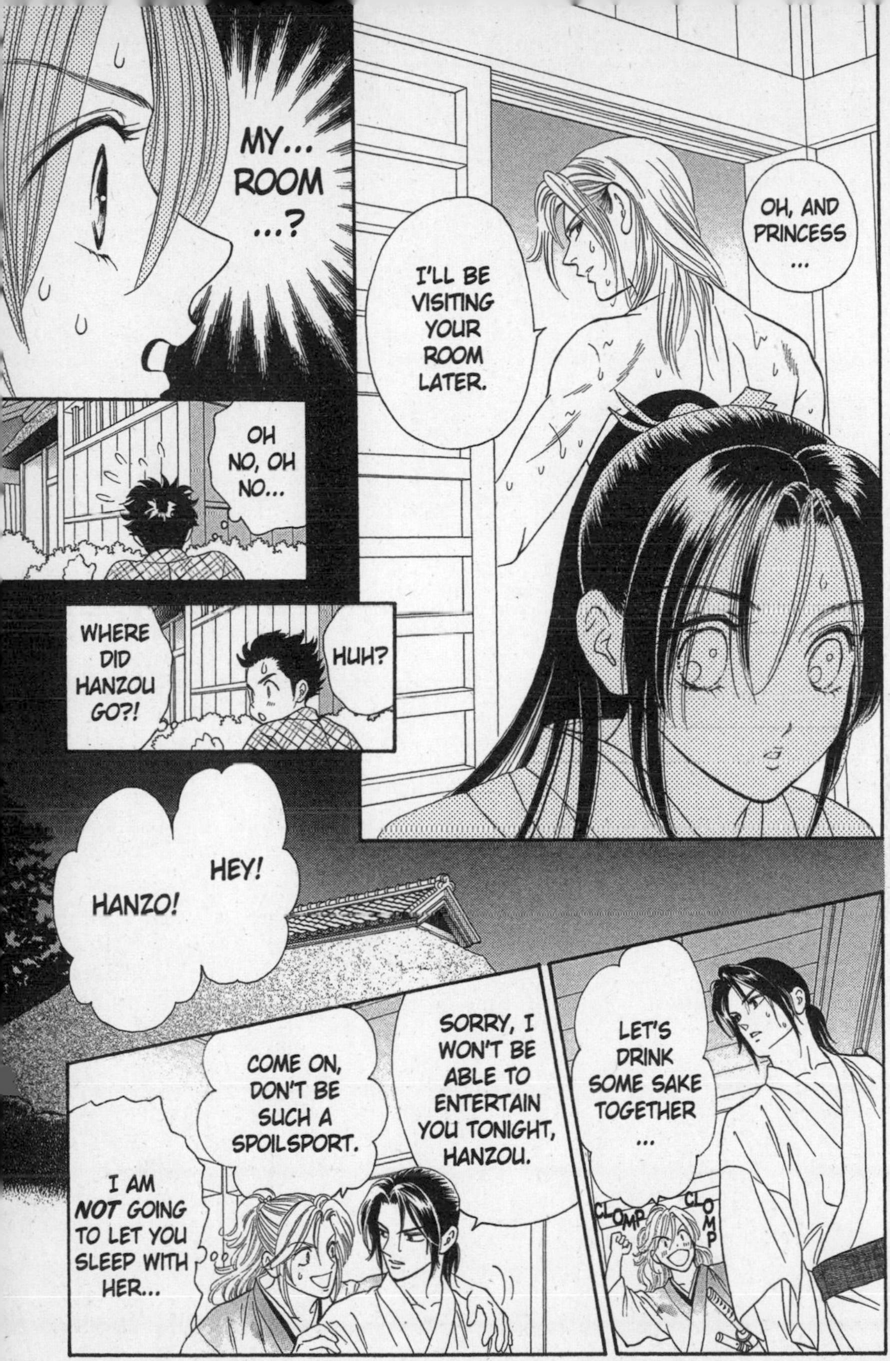
OH, AND PRINCESS...
I'LL BE VISITING YOUR ROOM LATER.
MY... ROOM...?
OH NO, OH NO...
HUH?
WHERE DID HANZOU GO?!
HEY!
HANZO!
LET'S DRINK SOME SAKE TOGETHER...
CLOMP
CLOMP
SORRY, I WON'T BE ABLE TO ENTERTAIN YOU TONIGHT, HANZOU.
COME ON, DON'T BE SUCH A SPOILSPORT.
I AM *NOT* GOING TO LET YOU SLEEP WITH HER...

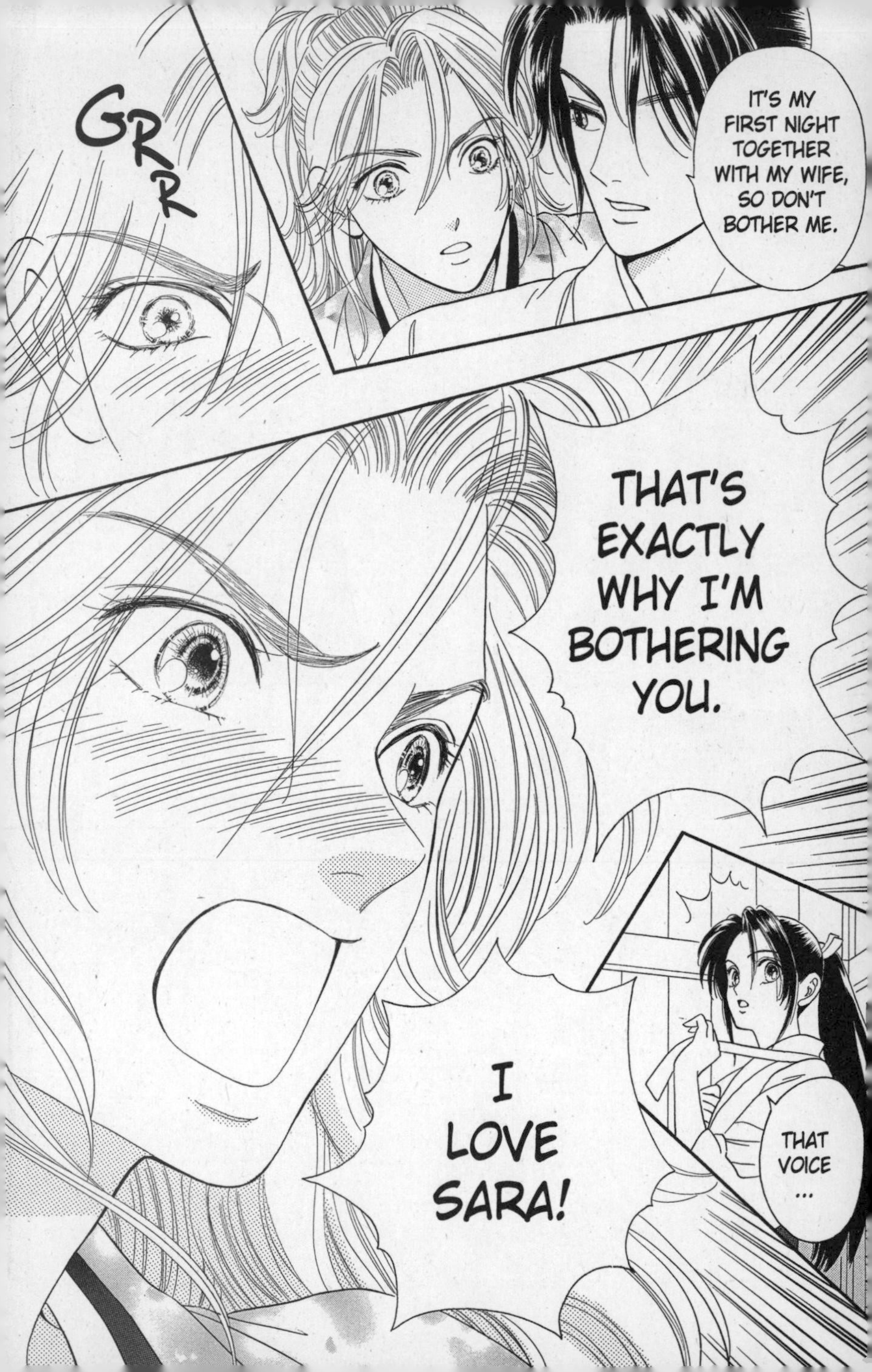
IT'S MY FIRST NIGHT TOGETHER WITH MY WIFE, SO DON'T BOTHER ME.
GRRR
THAT'S EXACTLY WHY I'M BOTHERING YOU.
I LOVE SARA!
THAT VOICE ...

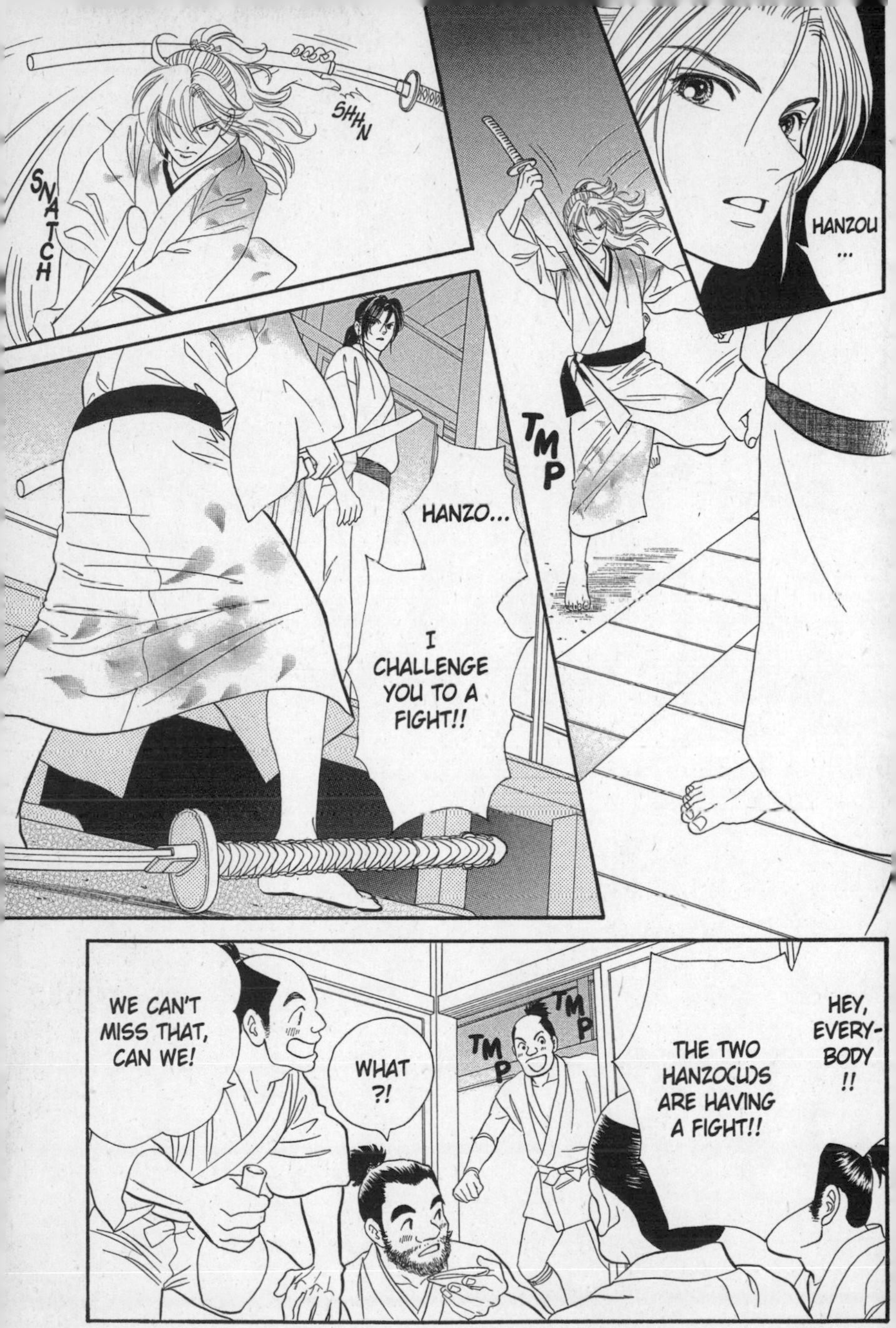
HANZOU ...
TMP
SHHN
SNATCH
HANZO...
I CHALLENGE YOU TO A FIGHT!!
HEY, EVERYBODY !!
THE TWO HANZO(U)S ARE HAVING A FIGHT!!
TMP
TMP
WHAT ?!
WE CAN'T MISS THAT, CAN WE!

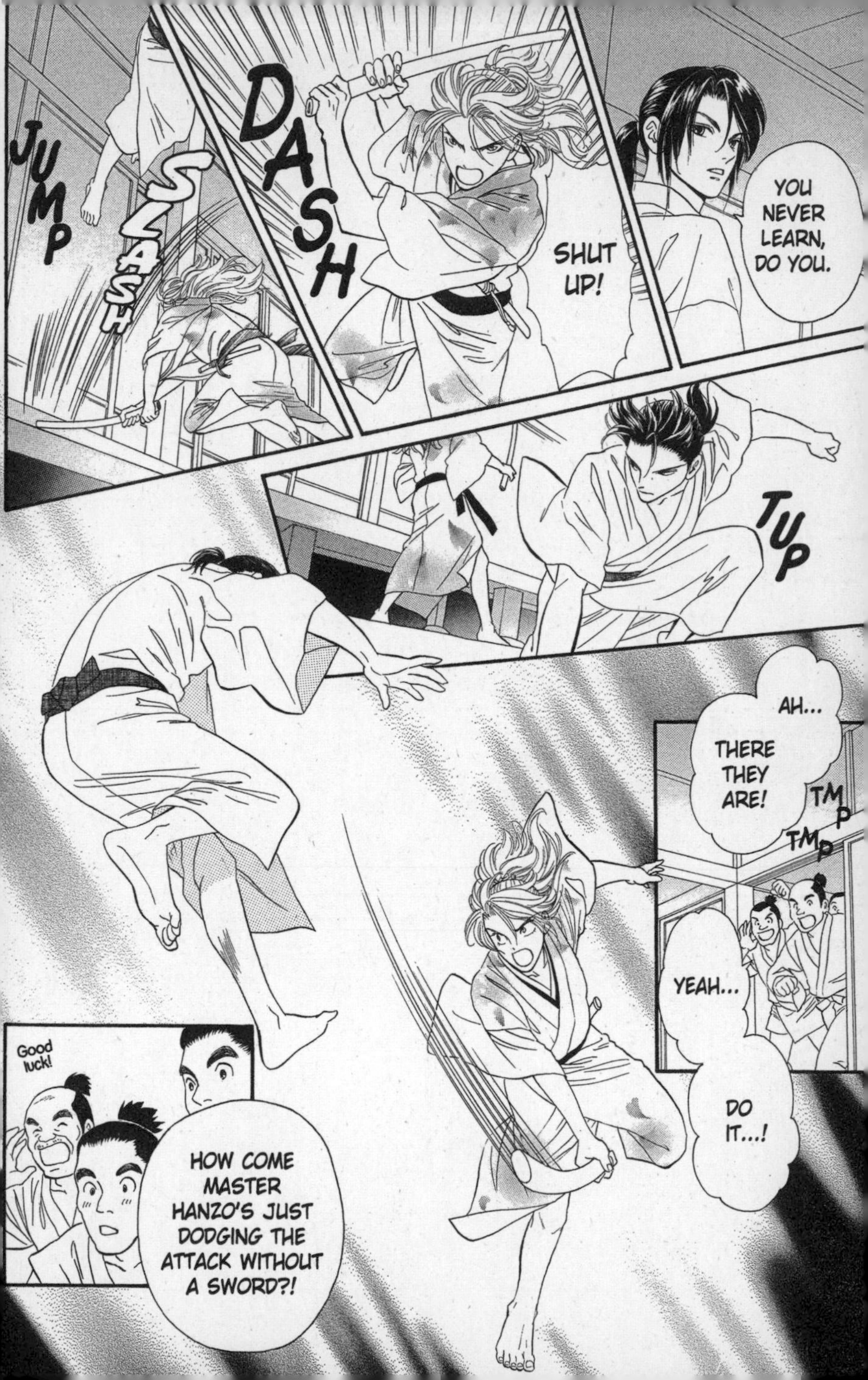
YOU NEVER LEARN, DO YOU.
SHUT UP!
DASH
JUMP
SLASH
TUP
AH... THERE THEY ARE!
TMP TMP
YEAH...
DO IT...!
Good luck!
HOW COME MASTER HANZO'S JUST DODGING THE ATTACK WITHOUT A SWORD?!

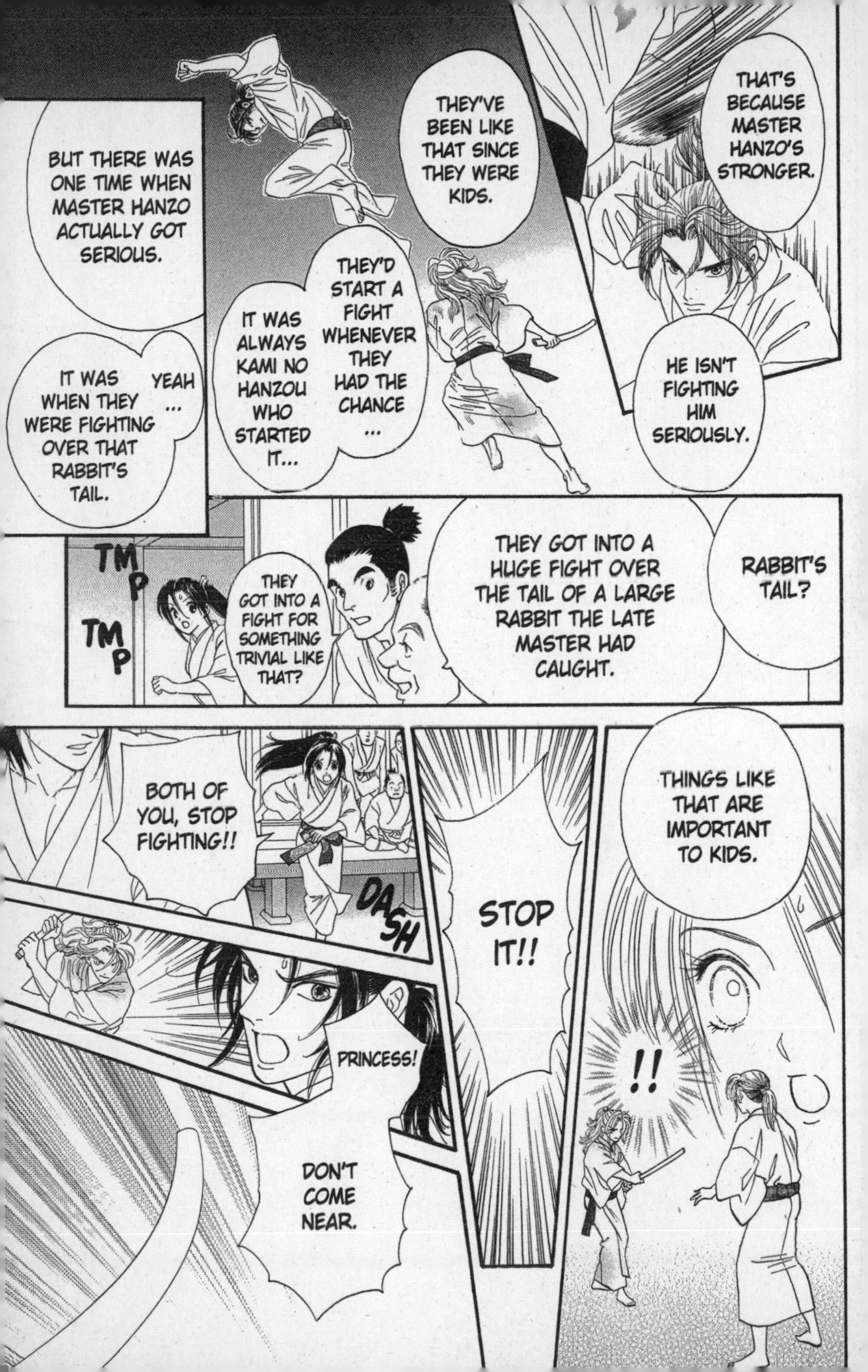
THAT'S BECAUSE MASTER HANZO'S STRONGER.
HE ISN'T FIGHTING HIM SERIOUSLY.
THEY'VE BEEN LIKE THAT SINCE THEY WERE KIDS.
THEY'D START A FIGHT WHENEVER THEY HAD THE CHANCE ...
IT WAS ALWAYS KAMI NO HANZOU WHO STARTED IT...
BUT THERE WAS ONE TIME WHEN MASTER HANZO ACTUALLY GOT SERIOUS.
YEAH ...
IT WAS WHEN THEY WERE FIGHTING OVER THAT RABBIT'S TAIL.
RABBIT'S TAIL?
THEY GOT INTO A HUGE FIGHT OVER THE TAIL OF A LARGE RABBIT THE LATE MASTER HAD CAUGHT.
THEY GOT INTO A FIGHT FOR SOMETHING TRIVIAL LIKE THAT?
TMP
TMP
THINGS LIKE THAT ARE IMPORTANT TO KIDS.
!!
STOP IT!!
BOTH OF YOU, STOP FIGHTING!!
DASH
PRINCESS!
DON'T COME NEAR.

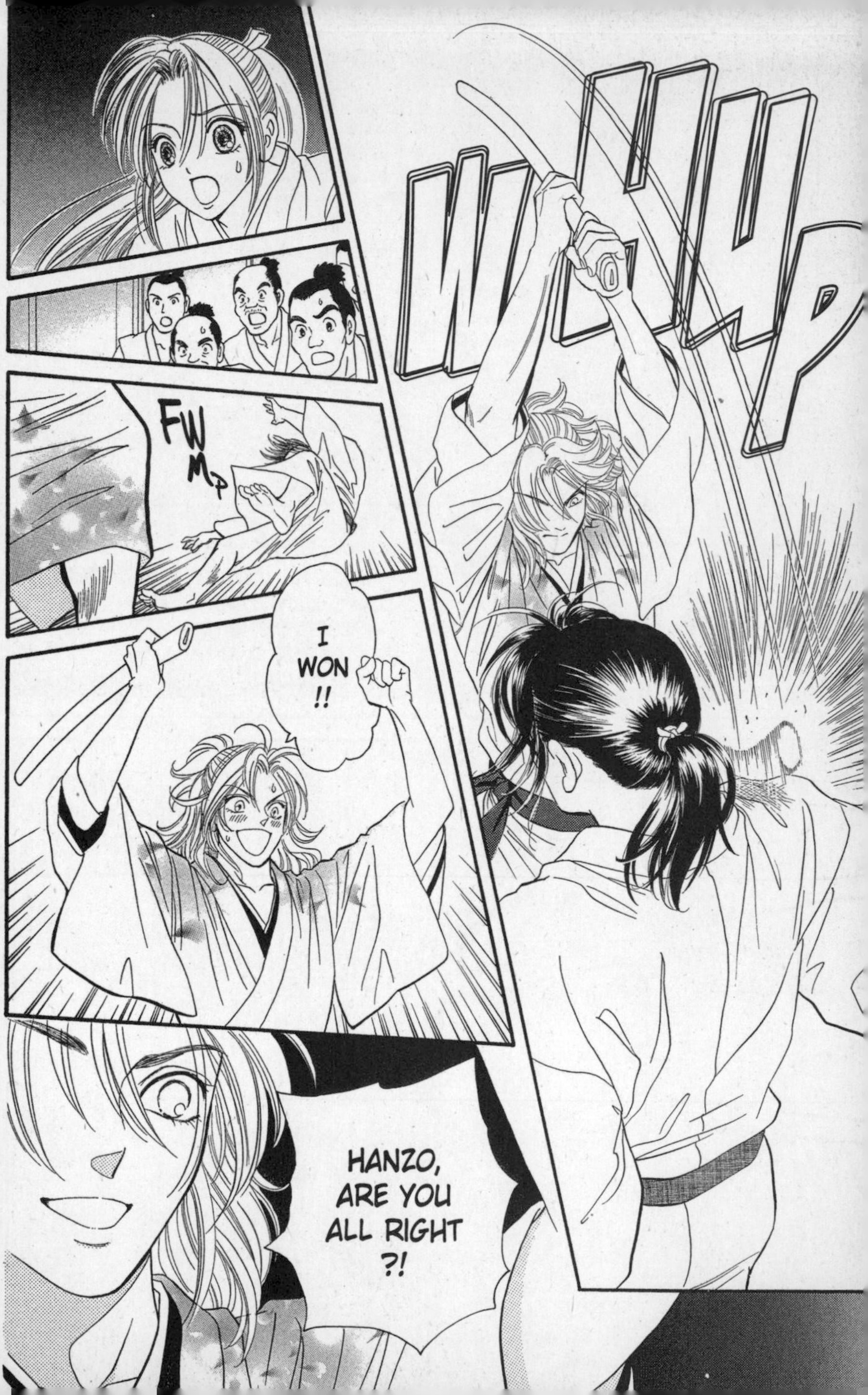
WHUP
FWMP
I WON !!
HANZO, ARE YOU ALL RIGHT ?!

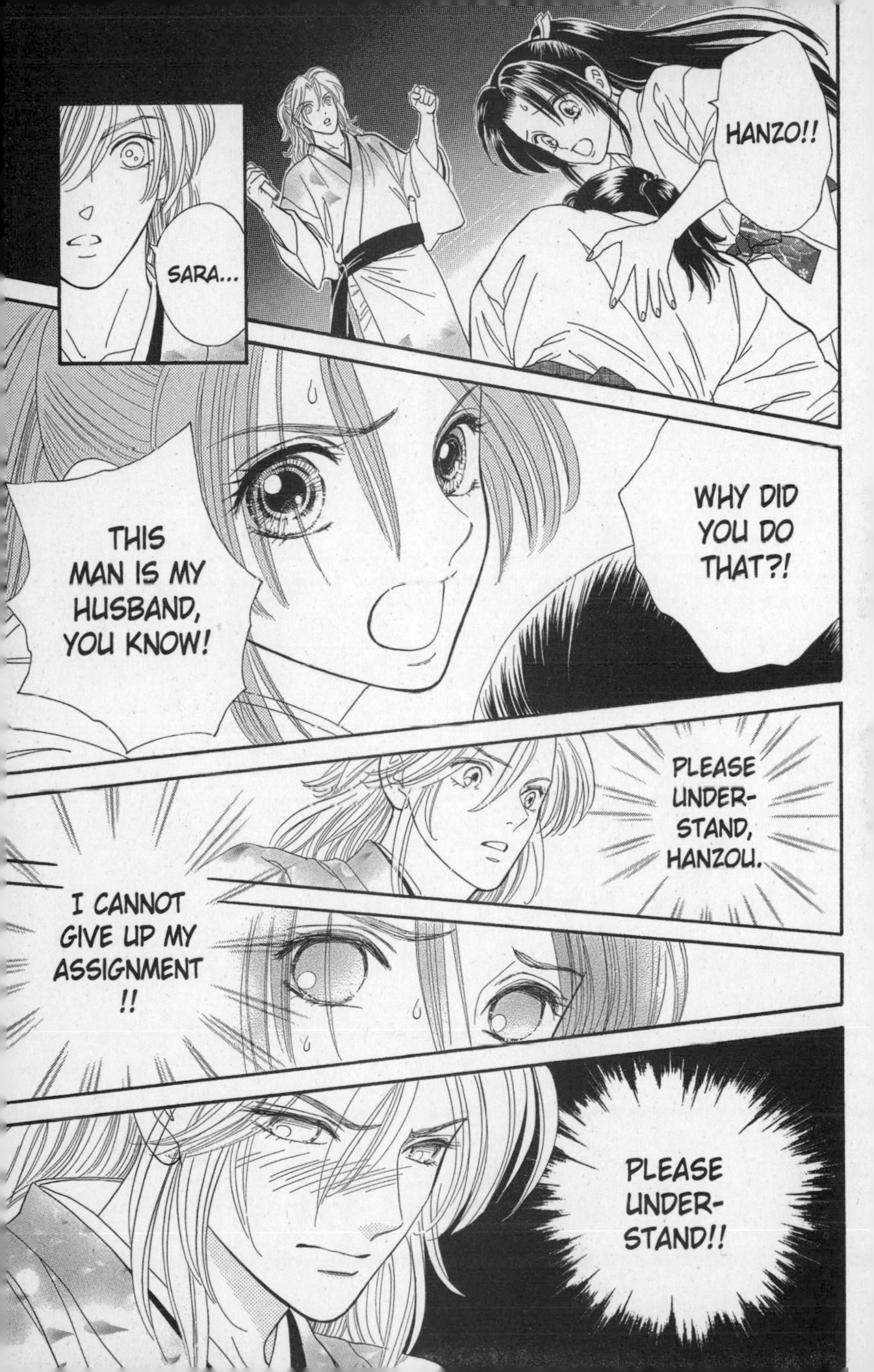
HANZO!!
SARA...
WHY DID YOU DO THAT?!
THIS MAN IS MY HUSBAND, YOU KNOW!
PLEASE UNDER-STAND, HANZOU.
I CANNOT GIVE UP MY ASSIGNMENT !!
PLEASE UNDER-STAND!!

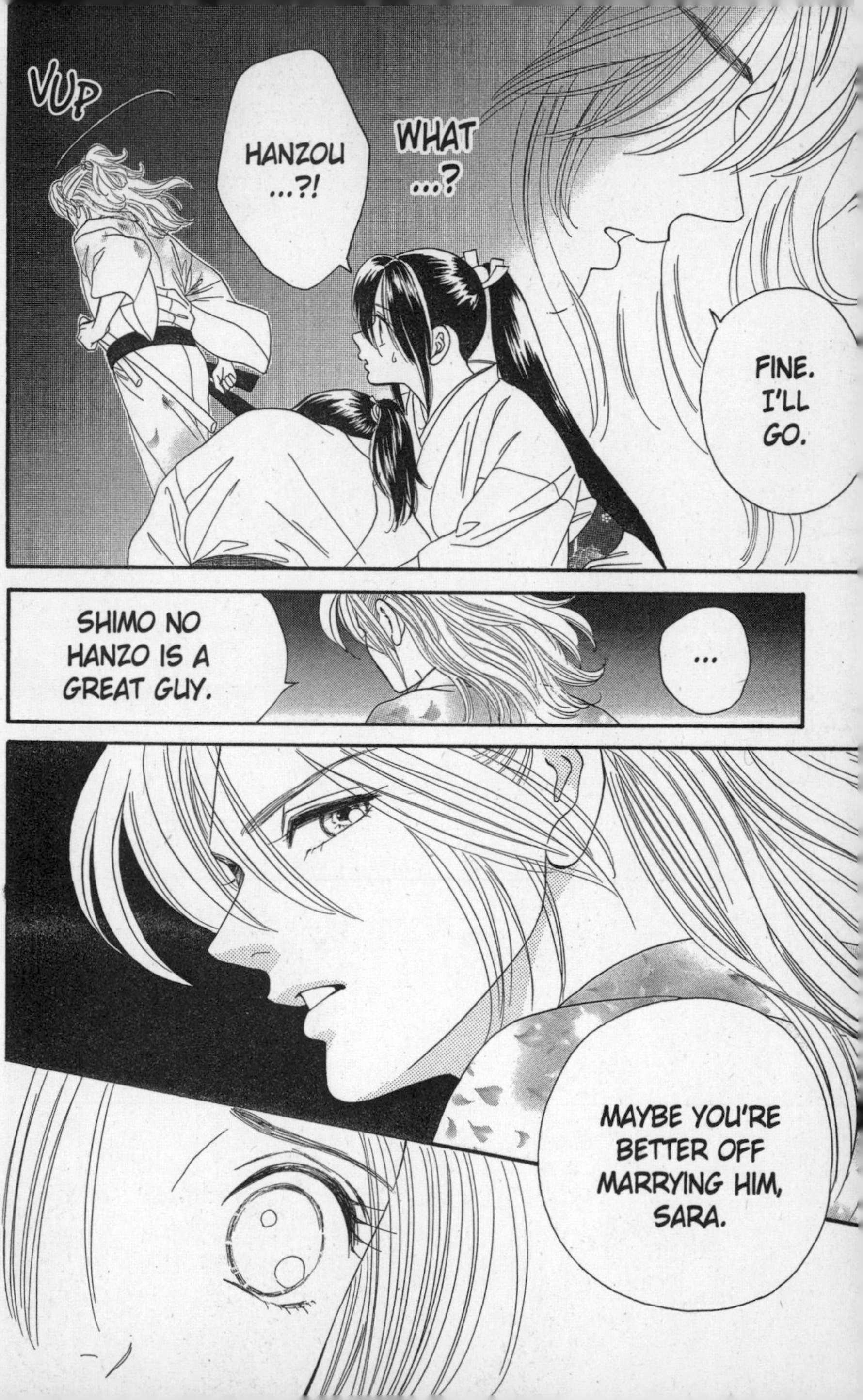
FINE. I'LL GO.
WHAT ...?
HANZOU ...?!
VUP
...
SHIMO NO HANZO IS A GREAT GUY.
MAYBE YOU'RE BETTER OFF MARRYING HIM, SARA.

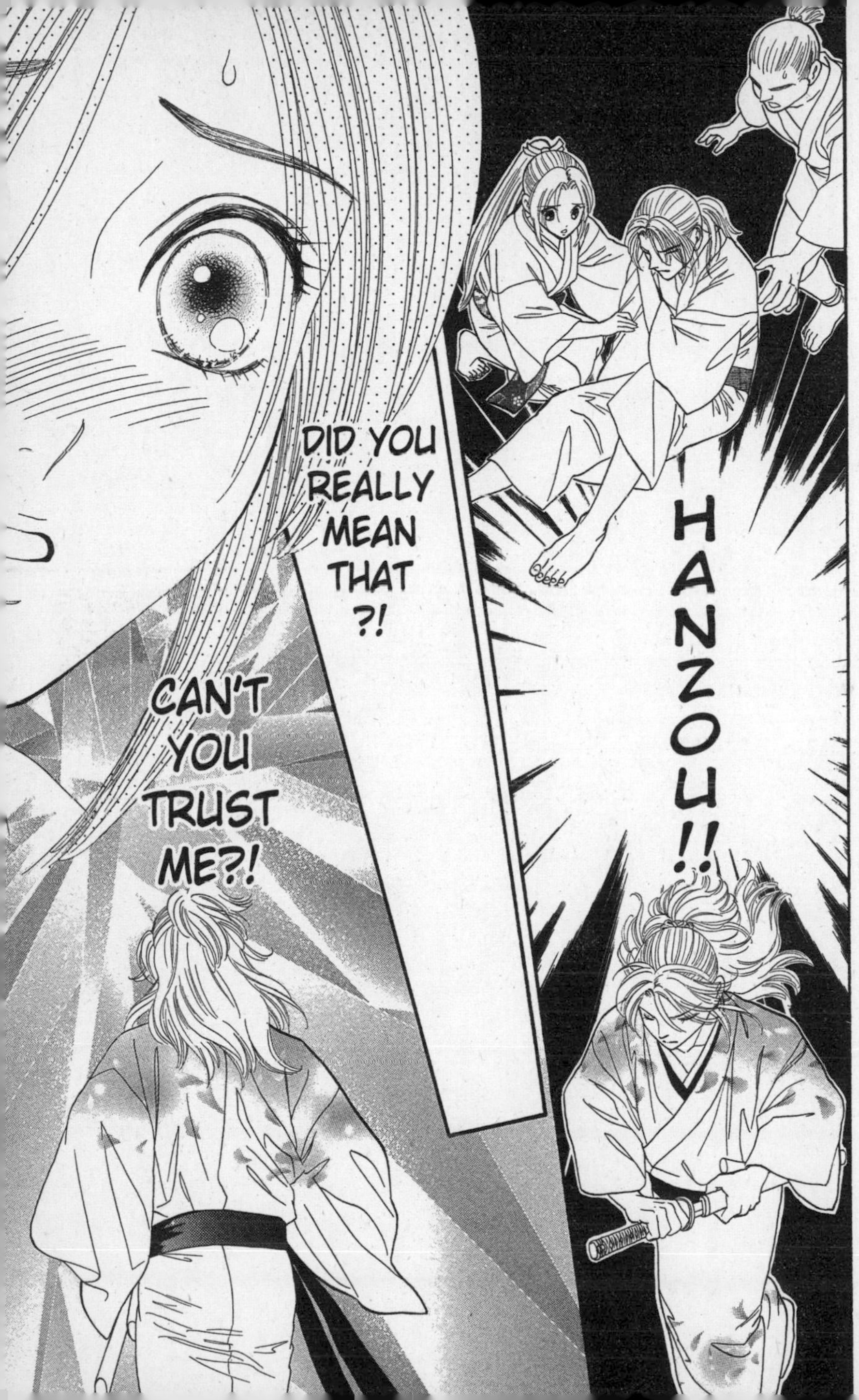
HANZOU!!
DID YOU REALLY MEAN THAT?!
CAN'T YOU TRUST ME?!

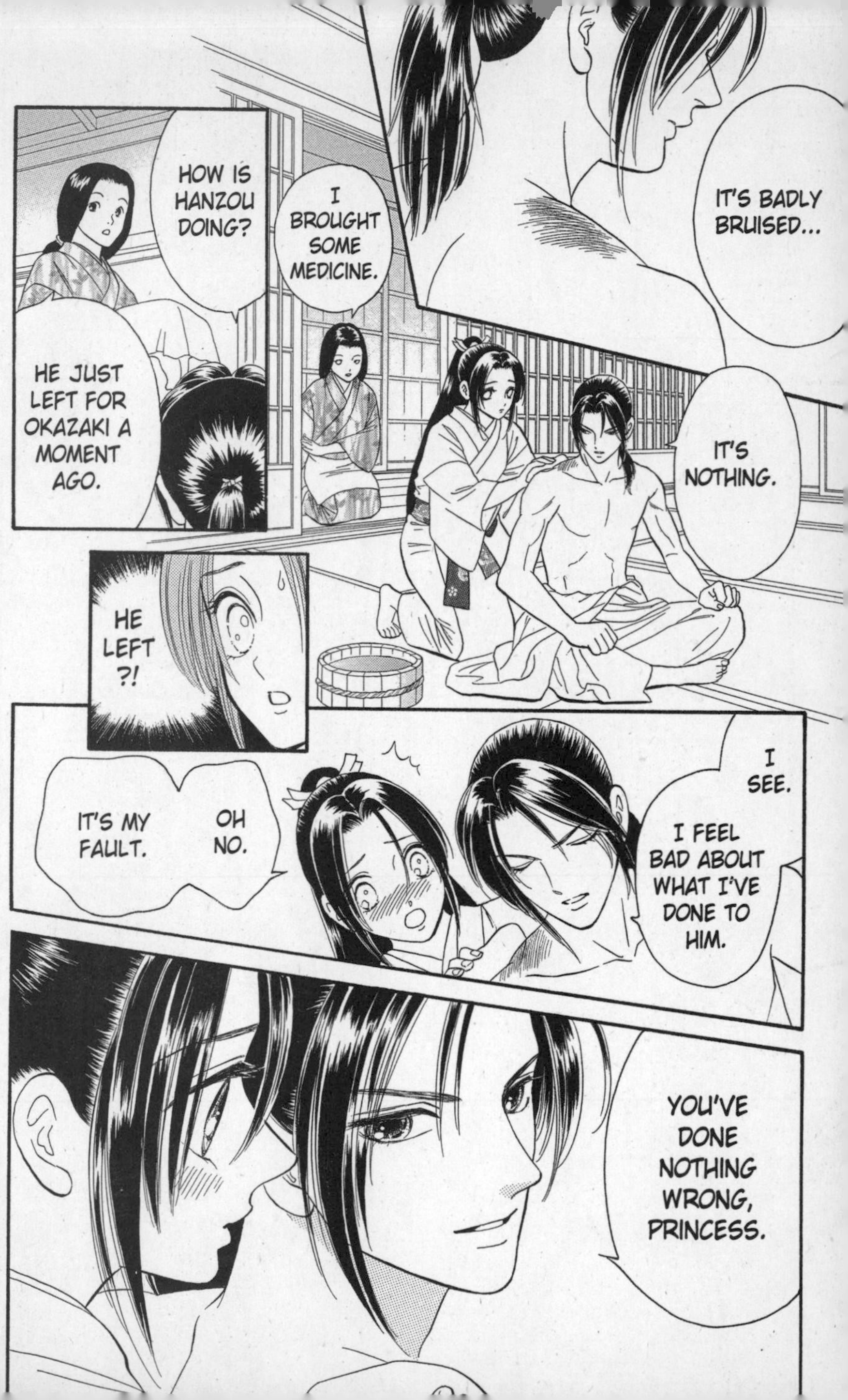
IT'S BADLY BRUISED...
IT'S NOTHING.
I BROUGHT SOME MEDICINE.
HOW IS HANZOU DOING?
HE JUST LEFT FOR OKAZAKI A MOMENT AGO.
HE LEFT?!
I SEE.
I FEEL BAD ABOUT WHAT I'VE DONE TO HIM.
OH NO.
IT'S MY FAULT.
YOU'VE DONE NOTHING WRONG, PRINCESS.

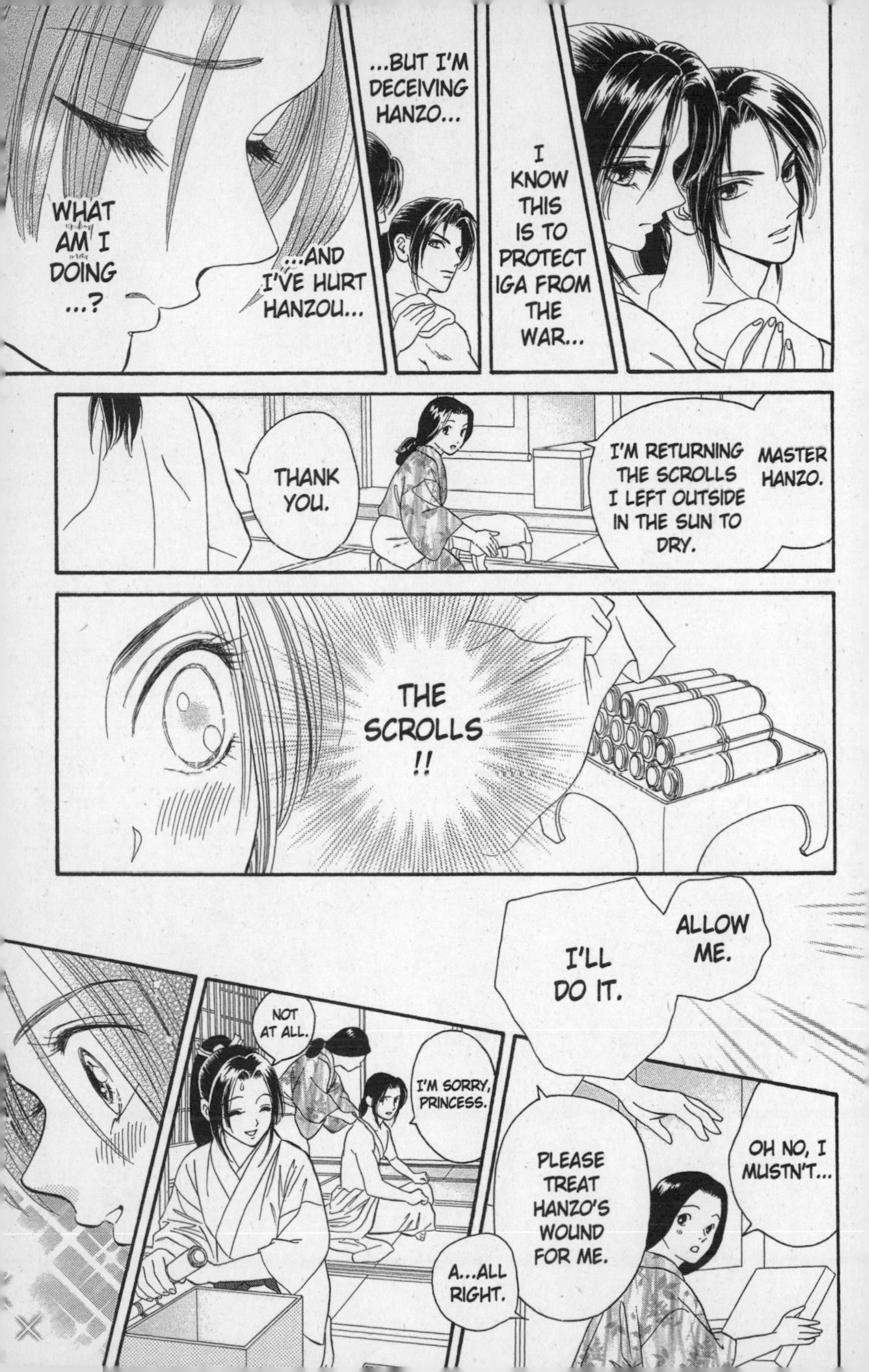
I KNOW THIS IS TO PROTECT IGA FROM THE WAR...
...BUT I'M DECEIVING HANZO...
...AND I'VE HURT HANZOU...
WHAT AM I DOING ...?
MASTER HANZO.
I'M RETURNING THE SCROLLS I LEFT OUTSIDE IN THE SUN TO DRY.
THANK YOU.
THE SCROLLS !!
ALLOW ME.
I'LL DO IT.
OH NO, I MUSTN'T...
PLEASE TREAT HANZO'S WOUND FOR ME.
A...ALL RIGHT.
I'M SORRY, PRINCESS.
NOT AT ALL.

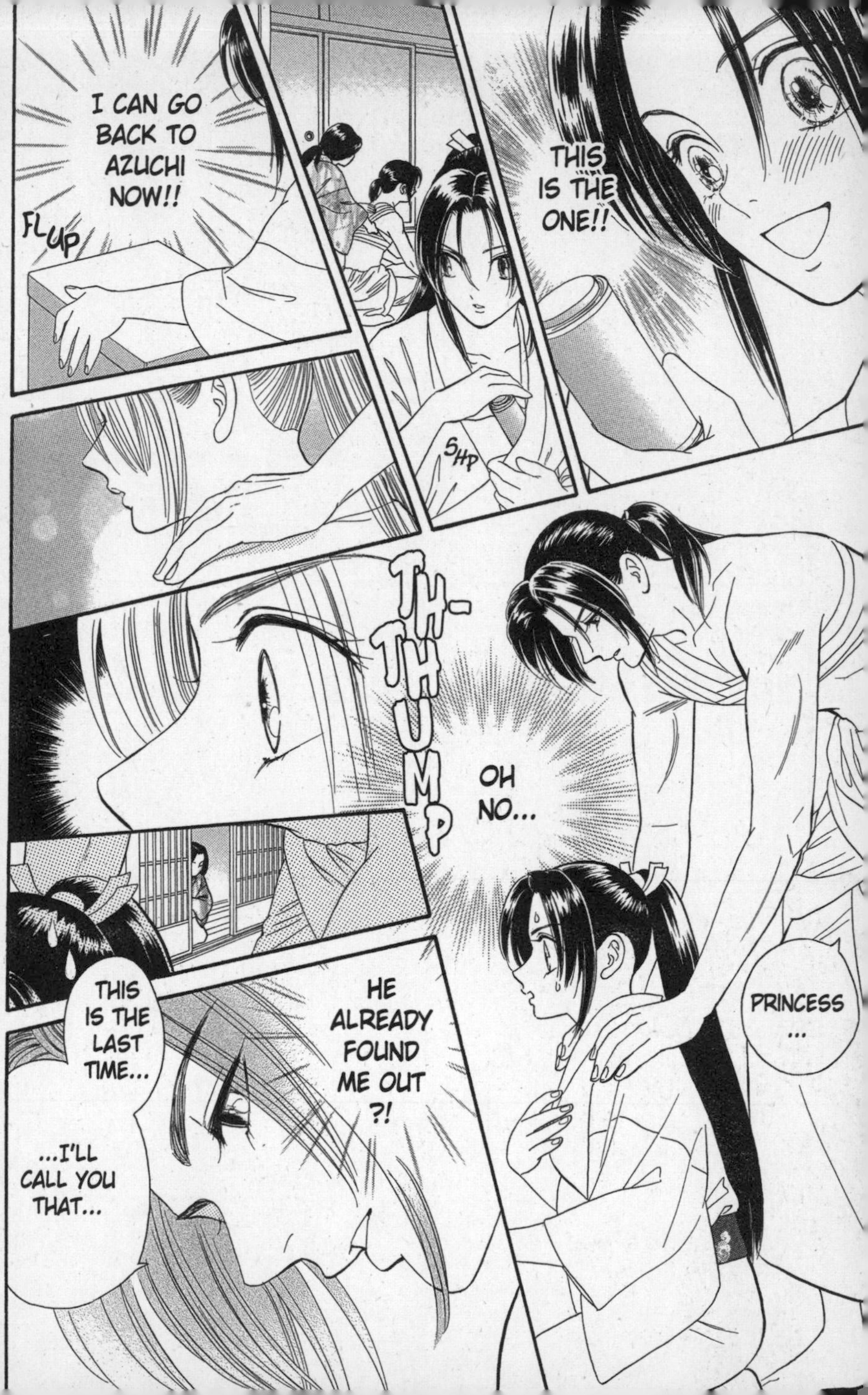
THIS IS THE ONE!!
SHP
I CAN GO BACK TO AZUCHI NOW!!
FLUP
PRINCESS ...
TH-THUMP
OH NO...
HE ALREADY FOUND ME OUT ?!
THIS IS THE LAST TIME...
...I'LL CALL YOU THAT...

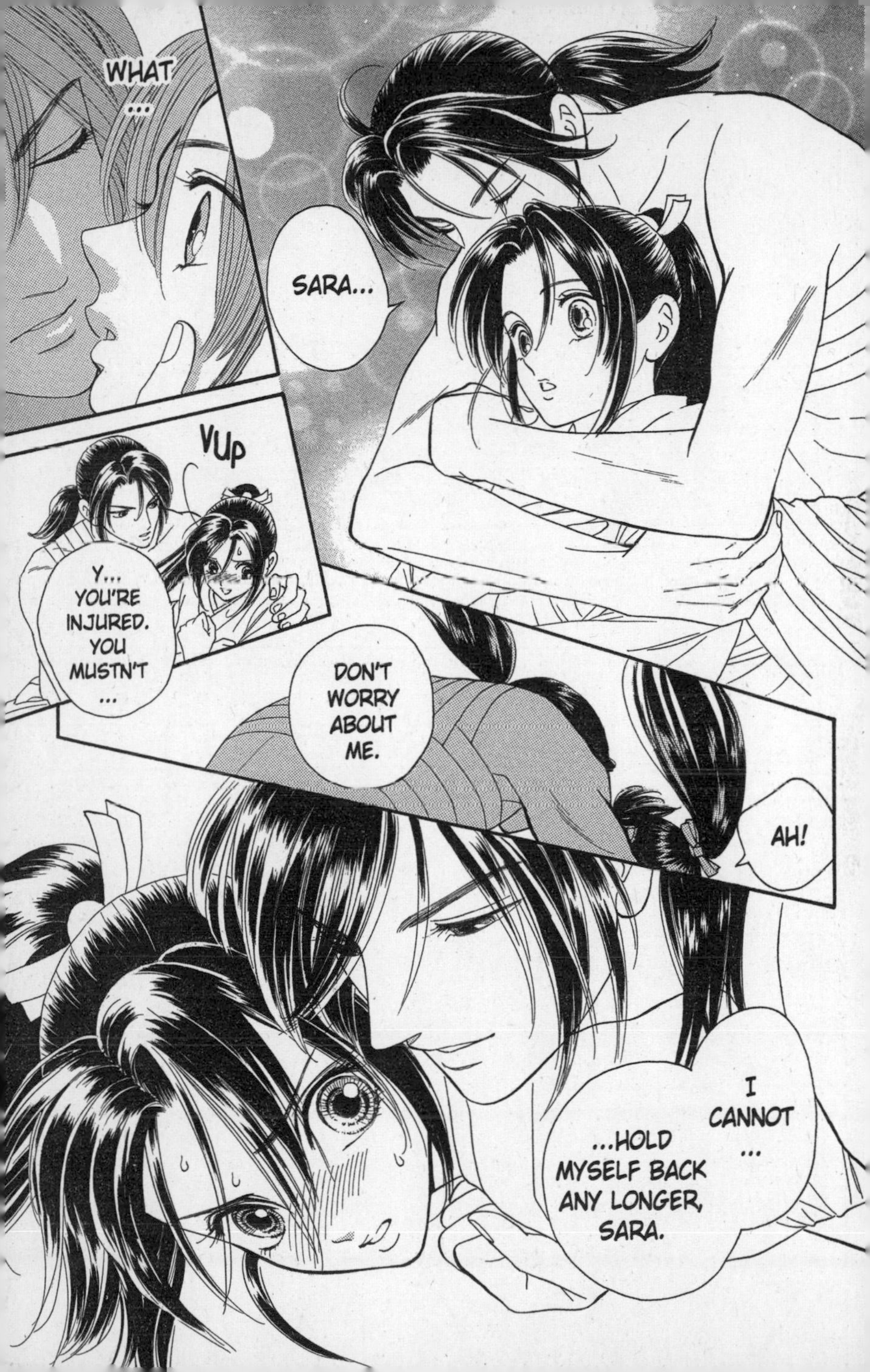
SARA...
WHAT ...
VUP
Y... YOU'RE INJURED. YOU MUSTN'T ...
DON'T WORRY ABOUT ME.
AH!
I CANNOT ...
...HOLD MYSELF BACK ANY LONGER, SARA.

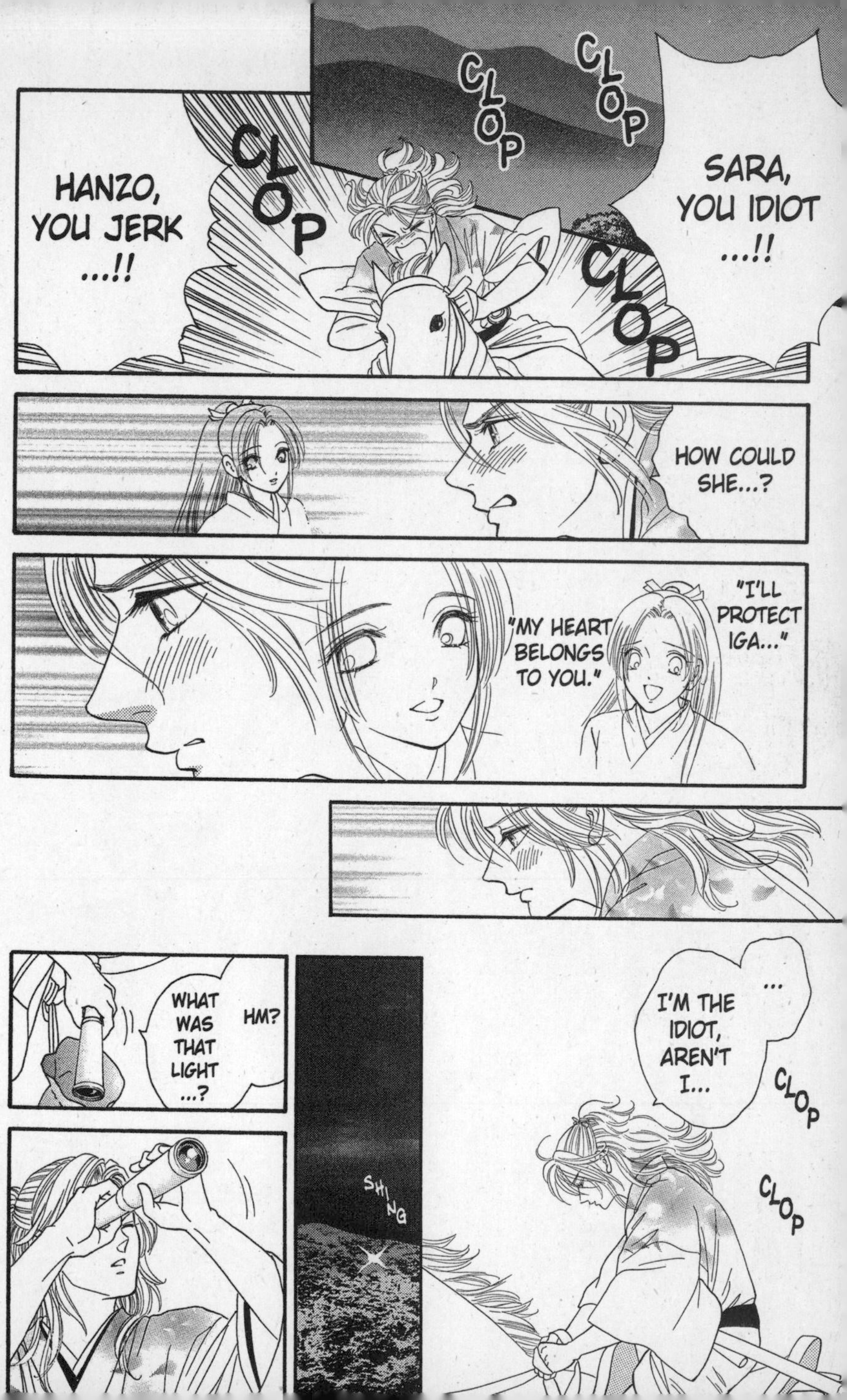

CLOP
CLOP
SARA, YOU IDIOT ...!!
CLOP
CLOP
HANZO, YOU JERK ...!!
CLOP
HOW COULD SHE...?
"I'LL PROTECT IGA..."
"MY HEART BELONGS TO YOU."
...
I'M THE IDIOT, AREN'T I...
CLOP
CLOP
SHING
HM?
WHAT WAS THAT LIGHT ...?

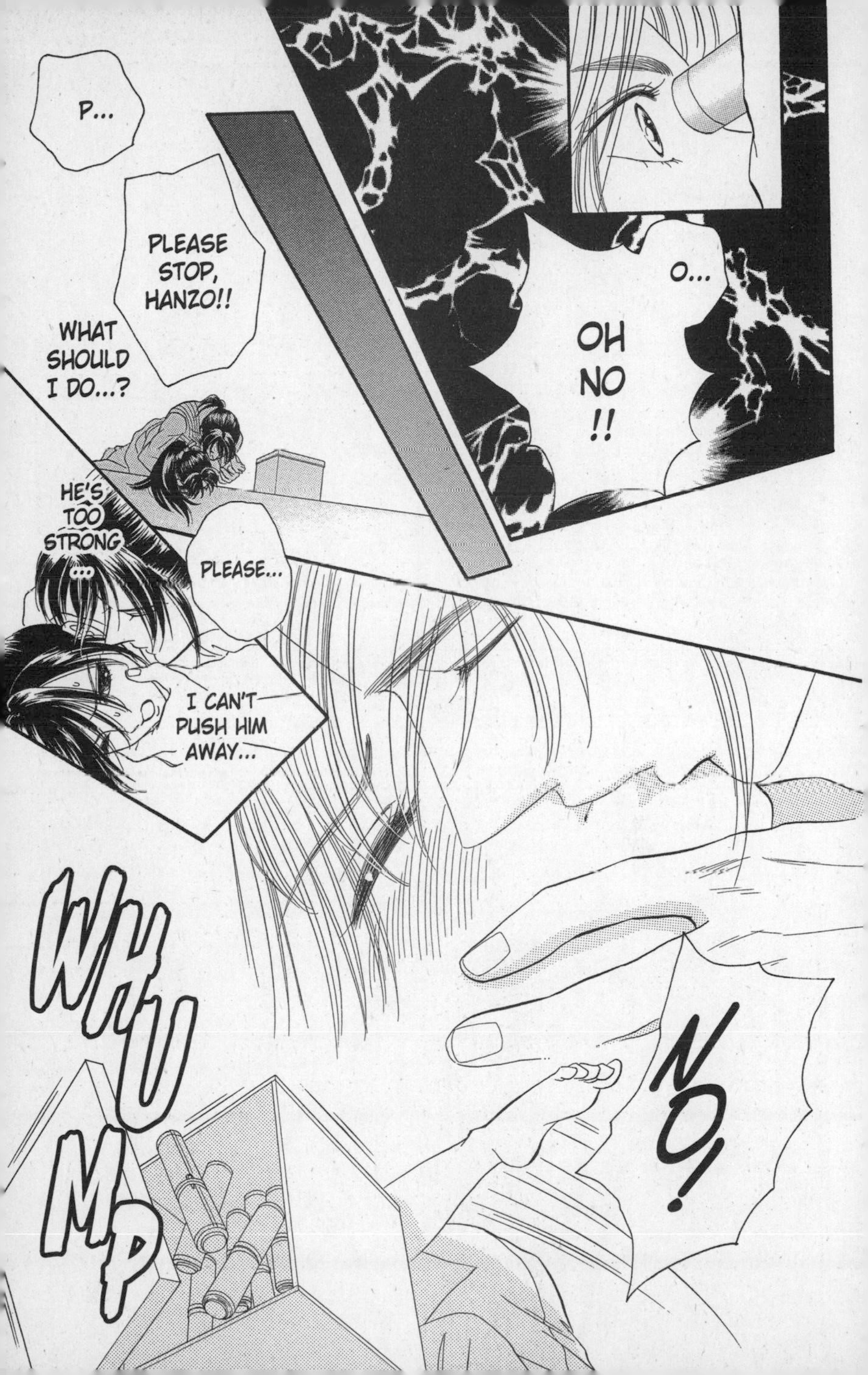
O...
OH NO!!
P...
PLEASE STOP, HANZO!!
WHAT SHOULD I DO...?
HE'S TOO STRONG...
PLEASE...
I CAN'T PUSH HIM AWAY...
NO!
WHUMP

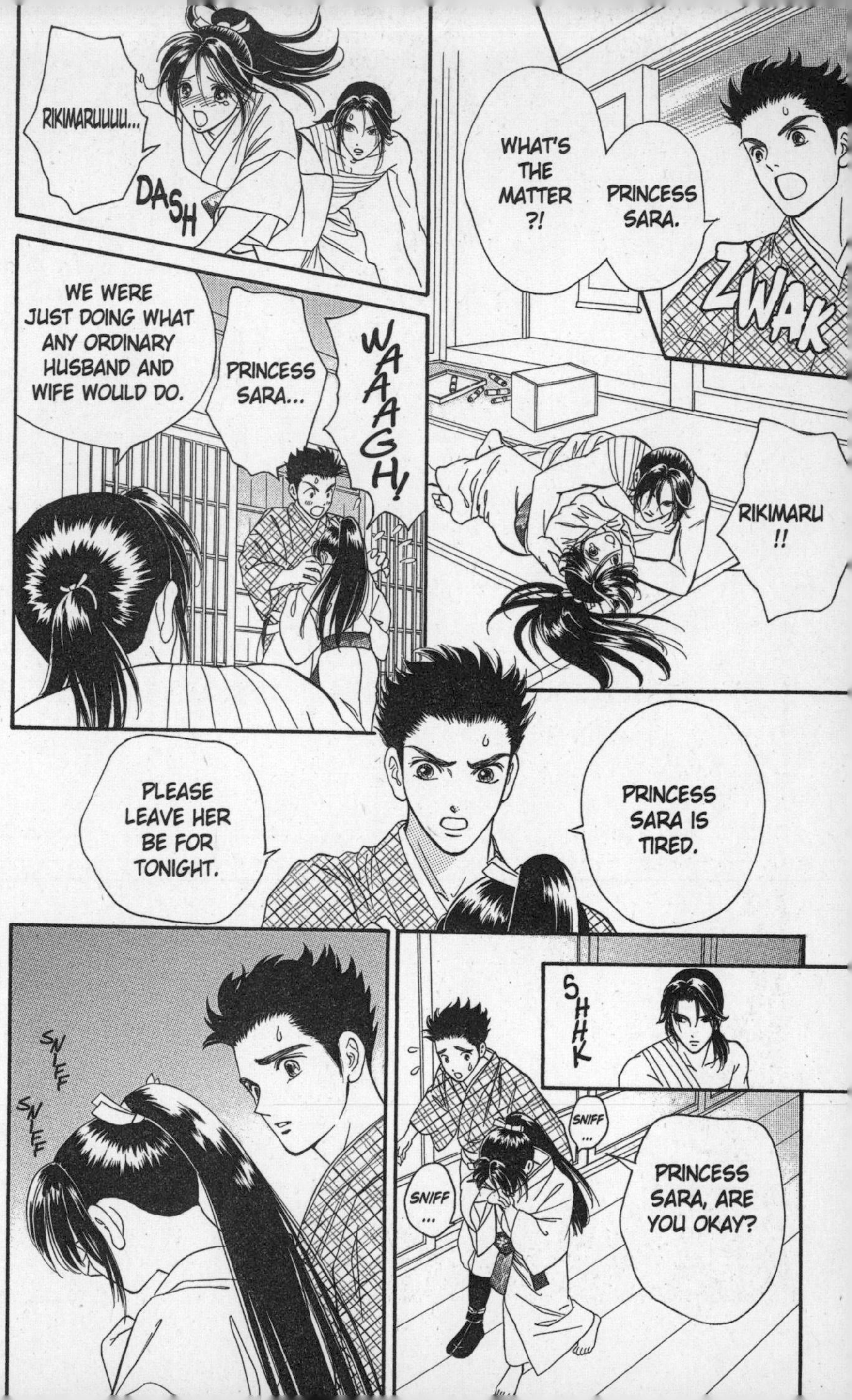
PRINCESS SARA.
WHAT'S THE MATTER ?!
ZWAK
RIKIMARU !!
RIKIMARUUUU...
DASH
WAAAGH!
PRINCESS SARA...
WE WERE JUST DOING WHAT ANY ORDINARY HUSBAND AND WIFE WOULD DO.
PRINCESS SARA IS TIRED.
PLEASE LEAVE HER BE FOR TONIGHT.
SHHK
PRINCESS SARA, ARE YOU OKAY?
SNIFF ...
SNIFF ...
SNIFF
SNIFF

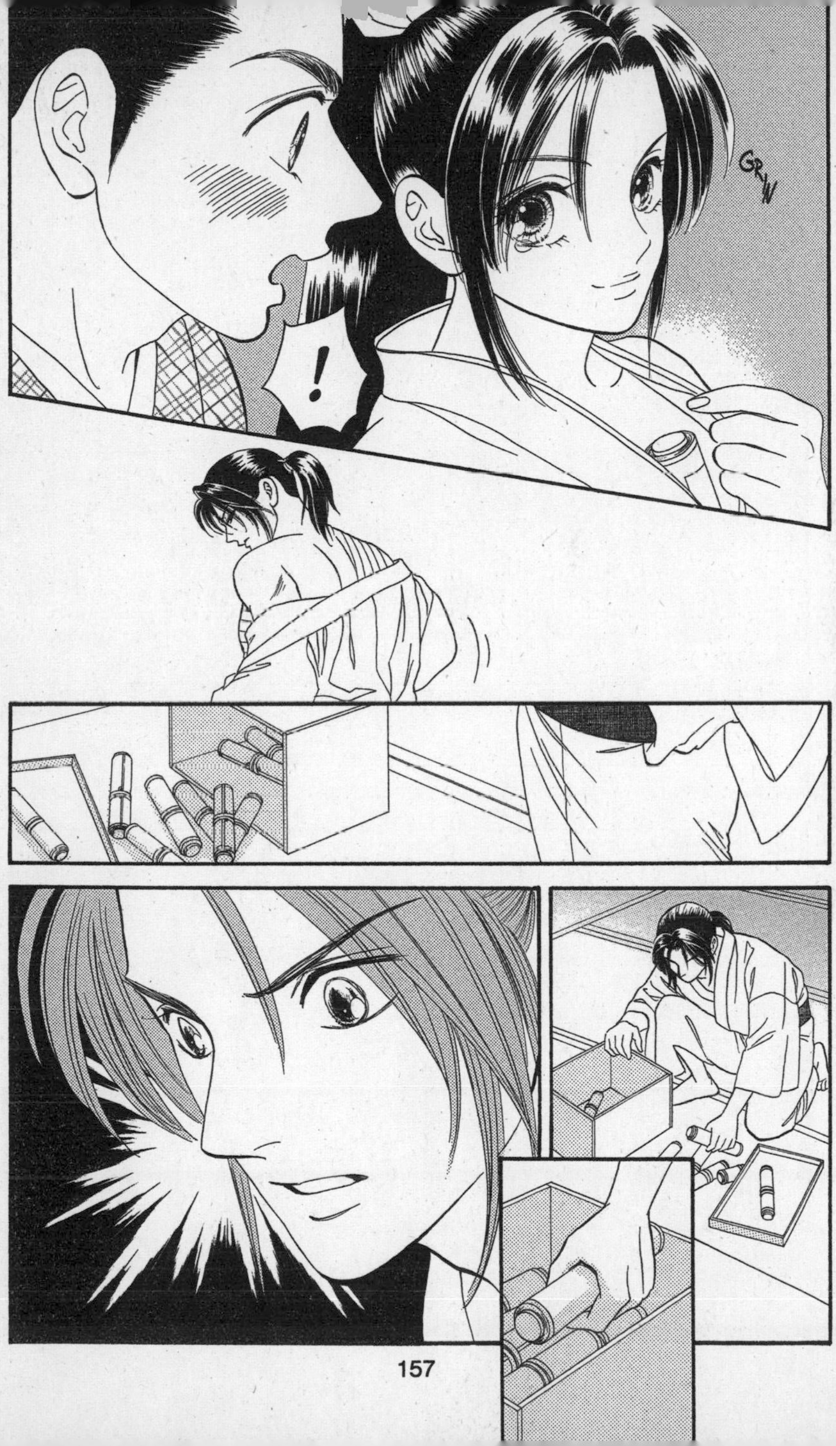
GR-W
!

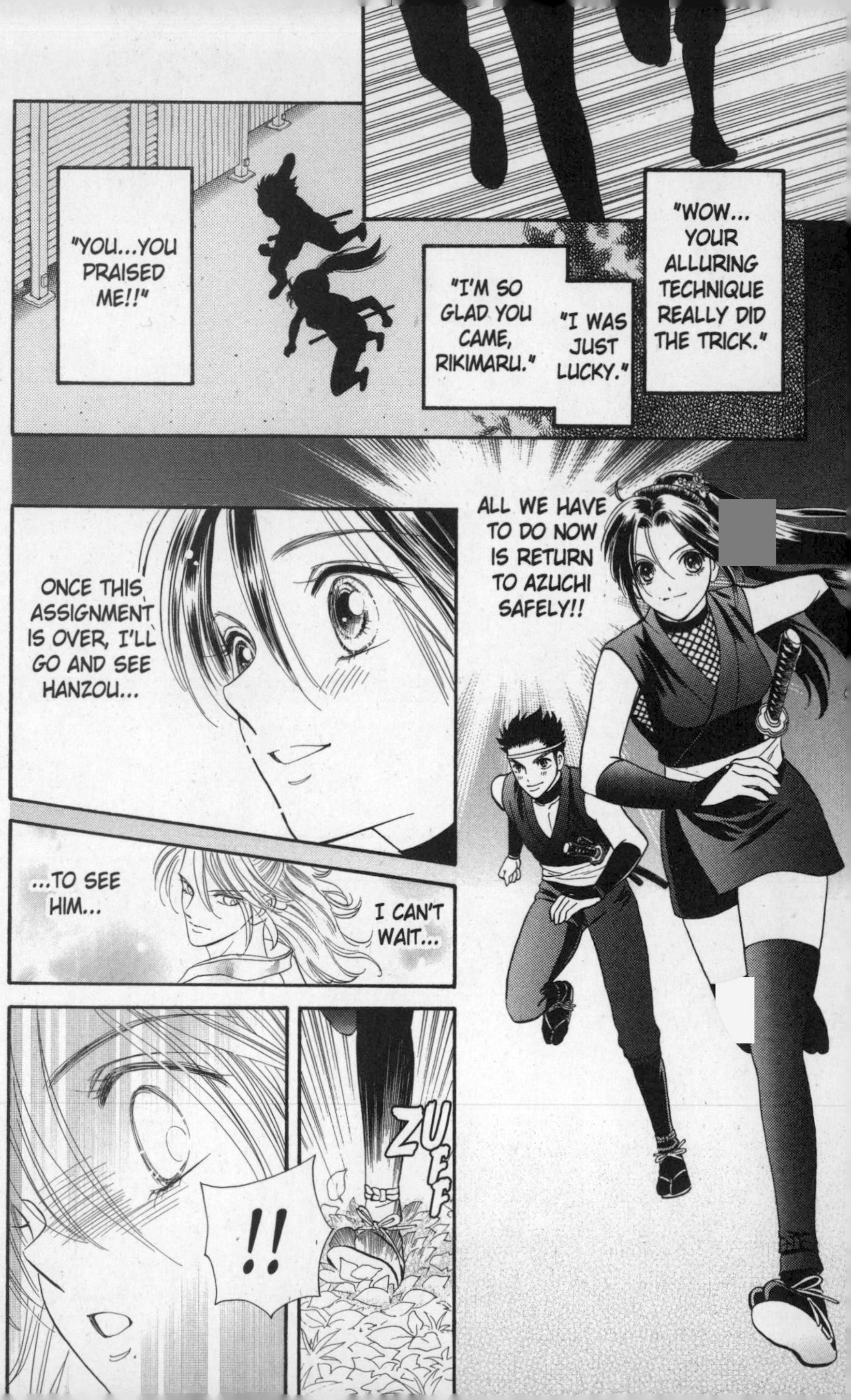
"WOW... YOUR ALLURING TECHNIQUE REALLY DID THE TRICK."
"I WAS JUST LUCKY."
"I'M SO GLAD YOU CAME, RIKIMARU."
"YOU...YOU PRAISED ME!!"
ALL WE HAVE TO DO NOW IS RETURN TO AZUCHI SAFELY!!
ONCE THIS ASSIGNMENT IS OVER, I'LL GO AND SEE HANZOU...
...TO SEE HIM...
I CAN'T WAIT...
ZUFF
!!

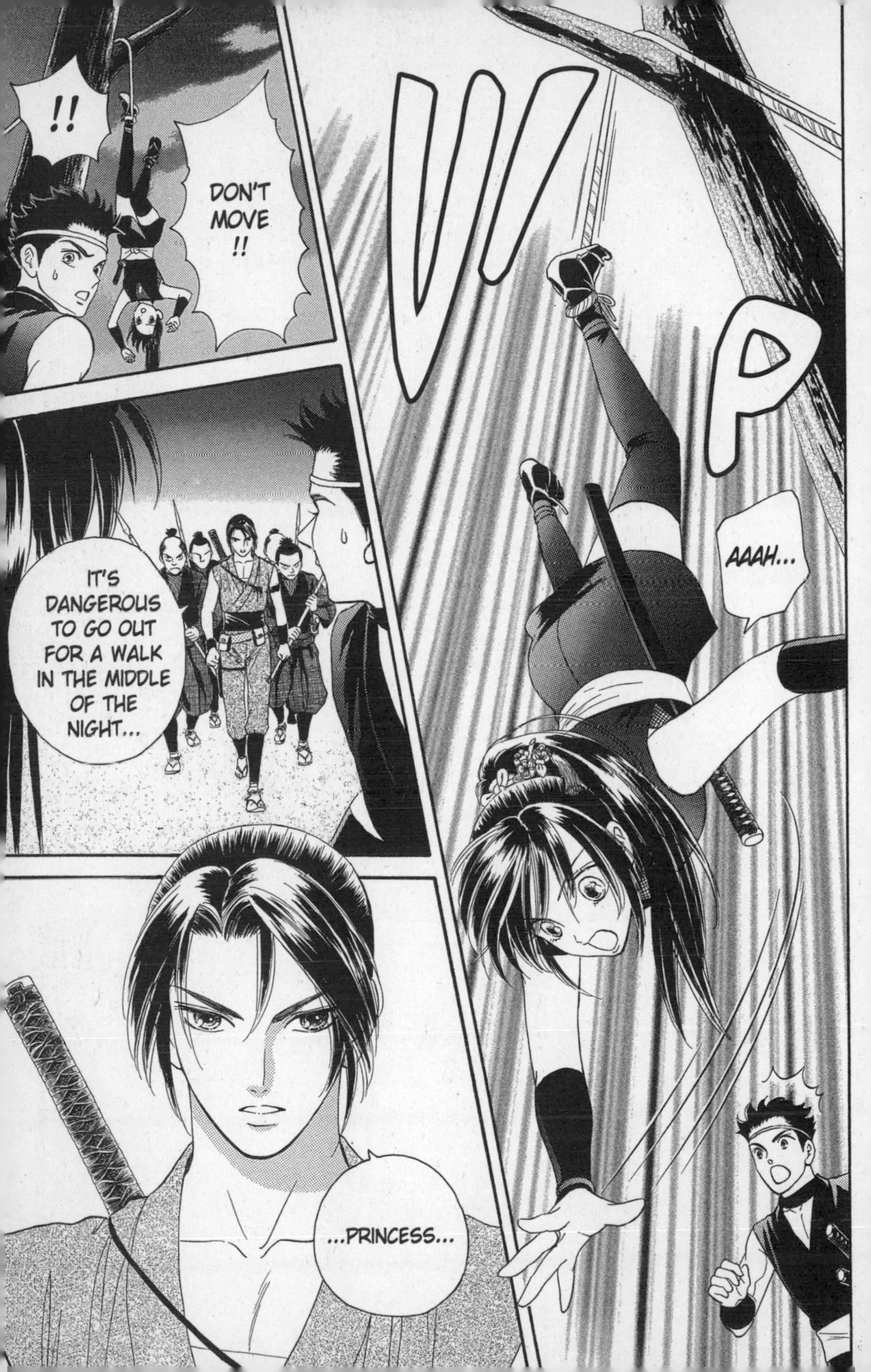
AAAH...
!!
DON'T MOVE !!
IT'S DANGEROUS TO GO OUT FOR A WALK IN THE MIDDLE OF THE NIGHT...
...PRINCESS...

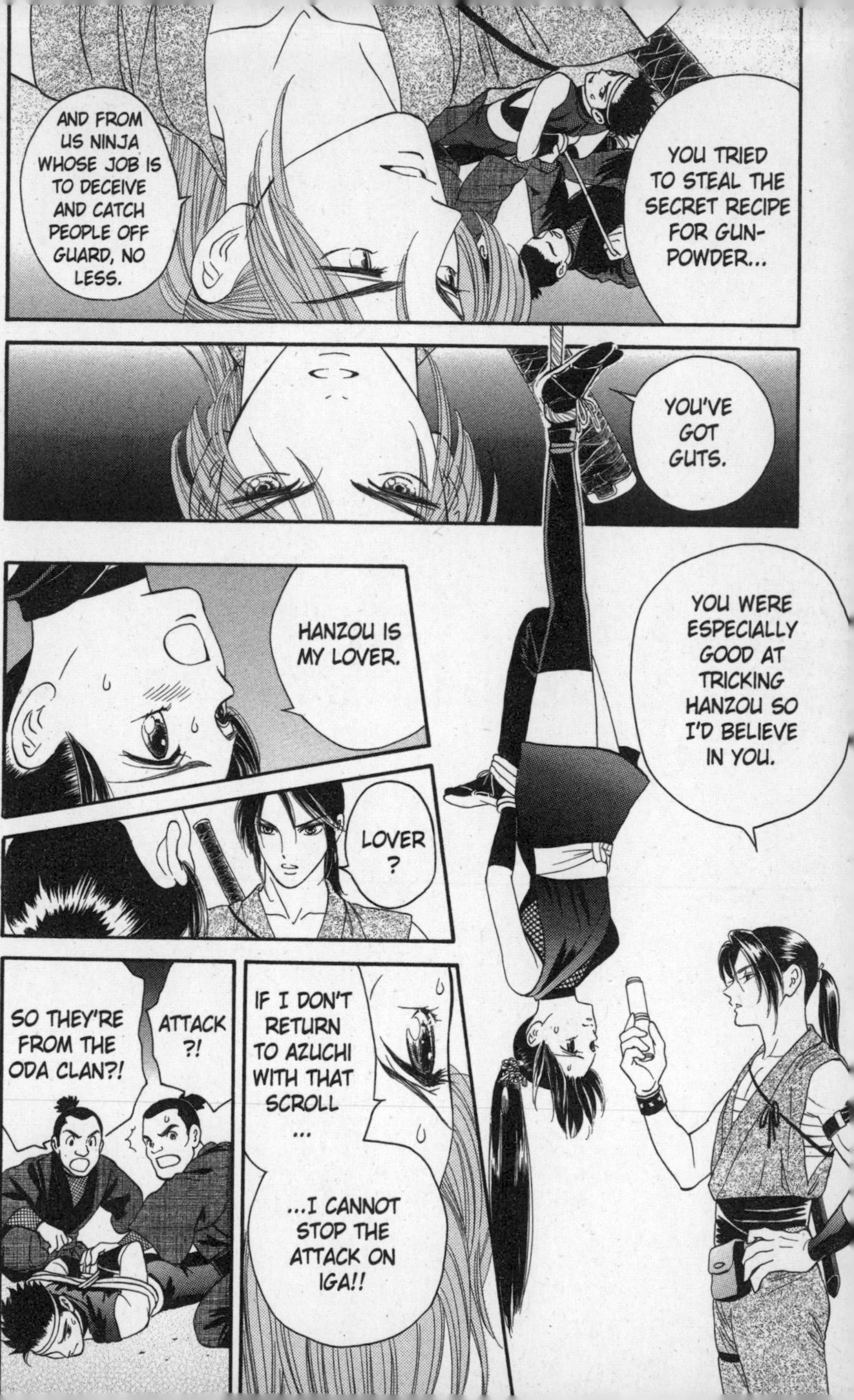
YOU TRIED TO STEAL THE SECRET RECIPE FOR GUN-POWDER...
AND FROM US NINJA WHOSE JOB IS TO DECEIVE AND CATCH PEOPLE OFF GUARD, NO LESS.
YOU'VE GOT GUTS.
YOU WERE ESPECIALLY GOOD AT TRICKING HANZOU SO I'D BELIEVE IN YOU.
HANZOU IS MY LOVER.
LOVER ?
IF I DON'T RETURN TO AZUCHI WITH THAT SCROLL ...
...I CANNOT STOP THE ATTACK ON IGA!!
ATTACK ?!
SO THEY'RE FROM THE ODA CLAN?!

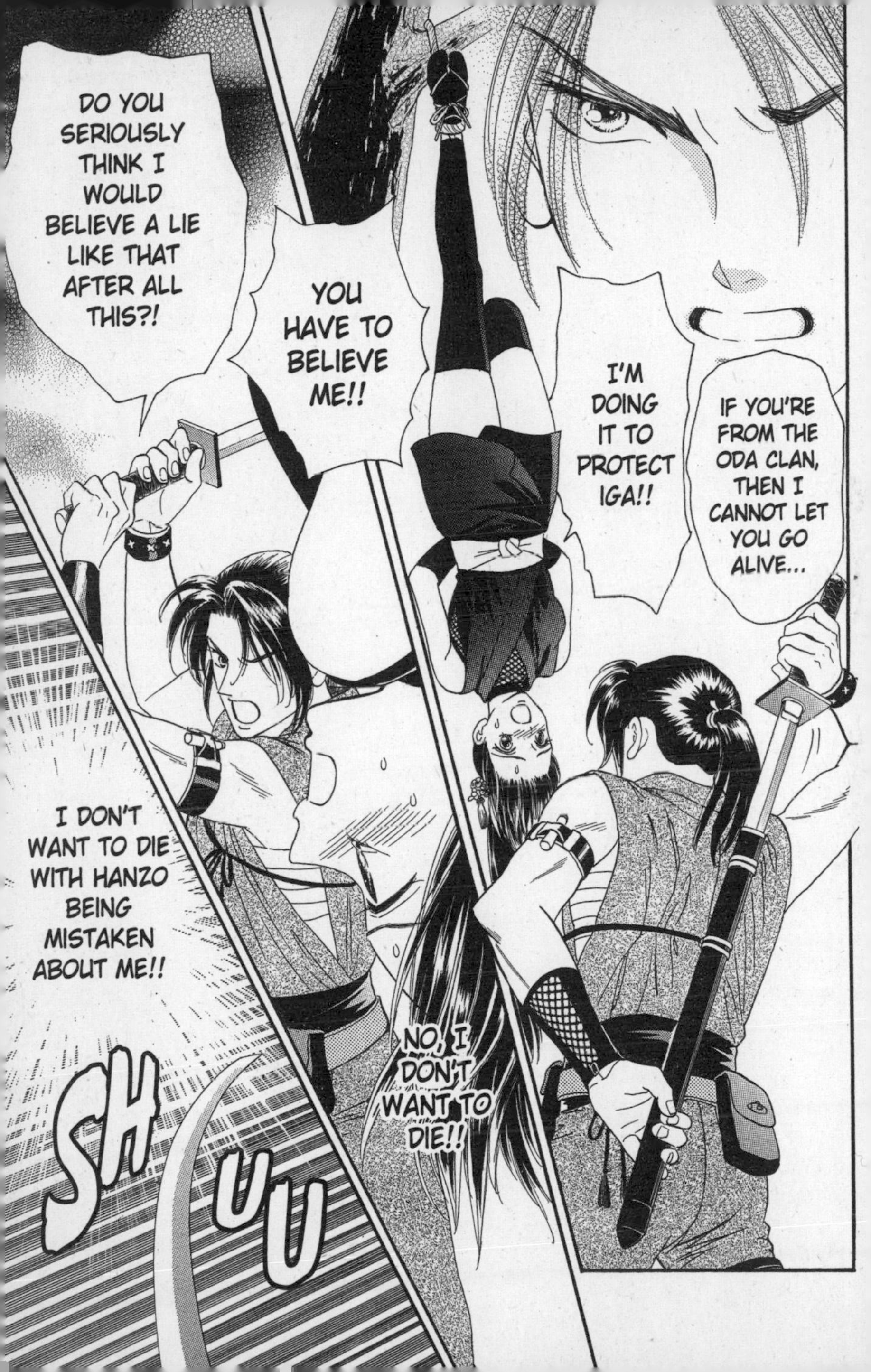
IF YOU'RE FROM THE ODA CLAN, THEN I CANNOT LET YOU GO ALIVE...
I'M DOING IT TO PROTECT IGA!!
YOU HAVE TO BELIEVE ME!!
NO, I DON'T WANT TO DIE!!
DO YOU SERIOUSLY THINK I WOULD BELIEVE A LIE LIKE THAT AFTER ALL THIS?!
I DON'T WANT TO DIE WITH HANZO BEING MISTAKEN ABOUT ME!!
SHUUU

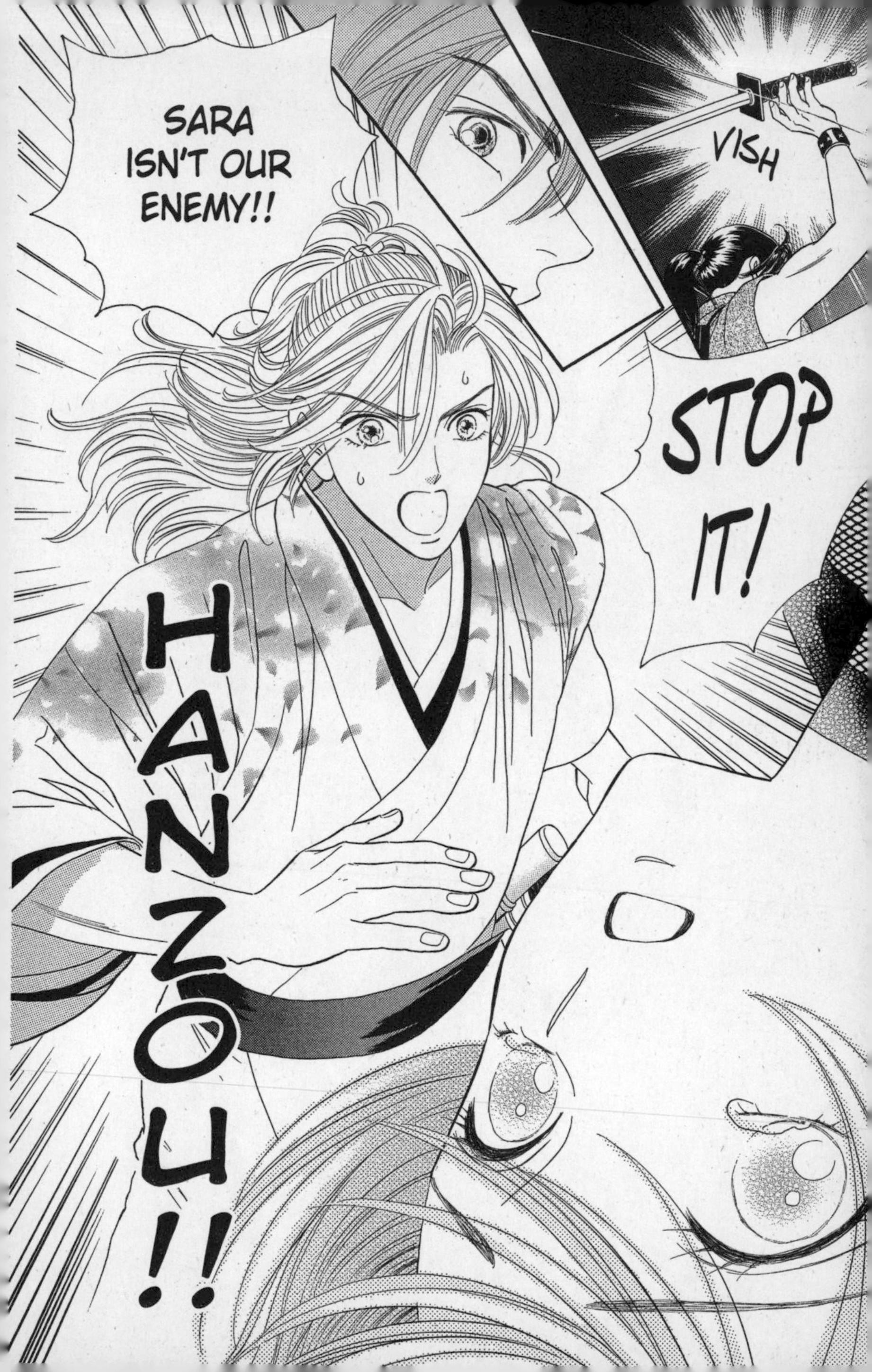
VISH
STOP IT!
HANZOU!!
SARA ISN'T OUR ENEMY!!

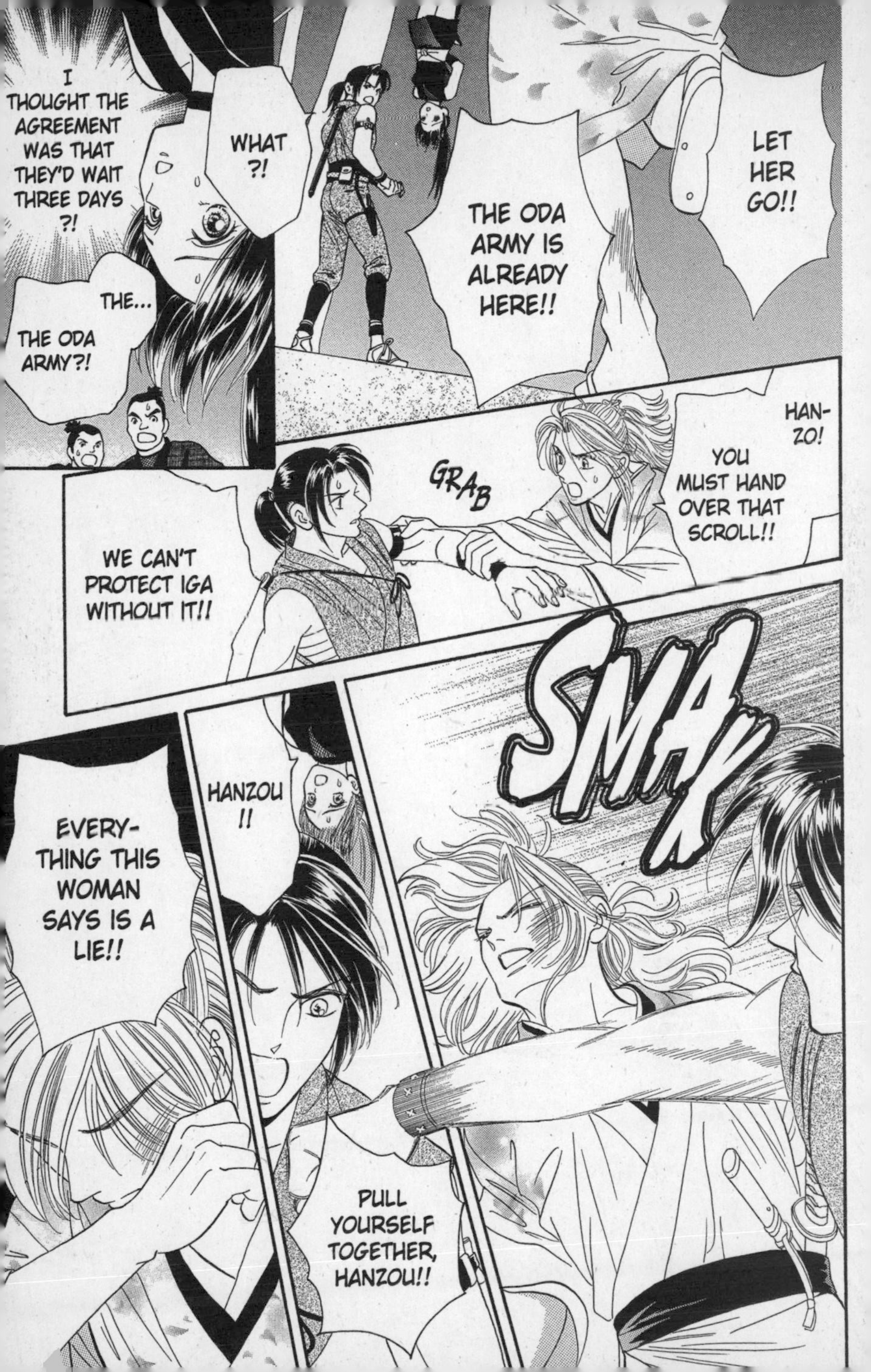
LET HER GO!!
THE ODA ARMY IS ALREADY HERE!!
WHAT ?!
I THOUGHT THE AGREEMENT WAS THAT THEY'D WAIT THREE DAYS ?!
THE...
THE ODA ARMY?!
HAN-ZO!
YOU MUST HAND OVER THAT SCROLL!!
GRAB
WE CAN'T PROTECT IGA WITHOUT IT!!
SMA
HANZOU !!
PULL YOURSELF TOGETHER, HANZOU!!
EVERY-THING THIS WOMAN SAYS IS A LIE!!

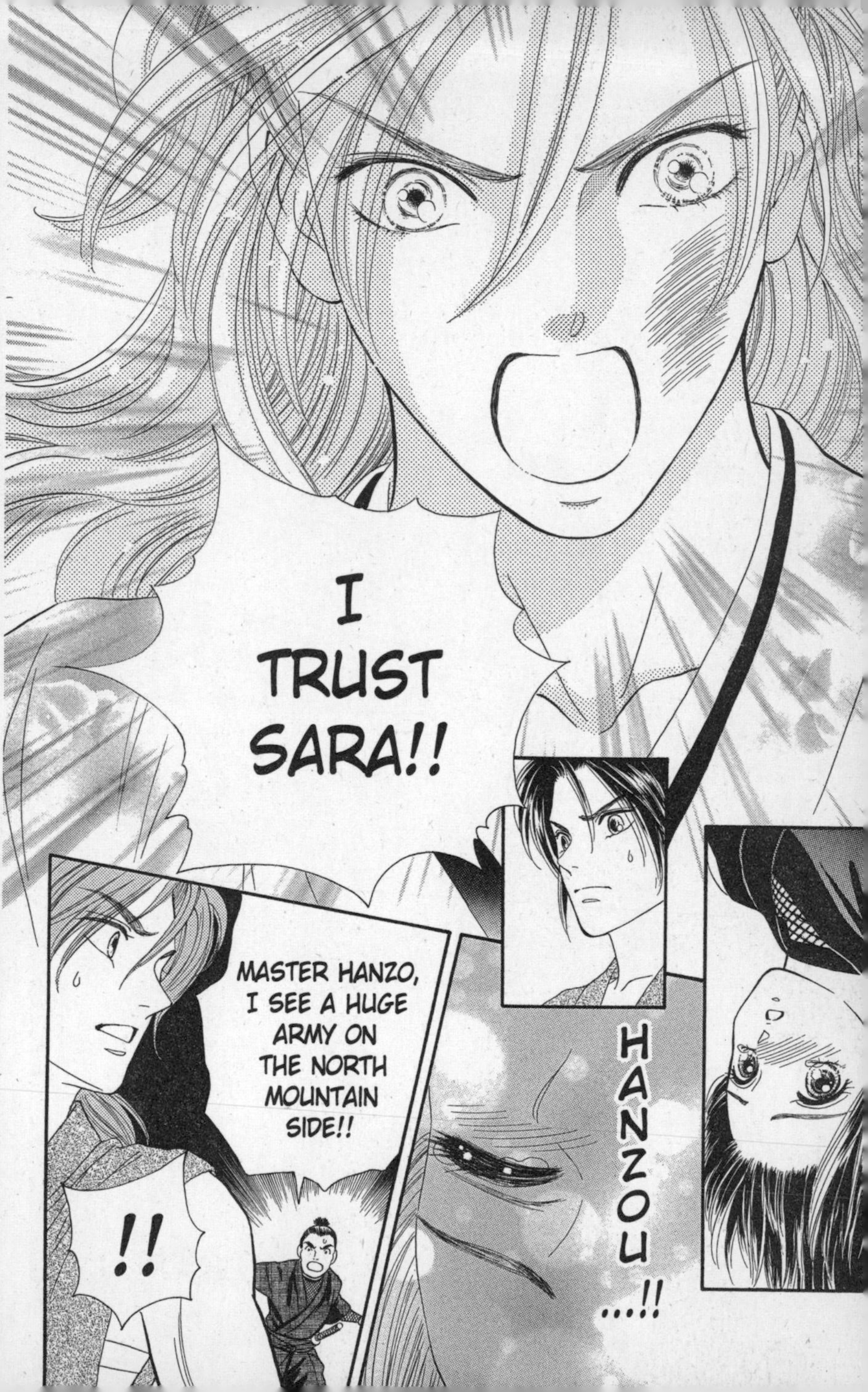

I TRUST SARA!!
HANZOU...!!
MASTER HANZO, I SEE A HUGE ARMY ON THE NORTH MOUNTAIN SIDE!!
!!

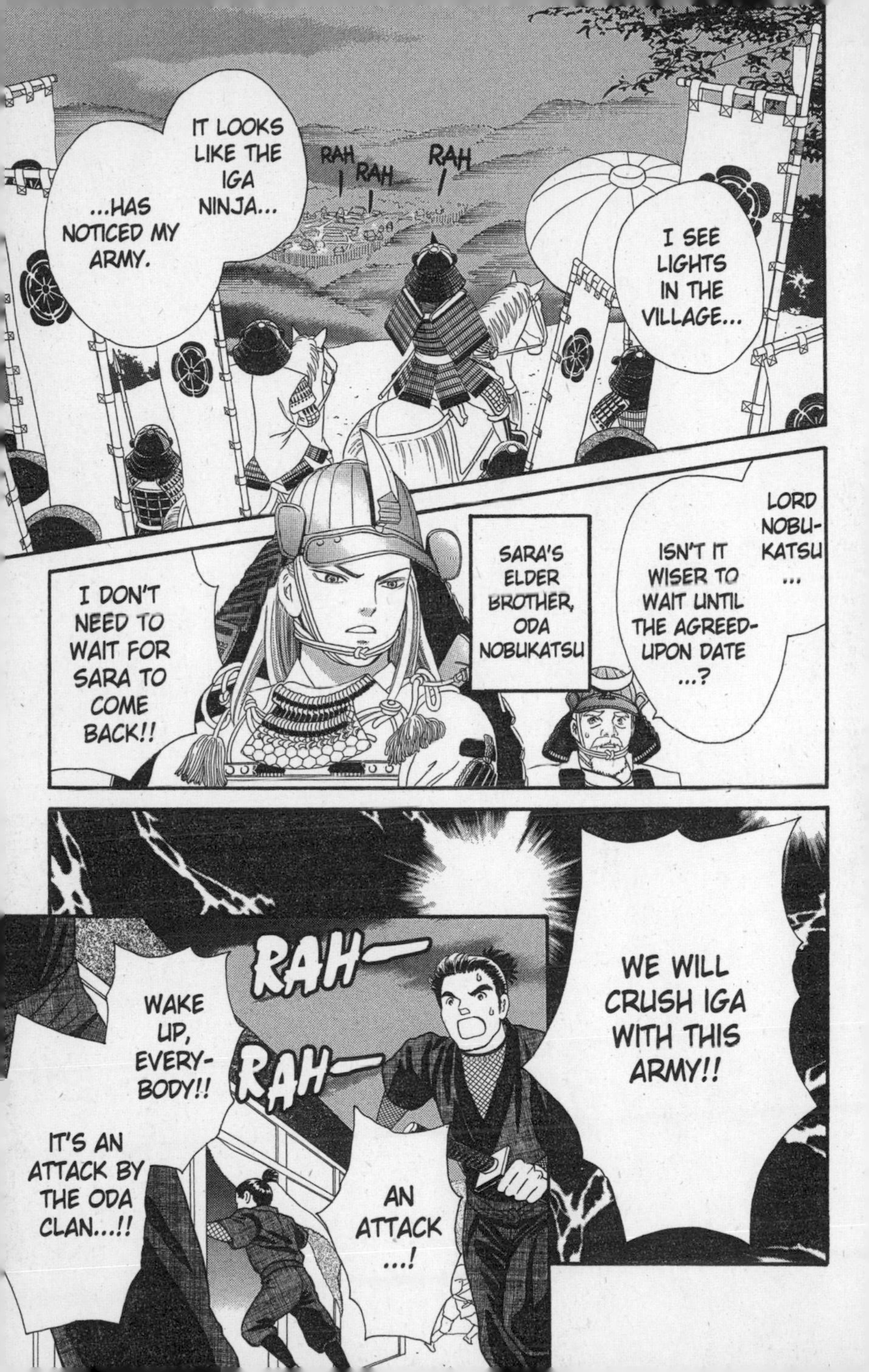
I SEE LIGHTS IN THE VILLAGE...
RAH
RAH
RAH
IT LOOKS LIKE THE IGA NINJA...
...HAS NOTICED MY ARMY.
LORD NOBUKATSU...
ISN'T IT WISER TO WAIT UNTIL THE AGREED-UPON DATE...?
SARA'S ELDER BROTHER, ODA NOBUKATSU
I DON'T NEED TO WAIT FOR SARA TO COME BACK!!
WE WILL CRUSH IGA WITH THIS ARMY!!
RAH—
RAH—
WAKE UP, EVERYBODY!!
AN ATTACK...!
IT'S AN ATTACK BY THE ODA CLAN...!!

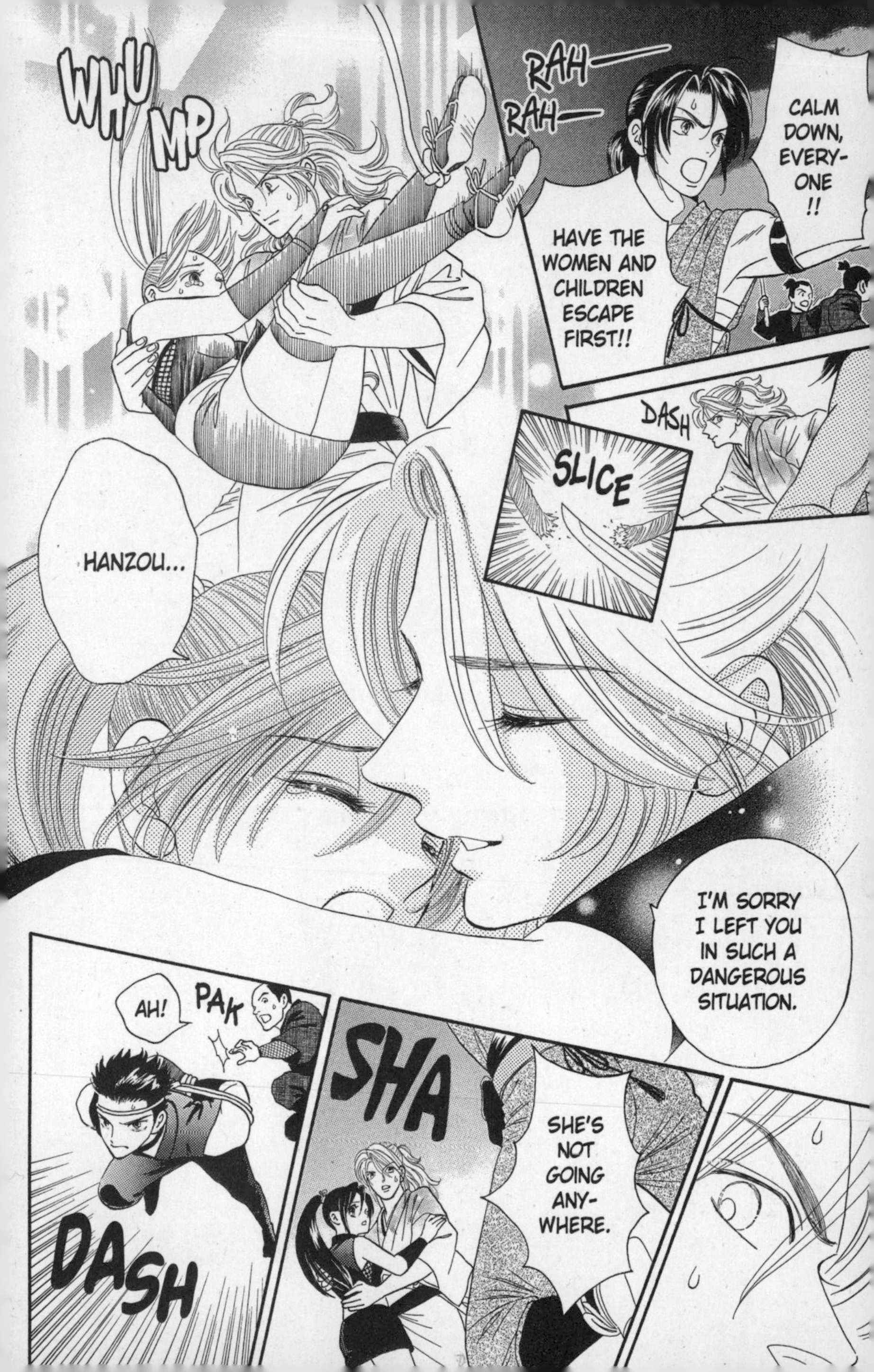
CALM DOWN, EVERY-ONE !!
RAH—
RAH—
HAVE THE WOMEN AND CHILDREN ESCAPE FIRST!!
DASH
SLICE
WHUMP
I'M SORRY I LEFT YOU IN SUCH A DANGEROUS SITUATION.
HANZOU...
SHA
SHE'S NOT GOING ANY-WHERE.
PAK
AH!
DASH

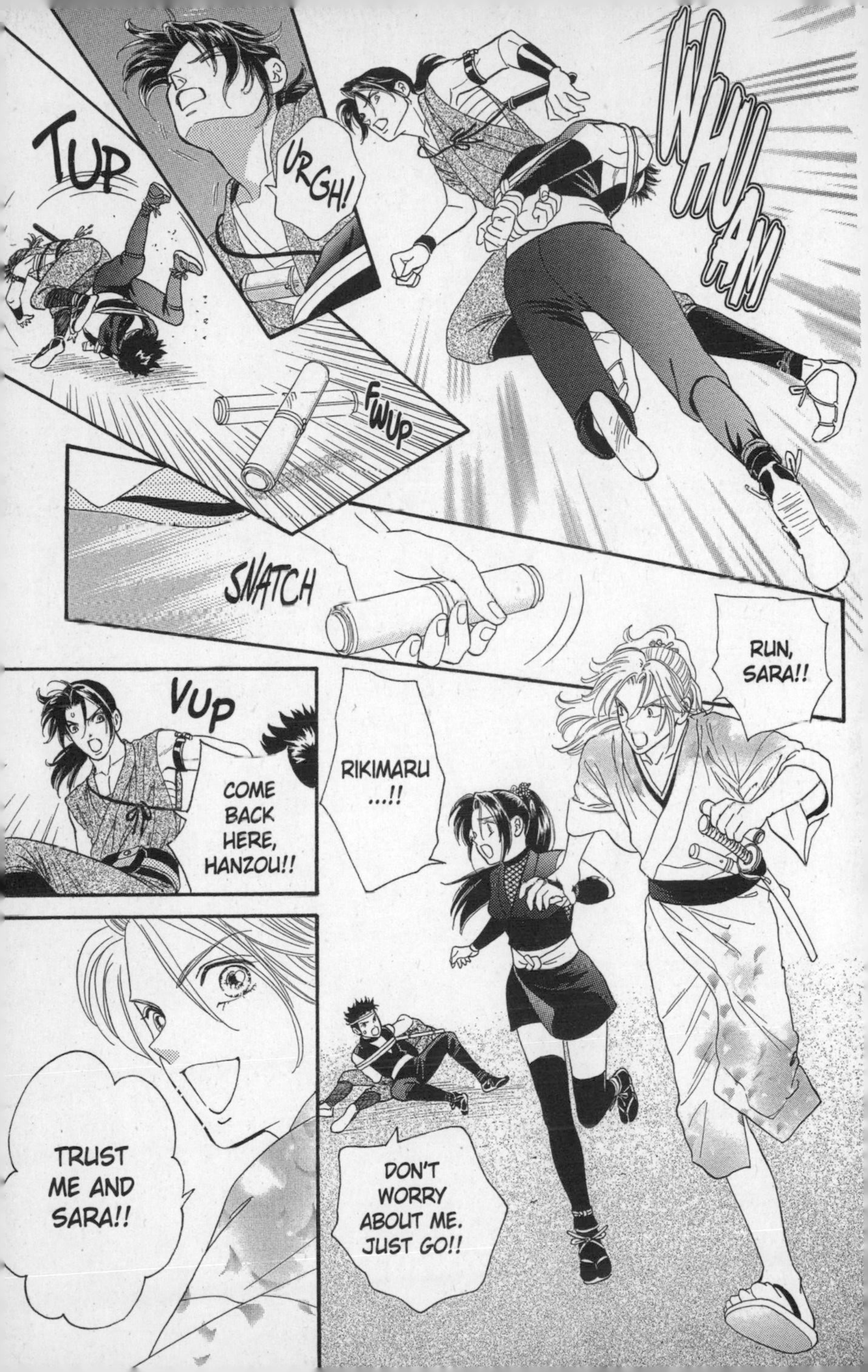
WHUAM
URGH!
TUP
FWUP
SNATCH
RUN, SARA!!
RIKIMARU ...!!
DON'T WORRY ABOUT ME. JUST GO!!
VUP
COME BACK HERE, HANZOU!!
TRUST ME AND SARA!!

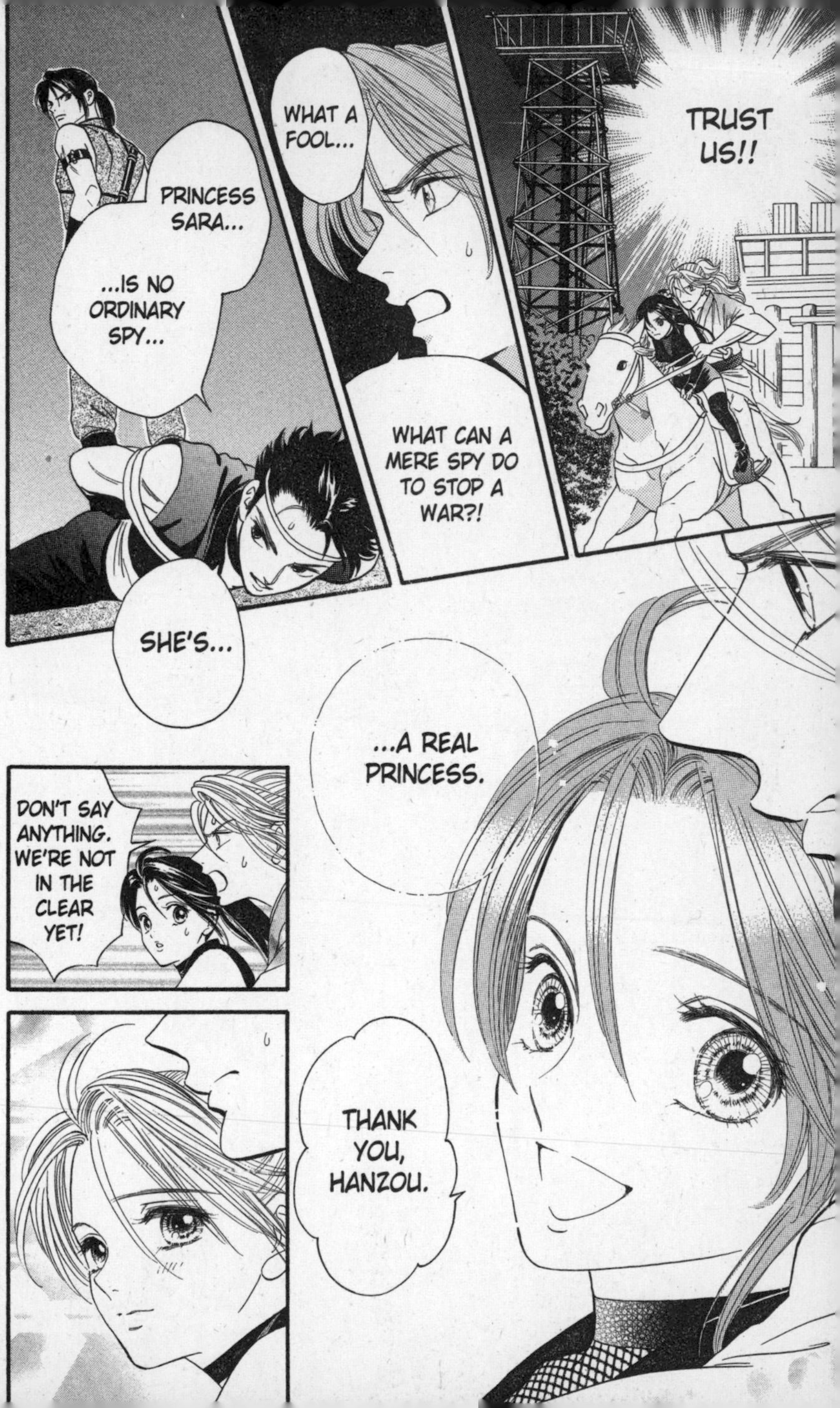
TRUST US!!
WHAT A FOOL...
WHAT CAN A MERE SPY DO TO STOP A WAR?!
PRINCESS SARA...
...IS NO ORDINARY SPY...
SHE'S...
...A REAL PRINCESS.
THANK YOU, HANZOU.
DON'T SAY ANYTHING. WE'RE NOT IN THE CLEAR YET!

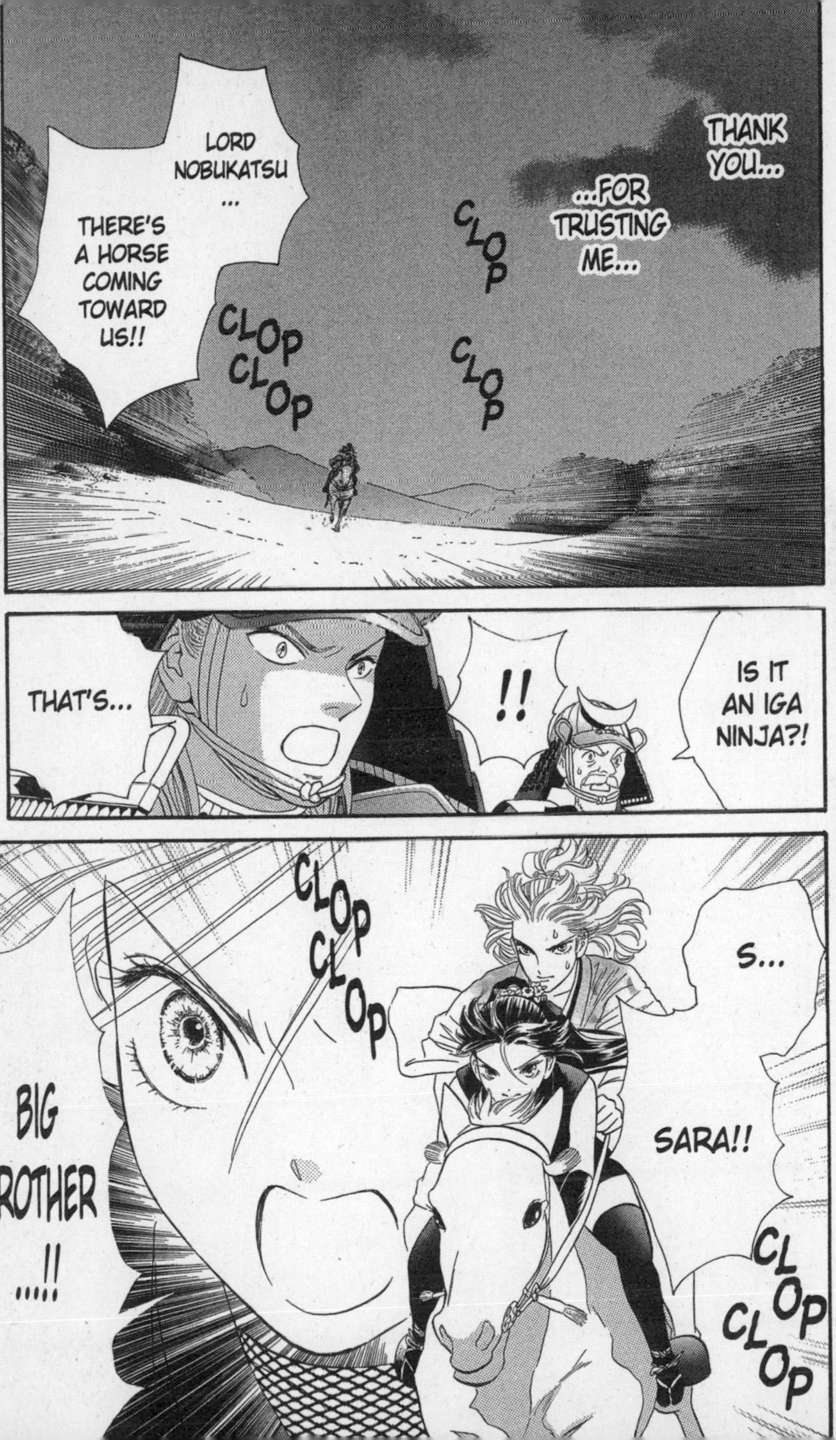
THANK YOU...
...FOR TRUSTING ME...
CLOP
CLOP
LORD NOBUKATSU ...
THERE'S A HORSE COMING TOWARD US!!
CLOP CLOP
IS IT AN IGA NINJA?!
!!
THAT'S...
S...
SARA!!
CLOP CLOP
CLOP CLOP
BIG BROTHER ...!!

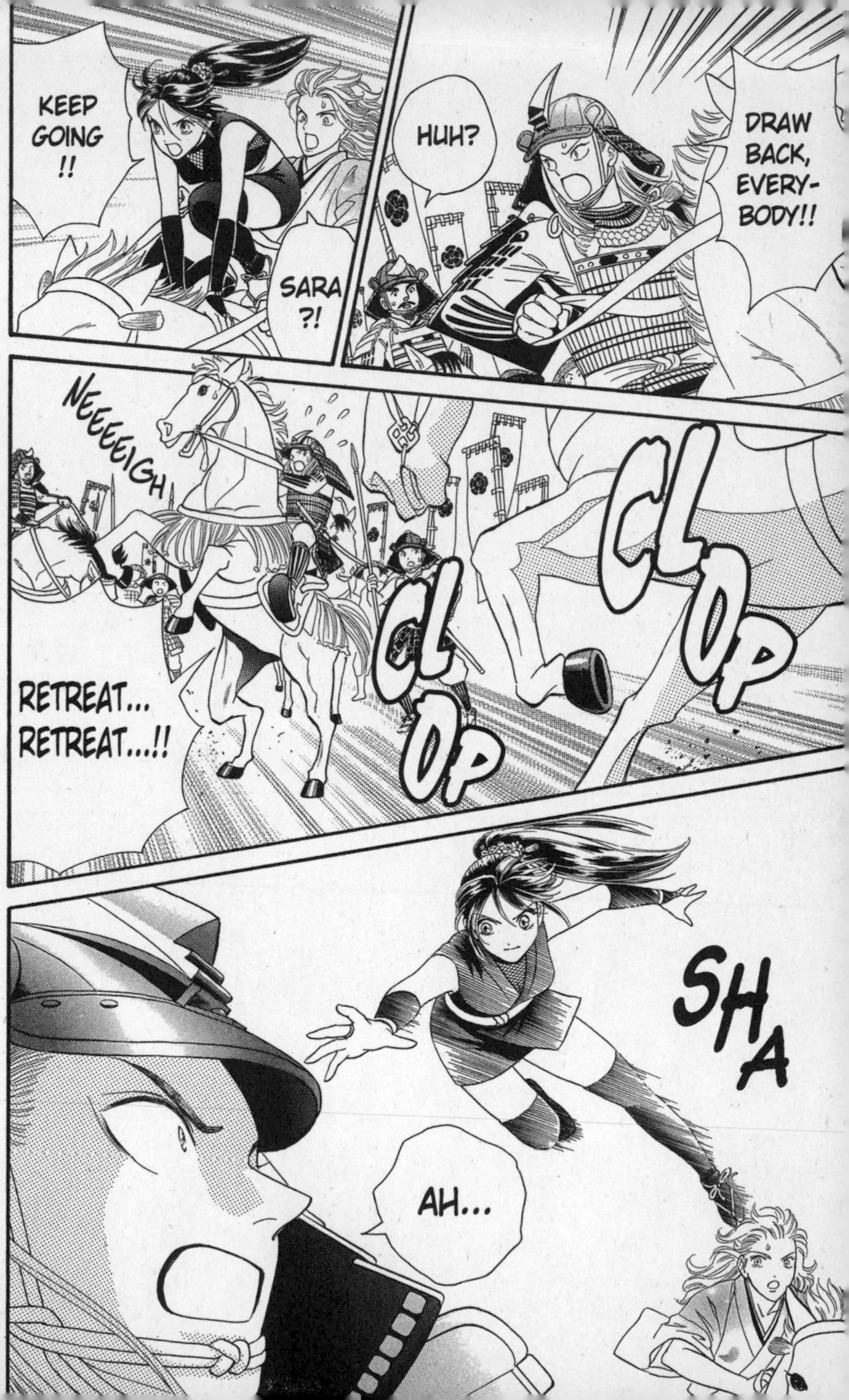
DRAW BACK, EVERY-BODY!!
HUH?
KEEP GOING !!
SARA ?!
CLOP
CLOP
NEEEEIGH
RETREAT... RETREAT...!!
SHA
AH...

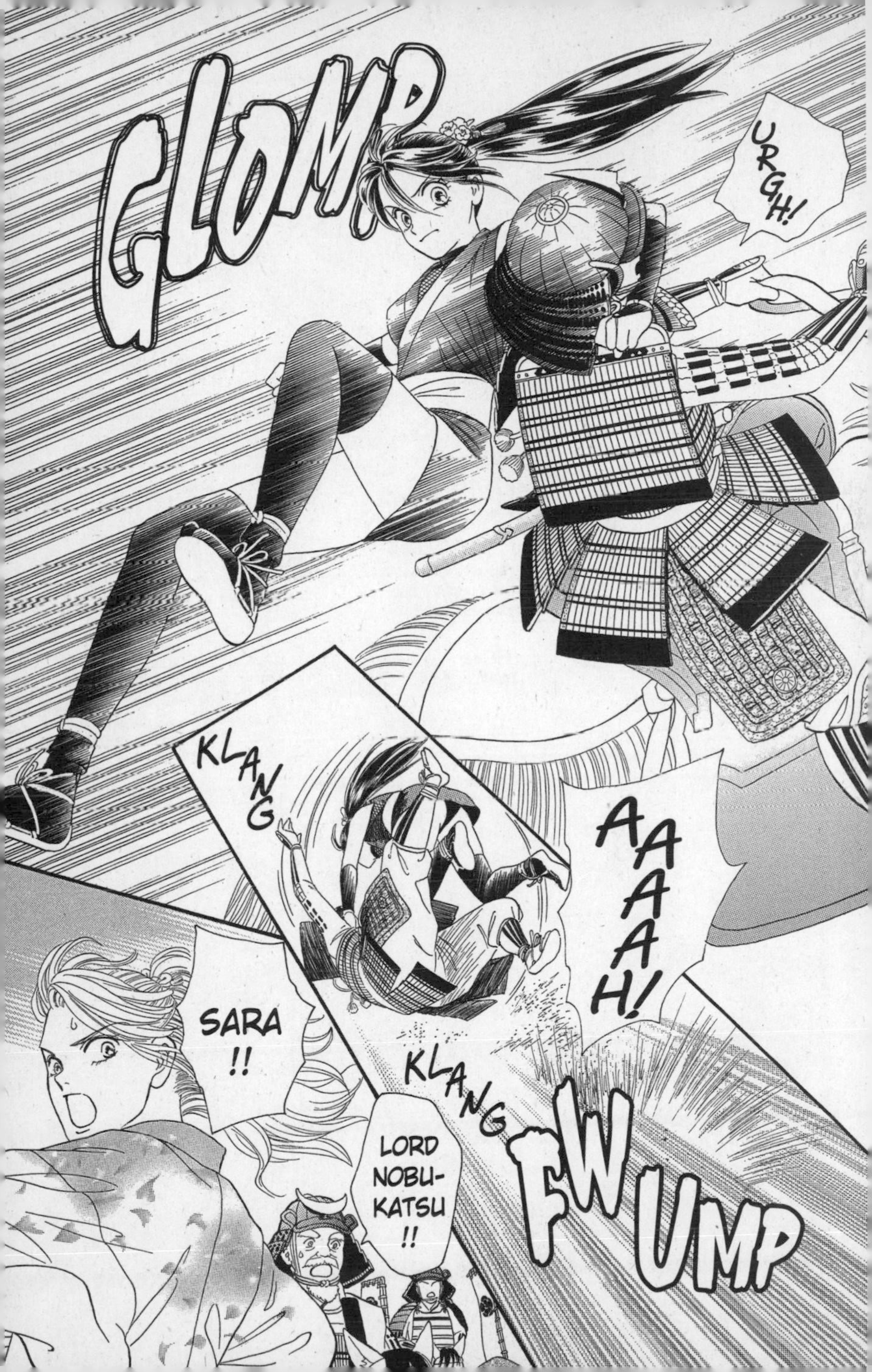
URGH!
GLOMP
AAAAH!
KLANG
KLANG
FWUMP
SARA !!
LORD NOBU-KATSU !!

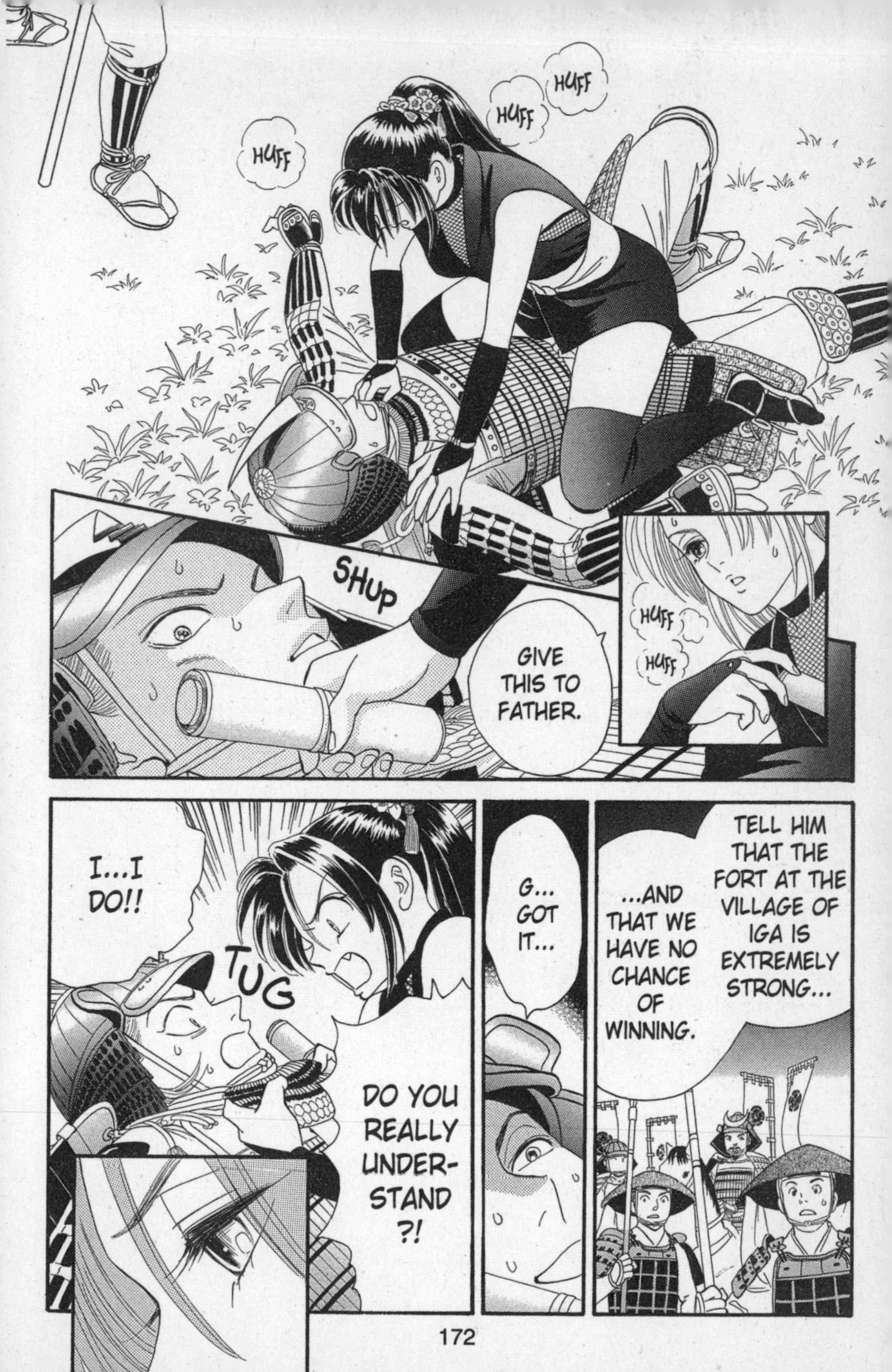
HUFF
HUFF
HUFF
HUFF
HUFF
SHUP
GIVE THIS TO FATHER.
TELL HIM THAT THE FORT AT THE VILLAGE OF IGA IS EXTREMELY STRONG...
...AND THAT WE HAVE NO CHANCE OF WINNING.
G... GOT IT...
TUG
DO YOU REALLY UNDER-STAND?!
I...I DO!!

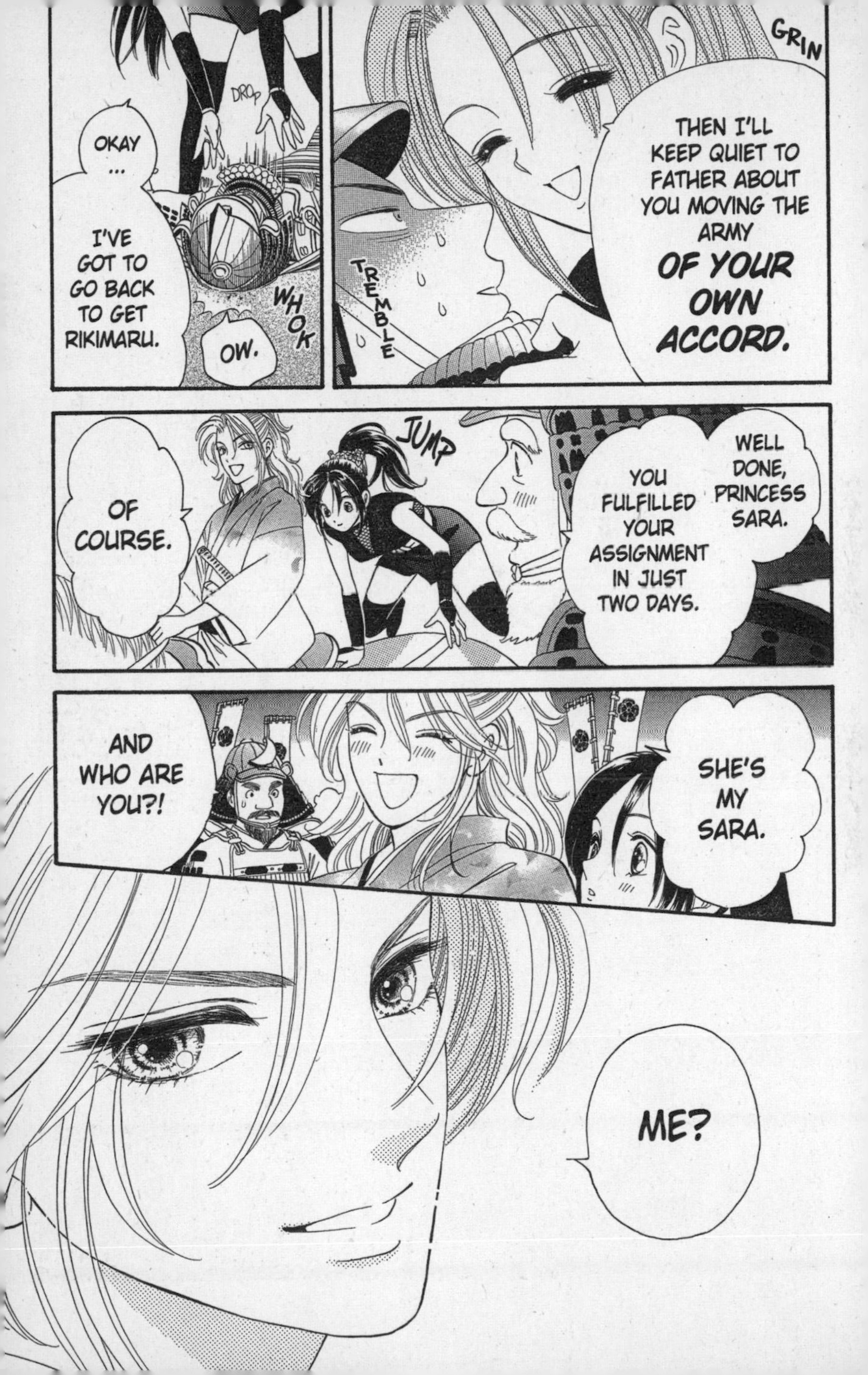
GRIN
THEN I'LL KEEP QUIET TO FATHER ABOUT YOU MOVING THE ARMY **OF YOUR OWN ACCORD.**
TREMBLE
DROP
OKAY ...
I'VE GOT TO GO BACK TO GET RIKIMARU.
WHOK
OW.
WELL DONE, PRINCESS SARA.
YOU FULFILLED YOUR ASSIGNMENT IN JUST TWO DAYS.
JUMP
OF COURSE.
SHE'S MY SARA.
AND WHO ARE YOU?!
ME?

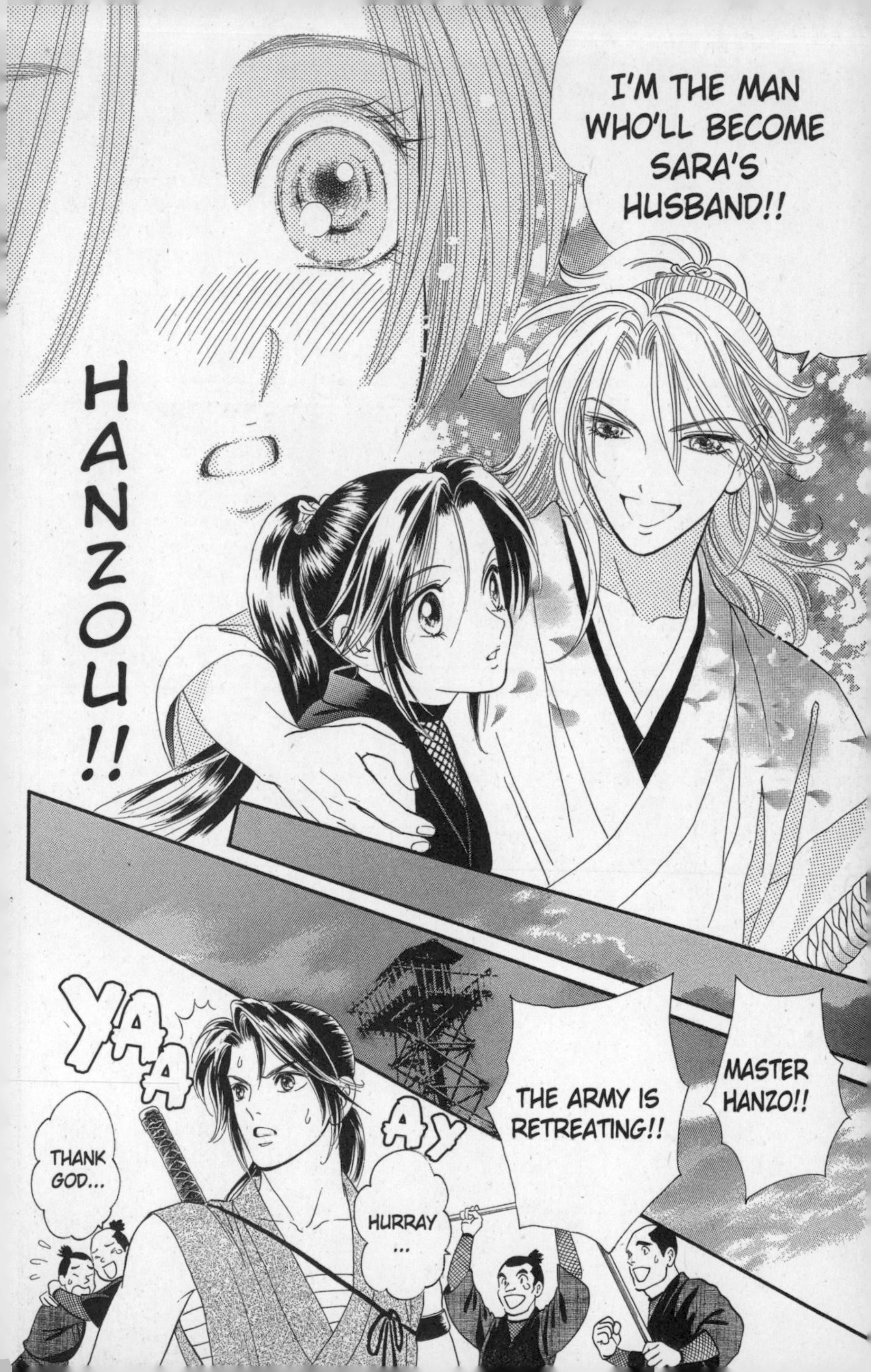
I'M THE MAN WHO'LL BECOME SARA'S HUSBAND!!
HANZOU!!
MASTER HANZO!!
THE ARMY IS RETREATING!!
YAAAY
HURRAY ...
THANK GOD...

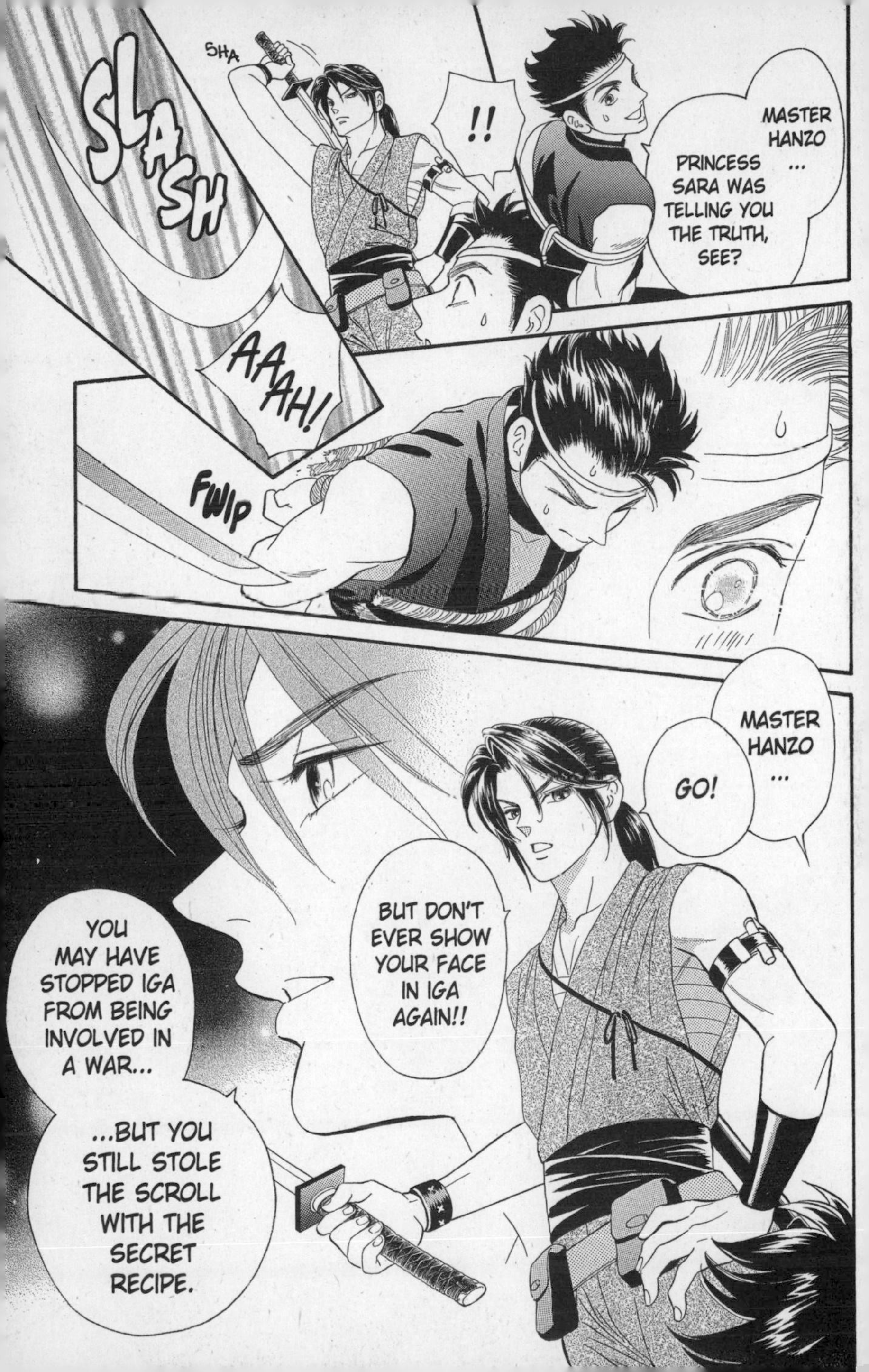
MASTER HANZO ...
PRINCESS SARA WAS TELLING YOU THE TRUTH, SEE?
!!
SHA
SLASH
AAAAH!
FWIP
MASTER HANZO ...
GO!
BUT DON'T EVER SHOW YOUR FACE IN IGA AGAIN!!
YOU MAY HAVE STOPPED IGA FROM BEING INVOLVED IN A WAR...
...BUT YOU STILL STOLE THE SCROLL WITH THE SECRET RECIPE.

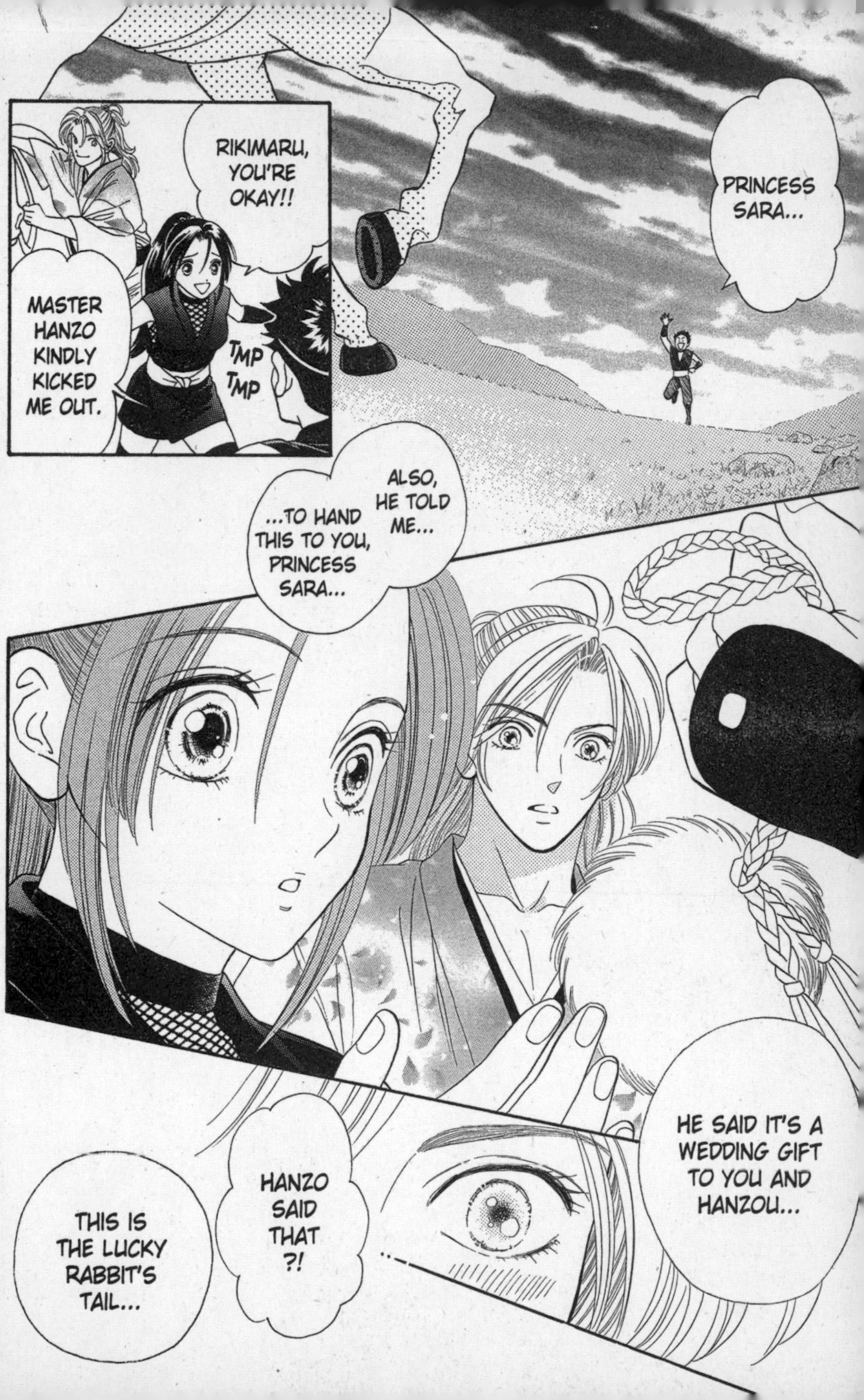
PRINCESS SARA...
RIKIMARU, YOU'RE OKAY!!
TMP TMP
MASTER HANZO KINDLY KICKED ME OUT.
ALSO, HE TOLD ME...
...TO HAND THIS TO YOU, PRINCESS SARA...
HE SAID IT'S A WEDDING GIFT TO YOU AND HANZOU...
...
HANZO SAID THAT?!
THIS IS THE LUCKY RABBIT'S TAIL...

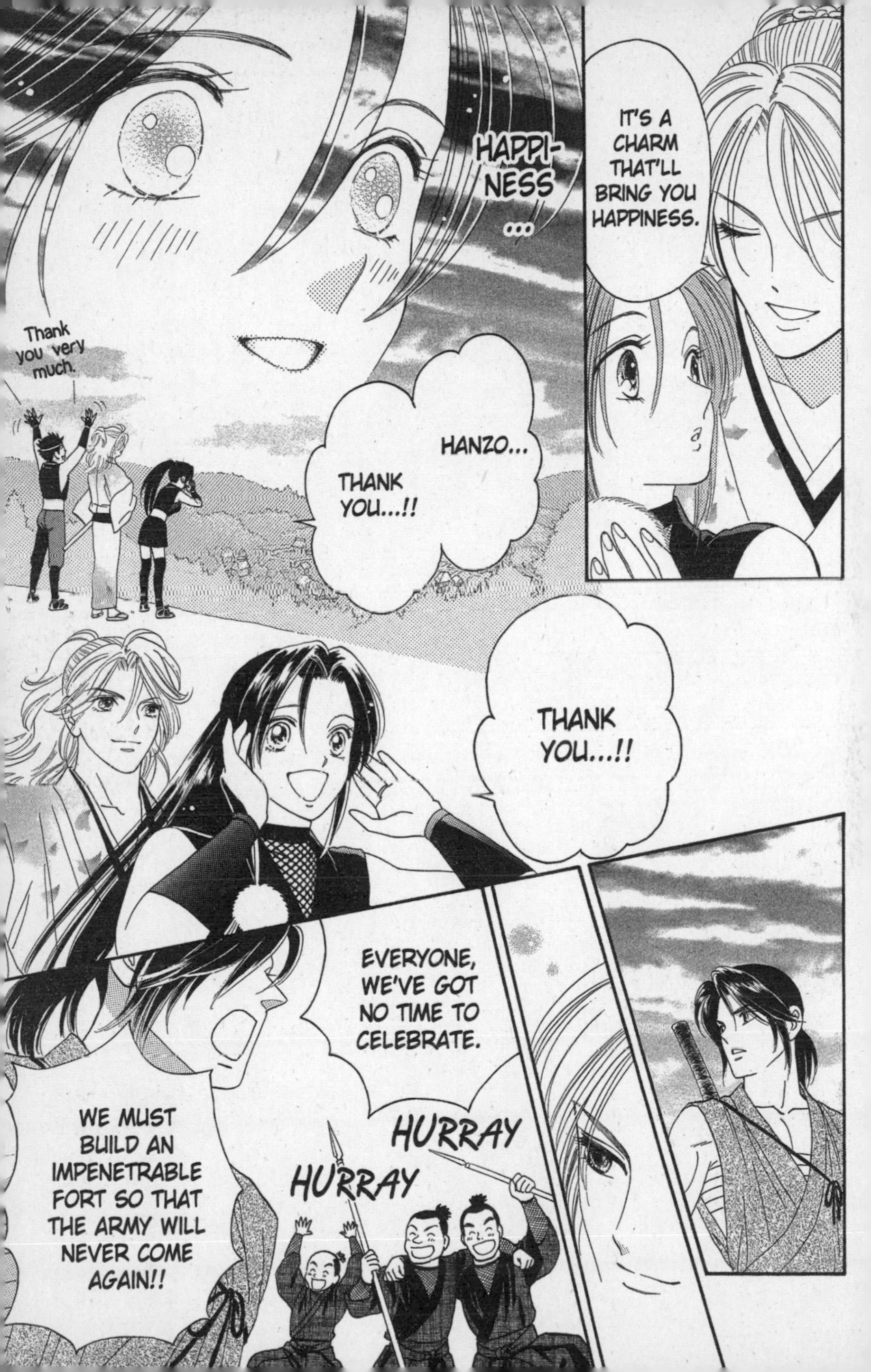
IT'S A CHARM THAT'LL BRING YOU HAPPINESS.
HAPPI-NESS ...
HANZO... THANK YOU...!!
Thank you very much.
THANK YOU...!!
EVERYONE, WE'VE GOT NO TIME TO CELEBRATE.
HURRAY
HURRAY
WE MUST BUILD AN IMPENETRABLE FORT SO THAT THE ARMY WILL NEVER COME AGAIN!!

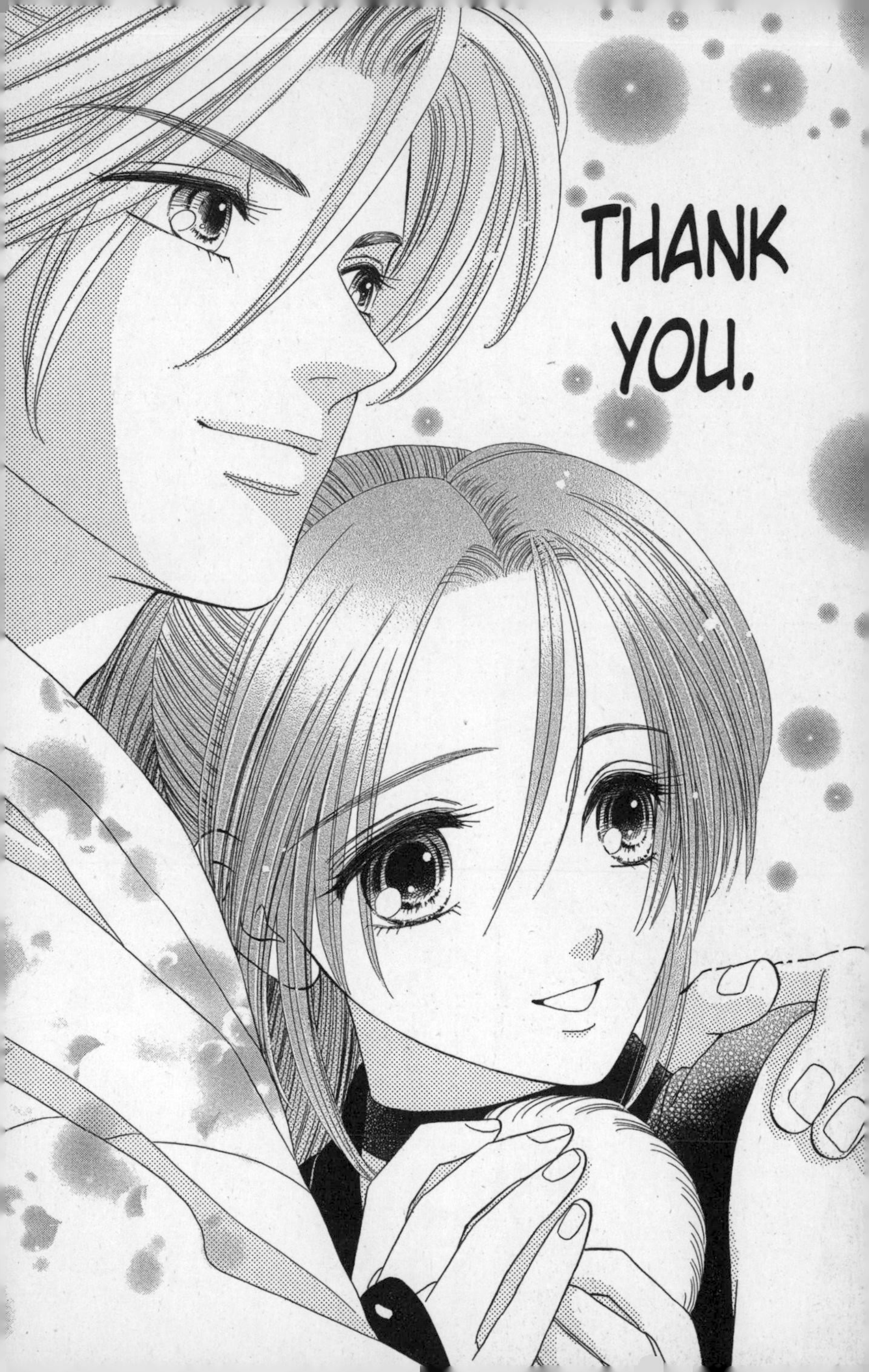
THANK YOU.

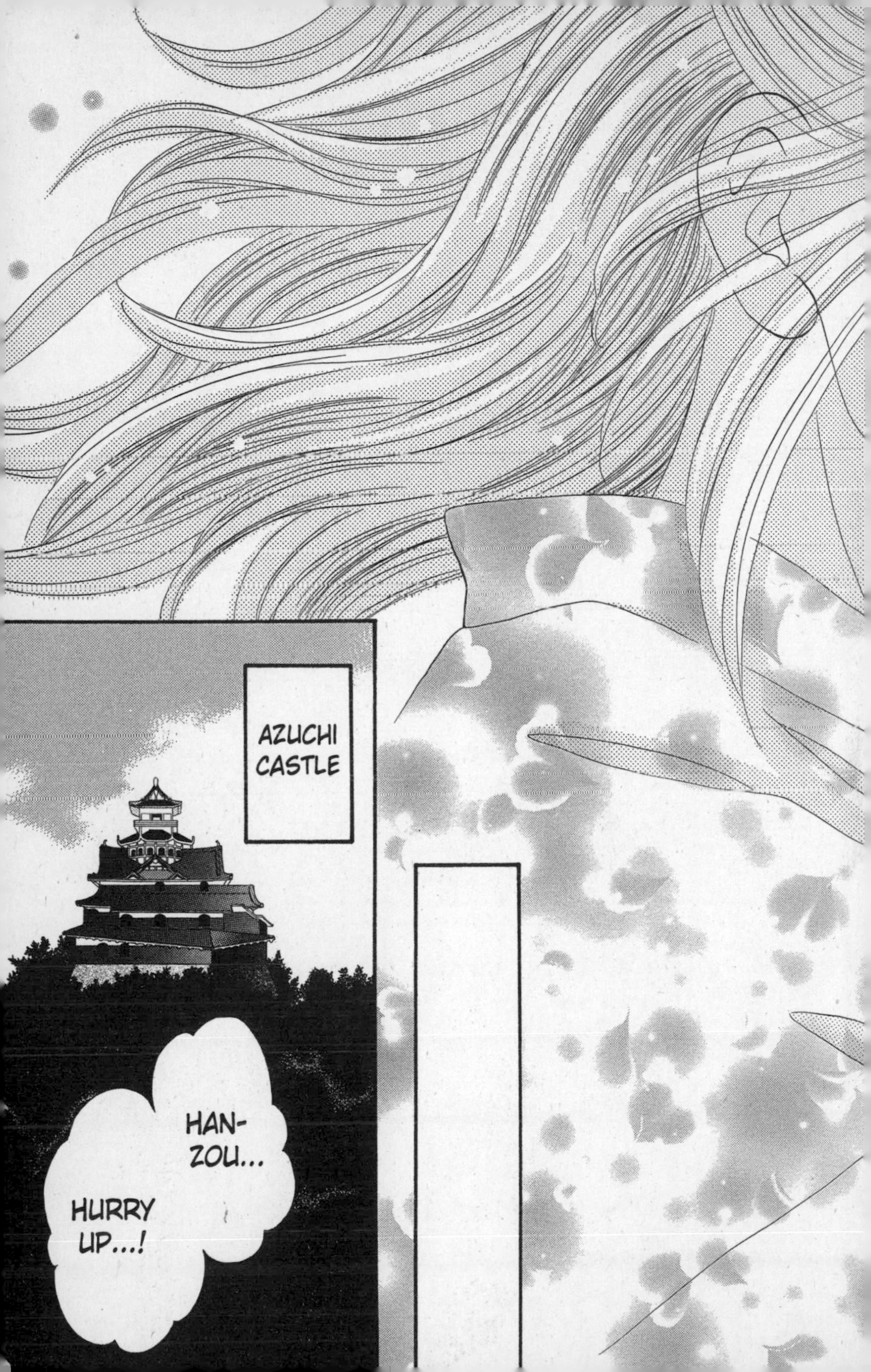
AZUCHI CASTLE
HAN-ZOU...
HURRY UP...!

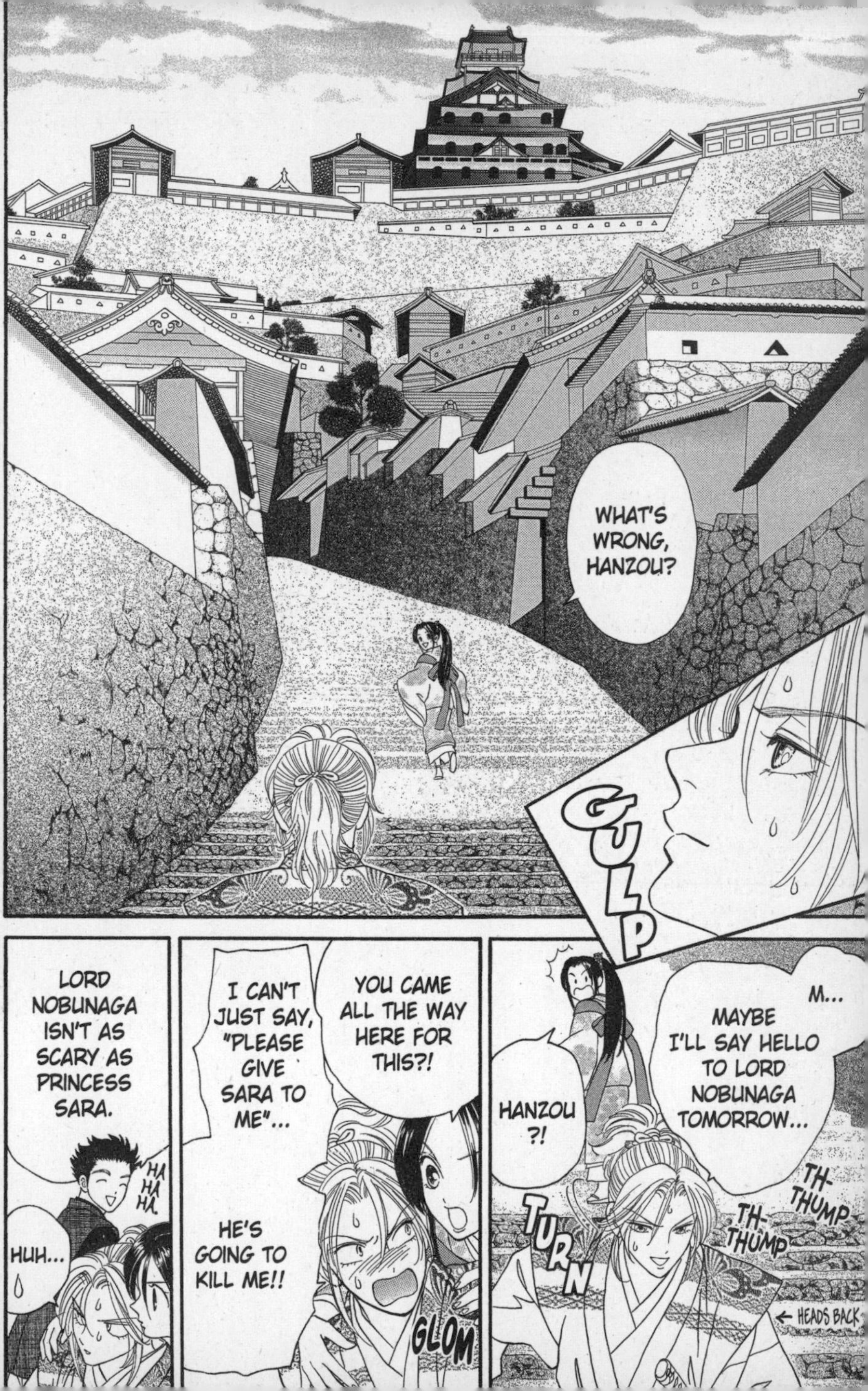
WHAT'S WRONG, HANZOU?
GULP
TH-THUMP
TH-THUMP
M... MAYBE I'LL SAY HELLO TO LORD NOBUNAGA TOMORROW...
HANZOU ?!
TURN
← HEADS BACK
YOU CAME ALL THE WAY HERE FOR THIS?!
I CAN'T JUST SAY, "PLEASE GIVE SARA TO ME"...
HE'S GOING TO KILL ME!!
GLOM
LORD NOBUNAGA ISN'T AS SCARY AS PRINCESS SARA.
HA HA HA.
HUH...

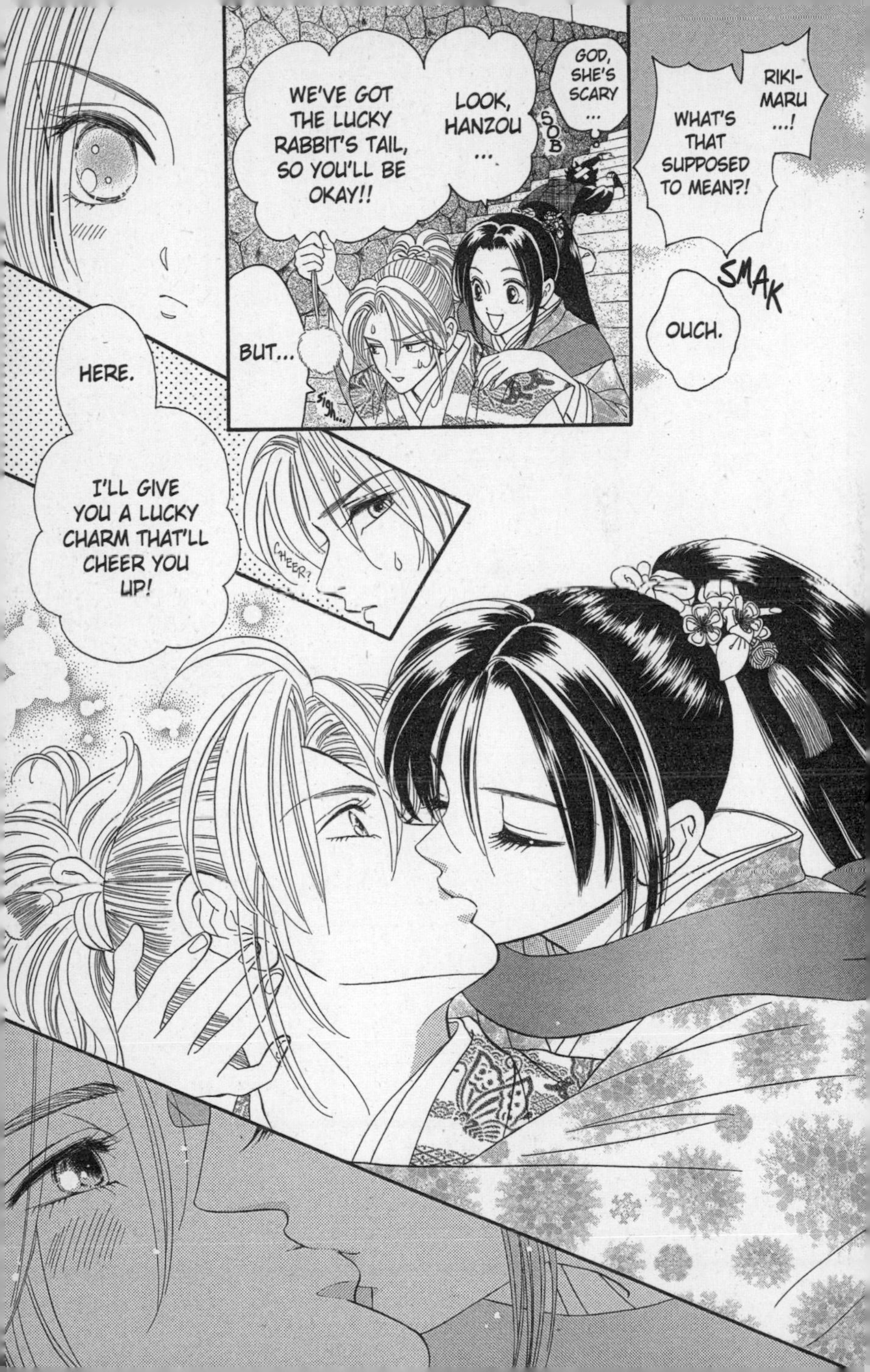
RIKI-MARU ...!
WHAT'S THAT SUPPOSED TO MEAN?!
SMAK
OUCH.
GOD, SHE'S SCARY ...
SOB
LOOK, HANZOU ...
WE'VE GOT THE LUCKY RABBIT'S TAIL, SO YOU'LL BE OKAY!!
BUT...
SIGH...
HERE.
I'LL GIVE YOU A LUCKY CHARM THAT'LL CHEER YOU UP!
CHEER?

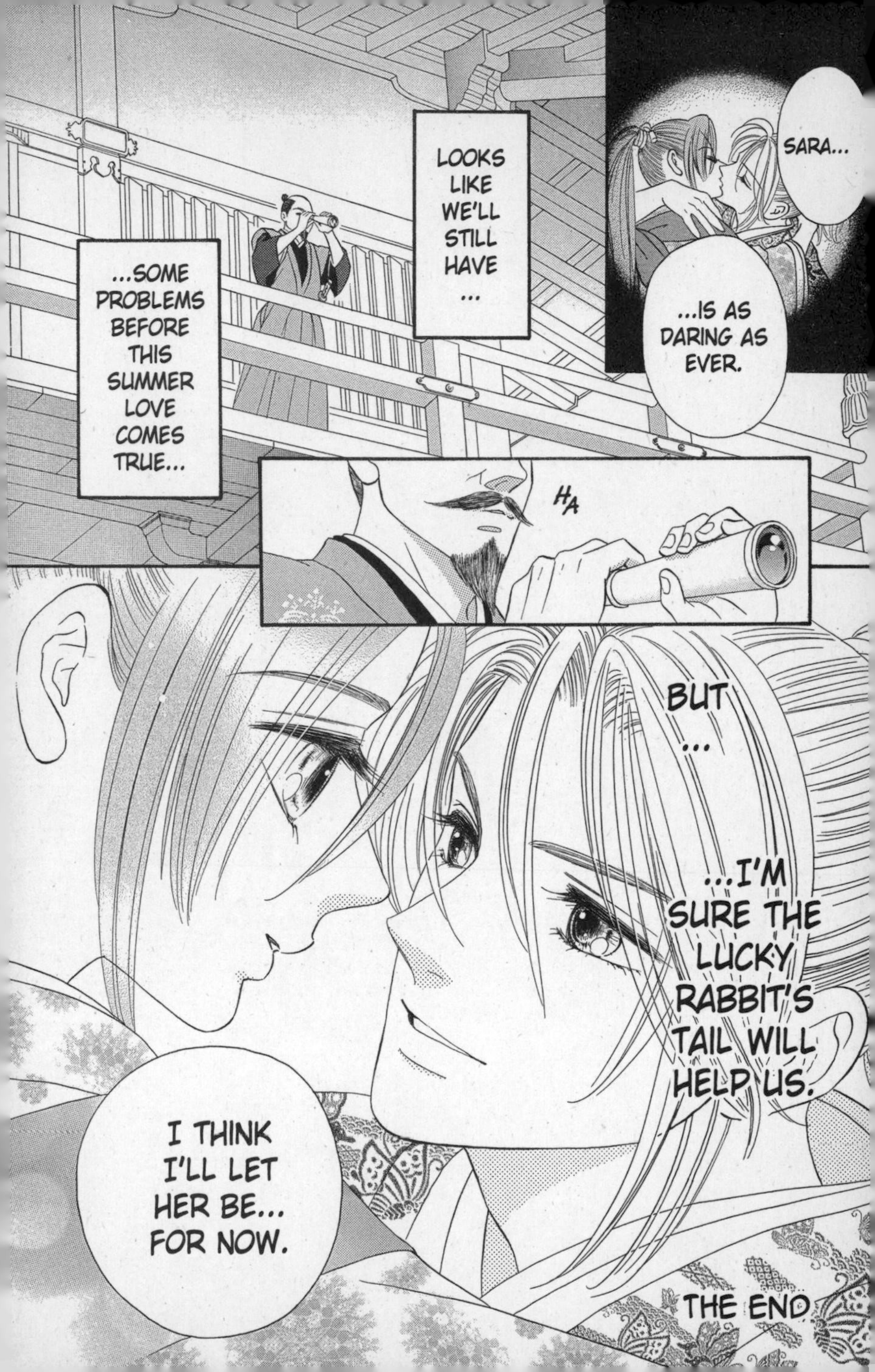
SARA...
...IS AS DARING AS EVER.
LOOKS LIKE WE'LL STILL HAVE ...
...SOME PROBLEMS BEFORE THIS SUMMER LOVE COMES TRUE...
HA
BUT ...
...I'M SURE THE LUCKY RABBIT'S TAIL WILL HELP US.
I THINK I'LL LET HER BE... FOR NOW.
THE END

Glossary

The Warring States Period was a fascinating time. Here is a glossary of terms to help you navigate the intricacies of that world.

Page 3, panel 1: Okazaki
Okazaki is in Aichi Prefecture on the main island of Honshu, about 22 miles from Nagoya.

Page 3, panel 4: Kaguya
The name Kaguya is a nod to the Japanese folktale about a childless bamboo cutter who finds a baby inside a bamboo stalk. He names her Kaguya-hime (Princess Kaguya) and raises her as his own. It turns out Kaguya-hime is from the moon, and she eventually returns to her true home.

Page 11, panel 2: Okazaki Castle
Okazaki Castle is in the city of Okazaki in Aichi Prefecture. This castle was home to various leaders throughout history, including Tokugawa Ieyasu. Though demolished in 1873, the castle was reconstructed in 1959.

Page 27, panel 2: Tokugawa Ieyasu
Tokugawa Ieyasu (1543-1616) was the first shogun of the Tokugawa Shogunate. In 1603, he built his shogunate in Edo and rose to power. Edo thrived and became a huge town, and was later renamed Tokyo, the present capital.

Page 27, panel 2: Oda Nobunaga
Oda Nobunaga lived from 1534 to 1582, and came close to unifying Japan. He is probably one of the most famous Japanese warlords, being the first to successfully incorporate the gun in battle.

Page 67, panel 4: **Takeda Clan**
The Takeda clan ruled the province of Kai and was one of Oda Nobunaga's most formidable opponents.

Page 89, panel 7: **Seppuku**
A form of suicide that involves cutting the belly open. Samurai used *seppuku* to demonstrate courage, self-control and strong resolve, as it was considered better to die by honorable means than to live in shame.

Page 104, panel 1: **Iga**
Iga is a region on the island of Honshu and also the name of the famous ninja clan that originated there.

Page 114, panel 1: **Kami No and Shimo No**
Kami no means "the upper" and can refer to geographic location in relation to an important city center, such as the capital. *Shimo no* means "the lower."

Page 165, panel 2: **Oda Nobukatsu**
Oda Nobukatsu (1558-1630) was the second son of Oda Nobunaga.

Page 179, panel 3: **Azuchi Castle**
Azuchi Castle was one of Oda Nobunaga's main castles. It is located near the shores of Lake Biwa in Shiga Prefecture.

♥ I just love historical dramas. In this story, the main character has amnesia, and it turns out she's actually a princess who's really strong. She falls in love with her enemy, and there's romance and action too! Everything about it is something I've always loved and have wanted to read myself, so I'm very happy to be able to publish this graphic novel.

—Rinko Ueda

Rinko Ueda is from Nara Prefecture. She enjoys listening to the radio, drama CDs, and Rakugo comedy performances. Her works include *Ryo*, a series based on the legend of Gojo Bridge; *Home*, a story about love crossing national boundaries; and *Tail of the Moon* (*Tsuki no Shippo*), a romantic ninja comedy.

Shojo Beat

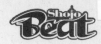

TAIL OF THE MOON

Prequel: The Other Hanzo(u)

The Shojo Beat Manga Edition

This manga volume contains material that was originally published in English in *Shojo Beat* magazine, April 2009 issue. Artwork in the magazine may have been altered slightly from what is presented in this volume.

STORY & ART BY
RINKO UEDA

Translation & Adaptation/Tetsuichiro Miyaki
Touch-up Art & Lettering/Mark McMurray
Design/Carolina Ugalde
Editor/Amy Yu

Editor in Chief, Books/Alvin Lu
Editor in Chief, Magazines/Marc Weidenbaum
VP, Publishing Licensing/Rika Inouye
VP, Sales & Product Marketing/Gonzalo Ferreyra
VP, Creative/Linda Espinosa
Publisher/Hyoe Narita

Printed in the U.S.A.

Published by VIZ Media, LLC
P.O. Box 77010
San Francisco, CA 94107

Shojo Beat Manga Edition
10 9 8 7 6 5 4 3 2 1
First printing, June 2009

VIZ media
www.viz.com
store.viz.com

RATED T+ FOR OLDER TEEN

PARENTAL ADVISORY
TAIL OF THE MOON is rated T+ for Older Teen and is recommended for ages 16 and up. This volume contains brief nudity and ninja violence.

ratings.viz.com

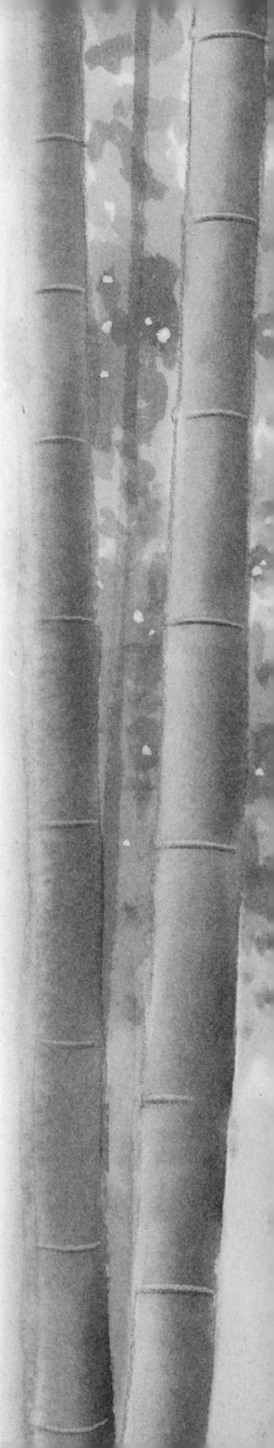

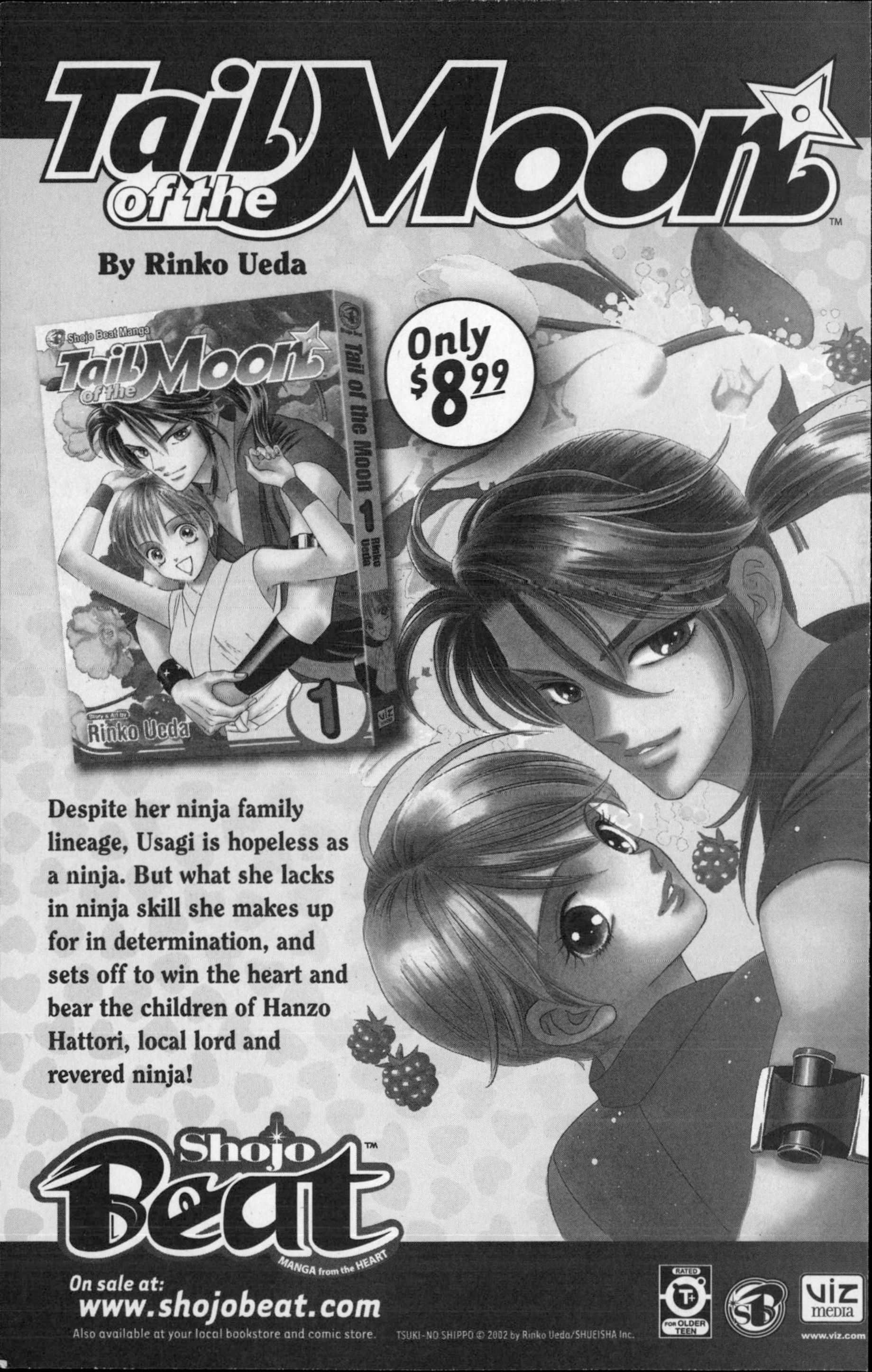
Tail of the Moon™
By Rinko Ueda
Shojo Beat Manga
Tail of the Moon
Tail of the Moon 1 Rinko Ueda
Story & Art by Rinko Ueda
1
Only $8.99
Despite her ninja family lineage, Usagi is hopeless as a ninja. But what she lacks in ninja skill she makes up for in determination, and sets off to win the heart and bear the children of Hanzo Hattori, local lord and revered ninja!
Shojo Beat™
MANGA from the HEART
On sale at:
www.shojobeat.com
Also available at your local bookstore and comic store.
TSUKI-NO SHIPPO © 2002 by Rinko Ueda/SHUEISHA Inc.
RATED T+ FOR OLDER TEEN
VIZ media
www.viz.com

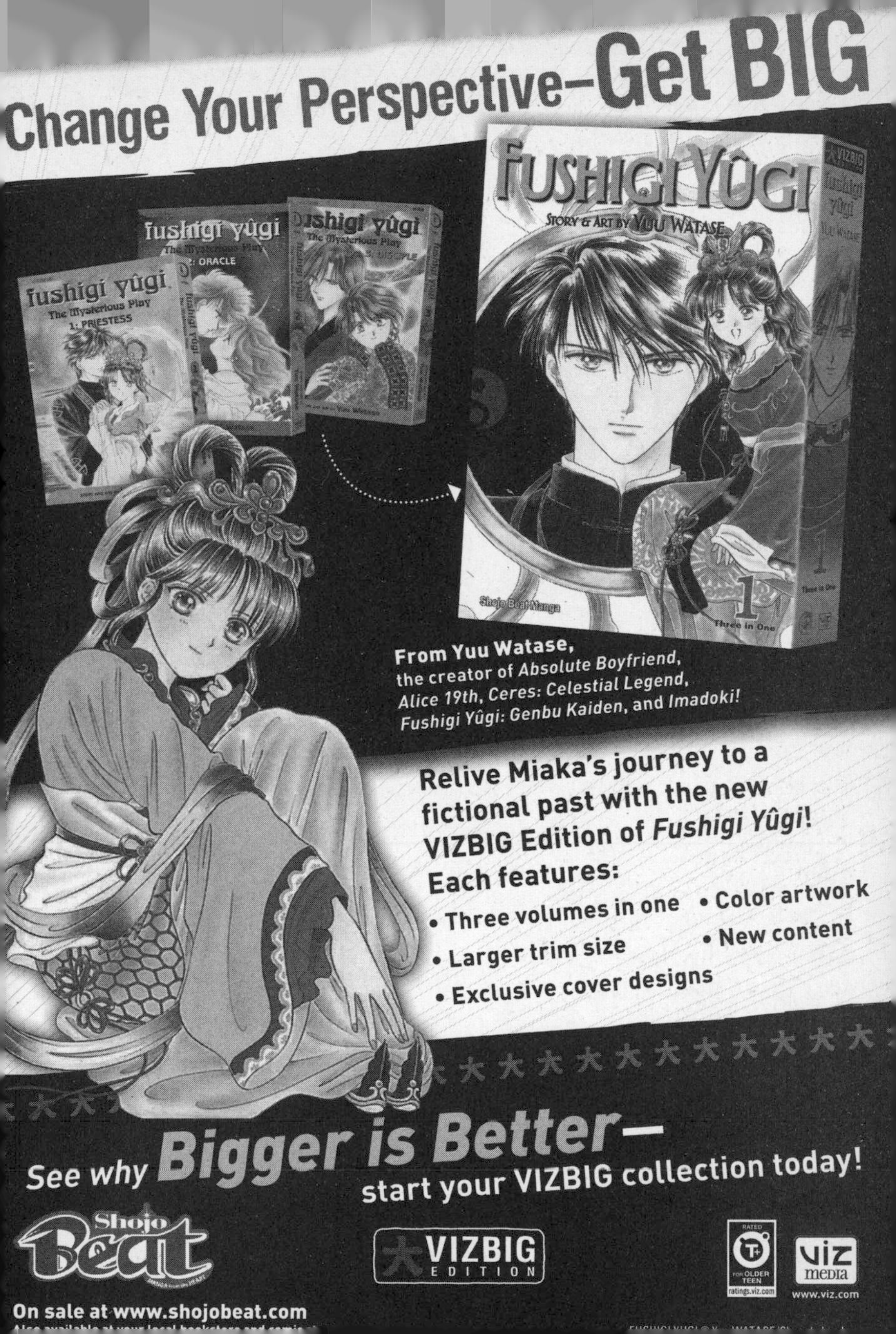
Change Your Perspective–Get BIG
Fushigi Yûgi
Story & Art by Yuu Watase
VIZBIG
Shojo Beat Manga
Three in One
fushigi yûgi
The Mysterious Play
1: PRIESTESS
2: ORACLE
From Yuu Watase,
the creator of *Absolute Boyfriend*, *Alice 19th*, *Ceres: Celestial Legend*, *Fushigi Yûgi: Genbu Kaiden*, and *Imadoki!*
Relive Miaka's journey to a fictional past with the new VIZBIG Edition of *Fushigi Yûgi*!
Each features:
• Three volumes in one
• Color artwork
• Larger trim size
• New content
• Exclusive cover designs
See why Bigger is Better—
start your VIZBIG collection today!
Shojo Beat
VIZBIG EDITION
RATED T+ FOR OLDER TEEN
ratings.viz.com
VIZ media
www.viz.com
On sale at www.shojobeat.com

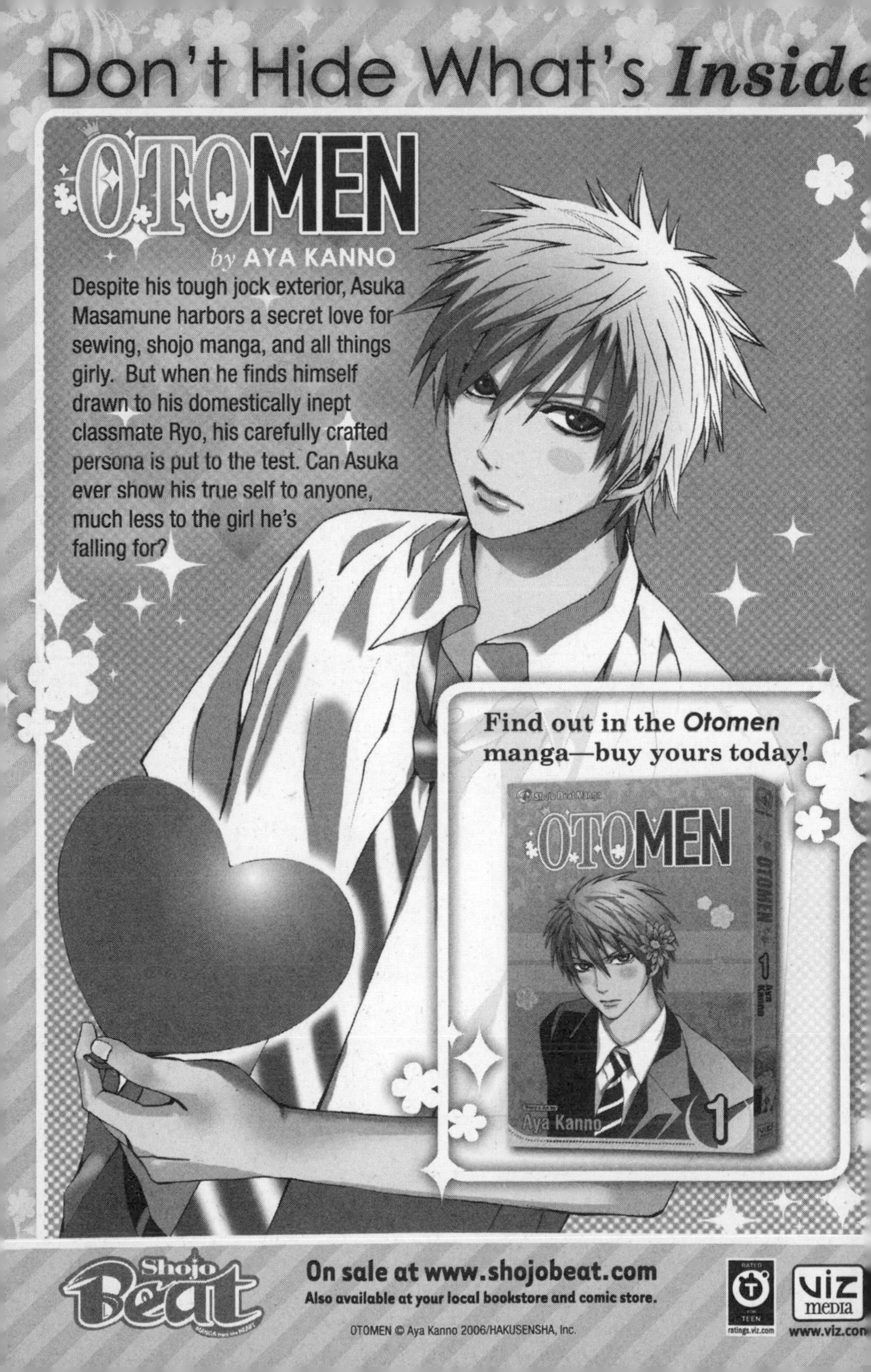
Don't Hide What's Inside
OTOMEN
by AYA KANNO
Despite his tough jock exterior, Asuka Masamune harbors a secret love for sewing, shojo manga, and all things girly. But when he finds himself drawn to his domestically inept classmate Ryo, his carefully crafted persona is put to the test. Can Asuka ever show his true self to anyone, much less to the girl he's falling for?
Find out in the Otomen manga—buy yours today!
Shojo Beat Manga
OTOMEN
Aya Kanno
1
Shojo Beat
On sale at www.shojobeat.com
Also available at your local bookstore and comic store.
OTOMEN © Aya Kanno 2006/HAKUSENSHA, Inc.
RATED T TEEN
ratings.viz.com
viz media
www.viz.com

Tell us what you think about Shojo Beat Manga!

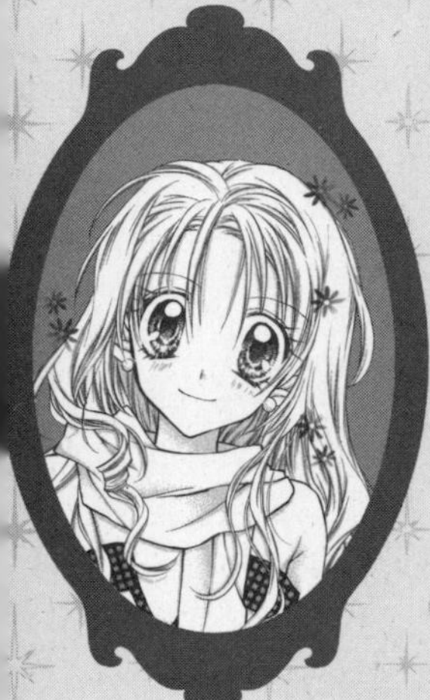

Our survey is now available online. Go to:

shojobeat.com/mangasurvey

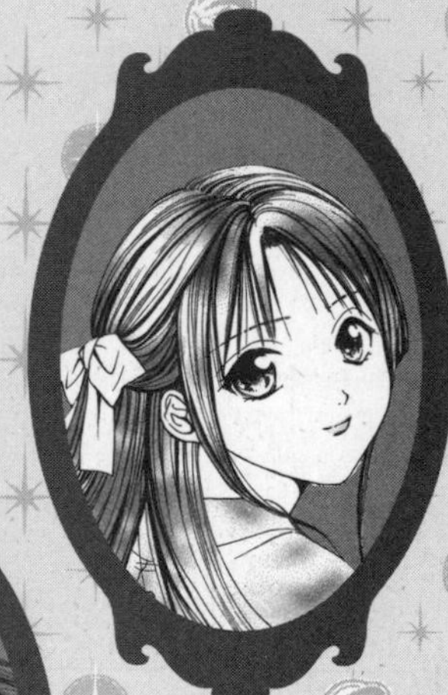

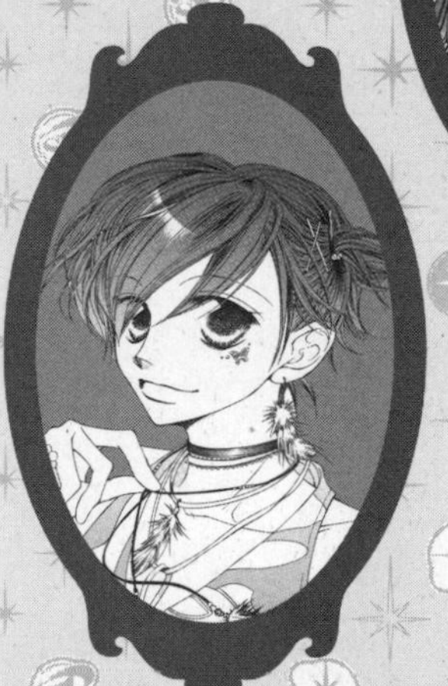

Help us make our product offerings better!

VIZ media

THE REAL DRAMA BEGINS IN... Shojo Beat

MANGA from the HEART

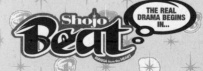